Nuclear Waste Stalemate

NUCLEAR WASTE STALEMATE

Political and Scientific Controversies

BY

ROBERT VANDENBOSCH

AND

SUSANNE E. VANDENBOSCH

THE UNIVERSITY OF UTAH PRESS
Salt Lake City

The Defiance House Man colophon is a registered trademark of the University of
Utah Press. It is based on a four-foot-tall, Ancient Puebloan pictograph (late PIII)
near Glen Canyon, Utah.

11 10 09 08 07   1 2 3 4 5

Library of Congress Cataloging-in-Publication Data

Vandenbosch, Robert, 1932-
  Nuclear waste stalemate : political and scientific controversies / by Robert Vandenbosch
and Susanne E. Vandenbosch.
     p. cm.
  Includes bibliographical references and index.
  ISBN 978-0-87480-903-9 (pbk. : alk. paper) 1. Radioactive waste disposal.
I. Vandenbosch, Susanne E. II. Title.
  TD898.V35 2007
  363.72'89—dc22
                              2007021526

Contents

Acknowledgments

We especially thank David Bodansky for a careful reading of the manuscript and for many valuable comments and discussions. We thank W. David Patton and Gregory R. Choppin, who reviewed the book and made helpful comments. We also thank Y. Chang, Russell Dyer, Allan Hedin, Mikhail Jensen, Makoto Kajikawa, John Kessler, Matthew W. Kozak, Robert Loux, Ken Marsden, Paul Maser, Ulrich Mosel, Brenda Murphy, Wesley Patrick, Charles P. Pray, Suzanne Struglinski, Peter Swift, Abe Van Luik, and Matthew L. Wald for helpful correspondence. The University of Washington Libraries, University of Arizona Libraries, University of Nevada–Las Vegas Library, Seattle Public Library, Borrego Springs Branch of the San Diego County Library system, and Pima County Library greatly facilitated our research.

We thank our copy editor Elisabeth A. Graves, especially for dealing with the numerous and varied endnotes. We also thank Acquisitions Editor Peter DeLafosse and Managing Editor Glenda Cotter at the University of Utah Press for facilitating publication of this book.

Preface

Nineteen years have passed since 1987 when the U.S. Congress selected Yucca Mountain, Nevada, as the only site to be studied further as the final resting place for spent fuel produced in civilian reactors. Since then, many new developments have taken place, both in the United States and abroad. In the United States, which has the largest amount of spent fuel, the secretary of energy recommended and the president approved Yucca Mountain as a geological repository. The State of Nevada vetoed this decision, but its veto was overridden by both the House and the Senate, and the proposal was signed into law by the president in 2002. Subsequently, the Yucca Mountain project has suffered delays in preparing a license application and encountered another roadblock in 2004 when a Federal Court of Appeals upheld a challenge by the State of Nevada and ruled that the 10,000-year compliance period for the isolation of radioactive waste was too short. At this point, the repository has not been licensed, and the possibility exists that it may never accept spent fuel from nuclear reactors.

The State of Nevada continues to wage a battle on all fronts using state and federal court challenges, budget cuts in Congress, holds on federal executive appointments, and public relations campaigns. The elevation of Senator Harry Reid (D-NV) to Senate minority leader gave Nevada much more influence than it had when Yucca Mountain was selected as the first repository site. Reid became Senate majority leader in 2007.

Furthermore, not only does the United States not have a permanent spent fuel storage site operating, it has not even approved of an interim storage facility. The lack of development of interim storage facilities in the United States is largely due to the fear of potential host communities that an interim storage facility will become a de facto permanent storage site. The lack of public trust, described by Luther Carter in 1987, remains an important factor in siting interim as well as permanent repositories. A consortium of private nuclear energy utility companies, discouraged by the lack of success of the Department of Energy in disposing of spent fuel, is trying to develop an interim storage facility on an Indian reservation in Utah. This effort is running into strong opposition from the State of Utah and thus far has been blocked. Meanwhile, with storage pools becoming overcrowded at many nuclear reactors, increasing use is being made of dry storage casks at nuclear reactor sites.

This problem is not unique to the United States. No other country in the world has opened a permanent spent fuel waste repository at this point. Some countries, including France, Japan, and the United Kingdom, reprocess spent fuel. Reprocessing still leaves large amounts of highly radioactive waste for ultimate disposal. Accidents at reprocessing facilities have led the United Kingdom to reexamine this approach. Germany and Sweden are investigating geologic disposal. Both of these countries, because of popular movements, plan to discontinue the use of nuclear power.

Spent fuel disposal problems and a decrease in public support for nuclear energy have slowed the development of nuclear energy as an energy source worldwide, and in many countries, including the United States, no new nuclear reactors have been built in recent years. It is unlikely that U.S. utilities will invest in new nuclear power plants until the waste disposal problem has been more effectively addressed. However, many observers feel that nuclear power will have to play a significant role in responding to global warming.

Spent fuel disposal problems involve many dimensions, including scientific, technical, political, historical, and environmental issues. Political institutions play a major role in determining the effectiveness of a country in dealing with spent reactor fuel disposal problems. These will be described and analyzed in this book.

Nuclear Waste Stalemate

Introduction

Permanent disposal of high-level nuclear waste, a problem since the beginning of the Manhattan Project in the early 1940s, was not addressed by Congress until passage of the Nuclear Waste Policy Act (NWPA) of 1982. The passage of this bill was prompted by a developing shortage of temporary storage for spent fuel and an increased awareness of the dangers of nuclear waste on the part of environmental groups and others. The League of Women Voters has pointed out that billions of dollars were spent on producing nuclear weapons and aiding the development of commercial nuclear power, whereas only a few hundred million dollars were spent on research on nuclear waste storage and disposal in the intervening decades between the beginning of plutonium production and passage of the NWPA.[1] By 2007, no country had implemented a permanent solution to the problem of disposing of spent fuel, even though some countries were much more dependent on nuclear power than the United States was. In France, for example, more than 70 percent of its electric power is provided by nuclear reactors.

The lack of attention to the problems of high-level nuclear waste disposal in the 1940s can be attributed to the urgency and secrecy that surrounded the development of an atomic bomb. There was widespread fear, which turned out to be unfounded, that the Germans would win the race to develop an atomic bomb. All too soon, because of security leaks and also the talent of Russian scientists, the race for even more powerful nuclear weapons began in the 1950s. Cold War fears led to the buildup of a massive arsenal of nuclear weapons and the enormous amount of spent fuel from plutonium-producing reactors. Again, priority was given to the production of weapons, with little concern for handling the extremely radioactive by-products.

At the same time that the race with the Russians was taking place there was a move to do something constructive with this powerful new source of energy. The ill-conceived Plowshare Project envisioned using nuclear explosives to dredge out harbors, to dig a new canal parallel to the Panama Canal, to free gas trapped in shale, and in other projects. Nuclear power, in the early stages of development, was touted by Atomic Energy Commission Chairman Lewis Strauss as a source of electricity that would be too cheap to meter.[2] Various incentives were provided to utilities to build nuclear power plants. An Atomic Energy Commission report for 1959 said that "waste problems have become completely manageable in the operations of the commission.... There is no reason to believe that proliferation of wastes will become a limiting factor in future development of atomic energy for peaceful purposes."[3] Initially, some thought of the fission byproducts as a resource rather than a waste problem. Historian Spencer Weart has said about the waste problem: "The press and the public gave the matter only passing attention, preferring to leave nuclear sanitary engineering to officials. Officials left it to nuclear experts, and nuclear experts left it alone."[4] Alvin Weinberg, one of the leading figures in reactor development for several decades and director of the Oak Ridge National Laboratory (ORNL) for many years, says in his autobiography that "I paid too little attention to the waste problem. Designing and building reactors, not nuclear waste, was what turned me on.... As I think about what I would do differently had I to do it over again, it would be to elevate waste disposal to the very top of ORNL's agenda."[5] The costs of disposal of spent fuel from nuclear power plants were not factored into the costs of nuclear power in its early stages of development.

In the 1970s momentum developed to permanently dispose of spent fuel in geological repositories, and this policy was adopted with the passage of the NWPA of 1982. Although many proponents of geological repositories envisioned that scientific and technical considerations would be paramount in the selection of repository sites, politics affected both the provisions of the act and its implementation. A great deal of effort was expended by participants in framing this landmark legislation, to include provisions that would exclude their state or region from serving as the host site for repositories. The most important and most debated provision is that allowing a selected state to veto its selection. This veto could be overridden, however, by a majority vote of both houses of Congress.

The public has long had a great fear of things nuclear, often attributed to the fact that radiation cannot be touched or seen.[6] Despite the fact that it cannot be seen, graphic depictions of the human consequences of the Hiroshima and Nagasaki bombs are seared in many people's memory. This underlying fear of things nuclear has contributed to the "not in my back-yard" mentality that has energized much of the political opposition to siting nuclear waste repositories in particular states or communities.

By 1987, several potential repository sites had undergone preliminary studies by the Department of Energy (DOE). Local awareness of these efforts had generated protests, particularly at eastern sites. Three western candidate sites had been selected for the first repository. Despite outraged responses, particularly of representatives from western states that had been selected as potential repository sites, the Nuclear Waste Policy Amendments Act of 1987 was passed, which established Yucca Mountain as the sole site to be studied further for the repository. This site is located in Nevada, the state with the least political power of the three repository finalist states. The Amendments Act is known colloquially as the "Screw Nevada" bill. If one looks in almost any public library in southern Nevada, one can find a copy of a book with the title *Screw Nevada*, a collection of cartoons by Jim Day of the *Las Vegas Review Journal.*[7] In addition to naming Yucca Mountain as the only site for further characterization for a permanent repository, the Amendments Act also suspended the requirement in the 1982 act to pursue an eastern site for a repository.

By early 2001 the DOE had completed a Draft Environmental Impact Statement and a Science and Engineering Report on the expected performance of Yucca Mountain. The secretary of energy was expected to recommend Yucca Mountain to the president before too long. In late spring 2001 an unusual shift of power occurred in the U.S. Senate. The Republicans had been in control, but then Senator James Jeffords announced that he was leaving the Republican Party and would vote with the Democrats to organize the Senate. This gave the Democrats control of the Senate, and one of the first statements incoming Senate Majority Leader Tom Daschle made was to declare, "I think the Yucca Mountain issue is dead. As long as we're in the majority, it's dead."[8] Early in 2002 Secretary Abraham recommended Yucca Mountain, and the president approved the recommendation. Nevada exercised its statutory power to veto the Yucca Mountain repository in April 2002. By this time Daschle had realized that the NWPA provided an unusual mechanism for bringing an override resolution to the floor without his support. The veto was overridden by both the House and Senate by mid-July 2002. The primary concern of most members of Congress in this post-9/11 period was to get rid of extremely radioactive spent fuel and other high-level nuclear waste that might be the objects of terrorist attacks. Representatives and senators from Nevada raised the issue that trucks and trains carrying nuclear waste could also be the objects of terrorist attacks. Analysis of the debates shows that the number of senators who were concerned about nuclear waste being stored in their states outnumbered the number concerned over transporting high-level nuclear waste. There was an overwhelming vote in both houses to override the Nevada veto and continue to develop the Yucca Mountain repository site.

Energy issues have received a renewed attention in the new millennium. One of the first initiatives of George W. Bush's administration was to form an Energy Task Force headed by Vice President Cheney. Among its recommendations was the encouragement of the expansion of nuclear energy. A number of subsidies were proposed as nuclear is not competitive with other energy sources in the present economic environment. A recent nongovernmental study led by the Massachusetts Institute of Technology found that creation of new generating capacity is appreciably more expensive for nuclear than for coal, gas, or oil. This cost disincentive may be considered less important in the future if global warming is taken more seriously. Unlike burning coal, oil, or gas, nuclear power does not create the greenhouse gas carbon dioxide. If the U.S. administration eventually recognizes the reality and implications of global warming, one result may be the imposition of a "carbon tax" on carbon dioxide emission. This would make nuclear power more economically competitive. It is generally thought, however, that utilities are unlikely to order any new nuclear power plants until the nuclear waste problem is resolved. Thus a study of the nuclear waste problem seems quite timely.

This book focuses on the politics of the disposal of nuclear waste. Many observers, particularly those with a technical background, believe that the nuclear waste problem is primarily a political problem. The political and scientific problems associated with developing a repository are interwoven, and in this study an effort has been made to describe and analyze both facets of this effort. As an indication of some of the issues to be discussed in this book, we list some of the major controversies that have arisen regarding nuclear waste disposal. Many of these issues have policy as well as technical aspects.

The political controversies include the power of the states to veto placement of a high-level nuclear waste repository, regional balance in placement of repositories, use of incentives for spent fuel acceptance, use of Indian reservations as host sites for spent fuel, use of regional interim storage sites, congressional versus executive branch control of a Nuclear Waste Fund, congressional versus judicial control of safety standards, and whether a state that does not have a nuclear reactor should be required to accept spent fuel. The scientific controversies include reprocessing versus direct burial of spent fuel, monitored surface storage versus permanent geological disposal, burial above or below the water table, assessment of improbable but potentially very serious seismic and volcanic events, health effects of radiation, how long one can and should assess the radiological hazards of a repository, and nuclear reactor transmutation versus accelerator-assisted transmutation of spent fuel.

NOTES

1. League of Women Voters Education Fund, *Nuclear Waste Primer: A Handbook for Citizens*, rev. ed. (New York: Lyons and Burford, 1993), 3.

2. "Abundant Power from Atom Seen: It Will Be Too Cheap for Our Children to Meter, Strauss Tells Science Writers," *New York Times*, September 17, 1954: 5.

3. Quoted in Göran Sundqvist, *The Bedrock of Opinion: Science, Technology and Society in the Siting of High-Level Nuclear Waste* (Dordrecht: Kluwer Academic Publishers, 2002), 66.

4. Spencer R. Weart, *Nuclear Fear: A History of Images* (Cambridge, MA: Harvard University Press, 1988), 296.

5. Alvin Weinberg, *The First Nuclear Era: The Life and Times of a Technological Fixer* (New York: American Institute of Physics Press, 1994), 183.

6. Weart, *Nuclear Fear*, 54.

7. Jim Day, *Screw Nevada: A Cartoon Chronicle of the Yucca Mountain Dump Controversy* (Las Vegas: Stephens Press, 2002).

8. Quoted in Keith Rogers, "Official Criticizes Lack of Final Plan for Repository," *Las Vegas Review Journal*, June 1, 2001, available at www.reviewjournal.com/lvjr_home/2001/Jun-01-Fri-2001/news/16225906.html (accessed April 23, 2007).

2

Alternatives for the Management
of Radioactive Waste

Before discussing specific alternatives for the disposition of radioactive waste, it seems appropriate to mention the principles that should guide our choice. We summarize here the most relevant conclusions drawn from statements issued by two broadly based international organizations. These are the International Atomic Energy Agency (IAEA) and the Organisation for Economic Co-operation and Development (OECD) Nuclear Energy Agency. Their reports and the implications drawn from them are discussed in more detail in an appendix.[1] The principles developed by these bodies require that waste be managed in such a way that predicted impacts on the health of future generations will not be greater than the relevant levels of impact that are acceptable today and that waste management not impose undue burdens on future generations. These two principles are often referred to as providing for intergenerational equity.

There are various ways to group or classify alternatives for waste management. One useful classification is not necessarily restricted to nuclear waste. In this classification the three alternatives are dilution and dispersal, storage and monitoring, and disposal by containment and isolation.[2] Dilution and dispersal are increasingly considered unacceptable options for any kind of waste and are particularly impractical and politically unacceptable for nuclear waste. Monitored storage has become a de facto short-term strategy in all nuclear waste–producing states. According to the principles mentioned above, monitored storage is not considered to be an acceptable long-term strategy, and intergenerational equity would seem to limit its acceptability to time periods of the order of a generation or two—and only if a process is in place for ultimate isolation. However, this consensus view is not accepted by all involved in waste management. In response to those advocating longer-term storage and monitoring, the "Collective

Opinion" report of the Nuclear Energy Agency of the OECD mentioned above calls attention to the fact that for the favored long-term strategy of deep geological disposal it will usually be possible, although perhaps costly, to retrieve waste from a "permanent" repository.[3] Finally, we are left with the disposal by containment and isolation option. In fact, the aforementioned principles lead us to conclude that this is the only appropriate long-term strategy.

In addition to the three strategies mentioned above, a fourth based on the destruction of hazardous species by nuclear transmutation is often mentioned. It is generally accepted, however, that the efficiency and economics of nuclear transmutation processes would not allow for the elimination of *all* long-term waste, and some long-term isolation would still be necessary. Transmutation is discussed in more detail in a later section of this chapter. We turn now to discuss in more detail short- and long-term disposal options.

SURFACE STORAGE AND DEEP GEOLOGICAL DISPOSAL

At-Reactor Storage

Originally it was envisioned that spent nuclear reactor fuel would be stored on-site underwater until it had sufficiently cooled (both thermally and radioactively) to be transported to central sites for eventual reprocessing or disposal. In the United States, the decision in the 1970s to forego reprocessing and the delay in developing a permanent repository have severely compromised this plan. Some nuclear reactors have found their underwater storage facilities filled to capacity and have added dry storage facilities. There waste is stored in robust casks resistant to accident and terrorism threats. Typically these casks have an outer concrete shell about two feet thick and an inner steel liner. The necessity of providing dry storage facilities on-site is not popular with reactor operators, and some have successfully sued the federal government for not fulfilling its commitment to start removing spent fuel by 1998. Creating a dry storage facility at a reactor site requires an additional capital investment and additional handling of highly radioactive spent fuel.

At-reactor storage has several temporary advantages. It avoids the transportation of nuclear waste. It places the burden and risk of hosting the waste on the geographic region that likely benefited most from the electrical power produced. However, at-reactor storage clearly becomes

impractical after reactor shutdown and decommissioning. The maintenance of technical competence and the cost of security become prohibitive
when distributed over many geographical locations.

Centralized Interim Storage (Monitored Retrievable Storage)

Rather than having to provide infrastructure at a lot of different localities,
centralizing interim storage has long had an appeal, especially to reactor
operators. It is generally recognized that this should not be a long-term
strategy, and therefore the waste should be readily retrievable. Such a facility is often termed a monitored retrievable storage (MRS) site. The creation of such a site at Oak Ridge, Tennessee, was attempted in the 1980s
but failed because of political opposition by the State of Tennessee, which
feared it would become a permanent facility. More recently, an attempt
to create an MRS at Yucca Mountain was vetoed by President Clinton in
2000, who felt it would reduce pressure to develop Yucca Mountain. Private Fuel Storage, a consortium of utilities, proposed an MRS in Utah
hosted by the Skull Valley Band of the Goshute Indian tribe. After many
years of controversy, this proposal received conditional approval from the
Nuclear Regulatory Commission (NRC) subject to the approval of the Bureau of Indian Affairs and resolution of some access and financing issues.
In September 2006, however, the Bureau of Land Management rejected a
necessary permit for rail or truck access to the site, and the Bureau of Indian Affairs announced that it would not approve of the lease of tribal land
for the facility. Thus barring a successful appeal, this proposal seems dead.
The history and politics of the Goshutes–Private Fuel Storage facility are
discussed in chapter 6.

The year 2006 also saw congressional interest in developing federal in-
terim storage in some or all of the states that have nuclear power reactors.
This proposal has received a cool reception from both the Department of
Energy (DOE) and the governors of possible candidate sites.

Spent fuel at interim storage sites is likely to be stored in steel containers inside a concrete shell similar to dry storage casks at reactors. The casks
proposed for the Private Fuel Storage facility would have an outer three-
quarter-inch carbon steel shell surrounding a two-foot-thick concrete shell
and a two-inch-thick carbon steel inner shell. The spent fuel assemblies
would be in a half-inch-thick stainless steel multipurpose canister loaded
at a reactor and transported in an NRC-approved transportation cask.[4]
These casks should present little environmental risk for periods as long as

several decades. Eventually structural degradation will occur, and the waste will have to be transferred to a disposal facility or repackaged for further storage. The International Atomic Energy Agency has concluded that surface "storage of radioactive waste has been demonstrated to be safe over some decades and can be relied upon to provide safety as long as active surveillance and maintenance is ensured."[5] Perpetual surface storage, however, "is not considered to be either feasible or acceptable."[6] A U.S. National Research Council panel has emphasized the difficulties of providing long-term institutional control of waste sites.[7]

The risk of a terrorist attack is comparable to that of at-reactor storage. Although economies of scale would suggest that it should be possible in principle to provide better security at a centralized site, Macfarlane has argued that, except for the case of decommissioned reactor sites, operating reactors will have to continue to provide security and the existence of a centralized site just adds another site that must be secured.[8]

There are also transportation safety issues associated with getting the waste to the facility and then moving it again to a permanent repository. Although the safety record for transporting spent fuel and high-level radioactive waste thus far has been very good, there are increased concerns since the terrorist attacks in recent years and because of the Baltimore tunnel fire, where temperatures exceeded those for which transportation casks had been tested. Transportation issues are discussed in more detail in chapter 11.

A safety concern specific to the Private Fuel Storage facility on the Goshute reservation is the possibility of an accidental crash of a single-engine F-16 fighter aircraft that would damage a waste container sufficiently to result in the release of a hazardous amount of radioactivity. Pilots from the Hill Air Force Base annually make some 7,000 flights down Skull Valley. A preliminary analysis of the risk of these flights led the Atomic Safety and Licensing Board of the NRC to reject the Private Fuel Storage proposal in 2003. Following a more extensive analysis of the risk, this board in 2005 reversed its previous decision, concluding that the likelihood of a crash causing a canister breach is less than one in a million per year.[9]

Siting a centralized interim storage facility will be difficult. The reaction of many governors, and state legislators, to a proposal by a Senate committee in 2006 to develop interim storage sites has been quite negative. In addition to the safety issues discussed above, there is also the concern of local officials that the storage site will become a de facto permanent repository.

There is an example of an operational MRS site in Sweden that has been in operation for over a decade. It is on the coast, as are all of Sweden's reactors, so that it has been possible to barge spent fuel from the reactor sites to the MRS. This facility uses underground water-filled pools rather than the aboveground dry storage envisioned in U.S. proposals. In October 2004 the Netherlands opened an interim storage facility at Haborg, where waste from the reprocessing of Dutch spent fuel in France will be stored for at least 100 years.[10]

Deep Geological Disposal

The general aim of this disposal method is to place the waste in an environment where there will be no need for custodial care of the site after emplacement of the waste and closure of the access portals. This requires that the combination of waste packaging and geologic surroundings prevent radioactivity from reaching the environment in amounts sufficient to appreciably affect human health. Since some of the radioactive species have half-lives as long as a million years, this means that even very low container leakage and radionuclide migration rates have to be taken into account in assessing the performance of the repository over the long time that the radioactivity persists. One must also choose a site where accidental human intrusion at some point far in the future is unlikely. For example, one would avoid geographical areas where there are important mineral or fossil fuel deposits that might be attractive to future generations after historical knowledge of the waste hazard has been lost. We first consider some of the geologic environments that have received attention as suitable media.

SALT DOMES AND BEDDED SALTS

Salt domes are formed by the uplift of bedded salt through the overlying rock layers. A salt deposit that is thicker in the vertical direction than it is wide is usually characterized as a salt dome. In the Gulf Coast area salt domes may be three to six miles thick in the vertical direction.

Salt is attractive for several reasons. The very existence of a salt bed indicates that water transport has not been important recently, as otherwise the salt would have dissolved. Many salt beds are believed to be over a million years old. Another attractive feature of salt is that it can slowly deform. Over a long period of time voids associated with waste emplacement will naturally be filled, sealing in the waste. This phenomenon, known as creep, is accelerated at higher temperatures and would be facilitated by the heat given off by radioactive waste.

The Waste Isolation Pilot Plant for transuranic wastes from military activities is located in a bedded salt site in New Mexico. (Transuranic elements are elements with an atomic number greater than that of uranium, Z = 92.) During early civilian waste site identification programs in the 1970s numerous bedded salt and salt dome sites were considered for a high-level waste repository. By the mid-1980s the number of sites under consideration had been narrowed to five, including a salt dome in Mississippi and bedded salt domes in Texas and Utah. The 1987 Nuclear Waste Policy Amendments Act terminated further considerations of any site other than Yucca Mountain, which is not a salt dome. The chronology of site selection in the United States is discussed in more detail in the following chapter.

A salt dome at Gorleben, Germany, was the leading candidate for a high-level waste repository until site characterization and selection activities were put on hold, mostly for political reasons, although there also had been a construction accident at the site.

PLUTONIC ROCK (GRANITE)

Plutonic rock is formed by the consolidation of magma (molten rock) deep below the surface of the earth. Under favorable conditions, with few fractures it has low water permeability, which is an advantage for minimizing transport of groundwater. Although suitable rock formations of this type probably exist in the United States, their investigation has not been extensively pursued, probably because suggested sites tend to be in the more populated and politically powerful regions of the country. The Canada Shield formation in Canada has been suggested as a possible repository site for Canadian waste. Sweden plans to locate its repository in granite.

BASALT

Basalt results when magma solidifies on or near the earth's surface. It is generally less dense than other rock types and can be rather porous to water transport. Despite these limitations, a site near Hanford, Wash., made its way into the final three sites being considered when Congress selected Yucca Mountain. Its inclusion in the list of three sites may have reflected government ownership of the land, the experience of Hanford workers with high-level nuclear waste, and presumed community receptivity as much as geologic suitability. The ability of basalt to protect the nearby Columbia River from leaking radioactivity was questioned by both the NRC and the U.S. Geological Survey as early as 1983, well before the Hanford site was retained on the short list of three possibly suitable sites for a repository.[11]

TUFF

Tuff results from volcanic explosions. Depending on the temperature and depth of deposit, the material may consolidate to form either welded or unwelded tuff. The Yucca Mountain repository emplacements would be below a layer of unwelded tuff and in a layer of welded tuff. Tuff is subject to fracturing, and water transport from the surface to the nuclear waste containers is likely to be dominated by transport through fractures. In chapters 7 and 10 we discuss some evidence that surface water has been transported through the 700 vertical feet of overburden to the exploratory tunnel at Yucca Mountain in less than 50 years. The realization that there will be considerable moisture in the vicinity of the waste canisters has led the DOE to design drip shields to protect the canisters from water contact.

CLAY

Clay deposits can vary greatly in the degree to which they have been compacted, their chemical composition, and their hardness. Some clays are rather plastic and can approach the behavior of salt in terms of their self-healing properties. In general their porosity is low. What water conductivity is present tends to be least in the direction perpendicular to the bedding structure. Clay has an especially high sorption capacity that retards the migration of many radionuclides, especially plutonium and other transuranic elements. Colloidal particle transport is strongly retarded. These latter properties have led to the consideration of using a clay buffer around canisters placed in harder rock.

One difficulty with clay is that construction of the access and emplacement tunnels is more difficult. Tunnel supports and lining are generally necessary. Clay has been or is being considered for a repository in several countries, including Belgium, Switzerland, and France. The organization responsible for waste disposal in Switzerland, the National Cooperative for the Disposal of Radioactive Waste, has recently recommended a clay site for its repository. This recommendation awaits government approval.[12] An underground research laboratory in clay has been in operation in Belgium (Mol) for some time.[13]

SUBSEABED

Bodansky has recently discussed both the technical and geopolitical aspects of subseabed disposal.[14] The political and environmental aspects of radioactive waste disposal at sea have been discussed at greater length by Ringius.[15] There are large mid-oceanic regions away from tectonic plate boundaries where the ocean floor is covered by a mud-clay layer thick enough to envision placing the waste 100–300 feet deep in the mud.[16] The idea would be to emplace canisters by direct injection into this mud or into predrilled holes. Once the waste containers are emplaced the entry holes would be filled with the same muddy material, forming a homogeneous environment. The canisters would not be expected to retain their integrity for the long time that some of the waste is hazardous, but the migration rate of some radionuclides, particularly plutonium and other transuranic elements, is very small because of the tendency of these species to bind chemically to the clay substituents.[17] Perhaps the greatest concern has to do with a possible accident during transport on the high seas or during the emplacement process, at which time it would be very difficult to contain any radioactive material leakage.[18]

Subseabed disposal, however, is not possible at the present time because of an international agreement known as the London Dumping Convention and in particular a 1996 protocol to the convention that specifically prohibits subseabed storage of wastes.[19] The original London Dumping Convention was motivated primarily by concern about nonradioactive wastes and reflects widespread public opinion that the ocean should not be used as a waste dump. It seems unlikely that it will be substantially modified in the foreseeable future, particularly in a way that would allow the disposal of waste as politically "toxic" as radioactive waste. If the protocol was weakened, one might worry that less responsible states would engage in less careful practices.

OTHER CONSIDERATIONS

We have mentioned the transport of water in connection with several of the geologic media. Not only is the migration of water to the canister sites of concern; the migration of any radioactive species that escape from the canister to the biosphere is of importance. Radionuclide transport in homogeneous bulk matter is determined by the porosity, density, and sorption coefficient of the rock type. In available environments transport may be dominated by inhomogeneities and fractures. This means that it is necessary to characterize in some detail any proposed site to assess its likely performance. This is perhaps less true for salt, where large homogeneous deposits may be found.

Another issue common to all rock types is the way that the radioactive waste is introduced into the geologic medium. Most well-developed engineering concepts for deep geologic disposal are based on tunnel excavations. An alternative to tunnel technology is deep borehole emplacement. The waste canisters would be lowered into cylindrical boreholes. Without the need to introduce personnel or equipment into the borehole it becomes practical to consider much deeper placement than with tunnel excavation. A Massachusetts Institute of Technology (MIT) study report includes a recommendation that more attention should be given to deep borehole emplacement.[20] It is suggested that waste be placed several kilometers below the surface in stable crystalline rock. It is claimed that at this depth there are many locations where the rock has experienced no tectonic, volcanic, or seismic activity for billions of years. The main advantages listed by the report are (a) the much longer migration pathway from the waste location; (b) the low water content, porosity, and permeability of rock at this depth; (c) the suppression of upward migration of any water present because of its typical higher salinity compared with higher-lying freshwater; and (d) the ubiquity of potential suitable sites.[21]

One of the problems associated with deep borehole emplacement is the difficulty in retrieving waste if problems arise or if the plutonium and unburned fuel become needed by a future society. This retrieval difficulty would, however, be an advantage with respect to proliferation concerns. Another problem is the greater difficulty and expense in characterizing the geologic and hydrologic environment at the great depths involved. It seems to us that this latter aspect will limit the number of sites that can be employed and would make it unlikely that colocation of borehole sites with reactor sites, a possibility mentioned in the MIT study report, could be a general practice.

Still another issue common to several rock types is whether to place the waste above or below the water table. If it is placed above the water table, the presence of air leads to a chemically oxidizing environment. Below the water table the environment is chemically reducing. The water solubility of several troublesome long-lived species, particularly Np-237 and Tc-99, is orders of magnitude less in a reducing environment than in an oxidizing environment.[22] Uranium and plutonium are also much less soluble in a reducing environment.[23] The robustness of the outer fuel container also depends on the chemical environment, with the copper proposed for the below–water table Swedish and Finnish repository designs generally expected to retain its integrity much longer than the Ni-based Alloy-22 proposed for the above–water table Yucca Mountain repository. The United States is unique in its choice of a site in the unsaturated zone above the water table.[24]

REPROCESSING OF SPENT FUEL

There are two dramatically different ways to manage nuclear reactor spent fuel. The first of these is to keep the fuel rods intact and, after a cooling period of one or more decades, to encapsulate the unprocessed spent fuel rods in metal canisters and permanently place them in a geological repository. The second approach is to chemically process the spent fuel. The plutonium can be chemically isolated and be either used in conjunction with uranium as power reactor fuel (mixed oxide [MOX] fuel), destroyed in a specialized reactor, or disposed of as waste. Recycling the plutonium in MOX fuel makes only a modest contribution to the waste disposal problem, as MOX fuel produces about two-thirds as much plutonium as it burns.[25] Most of the longest-lived fission products can also, in principle, be destroyed in an appropriately configured nuclear reactor (see later section on transmutation) or disposed of as high-level waste.

Each of these approaches has its advantages and disadvantages. The burial of unprocessed spent fuel has the advantage that the plutonium cannot be readily diverted for nuclear weapons production. No chemical processing and considerably less handling of high-level radioactivity are required. A disadvantage is that the spent fuel remains hazardous for hundreds of thousands of years, placing stringent demands on geological repository performance. Reprocessing alone does not alleviate the stringent demands on waste disposal. It must be followed by transmutation of the long-lived actinides and fission products in either reactors or accelerator-driven systems. Transmutation approaches are discussed in a later section of this chapter.

Reprocessing was historically attractive because it provides for somewhat more efficient utilization of nuclear fuel resources, both because the unused U-235 in spent fuel can be recovered and because the Pu produced can in principle be used as a fuel. Resource conservation has become a less dominant issue as uranium ore has been found to be more abundant and geographically distributed than initially thought. A recent estimate is that there is sufficient reasonably accessible terrestrial uranium to sustain four times the present rate of worldwide nuclear power generation for 80 years.[26] Reprocessing with uranium recovery and recycling of plutonium does not alone lead to significant conservation of uranium resources.[27] Less than a quarter of the original U-235 fuel is left in spent fuel, and the amount of Pu-239 in spent fuel is even smaller than the amount of remaining U-235. In order for nuclear energy to be sustainable for more than a century or two requires using the much more abundant (>99 percent for natural uranium) U-238. This requires a different kind of reactor than that presently used for power production. In light-water power reactors the average energy of the neutrons inducing nuclear reactions is very low, because of collisions with the neutron moderator. These collisions result in neutrons with a temperature approaching that of the moderator, and hence the neutron spectrum is called "thermal." In order to use the U-238, either by direct fission or by neutron capture leading to more easily fissionable Pu-239, the neutron energy must be much higher than the "thermal" energy of most of the neutrons in present-day power reactors. Reactors with higher energy neutrons are called "fast" reactors, reflecting the higher energies and hence higher speed of the neutrons.

There are a number of disadvantages to reprocessing spent fuel. At present it is more expensive to recover U-235 from spent fuel than to produce it from natural uranium.[28] Reprocessing is technologically challenging and results in a number of waste streams with considerably increased total volume. Historically there have been serious environmental problems associated with reprocessing both in the United States (Hanford, Wash.; West Valley, N.Y.) and in some countries abroad (Sellafield, U.K.; Mayak, Russia). There have been no reports of serious accidents at the La Hague facility in France. Both the Sellafield and the La Hague plants, however, routinely discharge some liquid radioactive wastes into the sea.[29] Ninety-nine percent of the long-lived I-129 in spent fuel is presently released out to sea in reprocessing at La Hague.[30] Another difficulty is that use of the Pu from the reprocessing of spent fuel would, for most U.S. power reactors, require modification of the reactor. Use of Pu in power reactors is also receiving mounting public opposition, particularly in Japan. There have been several incidents in Japan that have sensitized the public to nuclear issues, including the resignation of electric utility executives over the issue of falsified maintenance reports at nuclear reactors, as well as a criticality accident at a fuel preparation facility.

A small trial of the use of MOX fuel is under way at a power reactor in the United States. Four of the 103 assemblies in the Catawba reactor in South Carolina contain MOX fuel. The plutonium in this fuel is not from U.S. reprocessing of power reactor spent fuel but, rather, was fabricated in France from U.S. weapons plutonium. The trial is part of a joint U.S.–Russia plan to dispose of excess weapons plutonium. As part of this plan the United States is constructing a MOX fabrication plant. This plant was projected to cost $1 billion in 2002, but a more recent projection gives a cost of $3.5 billion and a completion date of 2015. The latter is six years later than originally anticipated.[31] Only in France is MOX fuel being used routinely.

The United States made a decision in the 1970s, largely on nonproliferation grounds, to forego spent fuel reprocessing. Although reprocessing is no longer banned in the United States, it has been unattractive on economic grounds. It receives attention from time to time, however, mostly motivated by the hope of reducing radioactive waste disposal problems. The impact of reprocessing on waste management is very complex. Although removal of the uranium can result in considerable reduction in the mass and volume of the high-level waste, other factors such as heat load have an important effect on repository capacity. A 2005 report of a Nuclear Energy Study Group of the Panel on Public Affairs of the American Physical Society has identified enrichment and reprocessing facilities as the principal proliferation concerns associated with nuclear power.[32] This report recommends that any U.S. decision on reprocessing be delayed for about a decade until further research on proliferation-resistant strategies and technology can be carried out.[33]

In spring 2006 the DOE suddenly proposed developing an alternative to direct disposal of spent fuel in a geological repository. This proposal involved reprocessing and recycling spent fuel. It appeared in the administration's fiscal year 2007 budget submission to Congress and is part of a broader initiative called the Global Nuclear Energy Partnership (GNEP).[34] In addition to proposing a complete reversal in the management of domestic spent fuel, this initiative proposes making new reactor fuel available to other countries and returning spent fuel to the United States for reprocessing. Briefly, the reprocessing and recycling aspects of this proposal involve an initial aqueous separation of plutonium and other actinides from the uranium and fission products and the transmutation of the neptunium, plutonium, and other actinides in a new generation of fast-neutron nuclear reactors, followed by further reprocessing by pyrochemical techniques. These technologies are discussed further later in this chapter. Fission products and some actinide waste would still have to be buried in a repository. Some comparisons of the advantages and disadvantages of the GNEP reprocessing and recycling proposal have appeared.[35]

Other countries planning to dispose of spent fuel directly without reprocessing include Canada, Sweden, and Finland. France, the United Kingdom, and Japan have adopted the reprocessing route. The longer-term sustainability of nuclear fission power has probably played a part in reprocessing decisions in some countries such as Japan. France has a major reprocessing capability and has reprocessed fuel for other countries as well as its own. Britain has also performed reprocessing for other countries. A plant has been built at Sellafield, England, to produce MOX fuel. It has experienced technical difficulties, and the first fuel order (for a Swiss utility) has yet to be fulfilled.[36] Japan is presently having its spent fuel reprocessed in Europe, but the separated plutonium and the nuclear waste are returned to Japan. Japan has built a large reprocessing plant that is undergoing initial testing. This construction project has taken considerably longer than anticipated. The ability to burn (in power reactors) all of the plutonium that will be extracted from spent fuel is questionable.

Reprocessing technologies can be divided roughly into aqueous and nonaqueous processes. In aqueous processing the fuel elements are dissolved in acid solution, and further processing takes place in the liquid state. All large-scale processing of power reactor fuel is currently based on a specific procedure known as PUREX (plutonium-uranium extraction). It was developed primarily to obtain plutonium for nuclear weapons. For this purpose it is important to remove neptunium and heavier actinides from the plutonium. The neptunium and other actinides and the fission products make up the waste stream. These liquid wastes are mixed with borosilicate glass and vitrified for long-term storage or disposal.[37] In most current applications of PUREX the plutonium recovered is mixed with uranium to form a mixed oxide that can be used as a fuel in power reactors.

A liability of the PUREX process is that the plutonium is not contaminated with other actinides and therefore could be used for making weapons. This gives rise to diversion and terrorism concerns. The suitability of recovered plutonium for weapons depends on the length of time the fuel rods are used in a reactor. To obtain weapons-grade plutonium the fuel rods should be used for only a relatively short time to avoid the buildup of isotopes of plutonium heavier than Pu-239. Heavier plutonium isotopes compromise weapon performance.

An alternative aqueous process known generically as UREX (uranium extraction) has been under development but has not been used as yet in large-scale processing. In this approach uranium is separated from the rest of the elements at an early stage. As part of the Bush administration's 2007 budget proposal, the DOE has proposed that a variant of the UREX scheme, UREX+, be investigated with respect to its use as part of a new closed fuel cycle. The UREX+ process is an aqueous process where the first step is dissolution in nitric acid. Later steps typically involve solvent extraction, where an organic reagent insoluble in aqueous solution is added and certain elements are preferentially removed by being captured by the organic reagent. Numerous versions of the UREX+ reprocessing scheme have been put forward, having product-plus waste steams varying in number from three to seven.[38] The scheme put forth by the U.S. administration following its 2007 budget proposal has three streams; a uranium stream accounting for most of the mass of spent fuel; a transuranic stream made up of Np, Pu, and higher atomic number transuranics such as Am and Cm; and a fission product waste stream.[39] The uranium could be saved for fuel for possible future fast (high-energy neutron) reactors, for eventual re-enrichment, or, if sufficiently free of contaminants, for disposal as low-level waste. It is proposed that the transuranics would be burned (largely destroyed) in a fast reactor, where some of the Np, Am, and Cm as well as the Pu could be made to fission. (Pu can be made to fission in conventional reactors, although with fairly low efficiency.) The proliferation resistance of this scheme would be that the Pu would never be separated from Np or Am and Cm and would therefore be much less useful in making a fission weapon. The fission products would go to a geological repository for final disposal.

With regard to proliferation and terrorist concerns associated with reprocessing, there are two distinct aspects that are often not clearly distinguished. The first has to do with the intense radioactivity of spent fuel, primarily due to the fission product radioactivity. This makes the acquisition and handling of spent fuel difficult and dangerous. The second has to do with the properties of the reprocessing product containing the Pu. In the PUREX process used presently the Pu is relatively pure and is suitable for making weapons without further chemical separations. In the UREX+ process the Pu is accompanied by Np, Am, and Cm. These latter elements compromise the performance of a possible weapon if not removed by further chemical separations.

An alternative to aqueous processing is to work at sufficiently high temperatures (typically above 600 degrees Centigrade) that one can perform electrolytic separations using molten metal or molten salt as the electrolyte. Different chemical species are deposited on the cathode depending on their reduction potential. The removal from the electrolyte of species to be deposited on the cathode is limited by thermodynamic considerations—100 percent removal is not possible.[40] A demonstration of this approach has been performed at Argonne West in Idaho using fuel rods from the experimental breeding reactor EBR-II. The fuel rods are rather unique in that the uranium is metallic rather than an oxide and have been infused by elemental sodium introduced between the fuel and the cladding. This fuel is not acceptable for direct repository disposal.[41] Apart from the general motivation for developing pyroprocessing methods, the particular motivation for EBR-II fuel reprocessing is fuel conditioning for disposal rather than the recovery of uranium or plutonium. As for the UREX schemes discussed above, it is hoped that the uranium will be of sufficient radiochemical purity that it can be disposed of as low-level waste. For example, this requires less than 0.001 percent contamination by mass of the long-lived fission product Tc-99.[42] After a demonstration run on 100 core assemblies of enriched uranium EBR-II spent fuel, the results were reviewed by a National Research Council–National Academy of Sciences review committee. The review is generally quite favorable, although it is mentioned that more work needs to be done to characterize the various waste streams to meet disposal acceptance criteria.[43] Looking to the future, the U.S. DOE sees pyroprocessing as promising for fuel preparation for possible transmutation systems and for dealing with fuel from possible fast-spectrum reactor systems.[44]

Pyroprocessing is being studied by quite a few countries, with Russia and Japan being important examples. There are a significant number of international collaborations working on various aspects of pyroprocessing.[45]

The main advantages and disadvantages have been summarized in the Nuclear Energy Agency/IAEA status report.[46] Some of the advantages are

1. compactness with a limited number of operational steps,
2. the inorganic molten salts are less sensitive to radiolysis hazards than are aqueous media, and
3. material with limited solubility in nitric acid can be more easily dissolved in molten salt.

Some of the disadvantages are
1. high temperatures and strongly corrosive reagents present difficult challenges for cell design,
2. current pyroprocesses have limited separation efficiency and are limited to batch mode (as contrasted with a continuous stream mode), and
3. the generation of process wastes outside the bounds of current standards (for example, uranium with too high fission product contamination for low-level waste disposal).

TRANSMUTATION OF RADIOACTIVE WASTE

Technical and Economic Issues

Spent nuclear fuel is much more radioactive than virgin uranium fuel because of the production of fission products and of transuranic elements in the power reactor. Fission products are the result of neutron-induced fission, and transuranic elements result from neutron capture by the uranium fuel followed by radioactive decay to elements with atomic numbers greater than 92. There are many different fission products produced with a broad distribution of yields and half-lives, as the mass ratio of the two products from splitting uranium can vary from one fission event to another. Of particular importance to nuclear waste disposal are two long-lived fission products, Tc-99 (half-life 220,000 years) and I-129 (half-life 17 million years). These two species dominate spent fuel fission product radioactivity after a few thousand years. The most troublesome transuranic elements present in spent fuel are Np-237 (half-life two million years) and Pu-239 (half-life 24,000 years).

The goal of transmutation of nuclear waste is to chemically separate out the most troublesome long-lived radioisotopes from spent nuclear fuel and transmute them in a neutron flux to shorter-lived and less toxic species in an intense neutron flux. The long-lived fission products are destroyed by neutron capture leading to short-lived radioactive species that quickly decay to stable species. The transuranic elements are destroyed either directly by neutron-induced fission or by neutron captures making heavier species that are then destroyed by fission.

Calculations suggest that ideally transmutation could reduce the ingestion toxicity of spent fuel by a factor of 100 for times longer than about 500 years. This would put appreciably fewer demands on the design of a permanent repository, perhaps reducing the period of time for secure storage from tens of thousands of years to hundreds of years. There are, however, major technical hurdles that must be overcome to make transmutation practical. Among these are the demanding chemical separation efficiencies and the challenging material requirements related to thermal and radiation stresses in the reactor. The need to separate Pu from uranium also raises proliferation and terrorism security issues.

Transmutation schemes are defined by their sources of neutrons. Three approaches have been considered. The first of these is to recycle the separated transuranics and troublesome fission products in conventional light-water power reactors. This is the most straightforward technically and has the least number of uncertainties in its implementation. However, the modest neutron flux of such reactors results in a rather slow rate of destruction of I-129 and Tc-99. The low average energy of the neutrons compromises the destruction of some transuranics. The second type of neutron source is the so-called fast-spectrum or fast reactor, characterized by more energetic faster-moving neutrons. These neutrons cause some transuranic species such as Np-237 to fission more efficiently. This is because the relative probability of fission as compared with capture is generally higher for fast neutrons. Fast reactor technology is much less mature than that of conventional power reactors, and some development projects such as one in France have been aborted. The third approach is to make neutrons by bombarding a suitable target with a proton beam from a high-energy accelerator. These neutrons would induce fission and hence produce additional neutrons from fissile material surrounding the target, leading to a subcritical reactor that would die out when the proton beam was shut off. The energy spectrum of the neutrons depends on the choice (mass, chemical composition, and whether liquid or solid) of the fuel and coolant.

Another application of transmutation beyond waste disposal is to extend the long-term sustainability of nuclear power by transmuting abundant U-238 into more easily fissionable Pu-239. This can be accomplished by putting the U-238 in a neutron flux where neutron capture leads to short-lived U-239. Within a period of days U-239 decays through Np-239 to Pu-239. A reactor that produces more fissile fuel than it consumes is called a breeder reactor. For technical reasons it is not possible to use conventional "thermal" reactors for breeding Pu-239 from U-238. One must turn to "fast" reactors. Thus fast reactor technology is common to both breeding and waste transmutation applications.

Fast reactors cannot use water or other light elements for the coolant, as thermalization of the fission neutrons must be avoided. Instead a liquid metal, typically sodium, is used as the coolant. Most fast reactor development projects were initiated several decades ago, and many have been terminated. France has had the most ambitious fast reactor program.[47] A small fast reactor, the Phenix, was put in operation in 1973 and was continuing to produce modest amounts of electricity into the 2000s. A more ambitious project was the construction of the SuperPhenix, which was shut down in 1998 because of technical problems after about a decade of intermittent operation. In Japan the Monju fast reactor, similar in size to Phenix, was shut down in 1995 after an accident where almost half of the sodium coolant leaked out. More recently the Japan Nuclear Cycle Development Institute has taken steps to obtain permission to restart the Monju reactor.[48]

Since the shutdown of the Experimental Breeder Reactor II (EBR-II) in Idaho and the Fast Flux Test Reactor in Washington no fast reactors have been operating in the United States. Fast reactors may play a more important role in future reactor development. Bodansky has reviewed the "Generation IV" program initiated by the U.S. DOE and now under international sponsorship.[49] The aim is to develop new reactors with improved economy, safety, and proliferation resistance that might be ready for deployment in two or three decades from now. Half of the six reactor systems proposed for primary development focus are fast reactors. The group working on fast reactors has as a goal for the systems under consideration the ability to recycle 99.9 percent of the actinides.[50]

We turn now to consider the use of high-energy accelerators as an alternative to fast reactors for producing energetic neutrons. Although less popular at the present time, this approach received a lot of attention in the last decade, not only in the United States but also in Europe and Japan. As alluded to above, the relative capture and fission cross sections for the neptunium, plutonium, and higher-Z transuranics for low-energy neutrons prohibit sufficiently complete burnup to make the use of conventional power reactors alone very practical. These cross sections are more favorable for a fast reactor neutron energy distribution, but then one runs into positive criticality problems unless one adds U-238. Such an addition reduces the net transuranic destruction rate.[51] These problems have led to the consideration of the use of a subcritical reactor sustained by neutrons produced by a high-energy proton accelerator. An accelerator system has the advantage that it can destroy radioactive elements without producing any neptunium or plutonium in the process.[52] The core of this reactor would contain the Pu and other transuranic elements and troublesome long-lived Tc and I fission products chemically extracted from the spent fuel. The Pu and other transuranics would be destroyed by neutron-induced fission, and the long-lived fission products would capture neutrons to make shorter-lived radioactive species that would more promptly decay to stable nuclei. Heat extracted from the core would be used to generate electricity, of which only a minor fraction would be required to power the accelerator and ancillary equipment. This approach is often designated Accelerator Transmutation of Waste or sometimes Accelerator-Driven Systems.

A number of variants of the Accelerator Transmutation of Waste approach are being considered by different groups and countries. We will initially focus our discussion on one presented in an October 1999 DOE report *A Roadmap for Developing Accelerator Transmutation of Waste (ATW) Technology: A Report to Congress.*[53] An independent effort in Europe by the European Technical Working Group on ADS has resulted in a report *A European Roadmap for Developing Accelerator Driven Systems (ADS) for Nuclear Waste Incineration.*[54] The U.S report laid out a 30-year, $10 billion research, development, and demonstration plan that begins with a research program, followed by pilot-scale transmutation demonstrations at a dedicated facility, and culminating in the operation of a half-scale plant prototype.

The Accelerator Transmutation of Waste "Roadmap" estimated that a full accelerator transmutation system capable of processing (over 60 years) the roughly 80,000 metric tons of spent fuel already produced or expected to be produced over the remaining lifetime of the presently licensed reactors would cost about $280 billion, and it optimistically suggests that the system could pay for itself from the electricity sold. The "Roadmap" envisions eight plants, each consisting of two accelerators and a chemical processing plant. An example of how a transmutation plant might work is as follows.[55] The spent fuel would first be fed to a chemical processing plant. In several steps five product streams would emerge. One would be the uranium from the spent fuel, which would constitute most of the mass but little of the radioactivity of the spent fuel. This could be stored for future use or be disposed of. A second stream would contain the transuranics, mostly plutonium but including troublesome long-lived neptunium. This would be fabricated into fuel for the transmuter. Also the Tc and the I from two additional product streams of the chemical separation facility would be fabricated for the blanket of the transmuter. I-129 and Tc-99 are long-lived fission products that are important contributors to the long-term toxicity of spent fuel. The final product stream would be other fission products, mostly short-lived or stable. This stream would be contaminated with about 5 percent of the I and Tc and 1 percent of the transuranics because of inefficiencies in the separation process. This product stream would have to be disposed of in a permanent repository.

The transuranics, Tc, and I fuel and blanket fractions would be placed around the target of the high-energy accelerator. The transuranics fuel would form a subcritical reactor, driven by the neutrons produced when the high-energy accelerator proton beam struck the tungsten target. After the transmuter fuel was about 30 percent consumed, it would have to be removed and cycled through the chemical processing plant again to separate out the new fission products from the transuranics.

At the present time Congress has made no commitment to the "Roadmap" plan. Appropriations in fiscal years 2001 and 2002 for general accelerator transmutation research were appreciably less than the figures envisioned in the "Roadmap." Congress in the fiscal year 2002 Appropriations Conference Report also directed the DOE to answer several questions regarding fuel processing and transmutation, including a comparison of accelerator-driven transmutation and fast reactor transmutation. A report in response to this directive was issued by the DOE in January 2003.[56] This report, reflecting in part the advice and input of the DOE Nuclear Energy Research Advisory Committee Subcommittee on Advanced Nuclear Transformation Technology, was less supportive of Accelerator-Driven Systems than the 1999 "Roadmap." In the years since 2003 the DOE has not put much emphasis on accelerator-based transmutation.

There are a number of technical challenges involved in reaching a practical facility. Existing accelerators in the desired energy range have a fairly high "trip rate," when the accelerator fails to deliver beam for periods of time ranging from seconds to hours.[57] Loss of beam for periods of more than a few seconds can cause problems associated with the fluctuation in electrical power delivered to the grid. Another challenge is associated with the chemical processing. The United States has less experience in this area because of the policy established some decades ago to forego reprocessing and opt for direct disposal of spent fuel elements. Not only the Pu and other transuranics but also specific fission product elements must be extracted. The hoped-for reduction of radiotoxicity of the wastes relies on a 99.5 percent separation efficiency. The volume of the waste stream must also be carefully considered.

Experimental work on the development of Accelerator-Driven Systems is most advanced outside of the United States. Japan is coupling a proton synchrotron to an old experimental reactor at Kyoto University's Research Reactor Institute at Kumatori to create the Kumatori Accelerator-Driven Reactor Test Facility. Protons will be fired into a cylinder of heavy metal surrounded by the reactor fuel. Another test facility is being pursued by France, Germany, and Italy at an experimental reactor in Rome. This project, dubbed TRADE, is not fully funded. A less ambitious experiment is planned at the Joint Institute for Nuclear Research at Dubna, Russia. A proton beam from an existing accelerator will be directed at a neutron production target.[58]

Both the economic and technical practicality of transmutation has been challenged.[59] An early but thorough review of separations and transmutation technologies was carried out by a committee of the National Research Council. This study had been requested by the secretary of energy. Its report, issued in 1995, was published by the National Academy of Sciences in 1996.[60] The report concluded that there was no evidence that applications of advanced separation and transmutation would have sufficient benefit for the U.S. high-level waste program to justify delaying the development of the first permanent repository for commercial spent fuel. The current policy of using the once-through (no reprocessing) fuel cycle for commercial reactors, with disposal of the spent fuel as high-level waste, should continue. N. C. Rasmussen, chairman of the committee that produced this 1995 report, along with committee member T. H. Pigford, summarized one of the conclusions of the committee by saying "to begin to have a significant benefit for waste disposal, an entire Separation and Transmutation system consisting of many facilities would have to operate in a highly integrated manner for several decades to hundreds of years."[61] With specific respect to Accelerator Transmutation of Waste concepts, the report emphasized the materials problems related to neutron fluxes at levels much larger than those for which there is previous experience.

In 2002, the Nuclear Energy Agency of the OECD released a report on an in-depth comparative study of accelerator-driven and fast reactor transmutation schemes.[62] Among the principal messages identified in the "Executive Summary" are the following:

- Fuel cycles with multiple recycling of the fuel and very low fuel losses are required to achieve the desired hundredfold radiotoxicity reduction.

- The accelerator-driven-based evolutionary and fast reactor–based innovative approaches appear to be attractive transmutation strategies, from both technical and economic viewpoints.

- The full potential of a transmutation system can be exploited only if the system is utilized for a minimum time period of about a hundred years.

A considerable amount of research and development on subcritical reactors, advanced fuels, and materials would be needed before accelerator-driven transmutation technology could be deployed. The report also notes that Accelerator-Driven System fuels "are particularly enriched in minor actinides and can probably be reprocessed only with the help of pyrochemical methods.... The introduction of pyrochemical processing technologies at the industrial level will require the development of new process flowsheets and the use of potentially very corrosive reagents in hostile environments. These processes will generate chemical and radiological hazards which will have to be mitigated."[63]

The aforementioned January 2003 DOE report to Congress questions the OECD report's estimates on the economic costs of transmutation. The DOE concludes that it is too early to estimate accurately the costs of spent fuel treatment and transmutation. The DOE also now considers its 1999

"Roadmap" for accelerator-driven transmutation as too costly and unrealistic. Its 2003 report to Congress outlines a "research program that will be required to enable an informed estimate of the potential benefits and cost of spent fuel treatment and transmutation technology."[64] Perhaps most relevant for the purposes of the present book, the report states that "even under the most successful scenario for this research, it will be necessary to proceed with all practical speed toward the establishment of a deep geologic repository to contain U.S. spent nuclear fuel and high-level radioactive wastes."[65]

A 2003 MIT study on the future of nuclear power evaluated the trade-offs of the present U.S. once-through fuel cycle (no reprocessing) with schemes involving separations and transmutation. The authors concluded that "we do not believe that a convincing case can be made on the basis of waste management considerations alone that the benefits of advanced fuel cycle schemes featuring waste partitioning and transmutation will outweigh the attendant risks and costs." They argue that for this conclusion to change "not only would the expected long-term risks from geologic repositories have to be significantly higher than those indicated in current risk assessments, but the incremental costs and short-term safety and environmental risks would have to be greatly reduced relative to current expectations and experience."[66] They are skeptical of the hope of some that by reducing the toxic lifetime of the waste the public would become more accepting of nuclear waste disposal. There can of course be another consideration besides that of waste management for a fuel cycle involving separation and transmutation if that cycle involves fast-spectrum neutrons. That is the possibility of extending our fuel supply by fissioning the much more abundant U-238 or breeding it to produce more fissionable Pu-239. However, the use of U-238 was not part of the "Roadmap" scheme discussed above.

A study on the economic future of nuclear power conducted by the University of Chicago and released in 2004 concluded that reprocessing would more than double the waste disposal costs compared with direct disposal of spent fuel.[67] In the same year, Bunn et al. concluded that direct disposal would remain significantly cheaper than recycling for at least the next 50 years.[68]

A study for Japan's Atomic Energy Commission was reported on October 6, 2004, to have concluded that reprocessing, at 1.6 yen/kWh, would be appreciably more expensive than direct burial, at 0.9–1.1 yen/kWh, when projected over the next 60 years. This estimate did not include the cost of eventually dismantling a reprocessing plant nearing completion at Rokkashomura.[69] In spite of this difference Japan's Atomic Energy Commission voted to proceed with the final commissioning and operation of the Rokkashomura plant. The reasons given included the stability it gives energy supplies, the lack of environmental risks, and the flexibility it affords energy policy.[70]

Public Acceptance Issues

Because transmutation involves reprocessing, issues related to reprocessing would be reopened. One concern about reprocessing is related to Pu and proliferation of nuclear weapons. This may not be a substantive issue as weapons-grade Pu would never be isolated in one plan envisioned.[71] Another issue is environmental safety, a matter that is of considerable public concern in view of past difficulties at reprocessing plants such as West Valley, N.Y., Hanford, Wash., and Windscale/Sellafield in Great Britain. With respect to global proliferation considerations, President George W. Bush in 2004 expressed his views that "nations of the Nuclear Suppliers Group should refuse to sell enrichment and reprocessing equipment and technologies to any state that does not already possess full-scale, functioning enrichment and reprocessing plants. This step will prevent new states from developing means to produce fissile material for nuclear bombs."[72]

Another issue is facility siting. Efforts to site both high- and low-level radioactive waste management facilities have encountered substantial, and often insurmountable, difficulties in gaining public acceptance. Part of the concern of neighbors to proposed sites is the possibility that they might become de facto long-term repositories. This fear has led to opposition to interim spent fuel storage facilities.

Finally, it should be noted that transmutation does not solve all of the problems of the transportation hazards associated with a geological repository, as the spent fuel would have to be transported to reprocessing and transmutation facilities, and some residual actinide and fission product waste would have to be transported to a final repository. The U.S. DOE has shown some sensitivity to this issue in its recent request for expressions of interest from the private sector for developing a reprocessing facility and a prototype fast-burner reactor as part of its GNEP initiative by encouraging colocation of these facilities.

NOTES

1. Nuclear Energy Agency, *The Environmental and Ethical Basis of Geological Disposal of Long-Lived Radioactive Wastes: A Collective Opinion of the Radioactive Waste Management Committee of the OECD Nuclear Energy Agency* (Paris: Organisation for Economic Co-operation and Development, 1995), available at www.nea.fr/html/rwm/reports/1995/ geodisp.html; International Atomic Energy Agency, *IAEA Safety Fundamentals: The Principles of Radioactive Waste Management* (Vienna: International Atomic Energy Agency, 1995). An extract of these principles from the Safety Series no. 111-F International Atomic Energy Agency publication is reproduced as Annexe I of the preceding Nuclear Energy Agency document.

2. Nuclear Energy Agency, *The Environmental and Ethical Basis of Geological Disposal of Long-Lived Radioactive Wastes*, 9.

3. Ibid.

4. Atomic Safety and Licensing Board, U.S. Nuclear Regulatory Commission, "Final Partial Initial Decision on F-16 Aircraft Accident Consequences," February 24, 2005, 2, available at www.nrc.gov/about-nrc/regulatory/adjudicatory/pfs-aircraft05.pdf.

5. International Atomic Energy Agency, *The Long Term Storage of Radioactive Waste: Safety and Sustainability* (Vienna: International Atomic Energy Agency, June 2003), 5, available at www-pub.iaea.org/MTCD/publications/PDF/LTS-RW_web.pdf.

6. Ibid., 13.

7. Commission on Geosciences, Environment and Resources, U.S. National Research Council, *Long-Term Institutional Management of U.S. Department of Energy Legacy Waste Sites* (Washington, DC: National Academy Press, 2000).

8. Allison M. Macfarlane, "Interim Storage of Spent Fuel in the United States," in *Annual Review of Energy and the Environment*, vol. 26, ed. Robert H. Socolow, John Harte, and Dennis Anderson (Palo Alto: Annual Reviews, Inc., 2001), 201–35.

9. Atomic Safety and Licensing Board, U.S. Nuclear Regulatory Commission, "Final Partial Initial Decision on F-16 Aircraft Accident Consequences."

10. "Headlines: International Briefs," *Radwaste Solutions* 11, no. 6 (November–December 2004): 11.

11. "Terms Worked Out for Nuclear Dump," *New York Times*, November 11, 1984: 40.

12. "Headlines," 11.

13. International Atomic Energy Agency, *Scientific and Technical Basis for Geological Disposal of Radioactive Wastes* (Vienna: International Atomic Energy Agency, 2003), available at www-pub.iaea.org/MTCD/publications/PDF/TRS413_web.pdf.

14. David Bodansky, *Nuclear Energy: Principles, Practices and Prospects*, 2nd ed. (New York: Springer-Verlag, 2004), 278–81.

15. Lasse Ringius, *Radioactive Waste Disposal at Sea* (Cambridge, MA: MIT Press, 2001).

16. Charles D. Hollister, D. Richard Anderson, and G. Ross Heath, "Subseabed Disposal of Nuclear Waste," *Science* 213, no. 4514 (September 18, 1981): 1321–27.

17. Charles D. Hollister and Steven Nadis, "Burial of Radioactive Waste under the Seabed," *Scientific American* 278, no. 1 (January 1998): 60–65.

18. Ibid., 64.

19. Bodansky, *Nuclear Energy*, 278.

20. Massachusetts Institute of Technology, *The Future of Nuclear Power: An Interdisciplinary MIT Study*, John Deutch and Ernest J. Moniz, cochairs (Cambridge, MA: MIT, 2003), 66–67, available at http://web.mit.edu/nuclearpower.

21. Ibid., 56.

22. Ibid.

23. William Miller, R. Alexander, N. Chapman, I. McKinley, and J. Smellie, eds., *Geological Disposal of Radioactive Wastes and Natural Analogues: Lessons from Nature and Archaeology* (Amsterdam: Pergamon, 2000), 82.

24. Paul P. Craig, "High-Level Waste: The Status of Yucca Mountain," in *Annual Review of Energy and the Environment*, vol. 24, ed. Robert H. Socolow, John Harte, and Dennis Anderson (Palo Alto: Annual Reviews Inc., 1999), 461–86.

25. Paul Rogers, sidebar, *Bulletin of the Atomic Scientists* 59, no. 5 (September–October 2003): 48–51.

26. Bodansky, *Nuclear Energy*, 225.

27. Nuclear Energy Agency, *Advanced Nuclear Fuel Cycles and Radioactive Waste Management*, NEA No. 5990 (Paris: Nuclear Energy Agency, Organisation for Economic Co-operation and Development, 2006), 139–41; Massachusetts Institute of Technology, *The Future of Nuclear Power*, 32.

28. Mathew Bunn, John P. Holdren, Steve Fetter, and Bob van der Zwaan, "The Economics of Reprocessing versus Direct Disposal of Spent Nuclear Fuel," *Nuclear Technology* 150 (2005): 209–29; see also University of Chicago, "The Economic Future of Nuclear Power," a study conducted at the University of Chicago, August 2004, available at www.anl.gov/Special_Reports/NuclEconSumAug04.pdf.

29. World Information Service on Energy (WISE)–Paris, *Possible Toxic Effects from the Nuclear Reprocessing Plants at Sellafield (UK) and Cap de La Hague (France)*, a study by WISE–Paris commissioned by the Scientific and Technological Options Panel of the European Parliament, November 2001, available at www.wise-paris.org/english/reports/STOAFinalStudyEN.pdf.

30. Pierre Bacher, quoted in Ann MacLachlan, "French Hail Strides in P&T but Question Strategy, Cost," *Platts Nuclear Fuel* 30, no. 5 (February 28, 2005): 10.

31. Lisa Zagaroli, "Program to Turn Plutonium Bombs into Fuel Hits Snag," *McClatchy Newspapers*, March 8, 2006.

32. Nuclear Energy Study Group of the American Physical Society Panel on Public Affairs, "Nuclear Power and Proliferation Resistance: Securing Benefits, Limiting Risk," May 2005, available at www.aps.org/policy/reports/popa-reports/proliferation-resistance/upload/proliferation.pdf.

33. Ibid., 20.

34. See U.S. Department of Energy, www.gnep.energy.gov.

35. Robert Vandenbosch and Susanne E. Vandenbosch, "Should the U.S. Reprocess Spent Nuclear Fuel?" *Forum on Physics and Society of the American Physical Society* 35 (2006): 7–9; Federation of American Scientists, "Global Nuclear Energy Partnership," 2006, available at www.fas.org/main/content.jsp?formAction=297&contentId=525.

36. Clayton Hirst, "Sellafield's Clean-Up Costs to Reach £1b Next Year," *The Independent (U.K.)*, October 31, 2004, available at http://news.independent.co.uk/environment/article31191.ece.

37. U.S. Department of Energy, *Report to Congress on Advanced Fuel Cycle Initiative: The Future Path for Advanced Spent Fuel Treatment and Transmutation Research*, January 2003, II-2, available at www.ne.doe.gov/pdfFiles/AFCI_CongRpt2003.pdf.

38. G. F. Vandegrift, M. C. Regalbuto, S. Aase, A. Bakel, T. J. Battisti, D. Bowers, J. P. Byrnes, M. A. Clark, D. G. Cummings, J. W. Emery, J. R. Falkenberg, A. V. Gelis, C. Pereira, L. Hafenrichter, Y. Tsai, K. J. Quigley, and M. H. Vander Pol, "Design and Demonstration of the UREX+ Process Using Spent Fuel," Argonne National Laboratory, presented at ATALANTE 2004—Advances for Future Nuclear Fuel Cycles, June 21–24, 2004, Nîmes, available at www.cmt.anl.gov/Science_and_Technology/Process_Chemistry/Publicatons/Atalante04.pdf; C. Pereira, G. F. Vandegrift, M. C. Regalbuto, S. Aase, Al. Bakel, D. Bowers, J. P. Byrnes, M. A. Clark, J. W. Emery, J. R. Falkenberg, A. V. Gelis, L. Hafenrichter, R. Leonard, K. J. Quigley, Y. Tsai,. M. H. Vander Pol, and J. J. Laidler, "Lab-Scale Demonstration of the UREX+2 Process Using Spent Fuel," presented at the WM'05 Conference, February 27–March 3, 2005, Tucson, available at www.wmsym.org/abstracts/pdfs/5410.pdf; Clay Sell, testimony before the Energy Subcommittee of the Senate Appropriations Committee, March 2, 2006, Washington, D.C., available at www.tmcnet.com/usubmit/2006/03/03/1428217.htm.

39. Sell, testimony before the Energy Subcommittee of the Senate Appropriations Committee.

40. H. F. McFarlane and M. M. Lineberry, "The IFR Fuel Cycle Demonstration," *Progress in Nuclear Energy* 31, nos. 1–2 (1997): 155–73.

41. U.S. National Research Council, *Electrometallurgical Techniques for DOE Spent Fuel Treatment: Final Report* (Washington, DC: National Academy Press, 2000), 42.

42. Nuclear Energy Agency, *Pyrochemical Separations in Nuclear Applications: A Status Report* (Paris: Organization for Economic Co-operation and Development, 2004), 150, available at www.nea.fr/html/science/docs/pubs/nea5427-pyrochemical.pdf.

43. U.S. National Research Council, *Electrometallurgical Techniques for DOE Spent Fuel Treatment*, 3–7.

44. U.S. Department of Energy, *Report to Congress on Advanced Fuel Cycle Initiative*, III-6.

45. Nuclear Energy Agency, *Pyrochemical Separations in Nuclear Applications*.

46. Ibid., 125–26.

47. Bodansky, *Nuclear Energy*, 190.

48. Mari Yamaguchi, "Court Upholds Japan Nuke Reactor Approval," Associated Press, May 30, 2005, available at www.nautilus.org/aesnet/2005/JUN0805/AP_Japan_Reactor.pdf.

49. Bodansky, *Nuclear Energy*, 470–75.

50. Nuclear Energy Research Advisory Committee and the Generation IV International Forum, *Generation IV Roadmap: R&D Scope Report for Liquid Metal-Cooled Reactor Systems*, GIF-005-00, Generation IV Nuclear Energy Systems, December 2002, available at http://gif.inel.gov/roadmap/pdfs/005_liquid_metal_reactors.pdf.

51. Weston M. Stacey, *Nuclear Reactor Physics* (New York: John Wiley and Sons, 2001), 239.

52. U.S. Department of Energy, *Report to Congress on Advanced Fuel Cycle Initiative*, III-8.

53. U.S. Department of Energy, *A Roadmap for Developing Accelerator Transmutation of Waste (ATW) Technology: A Report to Congress*, October 1999 (DOE/RW-0519), available at www.pnl.gov/atw/ReportToCongress/.

54. European Technical Working Group on ADS, *A European Roadmap for Developing Accelerator Driven Systems (ADS) for Nuclear Waste Incineration* (Rome: Ente per le Nuove technologie, l'Energia e l'Ambiente, 2001), available at http://130.237.70.51/reports/European%20Roadmap%20for%20developing%20ADS%20for%20Nuclear%20Waste%20Incineration-Full%20document.pdf.

55. U.S. Department of Energy, *A Roadmap for Developing Accelerator Transmutation of Waste (ATW) Technology*, "System Scenarios and Integration" (ANL-99/16), September 1999, Sec. 4.3.

56. U.S. Department of Energy, *Report to Congress on Advanced Fuel Cycle Initiative*, 2003.

57. W. Gudowski, "Transmutation of Nuclear Waste," *Nuclear Physics* A663–64 (2000): 169c–82c.

58. Dennis Normile, "Proton Guns Set Their Sights on Taming Radioactive Wastes," *Science* 302 (2003): 381.

59. Wolfgang Panofsky, "Mixed Message," *Bulletin of the Atomic Scientists* 54, no. 2 (1998): 45.

60. U.S. National Research Council, *Nuclear Wastes: Technologies for Separations and Transmutation* (Washington, DC: National Academy Press, 1996).

61. N. C. Rasmussen and T. H. Pigford, "Transmutation of Radioactive Waste: Effect on the Nuclear Fuel Cycle," International Symposium on Nuclear Fuel Cycle and Reactor Strategies: Adjusting to New Realities, International Atomic Energy Agency, June 3–6, 1997, Vienna, quoted in World Information Service on Energy–Paris, "The European Spallation Source Project and Nuclear Waste Transmutation," available at www.noah.dk/energi/ESS-WISE-Memo-271102-final.pdf.

62. Nuclear Energy Agency, *Accelerator-Driven Systems (ADS) and Fast Reactors (FR) in Advanced Nuclear Fuel Cycles: A Comparative Study* (Paris: Organization for Economic Co-operation and Development, 2002), available at www.nea.fr/html/ndd/reports/2002/nea3109.html.

63. Ibid.

64. U. S. Department of Energy, *Report to Congress on Advanced Fuel Cycle Initiative*, I-2.

65. Ibid., I-8.

66. Massachusetts Institute of Technology, *The Future of Nuclear Power*, 60.

67. See University of Chicago, "The Economic Future of Nuclear Power."

68. Bunn et al., "The Economics of Reprocessing versus Direct Disposal of Spent Nuclear Fuel."

69. United Press International, "Nuclear Fuel Reprocessing Too Costly," *Washington Times*, October 6, 2004.

70. "The Nuclear Power Challenge," Editorial, *Japan Times Online*, November 17, 2004, available at www.japantimes.co.jp/cgi-bin/geted.pl5?ed20041117a1.htm.

71. U.S. Department of Energy, *A Roadmap for Developing Accelerator Transmutation of Waste (ATW) Technology*.

72. George W. Bush, remarks, National Defense University, Fort Lesley J. McNair, February 12, 2004, Washington, DC.

3

Overview of Legislative and Executive Actions Concerning High-Level Radioactive Waste

EARLY EFFORTS REGARDING WASTE DISPOSAL

In the United States the responsibility for the handling of both commercial and defense nuclear waste has resided with the Atomic Energy Commission (AEC) and its successor agencies since the establishment of the AEC in 1946. By the early 1970s there was increasing public distrust with the AEC acting as both the promoter of nuclear power and the regulator of nuclear power. In 1974, Congress abolished the AEC and created two new agencies. The Energy Research and Development Administration took on most of the activities of the former AEC. The Nuclear Regulatory Commission (NRC) was given responsibility for the regulatory aspects. This reorganization was supported both by nuclear power proponents and by nuclear power opponents.[1] The proponents felt that resolving the apparent conflict of interest in the same agency promoting and regulating nuclear power would remove a liability. The opponents hoped that the division into separate agencies would result in better oversight of the nuclear industry and increased protection of public health and safety. In 1976, the Environmental Protection Agency (EPA) assumed responsibility for developing radiation protection standards for nuclear wastes. These included standards for both radioactivity releases and radiation exposures associated with the operation of waste facilities. In the early 1970s the Joint Committee on Atomic Energy, once a very powerful committee of the U.S. House and Senate, was losing power. This loss of power reflected changing public attitudes toward the safety and economics of nuclear power. The joint committee was abolished in 1977, in part because of "the general perception that the committee members were too close to the industry."[2]

The Arab oil embargo in the mid-1970s further emphasized the need for a comprehensive national energy policy. Reflecting the increasing importance of energy, the Energy Research and Development Administration was replaced in 1977 by the Department of Energy (DOE), a Cabinet-level department. In addition, the National Academy of Sciences (NAS) has been asked from time to time to provide scientific advice on such questions as reactor safety and radiation protection standards.

In the mid-1950s the National Academy of Sciences was asked to consider methods for the disposal of defense-related high-level radioactive waste. It concluded that radioactive wastes could be safely disposed of in a variety of geologic media and recommended salt as a potentially suitable host rock.[3] The features of salt that make it attractive for high-level nuclear waste disposal are described in the previous chapter. The NAS did recognize that significant research would be necessary to reach a final conclusion on the feasibility, reliability, and safety of geologic disposal. This early recommendation for salt as a host site was reaffirmed by the NAS in 1970, although further studies were suggested.[4]

The mid-1960s through the early 1980s was a period during which the AEC and its successor agencies, the Energy Research and Development Administration and the DOE, spent considerable effort in seeking suitable geological repository sites. Carter has given an excellent account of the technical and political aspects of this effort through 1986.[5] At first the emphasis was on identifying sites underlain by salt.

In an early effort the AEC investigated salt deposits near Lyons, Kansas (about 80 miles northwest of Wichita), for a permanent repository. As part of this investigation encapsulated spent fuel from an experimental AEC reactor was inserted into holes drilled in the floor of a salt mine.[6] Valuable information was obtained about the interaction between the waste form and the salt in which the waste was emplaced between 1965 and 1967. The experiment revealed that inclusions of moisture, or brine, in the salt beds have a tendency to migrate up a thermal gradient toward a heat source.[7]

In 1970, the AEC proposed the salt deposits near Lyons, Kans., for a permanent repository. Congress formalized this recommendation in a provision creating a National Radwaste Repository Program as part of the Atomic Energy Authorization Act of 1972.[8] The Lyons site, however, was abandoned soon thereafter for both technical and political reasons. On the technical side, a survey revealed that there were numerous boreholes associated with previous explorations for oil and gas.[9] On the political side, there was growing opposition to the site within Kansas. Congressman Joe Skubitz became strongly opposed to the project even though the site was several counties away from his district. At his urging, the two senators from Kansas were able to have the AEC's annual authorization bill amended to prevent any work at Lyons until a distinguished technical advisory committee could certify the proposed repository site as safe.[10]

After the failure of the Lyons, Kans., siting proposal, the Energy Research and Development Administration proposed the development of a retrievable surface storage facility at the Hanford Nuclear Reservation in the State of Washington. This proposal was dropped because of concerns that it would defer efforts for final geologic disposal. In the years since, several proposals for monitored retrievable storage (MRS) have been put forward, but they have usually died or been killed because of the same concern. The most active effort presently in this direction is a utility industry–sponsored initiative to develop a facility on Goshute Indian tribal land in Utah. This effort is discussed further in a later chapter.

Another site screening was attempted as part of the National Waste Terminal Storage Program in 1977. Both areas underlaid by salt and areas where radioactive materials were already present were considered. As part of the latter emphasis, site screening was initiated at the Hanford site and at the Nevada Test Site. Initially the Nevada Test Site exploration focused on finding a suitable structure of argillite (a clay-rich metamorphic rock) or of granite. In 1978 an exploratory borehole at a promising location was drilled to a depth of 3,000 feet without finding granite. Other studies indicated that possible granite blocks elsewhere in the vicinity might not be large enough and might contain deposits of precious metals. Still other studies indicated that argillite in the area was too structurally complex for definitive characterization. Emphasis then shifted to Yucca Mountain, at the western edge of the test site, where an exploratory hole confirmed the presence of thick tuff layers. Tuff had not previously been identified as a suitable host, so the DOE sought the advice of the National Academy of Sciences Committee for Radioactive Waste Management. This committee supported further investigation of tuff as a repository host rock. In parallel with the Nevada Test Site screening, studies of basalt inside or adjacent to the Hanford site were performed. Evaluation of sites outside the Hanford site did not locate sites obviously superior to those within the Hanford site, and a "reference repository location" within the site was identified.

Salt deposits continued to be of interest. Salt domes are found in the

Gulf Coastal plain region of Texas, Louisiana, and Mississippi. Bedded salt is found in the large Permian Basin, extending from southeast New Mexico across Texas and Oklahoma into Kansas; in the Paradox Basin in southeastern Utah; and in the Salina Basin, which extends from the lower Great Lakes region into New York and Pennsylvania. Investigations in the latter basin quickly ran into political opposition from the states of Ohio, Michigan, and New York. The governors of these states were able to stop further investigations in their states before exploratory drilling commenced: "Nothing beyond the preparation of literature surveys was ever accomplished."[11] The Energy Research and Development Administration and its successor, the DOE, abandoned efforts to explore the Salina Basin by the end of the 1970s.

In 1978 President Carter initiated an Interagency Review Group to conduct a comprehensive review of nuclear waste disposal policy. In the following year this group recommended proceeding with geologic disposal. It also recommended that alternative host rock environments in addition to salt be considered. In response, a national survey of crystalline rocks was undertaken, resulting in the identification of near-surface and exposed crystalline rock formations in 17 states.

President Ford decided in 1975 to forego reprocessing of commercial spent nuclear fuel. This decision was based on nonproliferation objectives. He feared that reprocessing would make plutonium more accessible for making nuclear weapons and hoped that if the United States did not reprocess, other nations would not proceed with their reprocessing plans.[12] The principal consequence of this decision for nuclear waste management is that larger quantities of plutonium would have to be disposed of, as the plutonium would not be separated and reused as a fuel in future reactors. The presence of the plutonium isotope Pu-239, with a half-life of 24,000 years, and of Np-237, with a half-life of 2.1 million years, means that release from the repository site must be held to an acceptable level for a period of time of the order of a million years. In 1977 President Carter reaffirmed the decision to forego reprocessing, again because of concerns about global nuclear proliferation.[13] He also proposed the acceptance of spent nuclear fuel at an away-from-reactor facility and the thorough investigation of several geologic repository sites from which the best would be picked later.[14] Although President Reagan in 1981 withdrew the ban on reprocessing, the policy of the United States has been to not reprocess used fuel.[15] This is contrary to the policy of most other nations with major nuclear power programs including France, the United Kingdom, Japan, and Russia. As discussed in the previous chapter, reprocessing is presently appreciably more expensive than the direct disposal of spent fuel. President Reagan also withdrew President Carter's away-from-reactor storage proposal.

THE NUCLEAR WASTE POLICY ACT OF 1982

In response to the lack of progress in dealing with the final disposal of high-level radioactive wastes, Congress in 1982 passed the Nuclear Waste Policy Act (NWPA).[16] This was a major piece of legislation that settled a number of issues and assigned responsibilities for siting, licensing, constructing, and operating a repository. Among the provisions of this act were the following:

1. Established the Office of Civilian Radioactive Waste Management within the DOE.
2. Adopted geological disposal for the final isolation of radioactive wastes.
3. Directed the DOE to nominate five sites as suitable for characterization for the first repository and to recommend three of the sites to the president for site characterization.
4. Directed that, following site characterization, the secretary of energy may decide to recommend a site to the president. If the secretary's recommendation is accepted, the president is to submit a recommendation to Congress. The site designation becomes effective 60 days after the president's recommendation, unless in the interim a Notice of Disapproval is submitted by the governor and legislature of the state in which the site is located or by the governing body of a Native American Tribe on whose reservation the site is located. If such a notice is submitted, the site would be disapproved unless within the first 90 days of a continuing session of Congress after the submittal, Congress passes a resolution of siting approval.
5. Directed that, if a site designation becomes effective, the DOE is to submit an application to the Nuclear Regulatory Commission within 90 days for a construction license. If approved and the repository is constructed, the DOE must apply for additional

licensing to begin accepting waste. Acceptance of waste is to begin by 1998.

6. Limited the quantity of waste to be emplaced in the first repository to 70,000 metric tons of heavy metal (uranium and the transmutation products neptunium and plutonium). A future second repository would have to be located in the eastern United States.

7. Established a Nuclear Waste Fund to cover the expenses of developing waste repository facilities. This is funded by a 1.0 mil per kilowatt-hour (0.1 cents/kWh) fee on the commercial generation of nuclear power. The secretary of energy is to review the fee amount annually.

8. Allowed for the recommendation to the president to be accompanied by an "environmental assessment," rather than a full environmental impact statement.

9. Endorsed monitored retrievable storage as a spent nuclear fuel management option.

10. Exempted waste resulting from defense activities from most provisions of the act.

In 1983 the DOE identified nine possible sites for the first repository. These were

- Vacherie dome, Louisiana   salt dome
- Cypress dome, Mississippi   salt dome
- Richton dome, Mississippi   salt dome
- Yucca Mountain, Nevada   tuff
- Deaf Smith County, Texas   bedded salt
- Swisher County, Texas   bedded salt
- Davis Canyon, Utah   bedded salt
- Lavender Canyon, Utah   bedded salt
- Hanford site, Washington   basalt flows[17]

The complex process of narrowing the list is described in the following chapter.

The last step in this period between the 1982 NWPA and the 1987 Nuclear Waste Policy Amendments Act was the secretary of energy's recommendation to the president of three sites for further characterization. These were Yucca Mountain, Nev., Deaf Smith County, Tex., and the Hanford site, Wash. The 1982 NWPA called for site characterization of all three. As discussed in a following chapter, Congress amended this act with the passage of the Amendments Act in 1987 and selected only one site, Yucca Mountain, for site characterization. A mandate of the 1982 NWPA to identify sites for a second repository was annulled with the passage of the 1987 Amendments Act.

THE NUCLEAR WASTE POLICY AMENDMENTS ACT OF 1987

Already by late 1986 it was clear that the schedule outlined in the Nuclear Waste Policy Act of 1982 could not be met. The approval of the three sites occurred almost a year and a half later than scheduled. Furthermore, the site selection had led to a great deal of controversy, including lawsuits initiated by the three affected states. Motivated in part by concern about program costs and the slippage in the time schedule, Congress reassessed the need to characterize three potential repository sites. It passed the Nuclear Waste Policy Amendments Act of 1987, which directed the DOE to limit its site characterization activities to Yucca Mountain.[18] Yucca Mountain was apparently selected at least in part because local opposition was thought to be less than at the other two sites. The accuracy of this perception is not clear. Statewide polls taken between 1986 and 1988 show that state residents in all three states opposed hosting a repository. The local communities of the Tri-Cities, Wash., and Beatty, Amargosa Valley, Nev., supported hosting a repository, whereas the agricultural counties of Deaf Smith and Oldham, Tex., opposed hosting a repository.[19] Another factor in this selection may have been that at this time Nevada's senators were low in seniority and Nevada had few representatives in the House because of its small population. The legislative skills of Senator J. Bennett Johnston (D-LA), who favored the selection of Yucca Mountain, played an important role.

By requiring the DOE to pursue site characterization only at Yucca Mountain, the 1987 Amendments Act also suspended the requirement to pursue a site for a second repository. It directed the DOE to report on the need for a second repository on or after January 1, 2007, but no later than January 1, 2010. It also directed the DOE to terminate all research programs on the suitability of crystalline rock as a potential repository host medium. This provision was a political decision advocated by congressional representatives of most eastern and Midwestern states, as crystalline rock, particularly granite, is the only likely medium in their geographical regions. Crystalline rock is the choice of Sweden and Finland for their repositories and is a leading candidate for a Canadian repository.

The Amendments Act also nullified a proposal from the DOE to locate a monitored retrievable storage facility in Tennessee. It restricted the DOE's ability to identify and develop an MRS site by requiring presidential approval of a proposed site, which could not be within the State of Nevada. Furthermore, construction of such a site could not commence until the NRC issued a license for the construction of a permanent repository.

The act had other provisions as well. It expanded external oversight of the DOE by establishing the Nuclear Waste Technical Review Board. It established an incentives program to entice states, local governments, and Indian tribes to support hosting a repository. (The implementation of the incentives program is described in chapter 6.) It defined certain units of government as "affected" because of their jurisdiction over proposed sites and required the DOE to provide financial assistance to such units to support their participation in defined activities. It required that packages for transport be certified by the Nuclear Regulatory Commission and that the DOE provide technical and financial assistance to states to train transportation public safety officials.

THE ENERGY POLICY ACT OF 1992 AND YUCCA MOUNTAIN RADIATION STANDARDS

Although this act did not deal extensively with waste issues, it did specify that the EPA would set unique standards for Yucca Mountain.[20] The EPA was directed to issue a new, health-based standard that could depart from EPA generic repository standards authorized by the 1982 NWPA and issued by the EPA in 1985.[21] (Part of this regulation was overthrown by a Court of Appeals decision in 1987.) In preparation for setting standards for Yucca Mountain, the 1992 act required the EPA to "contract with the National Academy of Sciences to conduct a study" and "provide findings and recommendations on reasonable standards for protection of the public health and safety."[22] The EPA was to use these findings and recommendations in establishing its new standards. The act directed the Nuclear Regulatory Commission to revise its regulations as necessary to be consistent with the EPA standards, once issued. This action by Congress to charge the EPA with establishing unique environmental standards to be met by the Yucca Mountain repository has been controversial, and attempts have been made to set it aside.

The National Academy of Sciences issued its recommendations on Yucca Mountain radiation standards in 1995.[23] These recommendations, as well as the EPA standards issued in response to them, are discussed in chapter 7.[24] Parts of the EPA regulations were challenged in court by Nevada, the Natural Resources Defense Council, and other petitioners. This lawsuit, as well as a Court of Appeals decision in 2004 to set aside the part of the EPA standards based on a 10,000-year compliance time rather than a longer time as recommended by the National Academy of Sciences, is discussed in chapter 10 on court appeals. At the present time the EPA is in the process of revising its standard, which must be approved by the court.

THE YEARS BETWEEN 1992 AND PRESIDENTIAL APPROVAL IN 2002

In the years following the Amendments Act, the complexity and cost of the site characterization process became more apparent. Progress was slow, and there was considerable congressional and constituent dissatisfaction with the program. In 1996 the Energy and Water Development Appropriations Act reduced program funding by 40 percent from 1995 levels.

In 2000 Congress passed a bill (S. 1287, "The Nuclear Waste Policy Act of 2000") that would have accelerated the schedule for transporting high-level nuclear waste to Yucca Mountain and blocked the EPA from setting radiation standards for the proposed repository. It would have directed the DOE to apply to the Nuclear Regulatory Commission for permission to store spent fuel at surface facilities at Yucca Mountain at the same time that it submitted an application for construction authorization.[25] President Bill Clinton vetoed the bill on April 25, and the Senate sustained the veto by one vote.[26] In his veto message Clinton criticized the requirement of further NRC and National Academy of Sciences review before the EPA could issue final regulations. He also criticized the bill for not authorizing the federal government to take title to spent fuel at reactor sites, which the administration believed would have offered a practical near-term solution to address the contractual obligation to utilities and would have minimized the potential for lengthy and costly proceedings.[27]

On November 14, 2001, the DOE issued final rules establishing policies for recommendation of repository sites.[28] The previously issued "General Guidelines for the Recommendation of Sites for Nuclear Waste Repositories" (10 CFR 960) was revised, and a new 10 CFR 963 "Yucca Mountain Site Suitability Guidelines" was issued. (Federal rules are codified in the *Code of Federal Regulations* [CFR]. The issuing agency is indicated by the number preceding CFR, and the particular part of the agency's regulations is indicated by the number following CFR.) The latter part 963 had to be in place before the secretary of energy could recommend Yucca Mountain to the president. These guidelines are discussed in appendix E.

THE CLOCK STARTS TICKING: 2002 APPROVAL OF YUCCA MOUNTAIN

Secretary Abraham's Recommendation to the President

On January 10, 2002, Secretary of Energy Spencer Abraham notified the governor of Nevada that he intended to recommend to President Bush that Yucca Mountain was a suitable site for a permanent repository. The recommendation was made February 14, 2002.

President Bush's Approval

The day following the secretary's recommendation, President Bush informed Congress that he was approving Yucca Mountain as the site for disposal of high-level waste. The president declared the site to be "qualified for application for a construction authorization for a repository." He further stated, "Proceeding with the repository program is necessary to protect public safety, health, and the Nation's security." He said that a "deep geologic repository.... is important for our national security and our energy future," mentioning that nuclear energy "must remain a major component of our energy policy in the years to come."[29] The president's approval set in motion the time schedule for possible state objection and congressional action as provided by the 1982 NWPA.

Nevada's Veto

Following President Bush's approval, Governor Kenny Guinn issued a Notice of Disapproval on April 8. This was the first time in U.S. history that a governor vetoed a presidential action. The disapproval, allowed for by the 1982 NWPA, would be effective unless Congress passed a resolution of siting approval within 90 days of "continuous session." Governor Guinn indicated some pessimism regarding Nevada's chance of getting Congress to disapprove the site. He said that he believed "our best opportunity is in the courts."[30] Within an hour of the president's approval Nevada filed a new lawsuit, "the third in nine months—charging that the President's decision was based on a flawed recommendation by the Department of Energy and asking that it be set aside."[31]

Congressional Override of Nevada's Veto

The House approved a resolution overriding Nevada's veto with a 306 to 117 vote on May 8. The Senate approved the resolution on July 9 with only two hours of floor debate. Post-9/11 anxiety about terrorist attacks on spent fuel storage facilities played a prominent role in the debate in both houses. In parliamentary maneuvering before the introduction of the resolution by Senator Murkowski (R-AK), it was agreed that a roll-call vote would be taken on whether to take up the resolution and that only a voice vote would be taken on the resolution itself. The vote to take up the resolution was 60 to 39, a larger margin than had been predicted in the days prior to the vote. President Bush signed the resolution approving Yucca Mountain on July 26, 2002.

The Way Forward

The next step is for the DOE to apply to the Nuclear Regulatory Commission for a license. According to the NWPA, the DOE was supposed to apply to the NRC for a construction license within 90 days after congressional approval of a repository site.[32] The NRC then would decide on the license application within three years of its submission, with the possibility of a one-year extension.[33] During the period in which it is considering the application the NRC has to provide an annual report to Congress on unresolved and contentious issues. For a number of years the DOE was expecting to submit a license application by the end of 2004 and start accepting waste by 2010. This timetable fell into disarray, however, primarily for reasons discussed in the following section.

In July 2006 the DOE announced a new schedule that would have a license application submitted by June 2008 and begin receipt of waste by 2017. This receipt date is 19 years after the receipt date originally mandated by Congress in 1982.

SETBACKS ON THE WAY TO A LICENSING APPLICATION

The Court of Appeals Overturns the Yucca Mountain Radiation Standards

As discussed further in the chapter on court appeals, the D.C. Court of Appeals in July 2004 rejected the EPA's 10,000-year compliance time in the Yucca Mountain radiation standards. The court directed the EPA to revise its standard to be consistent with the recommendations in the National Academy of Sciences report mandated by the 1992 Energy Act. That report recommended that the compliance time should extend to the time of projected peak dose. The peak dose is expected to occur between 100,000 and one million years from now. It is not clear when the EPA will issue its new final standard. The absence of a standard to measure up to makes it awkward to construct a license application. Furthermore, if the EPA were to keep the same maximum exposure limit and just extend the compliance time to that of the peak dose, the present design of the repository would not be adequate. The DOE has presented performance assessments that exhibit a peak dose (at approximately 300,000 years after closure of the repository) an order of magnitude larger than the 15 millirem per year (mrem/yr) dose limit of the original standards. Bodansky has pointed out that this peak dose is probably an overestimate because an outdated, excessively large dose-response coefficient for long-lived Np-237 was employed in these calculations.[34] Use of a more recent dose-response coefficient, however, would probably not bring the anticipated long-term performance within the 15 mrem/yr dose limit of the original 10,000-year standard.

The Environmental Protection Agency Issues Proposed New Radiation Standards

In mid-2005 the EPA proposed new standards in response to the Court of Appeals rejection of part of its earlier standards. These new standards are discussed in more detail at the end of the Yucca Mountain chapter. Briefly, the EPA proposed a two-tiered standard, retaining its earlier 15 mrem/yr dose limit for the first 10,000 years and proposing a much less stringent 350 mrem/yr dose limit between 10,000 years and one million years. The proposed new standards were open for public comment until late fall 2005. The EPA now has to review these comments and issue final standards.

Other Setbacks

The Nuclear Regulatory Commission requires as part of the licensing application process that the DOE construct an Internet-accessible documentation retrieval system that would contain all of the supporting data and reports. This system was supposed to be in place and certified by the NRC prior to formal submission of an application. The DOE found the generation of this Licensing Support Network (available at www.lsnnet.gov/) to be a larger challenge than anticipated and did not achieve certification sufficiently in advance of the date required for a December 2004 license application.

A third setback was the revelation in early 2005 of some e-mails generated by DOE contractor personnel indicating that some validation documentation had been fabricated. This matter is under investigation and was the subject of a preliminary hearing by a House subcommittee. It remains to be seen whether any ingredients of the performance assessment models were compromised or whether the alleged fabrication only involved the documentation of quality assurance.

Reconsideration of the Reprocessing Option in the United States

As mentioned in the previous chapter, the DOE has as part of a new Global Nuclear Energy Partnership initiative proposed developing reprocessing and fast-reactor technology that would reduce the amount of waste requiring geological disposal. It would not, however, eliminate the need for a permanent repository. Congress has yet to endorse this proposed major change in the direction of the U.S. spent fuel management program.

NOTES

1. Robert J. Duffy, *Nuclear Politics in America: A History and Theory of Government Regulation* (Lawrence: University Press of Kansas, 1997), 112–13.

2. Frank R. Baumgartner and Bryan D. Jones, *Agendas and Instability in American Politics* (Chicago: University of Chicago Press, 1993), 69.

3. U.S. National Academy of Sciences–National Research Council, *The Disposal of Radioactive Waste on Land*, report of the Committee on Waste Disposal, Division of Earth Sciences, Publication 519 (Washington, DC: National Academy of Sciences–National Research Council, 1957).

4. David Bodansky, *Nuclear Energy: Principles, Practices and Prospects*, 2nd ed. (New York: Springer-Verlag, 2004), 292.

5. Luther J. Carter, *Nuclear Imperatives and Public Trust: Dealing with Radioactive Waste* (Washington, DC: Resources for the Future, 1987).

6. U.S. Congress, Office of Technology Assessment, *Managing the Nation's Commercial High-Level Radioactive Waste* (OTA-O-171; Washington, DC: Office of Technology Assessment, March 1985), 237.

7. Colin A. Heath, "The Department of Energy Program for Long Term Isolation of Radioactive Waste," in *Radioactive Waste in Geologic Storage*, ed. Sherman Fried (Washington, DC: American Chemical Society, 1979), 2.

8. James H. Saling and Audeen W. Fentiman, eds., *Radioactive Waste Management*, 2nd ed. (New York: Taylor and Francis, 2001), 19.

9. Carter, *Nuclear Imperatives and Public Trust*, 69.

10. Ibid., 70–71.

11. Ibid., 149.

12. Ibid., 117.

13. Ibid., 118, 129.

14. Ibid., 117–18.

15. Ibid., 120; U.S. Department of Energy, Office of Civilian Radioactive Waste Management, "History of the Civilian Radioactive Waste Management Program," in *Civilian Radioactive Waste Management Program Plan, Revision 3* (Washington, DC: Office of Civilian Radioactive Waste Management, February 2000), app. B, 66, available at www.ocrwm.doe.gov/pm/pdf/pprev3.pdf.

16. Nuclear Waste Policy Act of 1982, Public Law 97-425, 97th Cong., 2d Sess. (January 7, 1983).

17. U.S. Department of Energy, Office of Civilian Radioactive Waste Management, "History of the Civilian Radioactive Waste Management Program," 67.

18. Budget Reconciliation Act of 1987, Public Law 100-203, 100th Cong., 1st Sess., Title V, Subtitle A, the Nuclear Waste Policy Amendments Act of 1987 (December 22, 1987).

19. See R. E. Dunlap, E. A. Rosa, and R. K. Baxter, "Local Attitudes toward Siting a High-Level Nuclear Waste Repository at Hanford, Washington," in *Public Reactions to Nuclear Waste*, ed. Riley E. Dunlap, Michael E. Kraft, and Eugene A. Rosa (Durham: Duke University Press, 1993), 141; R. S. Krannich, R. L. Little, and L. A. Cramer, "Rural Community Residents' Views," in *Public Reactions to Nuclear Waste*, ed. Riley E. Dunlap, Michael E. Kraft, and Eugene A. Rosa (Durham: Duke University Press, 1993), 273; J. G. Brody, and J. K. Fleishman, "Source of Public Concern about Nuclear Waste Disposal in Texas Agricultural Communities," in *Public Reactions to Nuclear Waste*, ed. Riley E. Dunlap, Michael E. Kraft, and Eugene A. Rosa (Durham: Duke University Press, 1993), 120.

20. The Energy Policy Act of 1992, Public Law 102-486, 102nd Cong., 1st Sess. (October 24, 1992). The Nuclear Waste Policy Act of 1982 as amended in 1987 and 1992 is codified at U.S. Code 42(2000), 10101 ff.

21. U.S. Environmental Protection Agency, "Environmental Radiation Protection Standards for Management and Disposal of Spent Nuclear Fuel, High-Level and Transuranic Radioactive Wastes; Final Rule," 40 CFR 191, *Federal Register* 50, no. 182 (September 19, 1985): 38066.

22. The Energy Policy Act of 1992, Sec. 801.

23. U.S. National Research Council, *Technical Bases for Yucca Mountain Standards* (Washington, DC: National Academies Press, 1995).

24. See U.S. Environmental Protection Agency, "Public Health and Environmental Radiation Protection Standards for Yucca Mountain, Nevada," 40 CFR 197, *Federal Register* 66, no. 114 (June 13, 2001): 32074.

25. *Congressional Record* 146 (February 10, 2000): S574.

26. Eric Pianin, "U.S. Sets Safety Rules for Yucca Nuclear Waste Site," *Washington Post*, June 6, 2001.

27. *Weekly Compilation of Presidential Documents* 36, no. 17 (May 1, 2000): 922, available at www.gpoaccess.gov/wcomp/.

28. U.S. Department of Energy, "General Guidelines for the Preliminary Screening of Potential Sites for Nuclear Waste Repositories," 10 CFR 960, *Federal Register* 66, no. 220 (November 14, 2001): 57304; U.S. Department of Energy, "Yucca Mountain Site Suitability Guidelines," 10 CFR 963, *Federal Register* 66, no. 220 (November 14, 2001): 57298.

29. George W. Bush, "Letter from Bush to House, Senate," *Las Vegas Review Journal*, February 16, 2002, available at www.reviewjournal.com/lvrj_home/2002/Feb-16-Sat-2002/news/18119294.html.

30. Steve Tetreault, Stephens Washington Bureau, "Nuclear Waste Repository: Bush Backs Yucca Plan," *Las Vegas Review-Journal*, February 16, 2002: 1A.

31. Ibid.

32. Nuclear Waste Policy Act of 1982, Sec. 114, available at www.ocrwm.doe.gov/documents/nwpa/css/nwpa.htm.

33. Ibid.

34. Bodansky, *Nuclear Energy*, 326.

: 4

The Nuclear Waste Policy Act of 1982: Adoption of a Policy for the Disposal of Spent Fuel from Commercial Reactors

FACTORS LEADING UP TO THE ADOPTION OF A
DISPOSAL POLICY FOR HIGH-LEVEL NUCLEAR WASTE

As more nuclear reactors were brought into production and existing reactors continued to produce power, the number of spent fuel rods increased. This gave rise to increased concern about dealing with this highly radioactive waste. The radioactivity of spent fuel is far too great to be released into rivers, lakes, or the atmosphere. Luther Carter has estimated that even after 1,000 years the amount of spent fuel produced by a single reactor in one year would have to be diluted with ten billion cubic meters of water to bring it up to drinking water standards.[1]

The nuclear industry was eager to get rid of the spent fuel. Initially people in the industry expected to ship it to reprocessing plants. This was done for the short period of time that a commercial reprocessing facility was operating at West Valley, N.Y. Although reprocessing facilities were being developed in South Carolina and Illinois, they never went into operation. Fears of proliferation led President Ford to propose a moratorium on reprocessing. President Carter formally imposed a moratorium during the first year of his administration. Although this moratorium was lifted during the Reagan administration, the reprocessing of spent fuel from commercial nuclear reactors was never resumed. This left nuclear utilities "holding the bag" with their spent fuel. In some cases, spent fuel rods were shipped back to nuclear reactor sites when the West Valley facility was shut down. The spent fuel was stored in pools of water, which provided thermal cooling, and radioactive decay continued to take place. These pools were getting crowded, and at some reactor sites the spent fuel rods were "reracked," placing them closer together.[2] Nuclear utility operators also had to pay for this storage, which added an economic dimension to their concerns over the storage of the waste.

Meanwhile, the public was becoming increasingly concerned about environmental pollution. Probably the person who did the most to alert people to environmental hazards was Rachel Carson. Carson called attention in the book *Silent Spring* to the fact that birds were dying as the result of the widespread use of the pesticide DDT.[3] In this book she also claimed that DDT was killing fish and getting into the human food chain. On April 22, 1970, Senator Gaylord Nelson sponsored Earth Day, which involved nationwide teach-ins about various environmental problems. Interest in the environment continued to grow as air and water quality deteriorated further, although concern about nuclear waste was not a top priority in the early 1970s.

In the nuclear area, the initial concern was over the thermal pollution cased by the discharge of waste heat into rivers. This was remedied, reluctantly, by the nuclear power industry, which constructed cooling towers and ponds. The next concern was over the discharge of radioactive gases into the air by routine releases. Still later, a controversy developed over reactor safety and the possibility of a core meltdown, the so-called China Syndrome. A few individuals and groups were concerned about nuclear waste disposal, but their concerns did not reach the level of becoming a movement.[4] An exception to this was an action in 1976 in the State of California that prohibited building any new nuclear reactors until the federal government demonstrated a means of disposal for high-level nuclear waste.[5]

An accident at a Three Mile Island nuclear reactor on March 28, 1979, heightened public concern over nuclear power and led to more interest group activity, increased government regulation, increased industry recommendations for changes related to reactor safety, and increased media coverage of nuclear power. This also translated eventually into more concern and action regarding nuclear waste.

The accident was initially triggered by a valve failure that eventually led to a partial meltdown of the core of the reactor. Although it did not cause much radioactive material to be discharged, the accident was not handled with a sure hand. Pregnant women and young children were evacuated on the advice of the governor after much uncertainty and vacillation over the decision. The media were unprepared for coverage of the accident, and this lack of preparation was conveyed to newspaper, radio, and television audiences. Even scientific experts disagreed on whether a hydrogen bubble posed a threat. There were fears also of additional radiation releases and complete meltdown of the core.

Polls taken shortly after the Three Mile Island accident by Gallup, Harris, and *New York Times*–CBS all showed a decrease in support for nuclear power.[6] The *New York Times*–CBS poll showed even a sharper dip in the willingness of respondents to have a nuclear reactor located in their neighborhood. Clearly, the accident diminished trust in the ability of government to regulate the new nuclear power industry. The wide publicity given the Three Mile Island accident, covered by about 300 journalists and support personnel from the United States and abroad, significantly increased the number of persons aware of problems with nuclear power.

After the Three Mile Island accident, the Nuclear Regulatory Commission (NRC) suspended the issuance of new construction permits and operation of new nuclear power plants for six months. This move preempted moves by Congress to impose a moratorium on nuclear power. Congress did pass some less drastic measures. Legislation introduced by Representative Jonathan Bingham required that the NRC report to Congress within 120 days describing how well each of the 72 reactors then in operation satisfied NRC safety requirements.[7]

The Kemeny Commission, appointed by President Carter, criticized the NRC for not paying enough attention to the process of assuring nuclear safety.[8] The NRC did assume more control over nuclear reactor construction and operation. This, however, led to construction and licensing delays. This and other factors increased the cost of nuclear power and made it even less competitive. The long-run aftermath of Three Mile Island is described by a business reporter for the *Washington Post*, Martha M. Hamilton, who states: "It drove a stake through the heart of new construction. No new nuclear plants have been built since then."[9] For years after the accident scientists struggled with the problems associated with the disposal of the irreparably impaired reactor. The process was both hazardous and very expensive.

THE POLITICS OF THE 1982 NUCLEAR WASTE POLICY ACT

Although nuclear reactors had been in operation for decades in the United States by the early 1980s, no provision had been made for permanent disposal of the highly radioactive wastes generated by the operation of these reactors. The United States was not alone in this. At this point in time no nation had developed a permanent repository for its nuclear wastes. In Japan, this situation was likened to building a house without a toilet.

In 1978, President Carter established the Interagency Review Group on Nuclear Waste Management.[10] This group, representing 14 different federal agencies and having received input from other interested entities and the public, found that there was a consensus on the following:

1. The responsibility for resolving military and civilian waste management problems should not be deferred to future generations.

2. The most promising technology for permanent disposal of high-level nuclear waste is geologic disposal.

3. The search for repository sites should consider a number of locations in a variety of geologic environments leading to the option of having at least two repositories, preferably in different regions of the country.

4. Interim storage should not be a substitute for progress on opening the first repositories.

These items influenced important provisions of the Nuclear Waste Policy Act (NWPA) of 1982.[11]

An attempt to pass a nuclear waste bill in 1979 and 1980 by the 96th Congress failed when the conference committee was unable to reconcile the House bill's insistence on geologic disposal as the first priority with the Senate's call for both interim away-from-reactor storage and indefinite monitored retrievable storage (as well as geological disposal).[12] The Senate's call for monitored retrievable storage (MRS) was put forward by Senator J. Bennett Johnston (D-LA). Luther Carter attributes Johnston's interest in MRS partly to the influence of the energy committee's staff director, Daniel Dreyfus, who had become discouraged about the likelihood of geological disposal.[13] Dreyfus is quoted by Carter as describing the problem as searching for a "technically appropriate subsurface with a politically compliant governor on top."[14] Some senators felt that spent fuel was still a valuable energy source and should be reprocessed in order to extract the remaining fissionable material.[15] Pressures to construct a permanent repository continued to build as spent fuel rods were accumulating in storage pools around the country and some storage pools were approaching their total capacity.

Examination of the floor debates reveals that most of the participants in the debate were from states that had large amounts of nuclear waste that they wanted to get rid of or were from states that had reason to believe that they would be selected for a repository. At this point there seems to have been little realization that regardless of which site or sites would be selected, the waste would have to be transported to the repository, and thus many other states would be affected.

Representatives from states that might be selected to host a repository made desperate efforts to include provisions in the bill that would guarantee that their state would be excluded from consideration for the high-level repository sites. Only a few were included, and Senator McClure made assurances that the bill had no provisions that would exclude any state from consideration for a repository site. Failed amendments include one sponsored by Senator Stennis from Mississippi and Senator Johnston from Louisiana, both from states with salt domes, which would make certain that the spent fuel repository would be located in states with low population density, thus eliminating their states. Senator Jackson (D-WA) from Washington, which has an enormous amount of military nuclear waste, made an effort to have the repository accept military waste. This also failed. Senator McClure from Idaho, which already had accepted nuclear waste and also had large amounts of wastes from its reactors, was actively involved in the debates. Senator Thurmond of South Carolina, who was in a similar situation, was also active in the debates.

Among the more important provisions of the act was the requirement that the Department of Energy (DOE) find, study, and designate potential sites both west and east of the Mississippi, that the repository be paid for by a tax of 0.1 cent per kilowatt-hour on the consumers of nuclear power, and that a site begin accepting high-level waste by 1998. The act also provided for development of an MRS facility. Mechanisms for the states to veto their selection and for Congress to override a veto were debated at length. Senator Proxmire (D-WI) wanted states to have an absolute veto over placing a repository in their state. This was rejected after considering the possibility that no state would accept it. A much weaker veto provision that gave states veto power but allowed a veto override by one house of Congress was debated. Senator Proxmire threatened to filibuster this provision, and a compromise requiring both houses of Congress to override a state veto was adopted. This would still allow a filibuster in the Senate by a state that had been selected for a repository.[16] Senator Lott's amendment banning placement of a repository within one square mile of an area with a population density of 1,000 or more was accepted. The act made the federal government responsible for transporting the high-level wastes from reactor sites to the repository. The act established deadlines, requiring the DOE to nominate five sites for the first repository and to recommend three of them to the president by 1985. Five sites for a second repository would have to be recommended by 1989. Senator James McClure (R-ID) filed a new version of the Nuclear Waste Policy Act of 1982 on December 13, 1982. On December 20, 1982, in the rush of legislative activity just prior to adjournment for Christmas vacation, Congress passed the act. Luther Carter has conducted interviews and has given valuable insights into the politics involved in passing the act.[17]

ANALYSIS OF THE 1982 NUCLEAR WASTE POLICY ACT

The establishment of the Office of Civilian Radioactive Waste Management in the NWPA of 1982 signaled that Congress felt it was necessary to have an entity within the DOE to provide more focus on the spent fuel disposal problem. The term Civilian in the title indicated that the primary concern of Congress was the disposal of spent fuel from commercial reactors and that the battle to include all military waste in the high-level nuclear waste program had been lost. Furthermore, the adoption of geologic disposal indicated that other alternatives such as reprocessing, shooting waste into space, subseabed disposal, and disposal in the Arctic were rejected.

Requiring the DOE to recommend five sites for the first repository indicated that Congress wanted the DOE to consider alternatives. It would be difficult to convince people that a scientific approach to the problem had been made if no alternatives had been considered. Requiring that only three sites be recommended to the president for further study indicated that Congress had some concerns about the cost of site characterization and also wanted the DOE to do the prioritizing. Introducing Congress into the process guaranteed that politics would enter into the site selection decision.

The site selection timetable did not allow sufficient time for public participation in the site selection process. One of the major findings of a panel of the National Research Council is that "the site selection timetable outlined in the Nuclear Waste Policy Act (NWPA) is likely to force the

DOE to choose between an open consultative approach to planning that fails to meet deadlines and a closed executive process that meets schedules. A decision to adhere to the tight schedule of the NWPA could contribute to insufficient attention to local concerns and participatory opportunities or result in inappropriate compromises."[18] The 60 days allotted for a state or Indian tribe to veto the siting of a repository within its territory was too short for states in which the legislature meets part-time or for Indian tribes that meet annually or less often.

The 90-day period for Congress to act after the veto of a state or Indian tribe would ordinarily be too short, especially for the Senate, which provides numerous opportunities for delaying consideration of legislation. However, proponents of the act were prescient in anticipating possible obstructionism and included provisions in the act that made obstructionism much more difficult. The most important was a provision that would allow any member of the Senate to bring the bill up for consideration, a power traditionally reserved to the Senate majority leader.

Allowing "site assessment" instead of "site characterization" reduced the cost of the preliminary work but at the same time left the DOE less prepared to submit a license application to the NRC. In fact, the DOE, when a site was finally selected in 2002, was unable to comply with the requirement in the act that an application for a license be submitted within 90 days of site selection.

Limiting the amount of waste in the first repository to 70,000 tons was a political and not a scientific decision. In 1982 no one knew which site would be selected, much less how much waste it could contain. The purpose of the limitation was to make certain that no one site would receive all of the spent fuel.

Also, considering the complexity of the studies necessary to ascertain that a geological repository would isolate highly radioactive waste, some of which would be radioactive for hundreds of thousands of years, the time allowed for narrowing the sites down to three in two years (the NWPA of 1982 was passed in late December 1982) was much too short. To put this in perspective, Congress took four years to pass the act.[19] The effect of this tight schedule, Luther Carter claims, was that the DOE was forced to consider only those sites that already were in its inventory.[20]

POLITICAL AFTERMATH OF THE 1982 NUCLEAR WASTE POLICY ACT

Acting so quickly that it can almost be described as a reflex, Wisconsin voters rejected hosting a high-level nuclear waste repository by an eight to one margin on April 5, 1983. This vote took place just 45 days after passage of the NWPA. The vote was on a referendum and was the first referendum on nuclear waste in the United States. The question on the referendum ballot asked: "Do you support the construction of a national or regional nuclear waste disposal site in Wisconsin?" At this point, Wisconsin had not yet been selected as a potential site. However, Representative Les Aspin (D-WI) advertised the fact that Wisconsin bedrock would be suitable for a repository and hence a likely candidate.[21]

On December 18, 1984, the DOE listed sites in 17 states as having the right kind of rock for the eastern repository. These were Michigan, Minnesota, and Wisconsin in the north-central region; Connecticut, Maine, Massachusetts, New Hampshire, New Jersey, New York, Pennsylvania, Rhode Island, and Vermont in the Northeast; and Georgia, Maryland, North Carolina, South Carolina, and Virginia in the Southeast.[22] By October 1985, strong opposition had already surfaced in the Northeast. In New Hampshire, town meetings, protests, and letter-writing campaigns were organized soon after Hillsboro, N.H., had been nominated as a site. New Hampshire Governor John H. Sununu (R-NH) vigorously opposed siting a nuclear waste dump in New Hampshire. When it was pointed out at a New Hampshire town meeting that it was inconsistent for him to oppose a nuclear waste "dump" at the same time he was championing a nuclear power plant at Seabrook, N.H., Sununu responded that the two were not connected.[23] At a joint meeting of the Atomic Industrial Forum and the American Nuclear Energy Council, Governor Sununu warned that the eastern site siting effort was generating such massive opposition that it was a threat to the entire nuclear industry.[24]

In Maine, the nuclear waste dump issue dominated the debate on a referendum to close down the Maine Yankee nuclear reactor. DOE officials told Maine residents that they had no right to oppose a nuclear waste dump while they were using electricity generated by a nuclear reactor. This approach proved to be ineffective, and Maine voters rejected shutting down the reactor while continuing to oppose a nuclear waste repository.

The level of protest in Maine over the nuclear dump was comparable to that experienced during the Vietnam era.[25] Maine's congressional delegation added its opposition to that of Maine residents. In a letter to the editor of the *New York Times* Maine representatives and senators stated that less spent fuel was being generated than originally estimated and that there was no need for a second repository.[26] Their claim that a second repository was not needed was contradicted by the April 23, 1986, testimony of an expert, Ben Rusche, head of the Office of Civilian Radioactive Waste Management in the DOE.[27] The most controversial site in Maine was the Sebago Lake batholith. Sebago Lake is located six miles from Portland and supplied 25 percent of its drinking water.

In North Carolina, Representative James T. Broyhill (R-NC), after two sites in North Carolina had been nominated for the spent fuel repository, announced that lowered projections for the amount of spent fuel that would be generated meant that the search for a second repository site could be discontinued.[28] Broyhill was one of the chief sponsors of the NWPA of 1982.[29] Broyhill was running for one of North Carolina's Senate seats in 1986.

At hearings before the Subcommittee on Energy Conservation and Power, House Energy and Commerce Committee, Representative Sikorski (DFL-MN) complained that there were over 8,000 lakes in the vicinity of a repository candidate site in Minnesota.[30] Jack Devine, administrative assistant to the lieutenant governor of Michigan, was concerned about a nuclear waste repository site in Michigan being a threat to the Great Lakes and also mentioned that the governor of Michigan would take advantage of the veto provisions of the 1982 act.[31] James G. Martin, governor of North Carolina, claimed that over 150,000 people lived within 12 miles of both sites identified in North Carolina. Governor Martin claimed that the rock formations in these areas were fractured. He also stressed that a second repository was not necessary.[32] Chairman Edward J. Markey (D-MA) observed that the reaction to the announcement of potential sites on January 16, 1986, was "astounding": "Within days…citizens sought the advice of geologists, seismologists, physicists and others…. Citizens have produced evidence of obvious aquifers and fault lines missing from the Department's maps. They have brought forth published studies that often contradicted key departmental assumptions about the geology."[33] In a May 1, 1986, hearing of the subcommittee a DOE spokesman discussing the proposal to prohibit consideration of crystalline rock for a repository testified that it was bad public policy to exclude any one rock type that may be suitable for a repository.[34]

There were many complaints about both the DOE's tardiness and its refusal to respond to requests for information by the states.[35] Nevada complained that the track record of the DOE in responding to requests for information ranged from 60 to 120 days.[36] Representative Al Swift (D-WA), frustrated over refusals to respond to requests for information, asked, "Are you telling me now that you interpret the law to mean that we have to subpoena the information in order to get a reply?"[37]

The procedure for identifying possible sites for the first repository and the sequence of events leading to a final recommendation to the president of three sites are presented in the following section. Opposition to the sites nominated for the first repository, with the exception of Washington State, tended to be confined to government officials, interest groups, and media rather than the general public. By December 1984 there were five sites still in the running. These were Davis Canyon, Utah; Richton dome, Miss.; Hanford, Wash.; Yucca Mountain, Nev.; and Deaf Smith County, Tex. The governors of Texas, Utah, and Nevada pledged to oppose repositories in their states. Environmental groups were active in opposing a dump in Washington State, but the Hanford community did not resist selection of the site. Resistance became much more pronounced after May 28, 1986, when President Reagan announced that studies of the second repository site would be indefinitely suspended and at the same time announced that the first repository would be built in either Texas, Nevada, or Washington.

In support of the suspension of siting efforts for a second repository Energy Secretary Herrington cited the decline in spent fuel generation but also mentioned the hope that Congress would authorize the MRS facility at Oak Ridge.[38] Brooks Yeager of the Sierra Club voiced his suspicion that political motives played a role in the indefinite suspension and mentioned the New Hampshire presidential primary in which Vice President Bush was expected to be a candidate.[39] Luther Carter also cites political motives for the postponement of the second repository, but his focus is on the legislative rather than the executive branch of the federal government. Carter suggests that the Reagan administration was worried that strong opposition to the second repository site would result in loss of Republican control of the Senate in the upcoming 1986 election. At stake were four Republican-held Senate seats in Wisconsin, New Hampshire,

Georgia, and North Carolina, all of which were still candidate venues for the second repository.[40] According to a *New York Times* editorial, "The action was widely seen as intended to help Eastern Republican candidates in last year's midterm elections and to protect George Bush's prospects in the New Hampshire primary. The decision shattered the 1982 compromise and angered Western states." It referred to the NWPA as an intricate political compromise that was wrecked by Energy Secretary Herrington.[41] The administration's action effectively eliminated a second repository without congressional approval.

The decision to suspend the search for an eastern repository site was also criticized on scientific grounds. David Berick, director of the Environmental Policy Institute's nuclear waste and safety project, expressed concern that the three western sites would not provide sufficient alternatives and felt that work should continue on the eastern crystalline rock sites.[42]

Senator Slade Gorton (R-WA), who had been in the forefront of the effort to have the NWPA of 1982 limit the amount of spent fuel accepted by the first repository until the second repository was opened, testified before a Senate committee that the second repository part of the act was an integral part of the act that could not be removed without jeopardizing the act. Furthermore, Gorton stated that if the DOE was going to disregard the requirement of the act for a second repository, the selection process for the first repository should be reopened and the DOE should conduct a nationwide search for the site.[43] In the 1986 election campaign, Senator Gorton's opponent, Brock Adams, made an issue of the Hanford site.[44] Adams charged Gorton with not resisting the repository strongly enough.[45] Senator Gorton lost the election to Adams. The Washington State legislature reacted to the postponement of the second repository by placing a referendum on the November 1986 ballot that would give Washington State the power to veto the site if selected for the first repository.[46] The referendum was passed by an 83 percent favorable vote.[47] This overwhelming support of the referendum occurred despite the expectation of legal experts that it would not survive a court test. Nevertheless, it sent a signal to the DOE that there was strong popular opposition to siting a repository in Washington State.

NARROWING THE LIST OF CANDIDATE SITES FOR THE FIRST REPOSITORY

The NWPA of 1982 set a time schedule for site selection, licensing, and initial operation of a geological repository:

1. The secretary of energy was to issue general guidelines for the recommendation of sites for repositories within 180 days after the date of the enactment of the act.

2. Subsequent to the issuance of guidelines the secretary of energy was to nominate at least five sites he determined suitable for site characterization.

3. The secretary of energy was to recommend to the president by January 1, 1985, three of the five nominated sites for site characterization.

4. Following DOE recommendation, the president was called on to recommend to Congress one site by March 31, 1987, with an option for a one-year extension.

5. The NRC was called on to approve or disapprove a license application for construction of a repository by January 1, 1989.

6. The DOE was to take title and begin disposing of spent fuel not later than January 31, 1998.

As a result of screenings and investigations that had been going on at varying levels of activity for quite a few years, the DOE was ready fairly soon after the passage of the NWPA to put forth a list of possible sites. The first step in site selection occurred in February 1983 when the DOE formally identified nine potentially acceptable candidate sites for the first repository: Vacherie dome, La. (salt dome); Cypress dome, Miss. (salt dome); Richton dome, Miss. (salt dome); Yucca Mountain, Nev. (tuff); Deaf Smith County, Tex. (bedded salt); Swisher County, Tex. (bedded salt); Davis Canyon, Utah (bedded salt); Lavender Canyon, Utah (bedded salt); and Hanford site, Wash. (basalt flows).[48] Note that no sites located in granite were included in this list. Jacob has reported that the DOE refused to study granite because it could delay the opening of the first repository by four years.[49] It has also been noted that the identification of these nine sites took place very shortly after the passage of the NWPA, before guidelines for site selection had been established.[50]

The NWPA required that two steps be taken before narrowing the list of potentially acceptable sites to those suitable for site characterization. At least five sites must be nominated as suitable. The first step was for the DOE to issue general guidelines to be used in determining site suitability. After NRC concurrence, these guidelines were finalized by the DOE in December 1984.[51] The second step was to prepare an environmental assessment based on these guidelines for each site proposed for nomination for site characterization. The narrowing of the list was mandated in part by the guideline requirement to group sites according to geohydrologic settings and to "select the preferred site on the basis of a comparative evaluation of all potentially acceptable sites in that setting."[52] A site could also be eliminated if it failed to meet some of the technical requirements of the guidelines. Draft Environmental Assessments were prepared for each of the nine sites mentioned above and issued for public comment in December 1984. These Draft Environmental Assessments proposed the following five sites:

GEOHYDROLOGIC SETTING	SITE
Columbia Plateau	Hanford, Washington
Great Basin	Yucca Mountain, Nevada
Permian Basin	Death Smith County, Texas
Paradox Basin	Davis Canyon, Utah
Gulf Coastal Plain	Richton Dome, Mississippi

The narrowing of the initial list of nine sites to five sites was based primarily on the basis of comparison between sites in the same geohydrologic setting. The Deaf Smith (Tex.) site was chosen as the preferred site in the Permian Basin (bedded salt) over the Swisher (Tex.) site mainly because it is farther from highly populated areas.[53] The Richton dome (Miss.) site was chosen over the other two salt dome sites, Vacherie dome (La.) and Cypress dome (Miss.), primarily because of its greater ability to ensure compliance with the waste-isolation requirements. Features of the Richton dome mentioned in this regard are the considerably larger size of the dome, the absence of known collapse features, and a limited potential for flooding of the dome area.[54] The selection of Davis Canyon (Utah) over Lavender Canyon (Utah) in the Paradox Basin (bedded salt) was based primarily on land-acquisition issues.[55] These two sites are only 1.5 miles apart, and other site issues are minor. Each of the five proposed sites was evaluated with respect to (a) postclosure technical guidelines (geohydrologic, geochemistry, climatic changes, tectonic, etc.); (b) preclosure radiological safety; (c) preclosure environment, socioeconomics, and transportation; and (d) siting, construction, operation, and closure cost. The overall ranking depends on the relative weighting given to each of the above considerations, but for most weightings considered, Deaf Smith, Hanford, and Yucca Mountain (in alphabetical order) were the top three.[56] Because of the sensitivity of the final ranking to the weighting of the different factors considered, "a unique preference ordering among these (top) three sites cannot be assigned."[57] The Draft Environmental Assessments go on to say these three sites "offer maximum diversity in geo-hydrologic settings and in rock types for the selection of the site for the first repository. Such diversity increases the probability that the sites suitable for site selection (recommendation for development as a repository) will be available even if studies should reveal a generic deficiency in one type of rock or geo-hydrologic setting."[58] It is difficult to pinpoint a specific issue that dominated the lower rankings of Richton and Davis Canyon. Richton was lowest ranked in the geochemistry, dissolution, and population density categories. Davis Canyon was lowest ranked in site ownership and control, meteorology, environmental quality, socioeconomic impacts, and transportation. On the other hand, Hanford was judged to have the highest cost.

Many comments were received in response to the issuance of the Draft Environmental Assessments. Of particular concern were the simple ranking methodologies presented in the drafts. Largely in response to this, a decision was made to adopt a formal decision analysis methodology and to prepare a single separate report. The methodology chosen is termed "Multiattribute Utility Analysis," an approach that has sometimes been used in siting dams and other energy facilities. The assumptions and conclusions of this exercise are given in a May 1986 report: "A Multiattribute Utility Analysis of Sites Nominated for Characterization for the First Radioactive-Waste Repository—A Decision-Aiding Methodology."[59] The analysis was broken into two parts, the preclosure performance and the postclosure performance. The preclosure analysis emphasized minimizing health and safety impacts before closure, adverse environmental and socioeconomic impacts, and construction and transportation costs. It turned out that the preclosure utility scores were quite similar for all sites, with the largest difference being attributed to larger costs at the Hanford site.

The postclosure analysis objective could be simply stated: to minimize the adverse health effects attributable to the repository. In hindsight, the analysis probably erred on the optimistic side. On a scale where 0 corresponds to meeting the Environmental Protection Agency (EPA) primary-containment standards and 100 is perfection, all sites had expected scores of 99.7 or better. A score of 99.7 corresponds to an average radiation release rate that is 0.003 of the EPA limits for 10,000 years. (The EPA limits at this time [codified in 40 CFR 191 on September 19, 1985] were less restrictive than later revised generic repository standards issued in 1993. As discussed in chapter 10, the present specific standards for Yucca Mountain, codified in 40 CFR 197, have been rejected in part by the Court of Appeals and have to be revised.) It must also be remembered that the available information on the sites was limited at this time—the purpose of the exercise was to identify the best sites for more complete characterization. The salt sites were judged to have smaller releases for unlikely disruptive scenarios than the other two sites. It was concluded that "a repository at the Hanford site would be slightly less favorable than that of a repository at the salt sites or at the Yucca Mountain site. The principal bases for this conclusion are technical judgments regarding the potential for waste dissolution, radionuclide travel time, and the possibility of the existence of unexpected features at the site."[60] A final composite analysis taking into account both preclosure and postclosure performance gave the same ranking as the preclosure analysis (Yucca Mountain, Richton dome, Deaf Smith County, Davis Canyon, and Hanford). It is emphasized in the report that this was an "initial" ranking and that a final ranking should take into account the diversity of geohydrological settings and the diversity of rock types.[61] It is interesting to note that the ranking from the Multiattribute Utility Analysis, based on essentially the same raw information, differs significantly from the earlier ranking in the Draft Environmental Assessments. Hanford was moved out of the top three, and Richton dome moved up from fourth place to second place. A greater emphasis on cost considerations may have contributed to this movement. (In 1987 Senator Reid of Nevada introduced an amendment to an Energy and Water Appropriations bill that would require the secretary of energy to give primary consideration to public health and safety in selecting study sites for a repository. The de-emphasis on cost might have moved Hanford higher in the ranking and the Yucca Mountain, Nev., site lower. The amendment was defeated, however.)[62]

In 1986 the secretary of energy recommended and the president approved three sites for further characterization. These were, in his final order of preference, Yucca Mountain, Nev.; Deaf Smith County, Tex.; and the Hanford site, Wash. The Yucca Mountain site is about 90 miles northwest of Las Vegas, the Hanford site is about 190 miles southwest of Seattle, and the Texas site is about 50 miles west of Amarillo. This action eliminated two of the semifinalists, Davis Canyon, Utah, and Richton dome,

Miss. All three of the recommended host states filed lawsuits challenging the administration's decisions and how they were reached.[63]

It should be noted that the recommended sites were the top three in the rankings of the 1984 Draft Environmental Assessments but not in the 1986 Multiattribute Utility Analysis, where Hanford was ranked fifth. Lemons, Brown, and Varner have reported that "some commentators suggested that DOE did not want to abandon its Hanford site for the Mississippi site, which was located in a state where there was strong public opposition to a repository."[64] They go on to say that the "DOE was accused of selecting sites on the basis of purely political, rather than environmental criteria."[65] Congressman Edward J. Markey (D-MA), commenting on Secretary Abraham's January 2002 decision to recommend Yucca Mountain, said, "During the 1980's...the Department of Energy put politics first and safety last. In some instances, the Department simply ignored environmental problems at potential sites for a permanent waste repository, such as Hanford, Washington, when it thought this site might be the most politically viable."[66] There may be some truth to these accusations, although the "purely political" characterization is clearly an overstatement. There is considerable documentation for the evaluations with respect to each of the subcategories in the Draft Environmental Assessments and the Environmental Assessments. It was the weightings of the different subcategories in making the final ranking that received the most criticism. Carter reports how two House subcommittee chairmen wrote Secretary of Energy John Herrington accusing the DOE of manipulating data and analytic techniques to arrive at a predetermined set of sites.[67] It is also interesting to note with regard to the Hanford site that the U.S. Geological Survey had warned already in 1983 that "the Columbia River Basalt...should be generally thought of as a series of semi-confined aquifers that are hydraulically connected to each other by semi-permeable confining beds. Overall, the system appears to be very leaky."[68]

An attempt to explain the basis for the choice of the three sites is given in the secretary's nine-page statement in which his recommendation is embedded.[69] This statement downplays the Multiattribute Utility Analysis, characterizing it as an "aid in determining the preferred ranking of the five nominated sites" and "providing only a partial and approximate accounting of the many factors important to the site-recommendation decision." It de-emphasizes differences in costs, stating that "post-closure performance of the sites and other technical factors should take precedence over costs."

The statement also minimizes differences in postclosure performance. It characterizes the difference between the sites with the highest (Hanford) and lowest radionuclide releases to the accessible environment as corresponding "to a very small change, i.e., from two one-thousandths (0.002) of the EPA limit to one ten-thousandth (0.0001) of the EPA limit." But this difference could also be described as saying that the radionuclide release for the Hanford site was estimated to be 20 times larger than for the best site. The secretary emphasized the DOE's siting provisions, "specifying diversity of geo-hydrologic settings and diversity of rock types shall be considered in determining a final order of preference for the characterization of such sites." With respect to geohydrologic settings, the recommendation makes a somewhat peculiar statement: "The five sites nominated as suitable for site characterization provide the maximum diversity in geo-hydrologic settings because each site is in a distinct geo-hydrologic setting. Any combination of three recommended sites will, therefore, provide the maximum diversity in geo-hydrologic settings." Achieving diversity in rock types was a factor in including Hanford in the final three in spite of its last-place ranking in the Multiattribute Utility Analysis. The Davis Canyon site was eliminated on the basis of being the least-preferred salt site with respect to preclosure performance measures. The recommendation acknowledges that "evaluating the relative performance of the Deaf Smith County site and the Richton Dome site is more difficult because their performance is comparable." The recommendation never really explains the basis of the choice, making the somewhat ambiguous statement with regard to different combinations of preclosure performance measures that "the Deaf Smith County site predominantly ranks in the top three sites in order of preference, whereas the Richton Dome site ranges from first to fourth in order of preference for the same combinations of pre-closure performance measures." This ambiguity is consistent with the charge mentioned above that political considerations played a role in the elimination of the Richton dome site. It is also worth mentioning that Mississippi had both of its senators on the Energy and Water Development Subcommittee of the U.S. Senate. Senator Stennis was also the ranking Democrat on the powerful Senate Appropriations Committee.

NOTES

1. Luther J. Carter, *Nuclear Imperatives and Public Trust: Dealing with Radioactive Waste* (Washington, DC: Resources for the Future, Inc., 1987), 222.

2. Ibid., 17.

3. Rachel Carson, *Silent Spring* (Cambridge: Riverside Press, 1962).

4. Samuel J. Walker, *Three Mile Island: A Nuclear Crisis in Historical Perspective* (Berkeley: University of California Press, 2004), 9–17.

5. Carter, *Nuclear Imperatives and Public Trust*, 84–87.

6. Walker, *Three Mile Island*, 24.

7. Robert J. Duffy, *Nuclear Politics in America: A History and Theory of Government Regulation* (Lawrence: University Press of Kansas, 1997), 141–43.

8. Ibid., 144.

9. Martha M. Hamilton, "Nuclear Power since Three Mile Island," *Washington Post*, March 30, 1999, available at www.washingtonpost.com/wp-srv/national/talk/archive/hamilton0330.htm.

10. Carter, *Nuclear Imperatives and Public Trust*, 135.

11. Thomas A. Cotton, "Nuclear Waste Story: Setting the Stage," in *Uncertainty Underground: Yucca Mountain and the Nations' High Level Nuclear Waste*, ed. Allison M. MacFarlane and Rodney C. Ewing (Cambridge, MA: MIT Press, 2006), 31–32.

12. Carter, *Nuclear Imperatives and Public Trust*, 204.

13. Ibid., 201.

14. Daniel Dreyfus, interview by Luther Carter, April 1983, quoted in Carter, *Nuclear Imperatives and Public Trust*, 202.

15. Cotton, "Nuclear Waste Story," 32–33.

16. Barbara Sinclair, "The '60-Vote Senate,' Strategies, Process and Outcome," in *U.S. Senate Exceptionalism*, ed. Bruce I. Oppenheimer (Columbus: Ohio State University Press, 2002), 249.

17. Carter, *Nuclear Imperatives and Public Trust*, 221–22. The reader is referred to this source for additional details.

18. Panel on Social and Economic Aspects of Radioactive Waste Management, Board of Radioactive Waste Management, National Research Council, "Social and Economic Aspects of Radioactive Waste Disposal: Considerations for Institutional Management" (Washington, DC: National Academy Press, 1984), 13.

19. Carter, *Nuclear Imperatives and Public Trust*, 195.

20. Ibid., 403.

21. Associated Press, "Nuclear Waste Site Decisively Rejected in Wisconsin Voting," *New York Times*, April 6, 1983: A16, available at http://topics.nytimes.com/top/news/national/usstatesterritoriesandpossessions/wisconsin/index.html?offset=90&s=oldest&.

22. United Press International, "17 States Are Chosen as Possible Dump Sites," *New York Times*, December 18, 1984: A24.

23. Joyce Maynard, "The Story of a Town," *New York Times Magazine*, May 11, 1986: 20.

24. Carter, *Nuclear Imperatives and Public Trust*, 411.

25. Matthew L. Wald, "Maine Saying No to Nuclear Waste Plan," *New York Times*, March 26, 1985: A1.

26. William S. Cohen, George J. Mitchell, Olympia J. Snowe, and Joseph E. Brennan, "Let's Dig One Nuclear-Waste Grave at a Time," *New York Times*, April 10, 1987: A34.

27. House Energy and Commerce Committee, Subcommittee on Energy Conservation and Power, *Hearing: Radioactive Waste Repository Program, DOE Implementation*, 99th Cong., 2d Sess. (April 23, 1986), 624.

28. Representative James T. Broyhill, "Washington Report," press release, April 21, 1986, cited in Carter, *Nuclear Imperatives and Public Trust*, 411.

29. Associated Press, "Reagan Expected to Sign Atomic Waste Burial Bill," *New York Times*, December 22, 1982: B15.

30. House Energy and Commerce Committee, Subcommittee on Energy Conservation and Power, *Hearing: DOE Radioactive Waste Repository Program*, 99th Cong., 1st Sess. (August 1, 1985), 6.

31. House Energy and Commerce Committee, Subcommittee on Energy Conservation and Power, *Hearing: DOE Radioactive Waste Repository Program*, 99th Cong., 1st Sess. (October 15, 1985), 408.

32. Ibid., 473–74.

33. Ibid., 471.

34. House Energy and Commerce Committee, Subcommittee on Energy Conservation and Power, *Hearing: DOE Radioactive Waste Repository Program*, 99th Cong., 2d Sess. (May 1, 1986), 1107.

35. Ibid., 865, 897–98.

36. Ibid., 865.

37. House Energy and Commerce Committee, Subcommittee on Energy Conservation and Power, *Hearing: DOE Radioactive Waste Repository Program*, 99th Cong., 1st Sess. (August 1, 1985), 22.

38. Carter, *Nuclear Imperatives and Public Trust*, 412.

39. Robert D. Hershey Jr., "U.S. Suspends Plan for Nuclear Dump in East or Midwest," *New York Times*, May 29, 1986: A1, A20.

40. Carter, *Nuclear Imperatives and Public Trust*, 411.

41. "Blundering over Nuclear Burial," Editorial, *New York Times*, March 16, 1987: A18.

42. Robert D. Hershey Jr., "U.S. Seeks Delay on Nuclear Dump," *New York Times*, January 29, 1997.

43. Senate Committee on Energy and Natural Resources, Subcommittee on Energy Research and Development, 99th Cong., 2d Sess. (June 16, 1986), cited in Carter, *Nuclear Imperatives and Public Trust*, 413.

44. E. J. Dionne Jr., "Parties Heighten Efforts to Bring Voters to Polls," *New York Times* (Late City Edition), November 2, 1986: 32.

45. "Nevada Chosen to Receive Nuclear Waste," *Congressional Quarterly Almanac, 1987*, 43 (Washington, DC: Congressional Quarterly, Inc., 1987), 309.

46. John Herbers, "The Political Campaign: From Gambling to Ecology, Voters in 43 States Take Up Ballot Issues Today," *New York Times*, November 4, 1986: A22.

47. See www.secstate.wa.gov/elections/initiatives/statistics_referendumbills.aspx.

48. U.S. Department of Energy, Office of Civilian Radioactive Waste Management, *Civilian Radioactive Waste Management Program Plan, Revision 3* (DOE/RW-0520; Washington, DC: Office of Civilian Radioactive Waste Management, February 2000), app. B, available at www.ocrwm.doe.gov/pm/pdf/pprev3.pdf.

49. Gerald Jacob, *Site Unseen: The Politics of Siting a Nuclear Waste Repository* (Pittsburgh: University of Pittsburgh Press, 1990), 36.

50. "High Level Radioactive Waste and Spent Nuclear Fuel Disposal," Policy Research Project Report 84 (Austin: Lyndon B. Johnson School of Public Affairs, the University of Texas, 1987), 135.

51. U.S. Department of Energy, "General Guidelines for the Recommendation of Sites for Nuclear Waste Repositories, 10 CFR Part 960," *Federal Register* 49, no. 36 (December 6, 1984): 47752–69.

52. Ibid., Sec. 960.3-2-2-2, 47758.

53. U.S. Department of Energy, Office of Civilian Radioactive Waste Management, "Draft Environmental Assessment, Swisher County Site, Texas" (DOE/RW-0015), December 1984.

54. U.S. Department of Energy, Office of Civilian Radioactive Waste Management, "Draft Environmental Assessment, Vacherie Dome Site, Louisiana" (DOE/RW-0016), December 1984.

55. U.S. Department of Energy, Office of Civilian Radioactive Waste Management, "Draft Environmental Assessment, Davis Canyon Site, Utah" (DOE/RW-0010), December 1984.

56. U.S. Department of Energy, Office of Civilian Radioactive Waste Management, "Draft Environmental Assessment, Reference Repository Location, Hanford Site, Washington" (DOE/RW-0017), December 1984; U.S. Department of Energy, Office of Civilian Radioactive Waste Management, "Draft Environmental Assessment, Yucca Mountain Site, Nevada Research and Development Area Nevada" (DOE/RW-0012), December 1984.

57. U.S. Department of Energy, Office of Civilian Radioactive Waste Management, "Draft Environmental Assessment, Yucca Mountain Site," ch. 7. (The same material of ch. 7 appears in the Draft Environmental Assessments for the other four sites.)

58. Ibid.

59. U.S. Department of Energy, "A Multiattribute Utility Analysis of Sites Nominated for Characterization for the First Radioactive-Waste Repository—A Decision-Aiding Methodology" (DOE/RW-0074; Washington, DC: Office of Civilian Radioactive Waste Management, 1986).

60. Ibid.

61. Ibid.

62. Joseph A. Davis, "Nevada Struggling to Fend Off Nuclear Dump," *Congressional Quarterly Weekly Report* 43 (November 14, 1987): 2815.

63. Carter, *Nuclear Imperatives and Public Trust*, 407.

64. John Lemons, Donald A. Brown, and Gary E. Varner, "Congress, Consistency and Environmental Law: Nuclear Waste at Yucca Mountain, Nevada," *Environmental Ethics* 12 (1990): 321.

65. Ibid.

66. Edward J. Markey, "News from Ed Markey," U.S. Congress, January 10, 2002.

67. Carter, *Nuclear Imperatives and Public Trust*, 407.

68. U.S. Geological Survey, "Review Comments on the Site Characterization Report for the Basalt Waste Isolation Project" (May 6, 1983), 5, 13, quoted in Carter, *Nuclear Imperatives and Public Trust*, 169.

69. U.S. Department of Energy, Office of Civilian Radioactive Waste Management, "Recommendation by the Secretary of Energy of Candidate Site for Site Characterization for the First Radioactive-Waste Repository" (DOE/S-0046; Washington, DC, 1986).

5

The Nuclear Waste Policy Amendments Act of 1987

The modest title of the Nuclear Waste Policy Amendments Act of 1987 belies the massive changes in nuclear waste disposal policies that took place in late 1987. The most important change was the curtailment of the selection process and the naming of Yucca Mountain, Nev., as the only site to be studied further for the first permanent repository. Other major changes included the indefinite postponement of the second (eastern) repository, the prohibition of studies of crystalline rock as a medium for a geological repository, and making the construction of a monitored retrievable storage (MRS) facility contingent on the licensing of a permanent repository. The act, in effect, reversed a decision made with the passage of the Nuclear Waste Policy Act (NWPA) of 1982 that mandated that selection of a repository site would be based purely on science and safety, not on politics.[1]

By 1986, the Department of Energy (DOE) had selected three possible sites for the western repository and had identified several possible sites for the eastern repository. Opposition to being selected was extremely strong in all of the states that had been identified. Strong opposition to hosting even a temporary storage facility underscored the mistrust of the DOE and the state of repository technology. States did not want to have a temporary facility built within their borders for fear it would become a de facto permanent storage facility.

Over 40 bills dealing with spent fuel disposal were introduced in the 100th Congress, 1st Session (1987). Most bills never reached the floor of the House or Senate. Although standing committee hearings were held on most issues that eventually were included in the Amendments Act, there were no hearings in these committees on the decision to select Yucca Mountain for the first permanent repository. Along with substantive issues, there were lengthy debates in committees over procedural issues.

These included the attempt of the DOE to abandon the second repository by changing the mission statement rather than by legislation and the site selection methodology used by the DOE. Unusual legislative maneuvering by Senator J. Bennett Johnston made it difficult for members of Congress to review the provisions of the Amendments Act. Yucca Mountain was selected as the only candidate for the first repository by a conference committee during the end-of-the-year rush before adjournment.

Passage of the Amendments Act left the country with a single site, Yucca Mountain, as the sole candidate for a permanent high-level nuclear waste repository and placed the country at risk of having no solution to the spent fuel disposal problem should this site prove to be unsatisfactory. A provision of the act prohibiting the study of crystalline rock as a host medium for a repository had no scientific basis. The processes that led to the passage of the Amendments Act will be described in greater detail below.

POSTPONEMENT OF THE SECOND REPOSITORY

In May 1986, Energy Secretary John Herrington announced that the DOE was going to delay indefinitely the search for a second repository and delay the opening of the first repository. According to a *New York Times* editorial, "The decision shattered the 1982 compromise and angered Western states."[2] The decision to delay the second repository was interpreted as a decision to drop the second repository. The NWPA of 1982 mandated that the DOE recommend three candidates for a second repository to the president by July 1, 1989. All of the members of the Senate Energy and Natural Resources Committee took exception to Energy Secretary Herrington's plan to make these changes by changing the DOE's Mission Plan rather than by asking Congress for new legislation. Herrington, former director of Presidential Personnel and a California lawyer, betrayed his ignorance of the prerogatives of the Senate by telling the members of the committee that if they did not overrule the new Mission Plan within 30 days he would assume that they accepted the new Mission Plan. According to Senator Daniel Evans (R-WA), former governor of the State of Washington: "With the Mission Plan Amendment the Department is boldly proceeding to modify the statute and intent of the 1982 Waste Policy Act that Congress passed after much deliberation. Then the Department has the gall to imply 'We'll go ahead and implement those changes if Congress doesn't act affirmatively in thirty days to overrule our game plan.' ... This is simple arrogance and bullheadedness."[3]

Secretary Herrington claimed that he had consulted a staff attorney and was told that modifying the Mission Plan was not illegal. He also listed scientific, technical, and economic factors that had led the department to reduce its estimates of the number of operating nuclear reactors and the amounts of spent fuel from those made in 1982, when the NWPA was passed. These included reduced rate of growth for electricity, financial constraints on utility companies, new regulations and safety requirements for nuclear reactors, delays in the construction of nuclear reactors, and cost escalations for building nuclear reactors.[4] Herrington also said that he was afraid that it would not be possible to get a bill through if they opened up or amended the NWPA of 1982. He did not mention other political factors thought to be important by many members of Congress, journalists, and scholars. The seven states east of the Mississippi River that had been identified as potential sites (Maine, New Hampshire, Wisconsin, Minnesota, Virginia, Georgia, and North Carolina) were actively opposed to hosting a repository.[5] Postponing or dropping a second repository would lessen the opposition to the whole repository program. Many members of the committee, including the ranking minority member, Senator James McClure (R-ID), indicated that to omit the second repository would be breaking faith with western state senators. These senators had been promised that the West would not get all of the high-level nuclear waste generated in the country.

The decision to drop the second repository was popular with representatives and senators representing states that were candidates for the second repository. In 1987, five bills were introduced in the House and two in the Senate calling for elimination of the second repository.

CANDIDATE STATES FOR THE FIRST REPOSITORY OBJECT

Soon after the passage of the Nuclear Waste Policy Act of 1982, the DOE selected nine candidate sites for the first repository. Most of these sites were in salt domes. By late 1984, the department had reduced the number to five and after ranking these, selected three sites. These three sites were in Deaf Smith County, Tex.; the Hanford Nuclear Reservation in Washington; and Yucca Mountain near the Nevada Test Site. All three sites were close to sites that already had radioactive waste generated by the nuclear weapons program. All three sites were formally recommended to President Reagan by the DOE on May 27, 1986. These selections were approved by the president only one day later, on May 28, 1986. This left virtually no time for House and Senate members representing the affected states, the governors of the affected states, or interest groups to influence the president's decision.

In 1987, four bills were introduced in the House and one in the Senate calling for suspension of the repository site selection process. These bills were introduced by three representatives and a senator who represented the three candidate states for the first repository.

Hanford, Washington

A major objection to the Hanford site was that the repository would be located close to the Columbia River (within six miles at the closest point). Military nuclear waste was already leaking from over 100 tanks into the Columbia River.[6] Although a repository with both engineered and basalt geological barriers would not be as leaky as these single-walled tanks, there was nevertheless concern that the basalt might not offer sufficient isolation. There were also angry protests over the site selection process. Hanford had ranked lowest among five sites after a preliminary site evaluation by the DOE. Secretary Herrington said it was selected over higher-ranked sites because the basalt rock type added to the rock diversity of the sites selected. The multiple attribute utility methodology was also criticized. This methodology, which used several factors, offered the opportunity to manipulate the outcome by adjusting the weighting of the factors. Senator Evans also complained that the first repository would not be taking any military waste and that there were no other facilities accepting military waste. Enormous amounts of military waste were generated during the massive nuclear arms buildup during the Cold War, and most of this was stored at Hanford. Melvin Sampson, chairman of the Tribal Council of the Yakama Indian Tribe, a tribe located in the vicinity of Hanford, cited a series of General Accounting Office reports critical of environmental practices at Hanford and other DOE nuclear facilities.[7] Senator Evans introduced a bill that would establish regional MRS facilities as an alternative to a high-level permanent repository.

Deaf Smith County, Texas

The chief drawback of the Deaf Smith County site was that it would be located beneath the Ogallala aquifer, the largest aquifer in the United States and a source of water for a large area including parts of eight states: Texas, Oklahoma, New Mexico, Colorado, Wyoming, Nebraska, Kansas, and South Dakota.[8] Access to the repository would be through a shaft passing through the aquifer to the repository located underneath the aquifer. There was concern that there would be leakage into the aquifer. The Deaf Smith site was a salt bed site similar to one being developed for a repository in Gorleben, Germany. On May 12, 1987, there was an accident in a shaft at the Gorleben site caused by the pressure of salt creep. Information about this accident was withheld from congressional committees with responsibilities for nuclear repository programs. According to Steve Frishman, director of Nuclear Waste Programs, Office of the Governor of Texas:

> We question why the DOE, as late as approximately two months after the Gorleben incident, had not informed interested and affected parties such as the State of Texas and Congress of this matter. The DOE closely observes the Gorleben nuclear waste project, in part because of the numerous similarities to the Deaf Smith County salt repository project. The Department of Energy has had numerous opportunities to inform us, the Congress, and the interested and affected public of this significant incident, yet we learned of the matter from an interested citizen in late June.[9]

Another objection was that Deaf Smith County was located in some of the best agricultural land in Texas. Not only farming but also farm machinery, food processing, and other businesses associated with agriculture would be affected.

Yucca Mountain, Nevada

Two main issues stand out in protests by Nevada senators and House members and Nevada officials over the increased chances that Yucca Mountain would be selected for the first repository. First, it was claimed that Yucca Mountain was not suitable from a scientific and technical point of view. There were over 30 identified earthquake faults in the vicinity, and there had been recent earthquake activity in the vicinity. Its location next to the Nevada Test Site raised the question of whether future nuclear testing activity would cause seismic activity in the area. Some previous tests had been associated with seismic activity. The rock in which the repository was to be located, tuff, was volcanic rock. This raised the question of whether there would be volcanic activity in the future along with geothermal activity commonly associated with volcanism. There were significant differences between the DOE and the State of Nevada estimates on groundwater transport time, with the state estimating faster flow rates and a higher rate of container corrosion. Second, it was felt that it was unjust to ask Nevada, which had no nuclear reactors and did not generate nuclear waste, to take nuclear waste from other states. Former governor Grant Sawyer testified: "Is it not patently unfair for one segment of the nation to be the primary user and beneficiary of nuclear power production and for a different segment to bear the risk and stigma of its by-products?"[10] These ethical issues were never raised by any hearing participants other than Nevadans.

Senator Chic Hecht (R-NV) introduced bills that called for studies of alternatives to Yucca Mountain including reprocessing and subseabed disposal. He also introduced a bill calling for a study of earthquakes at Yucca Mountain.

MONITORED RETRIEVABLE STORAGE

Plans for an MRS facility were made many years prior to the passage of the Nuclear Waste Policy Amendments Act of 1987. In 1979, Senator J. Bennett Johnston (D-LA) and Senator Henry Jackson (D-WA), chairman of the Senate Energy Committee, introduced legislation authorizing construction of an MRS facility. Senate Energy Committee Staff Director Daniel A. Dreyfus thought that the high-level nuclear waste problem could be solved by placing the facility in a state already accustomed to having nuclear waste in storage.[11] This idea, in fact, seems to have influenced the subsequent siting of all types of high-level nuclear waste facilities. Washington State was thought to be a promising site at that time. Senator Johnston, a strong supporter of the MRS concept, favored placing the facility at the Nevada Test Site. He felt that existing tunnels at the Nevada Test Site could be adapted for the storage of spent fuel and for other high-level nuclear waste. The DOE initially opposed the MRS concept but later became more favorably disposed toward it as it became apparent that completion of a geologic permanent repository would take longer than anticipated.

Compared with moving nuclear waste directly from reactor sites to a permanent repository, an MRS facility would involve additional handling, transportation, and cost. The nuclear industry favored the MRS facility but viewed it as only a temporary measure that should not be substituted for a permanent solution. Environmental groups opposed an MRS facility because they felt it would reduce the pressure to build a permanent repository and thus would continue to place the burden on future generations to solve the high-level nuclear waste disposal problem. The 1979 bill, which was not passed, favored an MRS facility over a geologic repository.

The NWPA of 1982, among other provisions, shifted the emphasis from an MRS facility to a geologic repository and furthermore stated that the MRS facility should not constitute an alternative to the disposal of high-level nuclear waste or spent fuel in a permanent geologic repository. This shift was largely related to the efforts of Senator James McClure (R-ID), who at that time was chairman of the Senate Energy and Natural Resources Committee.[12]

Although the MRS was not a top priority in 1987, it was nevertheless a significant issue, and extensive hearings were held by the Senate Energy and Natural Resources Committee on the issue. Senator J. Bennett Johnston, chairman of this committee, was a proponent of MRS facilities and introduced legislation to establish MRS facilities in 1987.

By 1987, two years later than the 1985 date mandated by the NWPA of 1982, the DOE had identified three sites for an MRS. Much to everyone's surprise and to the dismay of Tennessee officials, all three sites were located in Tennessee. One of the advantages of an MRS facility is that it could be built in any state because it could be built above ground and only required land and viable transportation routes. Even though the facility was only going to be temporary, fireworks followed the announcement of this decision. According to Ned R. McWherter, governor of Tennessee: "The proposal by the Department of Energy to construct a Monitored Retrievable Storage facility in Tennessee has resulted in the most important and emotional debate of our generation."[13] He also noted, "The people of Tennessee are prepared to accept their share of responsibility for the spent fuel produced at the state's nuclear plants. What they cannot justify is the construction of a facility designed to process waste from the entire country."[14]

Chief among the worries of Tennessee officials was the concern that an MRS facility, designed as a temporary holding facility, would become a de facto permanent storage facility. Cancellation of the second repository and delay of the first repository heightened these fears. There was also concern that safety was not a paramount concern of the DOE.

Senator Albert Gore Jr. (D-TN) questioned the need for an MRS facility. He said: "We cannot accept a justification of the need of the MRS

based on the DOE's inability to meet the Act's deadlines for completion
of a permanent repository. This road leads to a de facto permanent repository in Oak Ridge, Tennessee. I will do everything possible to stop DOE's
efforts to turn the MRS into a quick fix political solution to the real problem of final nuclear waste storage."[15] Officials representing local governments at the candidate sites were less opposed to an MRS facility than
were state officials. The City of Oak Ridge and the county in which the
city is located, Roane County, set up a study commission that came up
with proposals that would mitigate their fears about the facility. To prevent the MRS facility from becoming a de facto permanent facility, it proposed that no high-level nuclear waste be accepted by the MRS facility
until a permanent geological repository was licensed. To prevent the MRS
facility from storing all of the high-level nuclear waste, it advocated limiting the storage capacity of the facility to 15,000 metric tons. This would be
about one-third of the waste projected to be produced by 1998. Furthermore, the commission proposed that no more than 10,000 metric tons be
shipped to the MRS facility until a permanent repository was actually operating. Penalties for any spent fuel that remained at the site for more than
15 years were another demand. The commission also wanted to establish
an oversight board with strong local representation and the power to shut
down the facility if the oversight board deemed it necessary. The commission, alluding to the concerns of the people over the postponement of the
first repository, felt that two procedural provisions were necessary. The first
was that binding contracts between the DOE and state or local governments be issued. The second procedural provision was that any changes in
the first three items (metric ton limits etc.) could not be made unilaterally
by the DOE but would be subject to the same procedures that applied to
the initial authorization of the MRS facility. These included congressional
authorization, a state veto provision, and the possibility of a congressional
override.[16] Nevertheless, the State of Tennessee blocked construction of an
MRS facility in Roane County.

The DOE defended siting the MRS facility in Tennessee, claiming that
the east-central or southeastern part of the country is central to the majority of nuclear reactors. Thus siting the MRS facility in Tennessee would
minimize the total shipment miles in the movement of nuclear waste both
to the MRS facility and from the MRS facility to the permanent repository. Also, Tennessee borders eight states and offered good access via the

Interstate Highway system.[17] Federal ownership and control of the site by the DOE were other advantages that were listed. Additionally, the DOE claimed that the Oak Ridge site could be expanded to accept 70,000 metric tons, which was thought to be an advantage for the program if the permanent repository did not materialize. This was a disadvantage, as far as Tennessee was concerned. As Senator Wendell Ford (D-KY), the first member of the Senate Energy and Natural Resources Committee to pick up on this, said: "I do not know whether Oak Ridge is ready for it, but they had better grab hold of their britches because they are about to get all 70,000 tons, in my opinion."[18]

Representatives of two of the first repository candidate states, Senator Dan Evans of Washington and Senator Chic Hecht of Nevada, were both supporters of the MRS concept. Senator Evans proposed building three or four MRS facilities, each in a different region of the country. Senator Evans also advocated having the Department of the Interior, rather than the Department of Energy, select potential MRS facility sites. Powerful senators from both political parties, including the chairman of the Senate Energy and Natural Resources Committee, Senator Johnston (D-LA), and the ranking minority member, Senator James McClure (R-ID), were longtime supporters of an MRS facility. The final outcome was that the Nuclear Waste Policy Amendments Act of 1987 did authorize the DOE to build an MRS facility. However, construction could not start until a geological repository was licensed by the Nuclear Regulatory Commission (NRC). Also, limitations were placed on how much waste the MRS facility could accept. The MRS facility would be limited to 10,000 metric tons after licensing of a permanent repository and before it was operating and 15,000 metric tons after the permanent repository was operating. Thus the local study commission from the Oak Ridge site was influential in shaping important conditions and protections for potential MRS facility host communities. Nuclear utility companies and organizations were not successful in their efforts to oppose linking the construction of the MRS facility with the licensing of a permanent repository. They feared they would continue to be stuck with spent fuel if a permanent repository were not licensed. The NWPA of 1982 instructed the DOE to search for and identify MRS sites. The 1987 act did not amend this part of the 1982 act. The effort to establish a temporary nuclear waste storage facility did not end in 1987 but continues to be debated, without resolution, until the present time.

OFFERING INCENTIVES FOR A REPOSITORY

After realizing that no state would willingly host either an MRS facility or a permanent repository, Chairman Bennett Johnston and Senator James McClure, ranking minority member of the Senate Energy and Natural Resources Committee, introduced a bill, S. 839, that would provide incentives for hosting these facilities. This bill included provisions for offering $100 million per year to a state that would accept a permanent repository and $50 million per year to a state accepting an MRS facility. The funding was to be provided by funds that would be freed by the cancellation of site characterizations of two of the three permanent repository candidate sites. Any state or Indian tribe could apply for these facilities, but it would only have 12 months from the enactment of the bill, S. 839, to demonstrate the suitability of a site within the state or reservation. The state or Indian tribe chosen would have to give up the right to judicial review of the MRS site program and the right to veto the site. Although the bill was not passed out of committee, the hearings on this bill provide some interesting insights on attitudes toward these issues. Some provisions were included in the Amendments Act of 1987.

The provision requiring a waiver of judicial review reflected Chairman Johnston's frustration over delays with both the nuclear power program and the high-level nuclear waste disposal program. According to Chairman Johnston:

> We were at Forsmark, the Swedish facility, and in connection with it they have a nuclear plant which they built in four and a half years. You know how long it takes in this country?... It takes three times as long because we have to go to court. We have to ring all those legal bells and whistles and have all those paper tracks, and almost without exception they do not think it contributes to their safety. And I do not think it would contribute to the safety of nuclear waste. I do not mind spending billions of dollars for safety. But save me from my colleagues at the bar, who just want another lawsuit, another hearing, another series of briefs, another series of interrogatories. Lawyers do not know anything about nuclear matters, by and large.... The National Academy of Sciences and Ph.D.'s and those kind of people ought to do that.[19]

At the Senate committee hearings on the bill there was unanimous opposition to the provision that all candidate site states and affected Indian tribes must waive judicial review.

Troy Don Moore, chairman of the Waste Deposit Impact Committee, Deaf Smith County, Tex., testified: "With regard to S839, I still believe in the three branches of government. If something is not going right you need recourse. Sometimes lawyers may not be the best recourse, but nevertheless it is recourse. I think to get the local community to give it up is asking a lot."[20] Senator Cohen (R-ME) testified: "I cannot conceive of a state that is willing to suspend a procedure through which the Department of Energy can be held accountable for its actions, and suspend the right to judicial review."[21]

There was strong opposition also to abandoning scientific and technical guidelines required by the 1982 NWPA. Russell Jim, manager of the Nuclear Waste Program of the Yakama Indian Tribe, testified: "The Nuclear Waste Policy Act properly provides that detailed geologic considerations should be the primary criteria for the selection of sites for repositories. S839 would replace that geologic siting mechanism with a wheel of fortune or marketplace siting scheme. The sites for these facilities would be determined by the states or tribes that came forward first to claim the prize money."[22] Terry Husseman, director of the Nuclear Waste Office of the State of Washington, testified: "It changes the primary focus of the site selection process…from a scientific search to, are you willing to take the site if we give you enough money."[23]

Another provision that was strongly opposed was the requirement allowing only 12 months after enactment of the bill for states to accept a repository or a monitored retrievable storage facility. The Environmental Policy Institute took the position: "It is highly improbable and totally unrealistic that any state or tribe could demonstrate the suitability of an as yet unstudied site for characterization within twelve months."[24] Because the DOE was already planning to compensate affected communities for the economic impacts of constructing high-level waste facilities, the $100 million and $50 million incentives were viewed by some as bribes. Russell Jim of the Yakama Indian tribe testified: "The cynicism of this bill is revealed by its potential for abuse with respect to small, poor Indian tribes. Given the dismal economic conditions which characterize most Indian reservations, a small tribe might be tempted to enter into such an agreement, essentially selling out its reservation in return for what would be enormous per capita payments to its present members."[25] Nevertheless, there was support for the idea of compensating states and Indian tribes that agreed to host a repository or an MRS facility.

Although S. 839 was not voted on by the Senate Energy and Natural Resources Committee and was not voted on by the Senate, the waiver of judicial review and provisions for monetary incentives, albeit at a reduced level, were included in the 1987 Amendments Act. Including Indian tribes was attractive because their special legal status does not give states veto power over them.

To carry out the mission of seeking volunteers, the Office of Nuclear Waste Negotiator was established by the Amendments Act. This office was set up because the DOE was viewed as having little credibility with potential volunteers. The office was located in the executive office of the president. The negotiator was nominated by the president, required confirmation by the Senate, and served at the pleasure of the president. This arrangement offered several opportunities for politicization of the "incentives" approach to selecting nuclear waste storage sites. The negotiator was authorized to offer any "reasonable and appropriate" inducements to potential volunteers. These could include direct payments, tax breaks, highway and airport improvements, siting of favorable federal facilities, and higher education programs. Agreements required congressional approval. Funding for the incentives and for the operation of the Office of Nuclear Negotiator would come from the Nuclear Waste Fund.[26]

UDALL PROPOSES A MORATORIUM

In July 1987, Representative Morris Udall (D-AZ), chairman of the House Interior and Insular Affairs Committee, proposed a moratorium on the implementation of the Nuclear Waste Policy Act of 1982. Udall also favored the establishment of a presidential commission to study the siting recommendations during the moratorium.[27] Udall had played a major role in negotiating the 1982 act. He was particularly upset over the indefinite postponement of the second repository. Furthermore, Udall felt that politics had played a major role in the decision to postpone the second repository. According to Udall: "Today, just 5 years later, this great program is in ruins. To help a few office seekers in the last election, the administration killed the eastern repository program, shattering the delicate regional balance at the heart of the 1982 Act."[28]

Udall introduced H.R. 2888, a bill to establish the moratorium, on July 1, 1987. In addition to a moratorium on site selection activities, the bill prohibited expenditures from the Nuclear Waste Fund and set up a commission. The mandate of the commission was to study the nuclear waste disposal problem and the DOE's handling of it thus far. The commission would be required to submit a report within 18 months of enactment of the bill.[29]

On July 15, 1987, Udall introduced another bill, H.R. 2967, which included the provisions of H.R. 2888 with some modifications and also required an Environmental Impact Statement for a repository.[30] The Interior Subcommittee on Energy and the Environment chaired by Udall adopted the bill with some amendments. The major amendments included a provision that would give federal aid to state and local governments affected by site characterization and also directed the commission to study whether the DOE should continue to operate the nuclear waste disposal program. H.R. 2967 was approved by the subcommittee on October 20, 1987, and the full interior committee on October 28, 1987. It was put on the House calendar on November 5, 1987, but this bill was never called up for House debate. By this time, Udall was showing signs of Parkinson's disease and was "running out of steam."[31]

The provisions of H.R. 2967 represented the core position of the House in conference committee negotiation on the 1987 Nuclear Waste Policy Amendments Act.[32] The moratorium was initially supported by states that were candidates for permanent repository sites, as well as Tennessee, the state with three MRS candidate sites. Senator Johnston opposed the moratorium because he was concerned that it would drive employees away from the nuclear waste program and also because he wanted to speed the program up. A moratorium was also opposed by nuclear utility companies and by states that had not been selected for a potential repository site. The latter had no incentive to revisit the siting decisions.[33] The moratorium did not survive in the conference committee.

THE NUCLEAR WASTE TECHNICAL REVIEW BOARD

The Amendments Act also established the Nuclear Waste Technical Review Board. This board was created in response to concerns over the scientific decisions of the DOE relating to the management and disposal of spent fuel from civilian nuclear reactors. The 11 members of the board serve four-year staggered terms. To form the first board, the president selected the members from a list of at least 22 scientists and engineers submitted by the National Academy of Sciences. If there is a vacancy, two candidates must be submitted by the academy. There are no formal political criteria for the nominees; rather, the enabling legislation specified that they must be eminent in a field of science and engineering and must have an established record of distinguished service.

The Nuclear Waste Technical Review Board is financed by yearly appropriations by Congress from the Nuclear Waste Fund. The power of the president to select the chair of the board and to select members from a list presents opportunities to politicize the board. Both Congress and the president have the power to influence the level of funding of the board and thereby the ability to provide effective oversight. The board can issue reports and recommendations but has no teeth. It does not have the power to compel the DOE to implement its recommendations. It does, however, sometimes influence DOE policies.

SELECTION OF YUCCA MOUNTAIN FOR THE FIRST REPOSITORY

The Yucca Mountain site in Nevada was selected as the only site to be further characterized for the first permanent repository by a conference committee of Congress in a highly politicized process. This decision was approved by both houses of Congress and was implemented immediately after the passage of the 1987 Amendments Act. The dominant actor in this process was Senator J. Bennett Johnston (D-LA), chairman of the Senate Energy and Natural Resources Committee, the Senate committee with major responsibilities for nuclear waste disposal programs. Johnston was also chairman of the Appropriations Subcommittee on Energy and Water Resources, which recommends appropriations for nuclear waste disposal programs and many other programs. Prior to the passage of the Nuclear Waste Policy Amendments Act of 1987, Johnston conducted several committee meetings on nuclear waste disposal issues primarily related to the site selection of a permanent repository and an interim storage facility. Testimony was heard from DOE officials and other federal administrators; federal, state, and local officials; environmental interest groups; nuclear utility officials; and nuclear utility association representatives. Johnston's questions for witnesses were well focused and succinct and reflected an impressive grasp of technical and scientific issues. The hearings were conducted with fairness and were not rushed, offering ample opportunity for detailed input into the hearings. Having said that, his legislative maneuvers in the last two months of 1987 lacked transparency.

Johnston adopted a three-pronged approach to amending the Nuclear Waste Policy Act of 1982. The first was to introduce on September 1, 1987, a bill, S. 1688, that only dealt with nuclear waste disposal issues. This bill had been approved by the Senate Energy and Natural Resources Committee, which had also agreed to attach it to the Senate Budget Reconciliation bill, S. 1920. The second approach involved attaching the nuclear waste provisions of S. 1688 to the fiscal year 1988 Energy and Water Appropriations bill, H.R. 2700, a massive pork barrel bill. This bill, which had been passed in the House, was introduced in the Senate on September 16, 1987, with Johnston's nuclear waste riders attached. On November 12, 1987, an amendment introduced by Johnston that would phase out studies of crystalline rock as a potential repository host medium was passed by voice vote in the Senate. This was a political move that would eliminate potential eastern and Midwestern repository sites. No scientific justification was given.[34] The amendment did provide that if the secretary of energy decided to consider any sites in crystalline rock for characterization or selection as a repository, the secretary should consider seasonal increases in population, proximity to public drinking water supplies including those of metropolitan areas, and the impact on Indian tribal lands.

Senators Brock Adams (D-WA) and Harry Reid (D-NV) launched a filibuster on the bill. Reid emphasized that the Yucca Mountain site was scientifically unsound and that the selection process was procedurally unfair.[35] Senator Adams introduced an amendment to remove the nuclear waste provisions from the bill, claiming that it was an authorization that did not belong in an appropriations bill. Senator Reid introduced an amendment that would make health and safety the primary considerations in selecting a site, a measure that would position Nevada lower in the rankings. Reid lost the support of Adams after introducing this amendment. Both amendments were rejected.[36] The Senate Environment and Public Works Committee wanted surface-based testing of all three finalist sites, but an amendment requiring this failed.[37] H.R. 2700 was passed by the Senate on an 86 to 9 vote on November 18, 1987. The Senate changes to the appropriations bill were not acceptable to the House. House leaders, including Representative John Dingell (D-MI), powerful chairman of the House Energy and Commerce Committee, were opposed to bypassing the authorizing committees on nuclear waste disposal issues. The impasse between the House and Senate on H.R. 2700 was never resolved, and the bill was attached to the omnibus appropriations bill for fiscal year 1988 and passed by a continuing resolution in December.

After having failed to pass the nuclear waste provisions through the appropriations process, Johnston attempted to pass nuclear waste provisions through another omnibus financial bill, the Budget Reconciliation bill. The Senate version of the Budget Reconciliation Act, S. 1920, which had nuclear waste provisions attached, was introduced in the Senate on December 4, 1987. Johnston introduced an amendment to S. 1920 that would strike the nuclear waste provisions included in S. 1920 and substitute the nuclear waste provisions adopted by the Senate with the passage of H.R. 2700, the appropriations bill that was rejected by the House. Again, the House would not accept the Senate version of the Budget Reconciliation bill, and the House and Senate versions went to a conference committee.

There are no transcripts of the actions of the conference committee, and the following description of the conference committee politics that ensued depends on accounts of Senator Johnston and other conferees in the debates on the conference committee bill, statements of conferees, and interviews of conferees by journalists. One outcome of the conference committee was the indefinite postponement of the second repository. This concession was instrumental in gaining the support of senators and representatives from Maine, Vermont, New Hampshire, North Carolina, Georgia, Virginia, Michigan, Minnesota, and Wisconsin, potential candidate states for a second repository. Five Texas representatives wanted to ban placing a repository below an aquifer. This ban would eliminate both the Hanford, Wash., site and the Deaf Smith site in Texas. This was supported by House Speaker Jim Wright (D-TX) and House Majority Leader Tom Foley (D-WA), powerful leaders in the House.[38] The House wanted to name Yucca Mountain explicitly but was not interested in a monitored retrievable storage facility. To obtain the support of House conferees for an MRS and to avoid a House debate on the bill, Johnston agreed to name the Yucca Mountain site for the first repository and to make building an MRS contingent on the licensing of a permanent repository.[39] The placement of an MRS facility in Tennessee was annulled in the conference committee bill.[40] This agreement added Tennessee and South Carolina representatives to the growing band of supporters.

The conference committee bill was debated in the House on December 21, 1987. Representative Udall (D-AZ) stated that he supported the conference committee bill, though he complained that the Senate "butch-ered" the Nuclear Waste Policy Act of 1982.[41] Udall did not give his rea-sons for supporting the bill in the conference committee debate, although he did so in material inserted into the record. The material introduced into the record by Udall also gives the impression that Udall was not aware that the monetary incentives for volunteering to host a repository or MRS had been reduced by 80 percent.[42] Although there had been no previous de-bate on nuclear waste by the full House, there was very little discussion on the nuclear waste issue in the House debate on the conference commit-tee report. Limited debate on conference committee bills, including those containing provisions introduced by the conference committee, is not un-usual, and generally only one hour is allotted for floor debate of confer-ence committee bills.[43] In the Senate debates Senator Johnston voiced the opinion that although he was unhappy with the restrictions on building MRS facilities, he supported going ahead with the repository program. The conference committee bill was approved by the House at 10 p.m. on December 21 by a 237 to 181 vote and by the Senate at 1 a.m. on Decem-ber 22, 1987, by a 61 to 28 vote. Both houses were eager to adjourn. The conference committee bill was the first bill to designate Yucca Mountain as the candidate site for the first repository. None of the House or Senate bills had done so. Although new material is not supposed to be inserted at the conference committee stage, this norm has often been violated with other major legislation. President Reagan signed the bill, Public Law 100-203, December 22, 1987. Reagan supported nuclear power because he felt it could help meet the need for increased energy supplies.[44]

In the end, it was not the DOE, which had conducted extensive stud-ies of the sites, that picked the site but, rather, a conference committee that operated behind closed doors. The conference committee decisions also had the effect of eliminating any backup provision by canceling site characterization of the two possible alternative repository sites and prohib-iting the building of a monitored retrievable storage facility prior to the is-suance of a license for construction of the first permanent repository.

One could hardly blame Nevada representatives for calling the Nuclear Waste Policy Amendments Act of 1987 the "Screw Nevada" bill. Represen-tative Al Swift (D-WA) said, "We've done it in a purely political process.... We are going to give somebody some nasty stuff."[45] Nor could one disagree with the more general assessment that "Johnston has a solid technical mas-tery of energy policy.... The bargains he strikes generally leave all parties with something to show for their efforts, provided they stay alert while the deal is being struck."[46] Clearly, Senator Johnston dominated the processes involved in the passage of the 1987 Amendments Act. His power, expertise and interest very likely contributed to his dominance. Michael Kraft reports that Johnston received a large amount of political action committee funds from the nuclear power industry.[47] Cotton, however, maintains that given the information that Congress had at the time of the passage of the 1987 Amendments Act, Yucca Mountain was a reasonable choice if only one site was to be characterized.[48]

POLITICAL AFTERMATH OF THE 1987 ACT

Monitored Retrievable Storage Review Commission

The 1987 Nuclear Waste Policy Amendments Act called for the creation of a Monitored Retrievable Storage Review Commission. It was directed to prepare a report on the need for an MRS. The context of the charge was that the MRS might be an alternative to at-reactor storage of spent fuel prior to final disposal in a repository. The commission issued its report on November 1, 1989.[49] It concluded that from a technical perspective both an MRS and at-reactor storage are safe options. It concluded, however, that an MRS constrained by the linkage language of the Amendments Act of 1987 would not be justified. The commission did conclude that the construction of an MRS would be justified if "1) there were no linkages between the MRS and the repository; 2) the MRS could be constructed at an early date; and 3) the opening of the repository was delayed considerably beyond its present scheduled date of operation."[50] It is interesting to note that in a section on equity considerations in MRS or repository site selection, the commission said that "exempting a broad region from consideration for a controversial facility may be a natural political accommodation, but it appears to have little to do with equity as the concept is generally understood."[51] Geographical equity considerations have recently been suggested by Canada's Nuclear Waste Management Organization, as discussed in a later chapter. The commission also commented that "regardless of their size, payment to States, localities or Indian Tribes affected by a MRS or repository's location may not mitigate all of the cost of siting and its effects on individuals."[52]

The commission did make some specific recommendations for modest interim storage facilities. It recommended that Congress should authorize the construction of a Federal Emergency Storage facility with a capacity limit of 2,000 metric tons and a User-Funded Interim Storage facility with a limit of 5,000 metric tons. The first of these was to serve as a safety net if it were necessary to remove stored fuel from a reactor that suffered an accident, and the second was to serve as an overflow facility for any reactors that ran out of storage capacity. The differing priorities of Congress and the Review Commission are readily apparent. In its linkage language requiring progress on a geological repository before an MRS facility could proceed, Congress was trying to keep the pressure on for completing a permanent repository. It was also addressing the concerns of those who feared the MRS would become a de facto permanent repository. The Review Commission had as its first priority providing interim storage so that the existing reactors could remain in operation for their useful life. The recommendations of the Review Commission have not been acted on. Not only have no interim storage facilities been built, there is no federal commitment to build any.

Nevada Opposition: Filibusters, Holds, Radiation Standards

The Nevada congressional delegation has been opposed to the repository ever since Yucca Mountain became a candidate for this facility. Opposition to the repository is the "sine qua non" for election to Congress in Nevada, as is willingness to look out for gambling industry interests. Candidates from both parties try to outdo each other in their opposition to Yucca Mountain in their campaign rhetoric. Duffy describes high-level nuclear waste disposal as the "hot-button" issue in Nevada.[53] This causes Republican candidates to distance themselves on this issue from the National Republican Party, which is generally pro–Yucca Mountain. Members of Congress from Nevada have used a variety of strategies and tactics to obstruct progress in studying the repository. These include voting against the designation of Yucca Mountain for the nation's repository, cutting the Yucca Mountain budget both in committee and on floor votes, filibusters in the Senate, and holding up nominations. They have been especially active in the Senate, whose institutions make it much easier to obstruct legislation than is the case in the House. The Senate "has always operated under rules that vest enormous power in each individual. In holding the floor and in proposing amendments, senators face fewer constraints than the members of any other legislature in the world."[54] Members of Congress have been tireless in honoring their campaign promises to oppose the Yucca

Mountain repository. Furthermore, on this issue there has been outstanding cooperation and teamwork between Republican and Democratic representatives and senators.

Senator Harry Reid (D-NV) has been one of the most effective opponents and has been involved in the effort at the national level longer than any other elected official from Nevada. Reid is a moderate Democrat and has worked well with Republicans to get legislation passed.[55] He is also viewed as "a superb party tactician who has the capacity to unite his Democratic colleagues when an emerging consensus within the party appears possible."[56] Reid played a major role in persuading Senator James Jeffords to defect from the Republican Party in spring 2001, offering Jeffords his ranking member position on the Environment and Public Works Committee. Soon after the Jeffords defection Majority Leader Tom Daschle announced that as long as the Democrats were in control, the Yucca Mountain project was dead. Reid has served as the minority whip in the Senate and after the defeat of Minority Leader Tom Daschle, became Senate minority leader. Reid has extensive political experience both in Nevada and at the national level of government. He has served in the Nevada legislature, held the post of lieutenant governor of Nevada, and was chairman of the Nevada Gaming Commission, which because of the importance of the gaming industry in Nevada may well be the most important office in Nevada. He has served in the U.S. House of Representatives and in 2004 was elected to his fourth term in the Senate. His voting record is a unique one. He is a liberal on economic issues but a conservative on social issues, except for gambling measures. Reid was a cosponsor of a constitutional amendment to ban flag burning and voted for the ban on partial-birth abortions.[57]

Reid understands the legislative process and has positioned himself to help Nevada by getting on committees and subcommittees that have jurisdiction over policies affecting Nevada. Reid made a major effort to block the passage of the NWPA of 1987 in which the Yucca Mountain site was selected for the nation's sole high-level nuclear waste repository.

In 1989, Reid managed to get $15.4 million added to the Energy and Water bill to help the State of Nevada and some local units of government in Nevada to oversee the DOE's planning for the Yucca Mountain repository. Reid obtained the funds even though Senator Johnston said that he believed that the State of Nevada was using every possible means to frustrate and obstruct the plan.

In 1991, Reid threatened to filibuster a bill that would allow the federal government to preempt permit laws of the State of Nevada. Senator Reid wrote a letter to President George H. W. Bush claiming this provision violated state sovereignty. The DOE had complained that the State of Nevada had refused to issue permits necessary for studying the Yucca Mountain site. The bill also would allow a temporary nuclear waste storage facility for high-level nuclear waste to be built at the Nevada Test Site, adjacent to the Yucca Mountain repository site. This law would overturn a law that does not allow an interim high-level nuclear waste facility to be built until a permanent nuclear waste facility is licensed. Reid informed the Senate majority leader that he planned to put a "hold" on the bill. (Note, Senate rules allow a single member of the Senate to block consideration of a bill by putting a "hold" on it. Often, secret "holds" are put on bills.) Although there was strong support for it in the Senate Energy and Natural Resources Committee, this bill was not enacted into law.

Senator Reid continued his opposition to the Yucca Mountain project with mixed results in subsequent years. Thus, in 1992, when Senator J. Bennett Johnston inserted a provision in conference negotiation on an energy bill that would require that Environmental Protection Agency (EPA) radiation standards for Yucca Mountain be based on a study by the National Academy of Sciences, Senator Reid and Senator Richard Bryan (D-NV) announced plans to filibuster the conference report.[58] The filibuster effort was halted quickly and decisively by an 84 to 8 cloture vote by a Senate eager to adjourn.[59] The Energy Act of 1992 is discussed in chapter 8.

In 1996, another effort was made to establish a temporary high-level nuclear waste facility in Nevada. Reid and Bryan threatened to filibuster the bill.[60] In case the filibuster was terminated by a cloture vote, they had filed 229 amendments and planned to introduce them and cause further delay in consideration of the bill. They agreed to call off a filibuster and forego introducing the amendments in exchange for an extra week of delay in consideration of the bill. This delay was sufficient to deter the House from taking up the bill because there was not enough time to take up the bill and also override the veto that President Clinton had promised.[61] The bill passed the Senate by a 63 to 37 vote, which was a large but not veto-proof margin. Reid and Bryan's tactics were successful, and the House majority leader announced the death of the Interim Storage Facility bill on September 24, 1996. Proponents planned to revive the bill in 1997.[62]

Reid and Bryan introduced an amendment in 1997 that would forbid the shipment of nuclear waste through a state without the approval of the state's government. The adoption of this amendment would have made it impossible for either a permanent or temporary nuclear waste facility to accept spent fuel as no Nevada governor would approve of shipment of high-level nuclear waste through Nevada. This amendment failed.[63] In 1997 an interim storage facility in Nevada passed the House. Reid and Bryan again threatened a filibuster. Senator Murkowski introduced a motion to proceed that was a test vote for a cloture vote. He could only get 56 votes, and the bill was dropped.

In 1999, the Interim Storage Facility bill was taken up again. This time it included a provision that would allow the NRC to set radiation standards for Yucca Mountain, which presumably would be weaker than those already set by the EPA. Energy Secretary Bill Richardson opposed allowing the NRC to set radiation standards and said that he would recommend that President Clinton veto the bill if this provision was kept in the bill. With this provision the Senate might not be able to stop a threatened filibuster by Reid and Bryan, and the decision was made not to proceed with the bill.[64]

The radiation standards and nuclear waste storage issues came up again in 2000. A bill was introduced that would allow the EPA to set radiation standards but would require evaluation of the standards by the National Academy of Sciences and the NRC. Utilities were to be offered money to build interim storage casks for spent fuel. The Senate passed the Interim Waste Storage bill, and the House decided to take up the Senate bill to avoid a conference committee. A conference committee procedure would require resubmitting the conference committee agreement to the full Senate and risk various delaying maneuvers by Reid and Bryan. In March 2000 the House passed the bill by a 253 to 167 margin, which was short, by 27 votes, of the two-thirds majority necessary to override a presidential veto. The bill was vetoed by President Clinton on April 25, 2000, and subsequently the Senate failed to override the veto.[65] No issue was too minor for Reid, and in 2000 Reid succeeded in inserting language into the fiscal year 2001 Energy and Water Appropriations bill. The language that he inserted ordered the DOE to stop advertising bus tours to the Yucca Mountain site.[66] Soon after President-Elect Bush announced his nominees for major environmental posts in his administration, Reid placed a hold on three of these nominees.[67] In July 2006, Reid lobbied the Rules and

Bylaws Committee of the Democratic Party to move the Nevada caucus close to the beginning of the presidential nominating process. This would make the Yucca Mountain issue more prominent in the 2008 presidential campaign.[68] Reid's prominent role in trying to stop the Senate from overriding the Nevada veto of the Yucca Mountain repository is described in chapter 9.

NOTES

1. "Nevada Chosen to Receive Nuclear Waste," *Congressional Quarterly Almanac, 1987,* 43 (Washington, DC: Congressional Quarterly, Inc., 1987), 307–11.

2. "Blundering over Nuclear Waste," Editorial, *New York Times,* March 16, 1987: A18.

3. Senate Committee on Energy and Natural Resources, *On the Current Status of the Department of Energy Civilian Nuclear Waste Activities: Hearings,* 100th Cong., 1st Sess., Part I (January 29, 1987), 17.

4. Ibid., 66–71.

5. Joseph A. Davis, "Nuclear Waste: An Issue That Won't Stay Buried," in *Congressional Quarterly Weekly Report* (Washington, DC: Congressional Quarterly, Inc., March 14, 1987), 451–56.

6. Matthew L. Wald, "Slowdown in Program to Clean Up Nuclear Waste in Washington State Is Drawing Criticism," *New York Times,* Late Edition, March 6, 2005: sec. 1, 34.

7. Senate Energy and Natural Resources Committee, *On the Current Status of the Department of Energy Civilian Nuclear Waste Activities,* Part I (February 4, 1987), 272.

8. Erla Zwingle, "Ogallala Aquifer: Wellspring of the High Plains," *National Geographic* 183, no. 3 (March 1993): 80–109.

9. Senate Energy and Natural Resources Committee, "Appendix II. Additional Material Submitted for the Record, by Senator J. Bennett Johnston, Letter from Steve Frishman," in *On the Current Status of the Department of Energy Civilian Nuclear Waste Activities,* 100th Cong., 1st Sess., Part IV (July 14, 1987), 664.

10. Senate Energy and Natural Resources Committee, *On the Current Status of the Department of Energy Civilian Nuclear Waste Activities,* Part I (February 4, 1987), 169.

11. Luther J. Carter, *Nuclear Imperatives and Public Trust: Dealing with Radioactive Waste* (Washington, DC: Resources for the Future, Inc., 1987), 202.

12. Ibid., 201–24.

13. Senate Energy and Natural Resources Committee, *On the Current Status of the Department of Energy Civilian Nuclear Waste Activities,* Part II (April 29, 1987), 522.

14. Ibid., 529.

15. Ibid., 558.

16. Ibid., 532.

17. Ibid., 164.

18. Ibid., 213.

19. Senate Energy and Natural Resources Committee, *On the Current Status of the Department of Energy Civilian Nuclear Waste Activities*, Part III (April 29, 1987), 204–5.

20. Ibid., 269.

21. Ibid., 332.

22. Ibid., 292.

23. Ibid., 202.

24. Ibid., 154.

25. Ibid., 294.

26. Mark Holt, "Civilian Nuclear Spent Fuel: Temporary Storage Options," *Congressional Research Service Report for Congress*, March 27, 1998: CRS-38–39.

27. Michael E. Kraft, "Public and State Responses to High-Level Nuclear Waste Disposal: Learning from Policy Failure," *Policy Studies Review* 10, no. 4 (winter 1991–1992): 160.

28. Omnibus Budget Reconciliation Act of 1987, H.R. 3545, 100th Cong., 1st Sess., *Congressional Record* 133 (December 21, 1987): H11967.

29. Nuclear Waste Policy Commission Act of 1987, H.R. 2888, 100th Cong., 2nd Sess., *Congressional Record* 133 (July 1, 1987): H6019.

30. Ibid.

31. Alan Ehrenhalt, *Politics in America 2004: The 100th Congress* (Washington, DC: CQ Press, 2003), 54.

32. Omnibus Budget Reconciliation Act of 1987, H11967.

33. Douglas Easterling and Howard Kunreuther, *The Dilemma of Siting a High Level Nuclear Waste Repository* (Norwell, MA: Academic Publishers, 1995), 41.

34. U.S. General Accounting Office, *Nuclear Waste: DOE Has Terminated Research Evaluating Crystalline Rock for a Repository* (Washington, DC: General Accounting Office, 1989), GAO/RCED89–148.

35. "Nevada Chosen to Receive Nuclear Waste," 309.

36. Energy and Water Development Appropriations Act, H.R. 2700, 100th Cong., 1st Sess., *Congressional Record* 133 (November 18, 1987): S16415.

37. "Nevada Chosen to Receive Nuclear Waste," 308–9.

38. Elizabeth Weir, "A Weary Congress Clears Bill to Raise Taxes, Cut Spending," *Congressional Quarterly Weekly Report* 45, no. 50 (December 26, 1987): 3187.

39. Omnibus Budget Reconciliation Act of 1987, S18661.

40. Matthew L. Wald, "Nevada Is Expected as Congress Choice for Atom Waste Site," *New York Times*, December 15, 1987: A1.

41. Omnibus Budget Reconciliation Act of 1987, H11967.

42. Ibid., H11967–69.

43. Lawrence D. Longley and Walter J. Oleszek, *Bicameral Politics: Conference Committees in Congress* (New Haven: Yale University Press, 1989), 227.

44. Regina S. Axelrod, "Energy Policy: Changing Rules of the Game," in *Environmental Policy in the 1980's: Reagan's New Agenda*, ed. Norman J. Vig and Michael E. Kraft (Washington, DC: Congressional Quarterly Press, 1984), 209.

45. "Nevada Chosen to Receive Nuclear Waste," 307.

46. Ehrenhalt, *Politics in America 2004*, 600.

47. Michael E. Kraft, "Environmental Gridlock: Searching for Consensus in Congress," in *Environmental Policy in the 1990's*, ed. Norman J. Vig and Michael E. Kraft (Washington, DC: CQ Press, 1997), 110.

48. Thomas A. Cotton, "Nuclear Waste Story: Setting the Stage," in *Uncertainty Underground: Yucca Mountain and the Nation's High-Level Nuclear Waste*, ed. Allison M. MacFarlane and Rodney C. Ewing (Cambridge, MA: MIT Press, 2006), 36.

49. Monitored Retrievable Storage Review Commission, "Nuclear Waste: Is There a Need for Federal Interim Storage?" (Washington, DC: U.S. Government Printing Office, November 1, 1989).

50. Ibid., cover letter to House Speaker Thomas Foley and Senate President Pro Tempore Robert Byrd, November 1, 1989.

51. Ibid., 79.

52. Ibid., 78.

53. Robert J. Duffy, *The Green Agenda in American Politics: New Strategies for the Twenty-first Century* (Lawrence: University Press of Kansas, 2003), 137.

54. Barbara Sinclair, "The '60-Vote Senate' Strategies, Process and Outcomes," in *U.S. Senate Exceptionalism*, ed. Bruce I. Oppenheimer (Columbus: Ohio State University Press, 2002), 241.

55. Andrew Taylor, "Taciturn Reid Steps in to Lead a Leaner Democratic Caucus," *CQ Weekly* 43 (November 6, 2004): 2600.

56. Lawrence C. Dodd and Bruce I. Oppenheimer, eds., *Congress Reconsidered*, 8th ed. (Washington, DC: CQ Press, 2005), xxviii.

57. Michael Barone and Richard E. Cohen, *The Almanac of American Politics—2006* (Washington, DC: National Journal Group, 2005), 1032–35.

58. Holly Idelson, "Key Energy Conference Players," *Congressional Quarterly Weekly* 50, no. 39 (October 3, 1992): 3031–33.

59. "Nevada Chosen to Receive Nuclear Waste," 242.

60. Jonathan Weisman, "Persistent Opposition Imperils Planned Nevada Storage Site," *Congressional Quarterly Weekly* 54, no. 18 (May 4, 1994): 1217–18.

61. Jonathan Weisman, "Nevada Senators Allow Vote and Hope for a Veto," *Congressional Quarterly Weekly* 54, no. 30 (July 27, 1996): 2111.

62. Jonathan Weisman, "January Resuscitation Likely for Interim Yucca Site Bill," *Congressional Quarterly Weekly* 54, no. 39 (September 28, 1996): 2751.

63. Jonathan Weisman, "Senate, President Are Heading for Collision over Waste Site," *Congressional Quarterly Weekly* 55, no. 15 (April 12, 1997): 843.

64. Chuck McCutcheon, "Panel Pursues Nuclear Waste Storage Deal," *CQ Weekly* 57, no. 16 (April 17, 1999): 897.

65. Chuck McCutcheon, "Nuclear Waste Veto Override Fails in Senate," *CQ Weekly* 58, no. 19 (May 6, 2000): 1950.

66. Chuck McCutcheon and Alan Greenblatt, "Reid Blocks Yucca Mountain Ads," *CQ Weekly* 58, no. 39 (October 7, 2000): 2313.

67. Rebecca Adams, "Early Test for Chairman Jeffords: How to Handle Blocked EPA Nominees," *CQ Weekly* 59, no. 22 (June 2, 2002): 1302.

68. Jonathan E. Kaplan, "Yucca Mountain Prominent if Nevada Caucus Is Moved Up," *The Hill*, July 25, 2006, available at http://thehill.com/index2.php?option=com_content&task=view&id=60098&pop=1&page=0&Itemid=70\.

6

Attempts to Store Waste
on Indian Reservations

One of the provisions of the 1987 Nuclear Waste Policy Amendments Act created the position of nuclear waste negotiator, who had the responsibility of finding volunteers to host a permanent repository or a monitored retrievable storage (MRS) facility. From the outset, the emphasis of the negotiator was on finding volunteers for an interim storage site rather than a permanent repository site. If the negotiator was successful in finding a volunteer for an interim site, a waiver of the provision of the Amendments Act mandating that an interim storage facility could not be constructed until a permanent repository was licensed would have to be obtained.[1]

The first nuclear waste negotiator, David H. Leroy, was appointed by President George H. W. Bush in 1990. Leroy publicized the incentives program by mailing a call for participation to all 50 states and 565 Indian tribes in October 1991.[2] Leroy also publicized the incentives program at the Annual Meeting of the National Congress of American Indians in December 1991. Phase I grants of $100,000 were offered to any tribe, state, or community willing to consider an interim storage site. No states were interested in the incentives program. Sixteen Indian tribes and four counties applied for Phase I grants.[3] Four Phase I applications were denied by the nuclear waste negotiator. Of those receiving grants, four Indian tribes withdrew before the grants were disbursed, bringing the total cost of the Phase I grants to $1,200,000. Eight tribes dropped out after receiving the grants. The citizens of one participant county, Grant County, N.D., objected to the participation of their county and recalled all three commissioners who had participated in Phase I. The new commissioners kept the $100,000 but did not proceed to Phase II of the process. The governors of the states of the other three counties were opposed to allowing the process to go forward to Phase IIA. Nuclear Waste Negotiator Leroy was unwilling to negotiate with counties if the governor of the state in which the counties were located opposed siting a nuclear waste storage facility in the county.[4] In the U.S. federal system, Indian tribes have sovereignty, and governors could not veto the participation of Indian tribes in the nuclear waste facility siting program. This makes them attractive venues for siting many facilities prohibited by state law. Five Indian tribes applied for the $200,000 Phase IIA grants, which were to be used to fund site studies and evaluate community support for a facility. Four Indian tribes that had not applied for Phase I grants applied for Phase IIA grants, bringing the total number of applicants for Phase IIA grants to nine, at a cost of $1,800,000.[5] Only two tribes, the Mescalero Apache tribe in New Mexico and the Skull Valley Band of the Goshute tribe in Utah, applied for the much more substantial Phase IIB grants of $2,800,000 each. Phase IIB grants required the grantees to conduct much more detailed site studies and also to enter into dialogue with the nuclear waste negotiator.

Participation in the nuclear waste facility siting program generated a great deal of controversy within the Indian tribes. Some members were attracted to the prospect of financial incentives and jobs, whereas others were distrustful of federal government programs. Many were afraid that radiation from the nuclear waste would harm tribe members.[6] The Indian tribes that participated in at least one of the phases of the incentives program are listed in Table 6.1.

States were frustrated over the fact that they were unable to veto participation in the incentives program by Indian tribes located within their borders. After the Mescalero tribe applied for a Phase IIB grant, the governor of New Mexico and the congressional delegation were "horrified."[7] Senator Jeff Bingaman (D-NM) introduced an amendment to an Energy and Water Appropriations bill that would prevent the Department of Energy from awarding a grant to an Indian tribe unless an agreement had been reached with officials in the vicinity of a proposed MRS facility. In October 1993, the conference committee on the fiscal year appropriations bill went further than the Bingaman amendment and incorporated a provision in the appropriations bill that barred any further use of the Nuclear Waste Fund for study grants for nuclear waste facilities.

The Mescalero and Goshute tribes continued to work with the negotiator. The final blow to the incentives program came when Congress failed to reauthorize the Office of the Nuclear Waste Negotiator when it expired in December 1994. The interest of the Goshute and Mescalero tribes

TABLE 6.1. Indian Tribes Participating in the Incentive Program

TRIBE	STATE
Akhoik	AK
Tetlin Village Council	AK
Ute	CO
Prairie Island Community	MN
Mescalero Apache	NM
Fort McDermitt Paiute Shoshone	NV and OR
Absentee Shawnee	OK
Alabama Quassante	OK
Apache Development Authority	OK
Caddo	OK
Chickasaw Indian Nation	OK
Eastern Shawnee	OK
Miami	OK
Ponca Tribe	OK
Sac and Fox Nation	OK
Tonkawa	OK
Lower Brule Sioux	SD
Skull Valley Band of Goshute Indian Tribe	UT
Yakama Indian Nation	WA
Northern Arapahoe	WY

continued, and these tribes began working with a consortium of private power companies, Private Fuel Storage (PFS), headed by the Northern States Power Company and including New York's Con Edison, Georgia's Southern Nuclear, Pennsylvania's GPU, Illinois Power, Indiana's Michigan Power, and Wisconsin's Genoa Fuel Tech. PFS is incorporated in Delaware and is a limited-liability corporation, an arrangement that shields individual members of the consortium from any liability arising out of the actions of PFS.[8] Eventually, the financial terms of the consortium proved to be unacceptable to the financially secure Mescalero tribe, and it withdrew from the negotiations.

The impoverished Skull Valley Band of the Goshute tribe of Utah, numbering 125 members, continued to negotiate with the private consortium, and PFS submitted a license application to the Nuclear Regulatory Commission (NRC) on June 25, 1997. The project would be located on 98 acres of the sparsely populated Skull Valley Goshute Reservation, located about

70 miles south of Salt Lake City. The initial lease was for 25 years with possible renewal for another 25 years. The capacity of the facility would be 40,000 metric tons. It would be available to any U.S. nuclear facility in addition to the eight consortium members.[9] The area already contains "a low-level radioactive waste dump, a chemical weapons depot, a chemical and biological warfare proving ground, three toxic chemical sites and a magnesium factory that lets loose clouds of chlorine gas. The tribe's options for development are limited."[10]

Strong opposition by the governor and legislature of the State of Utah led to several actions. Utah Senate Bill 196, passed by the Senate and a unanimous vote of the lower House, required the private power consortium to pay the state a $5 million licensing fee and post a $2 billion cash bond before any nuclear waste could enter the state. The legislature appropriated $375,000 to finance the opposition effort.[11] In 2000, Governor Mike Leavitt created the Office of High-Level Nuclear Waste Opposition.[12]

Despite the strong opposition of Utah officials, the Goshute tribe and the private power consortium, PFS, pressed on with their plan and signed a lease in May 1997. This lease was approved by the Bureau of Indian Affairs superintendent, contingent on both the completion of an Environmental Impact Statement and licensing by the NRC. Using the federal Freedom of Information Act, the State of Utah requested a copy of the lease from the Bureau of Indian Affairs. It received an incomplete copy of the lease from which important sections had been deleted. Among the deleted sections were lease payment provisions, provisions governing termination of the lease, and sovereign immunity issues. The State of Utah appealed the deletions to the superintendent of the Bureau of Indian Affairs, who denied the appeal, citing Exemption Four of the Freedom of Information Act. This exemption prohibited disclosure of classified information or "trade secrets." The State of Utah then appealed to the Department of the Interior and when it had not received a reply in 20 days, sued the Department of the Interior in federal district court. The court, in a summary judgment, upheld the defendants. The state appealed to the 10th Circuit U.S. Court of Appeals and was defeated again, with the court ruling that the Goshute tribe and the PFS consortium could suffer competitive injury if the deleted sections were made public.[13] Winona LaDuke reports that the Skull Valley tribal chairman promised each tribal member $2 million if the PFS facility gets built.[14] The Goshute–PFS project has received a favorable Safety Evaluation Report from the NRC.[15] The State of Utah claims that the NRC has no right to license a privately owned nuclear waste facility and has filed suit in the U.S. District of Columbia Circuit Court of Appeals.[16]

On January 3, 2002, the NRC released the Final Environmental Impact Statement for the Goshute–PFS facility.[17] In March 2003, another entity involved in nuclear waste issues, the Atomic Safety and Licensing Board of the NRC, ruled that the risk of fighter jets from a nearby air base crashing into the PFS nuclear waste storage site from nearby Hill Air Force Base was too high. Further studies showed that the risk of release of radioactive materials from a plane crashing into casks and canisters was low, and the board reversed its earlier decision on February 24, 2004.[18]

The State of Utah experienced a setback when the U.S. 10th Circuit Court of Appeals ruled that Utah laws enacted from 1998 to 2001 to block the PFS facility conflicted with federal law, which supersedes state law.[19] The NRC denied Utah's final appeals on September 9, 2005, and authorized its staff to prepare to issue a license. By doing so the NRC seems to have been out of compliance with President Clinton's "environmental justice" Executive Order 12898 issued on February 11, 1994, which requires sensitivity to policies that have a disproportionately negative effect on minority and low-income populations.[20]

The NRC awarded a license on February 21, 2006, to PFS to build and operate a spent fuel storage facility.[21] The license is for 20 years and for 44,000 tons of spent fuel. Before the license can be used PFS must obtain financing and also approvals from the Bureau of Land Management, the Bureau of Indian Affairs, and the Surface Transportation Board.[22]

On September 7, 2006, the Department of the Interior rejected the plan of the Private Fuel Storage consortium to store spent fuel on the Skull Valley reservation in Utah.[23] The decision was contained in a 47-page report released to the Associated Press by the Office of Senator Orrin Hatch (R-UT). As of September 8, the PFS consortium had not received a copy of this report from the Department of the Interior.[24] The chairman of the Skull Valley Indian tribe, inexplicably, had not received a copy of the report by September 9, 2006.[25] The decision actually consisted of two separate decisions, one by the Bureau of Indian Affairs and the other by the Bureau of Land Management. The Bureau of Indian Affairs refused to grant the lease to use the Skull Valley reservation land for spent fuel storage. The Bureau of Land Management would not grant the right of way on public land to move spent fuel to the reservation site by truck from a proposed intermodal transport site with rail access.[26] Earlier direct rail access had been blocked by the Cedar Mountain Wilderness Act, passed in 2005. Senator Bennett (R-UT) and Representative Jim Matheson (D-UT) sponsored this act.

According to Robert Gehrke, Senator Hatch and Senator Bennett contacted Interior Secretary Dick Kempthorne about the PFS storage issue both before and after his confirmation hearings. Senator Hatch met with Secretary Kempthorne in June 2006 to explain his objections to the PFS project.[27] An Interior Department spokesman, Shane Wolfe, reported that Secretary Kempthorne did not make the decisions himself and that the decisions were made by two unnamed senior-level assistants.[28]

An editorial in the *Salt Lake Tribune* gives major credit for the program rejection to the efforts of the entire Utah congressional delegation: Senators Hatch and Bennett and Representatives Chris Cannon (R-UT), Rob Bishop (R-UT), and Jim Matheson (D-UT). The editorial claimed that the members of the delegation "pulled every lever" to accomplish the rejection of the PFS project. Also mentioned in the editorial was the opposition of the Healthy Alliance of Utah and the Church of Jesus Christ of Latter-day Saints (Mormon).[29] The argument used by the Mormon Church is that one state should not be required to store all of the nation's spent fuel. It was silent, however, for the 19 years during which all of the spent fuel was scheduled to be sent to Nevada. On November 15, 2006, the State of Nevada approved a payment of $844,000 to cover all of the $68,795 legal expenses incurred by the Skull Valley Band of the Goshute Indian tribe and 62 percent ($775,000) of the legal expenses incurred by PFS when they challenged five state laws designed to keep nuclear waste out of Utah.[30]

NOTES

1. Mark Holt, "Civilian Nuclear Spent Fuel: Temporary Storage Options," *Congressional Research Service Report for Congress*, March 27, 1998: 38.

2. David H. Leroy, letter to the editor, "Confronting the Nuclear Waste Problem," *Christian Science Monitor*, December 14, 1992: 20.

3. Douglas Easterling and Howard Kunreuther, *The Dilemma of Siting a High-Level Waste Repository* (Norwell, MA: Kluwer Academic Publishers, 1995), 71–80.

4. Rajeev Gowda and Douglas Easterling, "Nuclear Waste and Native America: The MRS Siting Exercise," *Risk, Health, Safety and the Environment* 9, no. 3 (summer 1998): 225–58.

5. Easterling and Kunreuther, *The Dilemma of Siting a High-Level Waste Repository*, 73.

6. Gowda and Easterling, "Nuclear Waste and Native America," 237–42.

7. Matthew L. Wald, "Nuclear Storage Divides Apaches and Neighbors," *New York Times*, November 11, 1993: A18.

8. Winona LaDuke, *All Our Relations: Native Struggles for Land and Life* (Cambridge, MA: South End Press, 1999), 104–5.

9. Mark Holt, "Civilian Nuclear Waste Disposal," in Warren S. Melfort, *Nuclear Waste Disposal: Current Issues and Proposals* (New York: Nova Science Publishers, 2003), 33–52.

10. Thomas Wellock, "Atomic Power in the West," *Journal of the West* 44, no. 1 (winter 2005): 52.

11. Associated Press, "Utah Posts 'Keep Out' Signs for Industrial Nuclear Waste," *Las Vegas Review-Journal*, March 4, 1998, available at www.reviewjournal.com/lvrj_home/1998/Mar-04-Wed-1998/news/7064591.html.

12. Judy Fahys, "Leavitt Creates an Office to Fight N-Waste Deal," *Salt Lake Tribune*, September 8, 2006: A1.

13. U.S. Court of Appeals, Tenth Circuit, *State of Utah v. the U.S. Department of the Interior*, No. 00-4018, July 10, 2001.

14. LaDuke, *All Our Relations*, 106.

15. Mary Manning, "Plan for Nuke Site in Utah Called Safe," *Las Vegas Sun*, October 9, 2000, available at www.lasvegassun.com/sunbin/stories/special/2000/oct/09/510881199.html.

16. Judy Fahys, "Utah Takes N-Waste Battle to D.C.," *Salt Lake Tribune*, February 13, 2003: B4.

17. See www.privatefuelstorage.com.

18. Associated Press, "Panel Backs Nuclear Waste Dump at Utah Reservation," *Las Vegas Review-Journal*, February 25, 2005, available at www.reviewjournal.com/lvrj_home/2005/Feb-25-Fri-2005/news/25938413.html.

19. Jessica Bledsoe, "Court Sides with Goshutes on Skull Valley Nuclear Storage Site," BYU NewsNet, August 5, 2004, http://newsnet.byu.edu/print/story.cfm/51647.

20. Dennis L. Soden, *The Environmental Presidency* (Albany: State University of New York Press, 1999), 89.

21. "NRC Ships License for Utah HLW Repository," *Inside Energy*, February 20, 2006: 161.

22. "NRC Issues License to Utility Group for Spent-Fuel Storage Site in Utah," *Inside Energy*, February 27, 2006: 177.

23. Associated Press, "Feds Reject Nuclear Waste in Utah," *New York Times*, Online, September 7, 2006, available at www.nytimes.com/aponline/us/AP-Indian-Nuclear-Dump.html?pagewanted=print (accessed September 8, 2006).

24. Paul Foy, Associated Press, "Hatch: Feds Killed Planned Nuke Storage Site in Utah," *Helena Independent Record* (MT), available at www.helenair.com/articles/2006/09/08/montana/c04090806 02.prt (accessed September 9, 2006).

25. Deborah Bulkeley and Suzanne Struglinski, "Decision to Deny PFS Lease Shocks 2," *Deseret Morning News*, September 9, 2006: A1.

26. Suzanne Struglinski, "Nuclear Waste Site Looks Doomed," *Deseret Morning News*, September 8, 2006: A01.

27. Robert Gehrke, "Hatch Jaw-Boned N-Dump Decision," *Salt Lake Tribune*, September 9, 2006, available at www.sltrib.com.portlet/article/html/fragments/print article.jsp?article=431d1408 (accessed September 9, 2006).

28. Ibid.

29. Editorial, "Politics Glows—Politicians Deserve Credit for Stopping PFS," *Salt Lake Tribune*, September 8, 2006, available at www.sltrib.com/portlet/article/html/fragments/print article.jsp?article=431089.

30. Glen Warchol, "State Forks over $844K for Goshute, PFS Lawyers," *Salt Lake Tribune*, November 15, 2006.

7

Yucca Mountain as a Repository

DESCRIPTION

Geologic Environment

Yucca Mountain is in southwestern Nevada, approximately 100 miles northwest of Las Vegas. Its location is shown schematically in Figure 7-1. The mountain is actually a series of north–south-running ridges, with the highest point in the repository site about 4,900 feet above sea level. The western side of the repository ridge is steep, whereas on the east the mountain slopes down more gently. The pattern of mountains and valleys has formed over the past 15 million years because of fault activity. The area is in the rain shadow of the Sierra Nevada, receiving only 7.5 inches of rainfall per year. It is arid, with evaporation exceeding the average rainfall. Groundwater in this region flows south. At the depth of the proposed burial tunnels the mountain is composed of volcanic tuff, originating from large-scale volcanic eruptions between about 14 and 7.5 million years ago. The water table lies approximately 2,000 feet below the surface, and the plan is to place the waste approximately 1,000 feet above the water table in the unsaturated zone. It should be remarked that the water table has not always lain this far down, as there have been cooler and wetter climates. But geologic evidence shows that over the past several million years the water table has not been more than about 400 feet higher than its present depth. The tuff is appreciably fractured, and the fractures provide the principal path for surface water to reach the emplaced waste. The movement of water through the aquifer is also primarily through fractures.[1]

The proposed site lies on federally owned land, with portions on the Nevada Test Site, the Nellis Air Force Range, and Bureau of Land Management land. It consists of approximately 200 square miles of territory. As part of the site characterization of Yucca Mountain, the Department of

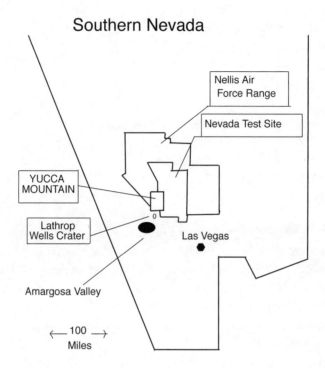

FIGURE 7.1. Schematic map of southern Nevada showing the Yucca Mountain site.

Energy (DOE) bored a five-mile U-shaped exploratory tunnel. One end of the tunnel is called the South Portal, and the other, the North Portal. These portals are on the Nevada Test Site side of the site. The Nevada Test Site, a 1,350 square mile site, was created in 1950 in response to the Korean conflict. This conflict, according to Atomic Energy Commissioner Gordon Dean, created a national emergency that required establishing a domestic nuclear-testing program.[2]

The waste containers will be placed in a series of parallel tunnels (called waste drifts) that are connected to service, exhaust, and performance-confirmation tunnels ("drifts"). A total of 35 miles of 18-foot-diameter emplacement tunnels (waste drifts) are required to accommodate the statutory allowed amount of waste, 70,000 metric tons (154,000,000 lbs.). A total subsurface area of approximately 1,100 acres will be needed. Access to the waste drifts will be from the exploratory tunnel.

As mentioned above, fractures in the tuff provide a significant path for water transport. The first indication that this transport could take place on a very short time scale was reported in 1990 using a new methodology based on Cl-36 measurements.[3] Chlorine as found in nature is primarily composed of the stable isotopes Cl-35 and Cl-37. Cl-36 is a radioactive isotope with a half-life of 300,000 years. It is found in nature in very small amounts related to production in the atmosphere by cosmic rays. Nuclear weapons testing in the Pacific in the 1950s produced greater amounts of Cl-36, which as part of the fallout traveled around the world. Thus there was a period during the 1950s and early 1960s when rainfall had an elevated amount of the Cl-36 isotope relative to the stable isotopes. This "bomb pulse," if seen in chlorine extracted from samples from deep underground, implies transport paths through the hundreds of feet of tuff in 50 years or less. In the study reported in 1990, samples taken from a borehole contained bomb-pulse Cl-36 as deep as 475 feet.[4] After construction of the exploratory tunnel, additional studies were undertaken. In one study samples were collected at regular intervals of 200 meters or less along the tunnel, with additional samples taken to target specific features such as damp zones, faults, and fractures.[5] Most of the samples did not exhibit elevated Cl-36. Except for two bedrock samples, samples with clearly elevated Cl-36 are from faults, fractures, or breccia zones.[6] The implication of very fast water transport to the repository depth raised concerns that during a wetter climate spent fuel containers could corrode more rapidly and release their contents much sooner than originally expected. Furthermore, the existence of fast pathways from the surface to the repository depth suggests that similar fast pathways might exist between the repository and the water table. This would result in more rapid transit of radioactivity from compromised spent fuel containers to well water utilized by nearby residents.

It should be noted that the Cl-36 findings are somewhat controversial. The Yucca Mountain Science and Engineering Report and its revision mention that the aforementioned Cl-36 findings have not been reproduced by some preliminary analyses by another laboratory.[7] The U.S. Geological Survey validation studies failed to find elevated Cl-36 in the samples they examined.[8] It is not clear whether this reflects methodological problems in one of the studies or whether it arises simply from differences in sampling location. This issue was still unresolved as of early 2007, in spite of a third attempt to clarify the situation.[9] In a March 5, 2003, letter to Margaret Chu, then director of the Office of Civilian Radioactive Waste Management, Michael Corradini, chairman of the Nuclear Waste Technical Review Board, reaffirmed its earlier recommendation that the

DOE resolve the contradictory Cl-36 analyses. The board, while recognizing that current modeling of the repository behavior takes a conservative approach by assuming the presence of fast flow paths, "continues to believe that the DOE should persist in its efforts to reach scientific consensus on the results of the chlorine-36 analyses and the implications of those results for fluid flow in Yucca Mountain."[10]

There has been considerable volcanic activity in this part of Nevada. The most recent episode occurred about 80,000 years ago, forming a feature 11 miles south of the repository site. Some 50 miles away across the California border sits the large Ubehebe volcanic crater, formed less than 10,000 years ago. A volcanic hazard analysis found a probability of 1.23 × 10^{-8} per year for an event with magma flowing through the repository and forming a volcano at the surface.[11] This corresponds to one chance in 8,000 of such an event occurring during the first 10,000 years and one chance in 80 during the first one million years. The recent identification of additional volcanic centers suggests there may be an increased probability for a volcano in the vicinity.[12]

There have also been several earthquakes in the area. In 1999 there was a magnitude 4.7 earthquake 28 miles east of the repository site, and on June 14, 2002, there was a magnitude 4.4 quake 12.5 miles southeast of the site. An aftershock of the 7.3 magnitude Landers, Calif., earthquake in 1992 led to a 5.6 magnitude movement at Little Skull Mountain, some dozen miles from Yucca Mountain. There is more concern about earthquakes occurring during the preclosure period and damaging surface facilities than about quakes occurring postclosure. Underground openings are not as likely to sustain damage as surface facilities because there is less shaking underground than on the surface.

Engineered Barriers

The engineered barriers are described in considerable detail in the Final Environmental Impact Statement and the Yucca Mountain Science and Engineering Report.[13] The details of the waste packages to be placed in the emplacement drifts depend on the type of waste to be placed in a particular package. Most of the waste will be spent fuel assemblies. The fuel rods themselves retain the structure they had in the reactor. They contain half-inch-long pellets of spent fuel, now consisting of highly radioactive fission products and transuranic elements plus unburned uranium. The cladding of the fuel rod is designed to survive the harsh reactor environment where high pressure and temperature are experienced. The Final Environmental Impact Statement describes a typical waste package for spent fuel from a pressurized water reactor. The fuel assemblies are held in a honeycomb structure ("fuel basket") of stainless steel. Interleaved with the carbon steel are neutron-absorber plates of borated stainless steel. Boron is a neutron absorber and is incorporated to reduce the possibility of criticality (a self-sustaining nuclear chain reaction). This fuel basket (or corresponding structure for other types of waste) will then be placed in a two-layer cylinder. The inner cylinder will be five-centimeter-thick stainless steel and will provide structural support. The outer cylinder will be about 2.3 centimeters thick and composed of a corrosion-resistant nickel-based alloy (Alloy 22) containing also Cr, Mo, W, Fe, and other minor constituents. This outer cylinder constitutes the principal long-term isolation of the waste from the environment. Considerable controversy has arisen over how long this component of the waste-isolation package will retain its integrity. A large extrapolation of laboratory corrosion rates is required to determine its behavior over the original 10,000-year compliance time. The waste packages have a modeled lifetime of 12,000 to over 100,000 years.[14] It is assumed that all of the containers will fail on the time scale of the decay lifetimes of the longest-lived radioactive species, such as Np-237, with a half-life of two million years.

Surrounding the top and sides of the waste package cylinders will be a 0.6-inch-thick titanium drip shield. The waste package will be installed remotely in the drifts using a gantry crane riding on rails. The rails are supported by a steel invert structure resting on the tunnel bottom. The bottom of the tunnel up to the top of the invert structure will be filled by crushed tuff. This will serve as a retarding barrier to the transport of radionuclides released after the deterioration of any waste package.

The Nuclear Waste Policy Act (Sec. 122) requires that the repository be designed so that spent nuclear fuel placed in the repository may be retrieved during an "appropriate period." The ability to retrieve emplaced materials will be maintained for at least 100 years and possibly for as long as 300 years. The drip shield will not be added until repository closure, expected to occur 100 to 300 years after emplacement of the waste packages. Closure activities would include sealing openings into the mountain such as access ramps, ventilation shafts, and boreholes.

As part of the site characterization, a major exploratory and test facility has been constructed at Yucca Mountain. A five-mile-long tunnel has been bored, off of which side tunnels will eventually be constructed to hold the waste containers. Numerous experiments on water transport, heat transport, and rock integrity have been performed. An account of a visit to the facility is given in an appendix.

Projected Performance

In order to determine whether the repository will meet health and safety standards, one must construct a model that incorporates all the pathways that the radioactive material might use to escape from the nuclear waste packages and reach the environment where human exposure is possible. This is a formidable task. It must characterize water flow in the unsaturated zone, waste package and drip shield degradation, radionuclide transport through the engineered barriers, transport through the unsaturated zone tuff down to the water table, and transport through the saturated zone. Finally it must account for contact with the biosphere and humans through soil and wells. All of these processes have to be followed as a function of time. The model used is called a Total System Performance Assessment (TSPA). It is a probabilistic model that assigns a probability distribution for each of the various things that might occur and picks a particular sequence of events for a "run" of the model. Many "runs" of the model are performed, each using random samples of uncertain parameters and each generally giving a somewhat different final dose to individuals. The TSPA used for Yucca Mountain is similar in form to that used for the Waste Isolation Pilot Plant, although the geological and engineered barrier inputs for the two repositories are of course very different. Performance assessment will form the basis for the Nuclear Regulatory Commission's consideration as to whether Yucca Mountain meets the Environmental Protection Agency (EPA) standards for human safety. It has served a broader purpose during site characterization, facilitating the identification of performance uncertainties and suggesting areas where additional work was needed.

The typical output of a particular run of the TSPA model is a curve of the dose to an individual living in close proximity to the repository. The full curve in Figure 7-2 shows the mean of the individual results for each of a large number of runs. The dashed curve is the median of these runs. It is the mean that the EPA has mandated for compliance considerations during the first 10,000 years. It can be seen that the repository is expected to easily meet the 15 millirem/year (mrem/yr) dose limit for the first 10,000

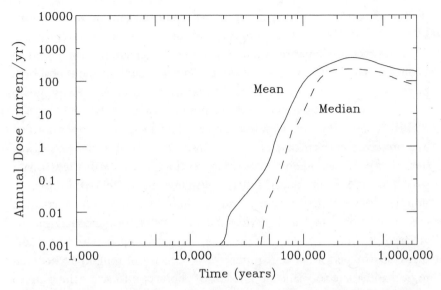

FIGURE 7.2. Total System Performance Assessment results prepared by the Department of Energy for the 2002 Yucca Mountain site recommendation. The solid-line and dashed-line curves represent the mean and the median, respectively, of the performance assessment results. Based on U.S. Department of Energy, Office of Civilian Radioactive Waste Management, *Yucca Mountain Science and Engineering Report Rev. 1: Technical Information Supporting Site Recommendation Consideration* (DOE/RW-0539-1; Washington, DC: U.S. Department of Energy, February 2002), fig. 4-187, available at www.ocrwm.doe.gov/documents/ser_b/index.htm.

years, the compliance time of the original (2001) EPA standards for Yucca Mountain.

As discussed elsewhere, the National Academy of Sciences had recommended that the standards be set for the time of peak risk, without suggesting a specific risk limit at that time. In limiting the compliance time to 10,000 years, the EPA did not respect the congressional mandate requiring it to construct standards consistent with National Academy recommendations. In 2004 the Court of Appeals threw out the compliance time part of the 2001 EPA standards. On August 22, 2005, the EPA published its proposed changes to the Yucca Mountain radiation standards in response to the Court of Appeals decision.[15] After a several-month comment period the EPA is preparing to issue its final standards. These will be subject to review and approval by the Court of Appeals.

In its new proposed rules the EPA puts forward a two-tiered standard. The 15 mrem/yr mean dose limit for the reasonably maximally exposed individual is retained for the first 10,000 years. Beyond 10,000 years but within the period of geologic stability (defined to end one million years after disposal) the dose limit jumps to 350 mrem/yr. The 350 mrem/yr figure is appreciably larger than one might have anticipated.[16] The results in Figure 7-2 show that the present design and modeling of the repository's performance lead to an expected dose that would meet the new proposed standards over the entire period of one million years.

There are a few other more technical changes in the proposed rules. The projected performance of the repository is given in terms of a distribution of possible outcomes. For times less than 10,000 years the standard would continue to use the arithmetic mean (average value) of this distribution. For longer times, the new standard would be based on the median of the distribution, which according to the results of performance assessments given in the Yucca Mountain Science and Engineering Report would further relax the performance requirement by a factor of roughly 10 between 10,000 and 100,000 years and a factor of about two for later times up to one million years. On the other hand, the new standard would require the consequences of unlikely but possible events such as volcanic activity to be included in the assessments performed for evaluating compliance.

It is likely that the DOE will present new performance assessments when it submits its application for a construction license to the Nuclear Regulatory Commission. The DOE might find that its performance assessment should be revised to take into account better knowledge about some ingredients of its model. Bodansky has called attention to one such possible ingredient, the dose coefficient for ingested Np-237.[17] The performance assessment presented in the Final Environmental Impact Statement uses an old dose coefficient that leads to an order of magnitude larger dose for a given amount of Np than obtained with more current dose coefficients. Another possibility for change in the performance assessment is that the fast water path implied by some Cl-36 measurements discussed in chapter 10 ("Court Appeals") would be found to be more important or less important on the basis of new Cl-36 measurements.

There has been a series of independent Total System Performance Assessments performed under the auspices of the Electric Power Research Institute (EPRI). Of course much of the input information for these assessments has been taken from DOE site characterization and engineered barrier designs. The latest version of EPRI's Total System Performance Assessment, designated IMARC 9, estimates a considerably smaller maximum dose to the "reasonably maximally exposed individual."[18] In this version the dose is about 0.02 mrem/yr and is still rising at one million years, the longest time for which the dose has been calculated. There are several reasons why the estimated dose is considerably less than in previous EPRI versions and in earlier DOE assessments. In the present version an attempt is made to provide a "best estimate" of the dose, whereas other approaches have often been based on conservative assumptions. (The DOE, in preparation for its license application to the Nuclear Regulatory Commission, is also moving toward a more realistic, less bounding assessment that would provide a "reasonable expectation" for repository performance.)[19] The latest EPRI model assumes a much lower solubility for neptunium and longer lifetimes for both waste packages and drip shields than in earlier assessments. The latter conclusion is partly related to the questionable assumption that manufacturing defect probabilities are so low that waste package failure is dominated by general corrosion. Bodansky has observed that the DOE calculation assumes a larger response-dose coefficient for Np-237 than the more up-to-date value used by EPRI.[20] These factors may contribute to the higher dose projected by the DOE assessments.

As mentioned at the beginning of this chapter, Yucca Mountain is located in a region of considerable volcanic and seismic activity. The DOE has examined these problems in considerable detail in its Science and Engineering Report prepared for site recommendation.[21] It has concluded that the probability of repository failure related to seismic activity is too small to meet the significance requirement for incorporation in the Total System Performance Assessment. In contrast to this, the consequences of a volcanic event are quite large and are the dominant contributions to the calculated dose for the first 10,000 years. Both intrusive events, where magma comes into contact with an emplacement drift and damages waste containers, and extrusive (eruptive) events, where material is ejected into the atmosphere, are included in the analysis. The calculated mean dose, when weighted by the probability of the event happening, never exceeds about 1/100th of the 15 mrem limit. However, if such an unlikely event were to happen, the expected dose could greatly exceed the regulatory limit for a period of time.

Another independent performance assessment has been carried out jointly by the Center for Nuclear Waste Regulatory Analyses and the Nuclear Regulatory Commission. The results presented so far are preliminary but are broadly consistent with the DOE assessments.[22] In this assessment the probability of an eruptive volcanic event is assigned a probability of one chance in a thousand of occurring during the first 10,000 years. This is a few times larger than in the DOE assessment.

At the request of the DOE, the Nuclear Energy Agency of the Organisation for Economic Co-operation and Development and the International Atomic Energy Agency assembled an International Review Team (IRT) to review and critically analyze the DOE's Total System Performance Assessment prepared for the site recommendation process. The DOE's assessment was completed in December 2000, and the ten-member IRT carried out its work between June and December 2001. With respect to the DOE's request that the IRT provide a statement regarding the adequacy of the TSPA for a site recommendation decision, the following statement was made: "Overall, the IRT considers that the implemented performance assessment approach provides an adequate basis for supporting a statement on likely compliance within the regulatory period of 10,000 years and, accordingly, for the site recommendation decision."[23]

The review team also concluded that the DOE's performance methodology conformed to international best practice. The review team was also asked by the DOE to provide detailed recommendations for improvements that would help the performance assessment better support the next programmatic decision point (the preparation and submission of a license application following site recommendation and approval). Among the suggestions made were that the performance of the geological barriers in their own right receive greater emphasis and that more attention be paid to factors that have little impact on the dose for the 10,000-year regulatory period in effect at the time of the review but are important for a full understanding of repository performance. It also recommended that a systematic methodology for identifying and quantifying uncertainties should be formulated. The International Review Team also suggested some areas where more experimental data should be obtained. These included long-term corrosion tests on waste package and drip shield materials.

Engineered Barriers versus Geologic Barriers

One of the arguments Nevada has used in opposing Yucca Mountain is that the DOE no longer is relying on the geological environment of the mountain, relying instead principally on engineered barriers. The Nevada opponents argue that if containment is primarily accomplished by engineered barriers, the repository could be located almost anywhere in the country. Robert Loux, executive director of the Nevada Agency for Nuclear Projects, in an article by Michael Schmidt in Inside Energy, says the DOE plans to rely on engineered barriers to contain 99.7 percent of the waste, relying on geologic barriers to contribute just 0.008 percent.[24] Arjun Makhijani, executive director of the Institute for Energy and Environmental Research, and Victor Gilinsky, a former Nuclear Regulatory Commission commissioner who is now a consultant to Nevada, have also said that the current Yucca Mountain design plan depends more on engineered barriers than on geologic barriers.[25]

At a hearing before the Senate Committee on Energy and Natural Resources on May 16, 2002, Chairman Bingaman asked Secretary Abraham, "To what extent will the repository rely on the geology of the mountain, and to what extent will it rely on waste packages, or drip shields, or other manmade barriers to ensure that the waste remains sealed in this repository?" Secretary Abraham's reply did not answer the question explicitly but implied that the natural barriers were most important.[26] The relative importance of engineered and natural barriers is an issue in one of Nevada's suits challenging the choice of Yucca Mountain and is discussed further in chapter 10.

A somewhat more quantitative understanding of the relative importance of geologic and engineered barriers can be deduced from the Yucca Mountain Science and Engineering Report, at least for times greater than 20,000–30,000 years. Figures in the section "Multiple Barrier Analyses" show that the increase in calculated dose rates assuming degradation of the natural barriers is less than when assuming degradation of the waste package barrier.[27] These results then support the claim that the present design for Yucca Mountain relies more heavily on the engineered barriers than the geological barriers. The Electric Power Research Institute assessment sheds some light on this issue also.[28] For the drinking water pathway the dose rate taking into account only engineered barriers exceeds the dose rate taking into account only natural barriers by several orders of magnitude at all times.[29] On the other hand, the importance of the engineered barriers can be seen in that they reduce the dose rate for natural barriers alone by a factor of 10,000 at all times between 10,000 and 100,000 years.[30]

LOCAL GOVERNMENT ENVIRONMENT: NYE COUNTY

The Yucca Mountain site lies in Nye County, a large and sparsely populated county with a population density of only 1.5 persons per square mile.

Nye County is larger in area than Massachusetts, Rhode Island, New Jersey, and Delaware combined. Only 7 percent of the land area is privately owned.[31] Most of the county residents live in or near Pahrump, a community located approximately halfway between Las Vegas and the repository site. The county seat is in the northwestern part of the county at Tonopah, which has a population of fewer than 3,000. There is speculation that the county seat may eventually move to the faster-growing and much more populated Pahrump area. Under the amended Nuclear Waste Policy Act, Nye County has certain rights of participation related to nuclear waste activities occurring within its boundaries.[32] These are carried out under the Nye County Nuclear Waste Repository Project Office. A principal activity initiated by this office is an Early Warning Drilling Program. Its purpose is to establish a groundwater-monitoring system in Amargosa and Pahrump valleys. Nye County also has received considerable compensation from the "Payments Equal to Taxes" program from the DOE.[33] The nearest year-round housing to the Yucca repository site is at the small crossroads community of Lathrop Wells in the Amargosa Valley, 14 miles south of the site. The closest communities to the site are Amargosa Valley to the south and Beatty to the west. Farther to the southwest is the larger town of Pahrump. The principal economic activities in this area are agriculture and mining. Unlike the state congressional delegation and the governor, who are strongly opposed to the repository, the residents of Amargosa Valley are more divided on the issue. Some local residents look toward economic benefits from the repository, whereas others are concerned with health and safety issues.

Nye County, like all of Nevada outside of the Las Vegas area, is served by a single member of the U.S. House of Representatives. That seat was held through 2006 by Republican Jim Gibbons, whose origins are in the Reno area. This district is presently represented by Dean Heller (R-NV).

POLITICAL ENVIRONMENT: NEVADA STATE AND YUCCA MOUNTAIN

Nevada is the fastest-growing state in the United States, with 2.2 million people according to the 2002 census. Most of the growth is in the Las Vegas area. Because of this growth it recently became entitled to a third representative in Congress. Two of the congressional districts are in Clark County, of which Las Vegas is the county seat. One district is represented by a Democrat, Shelley Berkley, and the other, by a Republican, Jon Porter. The senior senator is Harry Reid, a Democrat, and the junior senator is John Ensign, a Republican. Nevada went for George W. Bush in both the 2000 and 2004 elections.

Many Nevada leaders are opposed to having a high-level nuclear waste repository in Nevada. There are several sources of opposition to the Yucca Mountain repository. Some opposition stems from distrust of the Department of Energy. The precursor of the DOE, the Atomic Energy Commission, conducted 829 tests of atomic and thermonuclear weapons at the Nevada Test Site between 1952 and 1992. Of these, 106 tests were above ground. The above-ground tests produced radioactive fallout primarily north and northeast of the Nevada Test Site, exposing residents of Nevada and southern Utah. Residents of other states were also exposed to fallout but, generally, to a lesser degree. The largest bomb, detonated July 7, 1957, had an explosive power of 74 kilotons. This is nearly five times as powerful as the atomic bomb dropped on Hiroshima on August 5, 1945. The dirtiest bomb, that is, the one producing the most fallout, "Dirty Harry," was a 32-kiloton bomb detonated May 19, 1953. After the test the Atomic Energy Commission minimized the danger of fallout and denied that the death of animals and increased cancer rates among exposed residents was related to the testing. "Downwinders" organized in the 1970s but did not receive compensation from the federal government until the 1990s.[34] This experience has led many to feel that the DOE cannot be trusted either to operate a repository safely as far as their health is concerned or to compensate victims if their health and safety are affected by operation of a repository. Some feel that Nevadans have done more than their share for the country by hosting the nuclear weapons tests and that it is unfair to ask them to do more.

Adding to the concerns of Nevadans about importing additional sources of radiation into the state is the dismal record of management of defense nuclear wastes by the DOE. Many Americans, not just Nevadans, in fact, are wide-eyed over the trashing of defense nuclear waste facilities. At the Hanford, Wash., site, where most of the plutonium for nuclear weapons was produced during the Cold War, high-level nuclear waste was stored in 177 tanks. Of these, 149 tanks were single-walled tanks, 67 of which have developed leaks. Approximately 100 million gallons of radioactive waste leaked into the subsoil and groundwater.[35] Scientists had warned as early as 1948 that single-walled tanks were inadequate, but nothing was done.[36] In the early days of the project some waste was injected directly into the ground.[37] Some of this waste has migrated to the Columbia River. Isotopes found in the Hanford reactor effluent of particular concern included P-32, As-76, Zn-65, Cr-57, and Np-237, which affect reproductive organs, blood-forming organs, bones, and the GI tract. Evidence for these isotopes was found in shellfish in Washington's Willapa Bay and Oregon's Tillamook Bay, both located along the Pacific Ocean coast near the mouth of the Columbia River, hundreds of miles from Hanford.[38] The situation was of sufficient concern that the U.S. Public Health Service issued an alarm.[39]

Also at Hanford, 500,000 curies of Iodine-131 were released into the atmosphere between 1945 and 1955. During a two-day "Green Run" in early December 1949 nearly 8,000 curies of Iodine-131 were released at Hanford.[40] This isotope, Iodine-131, has an eight-day half-life and concentrates in the thyroid gland and sometimes causes cancer. As a result of the "Green Run," Iodine-131 levels at Kennewick, Wash., reached 1,000 times the permissible level.[41] The purpose of the "Green Run" experiment was to help the U.S. military develop techniques for detecting plutonium production in Soviet reactors.[42]

At Savannah River, another site at which reprocessing has taken place, nine of the 16 single-walled tanks have leaked, contaminating the soil around them.[43] Incomplete records have made it difficult to estimate cleanup costs. The General Accounting Office has estimated the cleanup costs at approximately $200 billion.[44]

Sagebrush Rebellion

Another objection to the placement of the nuclear waste repository in Yucca Mountain is that it will increase the size of the federal presence in Nevada. The federal government controls 87 percent of the land in Nevada, which is a larger percentage than in any other state except Alaska. Approximately 70 percent of the land in Nevada is controlled by the Bureau of Land Management. In 1979, Nevada led 13 western states in which federal land ownership is high in the Sagebrush Rebellion. This led to the passage in July 1979 of Nevada's Sagebrush Rebellion Act, in which the State of Nevada claimed jurisdiction over 49 million acres of land controlled by the federal Bureau of Land Management.[45]

Other western states that subsequently passed bills similar to the Nevada Sagebrush Rebellion Act of 1979 included Arizona, New Mexico, and Utah.[46] The Sagebrush Rebellion was supported by California Governor

Ronald Reagan and was an issue in his 1980 presidential campaign.[47] Senator Orrin Hatch (R-UT) introduced a bill that would transfer lands under federal control to the states. Hatch's bill was supported by the Western Conference of Governors and the Western Region of the National Association of Counties.[48] This bill was not enacted into law.

The forces in Nevada backing the Sagebrush Rebellion included ranchers; mining interests; state, county, and local governments; developers; and "states' rights" advocates.[49] Ranchers opposed new Bureau of Land Management regulations that included reducing the amount of grazing on federal land. Ranchers also opposed environmental movement–inspired efforts to preserve land. Local governments and the State of Nevada were concerned about the effect that extensive federal landholdings had on economic growth and development and on their tax base. Landlocked cities claimed that the federal government was unnecessarily slow in making land transfers necessary for the expansion of cities. Developers were loath to see choice parcels of land unavailable for development. Oil and mining exploration interests felt that federal ownership of land unduly restricted their activities. In addition, some with no economic stake in the issue supported "state rights" for ideological reasons.

The issues previously mentioned had been simmering for some time and may not have come to a head in 1979 if it had not been for two new developments in the late 1970s. In the 1970s the country had become much more sensitive to environmental concerns, and in 1976 the federal Land Policy and Management Act of 1976 was passed. This act gave the Bureau of Land Management its first modern mandate for administering federal land under its jurisdiction. The legislation provided for multiple land use and also directed the Bureau of Land Management to select areas from all of its holdings that might be suitable for designation as wilderness areas. These provisions had the potential for reducing the amount of grazing land available.[50] The second development leading to the Sagebrush Rebellion was President Jimmy Carter's announcement of a plan to base an MX missile system in the Great Basin area of Nevada and Utah. Two-thirds of the area affected would be in Nevada, and the remaining third, in Utah. The MX missile system would consist of 200 intercontinental ballistic missiles, each carrying ten nuclear warheads, for a total of 2,000 nuclear warheads in the Great Basin. These 2,000 ballistic missiles would move continuously on tracks through 200 tunnels among 4,600 sites.[51] Building it would be a massive undertaking estimated to cost $30 billion.

A Pentagon team that tried to sell the MX program at a town hall meeting in Ely, Nev., found that the residents were uncomfortable with the idea of 2,000 nuclear weapons racing around in their neighborhood. The Pentagon officials attributed the resistance of Ely residents to the "Sagebrush Rebellion."[52] A former governor, Paul Laxalt, expressed concern that just the presence of the MX missile system would make the area a high priority for a massive first-strike nuclear attack by the Soviet Union. Some voiced concern that it would reduce the amount of grazing land and use up too much water in construction of the system. State of Nevada, county, and city government officials were concerned that the boomtowns created would put stress on the school systems and services provided by these units of government. President Reagan decided in 1981 to build a greatly modified missile defense system in the upper Midwest rather than in the Great Basin area.

The Bureau of Land Management decided to ignore the Sagebrush Rebellion Act of 1979.[53] Fearing an unfavorable decision by the U.S. Supreme Court, the Sagebrush Rebels did not go to court to implement the Sagebrush Rebellion Act. The Sagebrush Rebellion Act of 1979 was declared unconstitutional by a U.S. District Court judge in 1996.[54] The Sagebrush Movement, though weakened, did not die out completely, and efforts continue to hold down grazing fees. To this day Bureau of Land Management and Forest Service employees experience threats, and some drive their own cars rather than government vehicles to avoid being targeted.[55]

Nevada Resistance to the Repository

Most of the organized opposition to the Yucca Mountain repository comes from the State of Nevada and from Las Vegas. Although health and safety are concerns associated with both the presence of the repository and the transportation of the waste to the repository, a large component of the opposition stems from economic concerns. Most of the economic activity in the state centers around the gambling industry (or "gaming" as it is termed in Nevada) in Las Vegas and to a lesser extent in Reno. In 2001, 35 million tourists, some also attracted by top Hollywood performers, visited Las Vegas, and five million visited Reno, outnumbering the two million residents by a factor of 20. These tourists spent $39 billion in these areas in 2001. The state levies a 6.25 percent tax on gambling, making it the chief source of revenue for the state government. Nevada has neither an individual nor a corporate income tax.[56] Additional evidence for the importance of the gambling industry in Nevada is the fact that both U.S. senators and all three members of Congress of both parties vote to protect the interests of Nevada on gambling legislation. A recent example of this is their effort to block a bill that would prohibit betting on college and amateur sports. Nevada presently allows such bets.[57]

An accident either transporting spent fuel or at the site of the Yucca Mountain repository might deter tourists from visiting Nevada and cut deeply into state, casino, hotel, restaurant, and shopping mall revenues. At Three Mile Island, over 200,000 residents left the area temporarily after the reactor accident. With the recent development of casino gambling on Indian reservations providing other alternatives for those who "need" to gamble, the economic risks have become even greater for Nevada. The fact that Nevada U.S. senators and representatives continue to support and actually advocate expenditures for the Nevada Test Site indicates that the economic roots of opposition to Yucca Mountain are probably paramount. Over 800 atomic and hydrogen bomb tests were conducted at the Nevada Test Site between 1952 and 1992. These tests generated radioactive fallout and left pools of radioactive material in craters throughout the Nevada Test Site. The George W. Bush administration has mentioned resuming nuclear weapons testing, which presumably would take place at the Nevada Test Site. The Yucca Mountain repository site is adjacent to the Nuclear Test Site. As long as the Nevada Test Site is not decommissioned, this remains a possibility. Nevada senators and representatives have not made an effort to shut down this site. In their campaigns opposing Yucca Mountain neither the governor nor the congressional delegation has cited the economic risks to Nevada, preferring to emphasize the risks to the country in transporting high-level nuclear waste and the defects of the proposed repository. The executive director of the Nevada Office for Nuclear Projects, Robert Loux, did mention the risks to the Nevada economy in testimony before a Nevada official, who subsequently denied a water permit for building and operating the repository.

The Nevada Agency for Nuclear Projects

The Nevada Agency for Nuclear Projects, located in the Office of the Governor in the state capital, Carson City, Nev., has been the lead state agency involved in opposing the repository. This agency receives both federal and state funds and was established by the state legislature in 1985. Robert Loux has been the executive director of this agency since its establishment. Loux supervises the agency, acts as the spokesman on repository and other nuclear issues, and provides testimony at congressional committee and agency hearings and at state and federal court hearings.

The main arguments used by the Nevada Agency for Nuclear Projects prior to 1995 focused on potential problems with the repository itself. These included the possibilities of earthquakes, volcanic activity, hydrothermal activity, and leakage of water through fractures in the rock that would hold the repository. After 1995, and especially after 9/11, focus was on the risks of transporting the highly radioactive spent nuclear fuel from nuclear power plants all over the country (but principally east of the Mississippi). Only at the state level did the Nevada Agency for Nuclear Projects testify that building a high-level nuclear waste repository at Yucca Mountain would have a negative impact on southern Nevada tourism.[58] The agency advocated denial of a water permit by the State of Nevada for the DOE to build and operate a repository at Yucca Mountain.[59]

Funds for the Nevada Agency have been temporarily cut at times by the federal government as some of the funds were improperly used. Before the funds were actually cut, funding for the agency was challenged a number of times. The first challenge came in 1988 from Senator J. Bennett Johnston, who objected to Nevada duplicating the studies of the DOE. Johnston claimed the money should only be used to review the work of the DOE.[60] In 1990, the General Accounting Office of the federal government audited the expenditures of the Nevada Agency for Nuclear Projects and identified certain activities that seemed improper. Although the General Accounting Office claimed that over $1 million was improperly spent, the Nevada Agency received funds from the federal government from 1983 until 1995. In 1995, Republicans gained control of Congress, and funding for the agency was terminated. Funds were restored in 1996. The 1996 audit of the agency found that the Nevada Agency for Nuclear Projects did not have the authority to spend $697,000 for consultants and for the production of a video on nuclear wastes for viewing by students.[61] In 1997, Congress passed a bill granting $5 million for counties near Yucca Mountain but did not include funds for the Nevada Agency for Nuclear Projects. Executive Director Robert Loux appealed to the Interim Finance Committee of the Nevada State legislature to make up some of the lost funds. His appeal received a lukewarm reception. A Nevada State legislative audit of his agency found that Loux had failed to solicit bids on $17 million in contracts and had paid some people $125 per hour for clerical work that included clipping newspapers.[62] The legislative Interim Finance Committee only granted $240,000 of the $860,000 requested by Loux. The committee cited federal and state audits that found Loux misused $700,000 in state funds. A specific improper activity cited by the committee was Loux's decision to send staff members around the country to drum up opposition in the media to the Yucca Mountain repository.[63] Senator Harry Reid (D-NV), senior senator from Nevada, has claimed that the actions of Loux made it increasingly difficult to obtain funds for the Nevada Agency for Nuclear Projects.[64] Loux is quoted as saying, "There is no question that we pushed the envelope about allowable uses of money."[65]

Loux was also associated with the "Mobile Chernobyl" campaign. This involved transporting a replica of a nuclear spent fuel cask around Nevada and other western states during summer 2000.[66] This called attention to the worst nuclear accident in history at the Chernobyl plant in Russia in 1986. The Chernobyl accident resulted in numerous deaths and radioactive contamination of parts of Russia. The subsequent fallout has been linked to leukemia and thyroid cancer deaths. (The particular kind of accident at Chernobyl would not be possible at any U.S. power reactors, as the latter have a negative temperature coefficient that shuts down the reactor if faulty operation allows the reactor to overheat sufficiently.) Federal funds had been used to finance the Mobile Chernobyl propaganda campaign. Undeterred by previous federal and state economic sanctions, the Nevada Agency for Nuclear Projects awarded a $90,000 grant to Nuclear Information and Resource Service, a Washington, D.C., antinuclear group. This group paid part of the salary of Kevin Kamps, who drove an 18-foot replica of a spent nuclear fuel cask on a flatbed truck on U.S. highway routes that would be used to transport waste to the Yucca Mountain repository. He also drove the flatbed truck and cask on the Washington, D.C., Beltway in 2001 and early 2002. Kamps, who has visited the Chernobyl site, had spent two years running a small program that brought Russian children from the Chernobyl area to the United States for medical care.[67]

Recently, the state legislature has not played an important role in opposing Yucca Mountain. Some members feel that the state should negotiate for compensation for accepting the repository instead of spending time opposing it. Some feel that it is hopeless to oppose the federal government.

The Creation of Bullfrog County

In 1987, the Nevada State legislature passed and Governor Richard Bryant signed into law a bill that created a new county, Bullfrog County, at the site of the Yucca Mountain repository.[68] Unlike all other counties in the United States, this county had no population. The county seat was located outside of the county in Carson City, the state capital, 270 miles away from Bullfrog County. All three county commissioners of this new county were to be appointed by the governor, and furthermore, despite the absence of population, this county was assigned the highest tax rate in Nevada.[69] Both the name and the features of this new county attracted the attention of the national media, including the *New York Times* and the *Washington Post*. There are varying accounts of the origin of the name "Bullfrog County." The most commonly cited is that it is named after the Bullfrog Mining District. One can see this district from the top of Yucca Mountain. Some of the ore from the Bullfrog Mining District is greenish colored with flecks of gold and resembles bullfrogs.[70] Dayton Duncan claims that it was named after the aborted attempt to form a county with this name near Death Valley mines in the early 1900s.[71] The purpose of the legislation creating Bullfrog County was to divert federal mitigation money from Nye County, the county in which the repository would be located, to the State of Nevada. Section 116 C.3.A. of the Nuclear Waste Policy Act of 1982 (P.L. 97-425) specified that the DOE make payments during the site characterization, development, and operation of the repository. These payments were intended to offset losses of property taxes by state and local governments because of the presence of the repository.[72]

Governor Bryan distanced himself from the Bullfrog County scheme after the Nevada attorney general stated that the law establishing Bullfrog County was unconstitutional. Nye County sued the State of Nevada, claiming that the Bulldog County Act was unconstitutional. The judge hearing the case ruled that the law was unconstitutional, as the county commission was appointed instead of elected and it made no provision for legislative representation or for a judicial district.[73] The law establishing Bullfrog County was repealed in May 1989 by a 15 to 5 vote of the State Senate, by a unanimous vote of the Nevada Assembly, and by the signature of the acting governor.[74]

Nevadans who were utterly opposed to placing the repository in Nevada felt that the passage of the Bullfrog County law had sent a message to Congress that Nevada was willing to accept the repository if the price was right. Those who supported the bill felt that it was inevitable that Nevada would get the repository and they might as well try to get as much money as possible from the federal government. Senator Chic Hecht accused Governor Bryan of causing embarrassment for the State of Nevada. It is possible that the act was supported by some as a form of "gallows humor." It is hard to believe that a bill with so many loose ends represented a serious effort. In any event, the state legislature played a very minor role, subsequently, in opposing Yucca Mountain. The Nevada legislature is a part-time legislature that spends 60 days or less in session. This makes it difficult to effectively oppose federal legislation, executive orders, agency rulings, and court rulings promulgated by full-time federal officials. Governor Bryan did not suffer repercussions from his association with the Bullfrog County endeavor and replaced Hecht as U.S. senator from Nevada in 1988.

NOTES

1. U.S. Department of Energy, *Yucca Mountain Science and Engineering Report Rev. 1: Technical Information Supporting Site Recommendation Consideration* (DOE/RW-0539-1; U.S. Department of Energy, Office of Civilian Radioactive Waste Management, February 2002), Sec. 4.2.1.3.1.4, available at www.ocrwm.doe.gov/documents/ser_b/index.htm.

2. Tom Vanderbilt, *Survival City: Adventure among the Ruins of Atomic America* (New York: Princeton Architectural Press, 2002), 81.

3. A. E. Norris, H. W. Bentley, S. Cheng, P.W. Kubik, P. Sharma, and H. E. Gove, "^{36}Cl Studies of Water Movements Deep within Unsaturated Tuffs," *Nuclear Instruments and Methods in Physics Research* B52 (1990): 455–60.

4. Ibid.

5. J. T. Fabryka-Martin, A. V. Wolfsberg, J. L. Roach, S. T. Winters, and L. E. Wolfsberg, "Using Chloride to Trace Water Movement in the Unsaturated Zone at Yucca Mountain," in *High Level Radioactive Waste Management: Proceedings of the Eighth International Conference* (La Grange Park, IL: American Nuclear Society, 1998), 264–68.

6. S. S. Levy, J. T. Fabryka-Martin, P. R. Dixon, B. Liu, H. J. Turin, and A. V. Wolfsberg, "Chlorine-36 Investigations of Groundwater Infiltration in the Exploratory Studies Facility at Yucca Mountain, Nevada," in *Scientific Basis for Nuclear Waste Management XX—Symposium*, ed. W. J. Gray and I. R. Triay (Pittsburgh: Materials Research Society, 1997), 901–8.

7. U.S. Department of Energy, *Yucca Mountain Science and Engineering Report: Technical Information Supporting Site Recommendation Consideration* (DOE/RW-0539;

Washington, DC: U.S. Department of Energy, Office of Civilian Radioactive Waste Management, May 2001); U.S. Department of Energy, *Yucca Mountain Science and Engineering Report Rev. 1.*

8. J. B. Paces, Z. E. Peterman, L. A. Neymark, G. J. Nimz, M. Gascoyne, and B. D. Marshall, "Summary of Chlorine-36 Validation Studies at Yucca Mountain, Nevada," in *Proceedings of the 10th International High-Level Radioactive Waste Management Conference (IHLRWM)* (La Grange Park, IL: American Nuclear Society, 2003), 348.

9. James Cizdziel, *Bomb-Pulse Chlorine-36 at the Proposed Yucca Mountain Repository Horizon: An Investigation of Previous Conflicting Results and Collection of New Data* (Technical Report TR-06-002, Rev. 0; Las Vegas: Nevada System of Higher Education, July 28, 2006), available at www.ocrwm.doe.gov/documents/design/48886/48886.pdf.

10. Michael Corradini, Chairman of the Nuclear Waste Technical Review Board, letter to Margaret Chu, Director of the Office of Civilian Radioactive Waste Management, March 5, 2003, available at www.nwtrb.gov/corr/mlc006.pdf.

11. U.S. Department of Energy, *Yucca Mountain Science and Engineering Report Rev. 1.*

12. V. A. Perry et al., *Geological Society of America Abstracts with Programs* 36, no. 5 (2004): 33, quoted in E. I. Smith and D. L. Keenan, *Eos, Transactions of the American Geophysical Union* 86, no. 35 (August 30, 2005): 317–21.

13. U.S. Department of Energy, Office of Civilian Radioactive Waste Management, *Final Environmental Impact Statement for a Geologic Repository for the Disposal of Spent Nuclear Fuel and High-Level Radioactive Waste at Yucca Mountain, Nye County, Nevada* (DOE/EIS-0250F), February 2002, available at www.ocrwm.doe.gov/documents/feis_a/ index.htm; U.S. Department of Energy, *Yucca Mountain Science and Engineering Report Rev. 1.*

14. U.S. Department of Energy, *Yucca Mountain Science and Engineering Report Rev. 1,* Sec. 4.5.4.

15. U.S. Environmental Protection Agency, "Public Health and Environmental Radiation Protection Standards for Yucca Mountain, NV, Proposed Rule, 40 CFR Part 197," *Federal Register* 70, no. 161 (August 22, 2005): 49014–65.

16. Benjamin Grove, "EPA Radiation Options for Yucca Met with Criticism," *Las Vegas Sun,* March 11, 2005, available at www.lasvegassun.com/sunbin/stories/lv-gov/2005/mar/11/518433625.html.

17. David Bodansky, *Nuclear Energy: Principles, Practices and Prospects,* 2nd ed. (New York: Springer-Verlag, 2004), 115–17.

18. J. H. Kessler, M. W. Kozak, M. J. Apted, W. Zhou, and G. Mungov, "EPRI's Total System Performance Assessment of Yucca Mountain Using IMARC 9," in *Proceedings of the 11th International High-Level Radioactive Waste Management Conference*

(IHLRWM 2006), April 30–May 4, 2006, Las Vegas (La Grange Park, IL: American Nuclear Society, 2006), 990–95.

19. A. Van Luik and E. Zwahlen, "Treatment of Uncertainty in the US Department of Energy's Yucca Mountain Repository Total System Performance Assessment (TSPA)," in *Management of Uncertainty in Safety Cases and the Role of Risk*, NEA No. 5302 (Paris: Nuclear Energy Agency, Organisation for Economic Co-operation and Development, 2004), 81–95.

20. Bodansky, *Nuclear Energy*, 326.

21. U.S. Department of Energy, *Yucca Mountain Science and Engineering Report Rev. 1.*

22. Sitakanta Mohanty and Richard Blake Codell, "Independent Postclosure Performance Estimates of the Proposed Repository at Yucca Mountain," *Nuclear Technology* 148 (2004): 109.

23. International Atomic Energy Agency and Organisation for Economic Co-operation and Development Nuclear Energy Agency, *An International Peer Review of the Yucca Mountain Project TSPA-SR* (Paris: Organisation for Economic Co-operation and Development, 2002), available at www.nea.fr/html/rwm/reports/2002/nea3682-yucca.pdf.

24. These figures were taken by Loux from a presentation by Dennis Williams to the January 1999 meeting of the Nuclear Waste Technical Review Board (R. Loux, personal communication).

25. Jeff Johnson, "Yucca Mountain," *Chemical and Engineering News* 80, no. 27 (July 8, 2002): 22.

26. Senate Energy and Natural Resource Committee, "Yucca Mountain Repository Approval Act," Hearings on S.J. Res. 34, 107th Cong., 2nd Sess. (May 16, 2002), 18.

27. U.S. Department of Energy, *Yucca Mountain Science and Engineering Report Rev. 1*, Secs. 4.5.3, 4.5.4.

28. J. H. Kessler and J. A. Vlasity, "Potential Importance of Diffusive Releases," in *Proceedings of the 10th International High-Level Radioactive Waste Management Conference (IHLRWM)* (La Grange Park, IL: American Nuclear Society, 2003), 932–37.

29. John Kessler, "Integrated Yucca Mt. Safety Case and Supporting Analysis: EPRI's Phase 7 Performance Assessment," *EPRI Technical Report* 1003334 (December 2002).

30. J. H. Kessler and J. A. Vlasity, "EPRI Performance Assessment Results for the Yucca Mountain Repository," in *Proceedings of the 10th International High-Level Radioactive Waste Management Conference (IHLRWM)*, March 30–April 2, 2003, Las Vegas (La Grange Park, IL: American Nuclear Society, 2003), n. 30, fig. 3.

31. See Nye County website, www.nyecounty.net.

32. Ibid.

33. See www.nevadaalliance.com/ymp-fact-sheet-10.doc.

34. Michael Light, *100 Suns: 1945–1962* (New York: Alfred Knopf, 2003).

35. Walter A. Rosenbaum, *Environmental Politics and Policy*, 5th ed. (Washington, DC: CQ Press, 2002), 291.

36. Bill Dietrich, "Fifty Years from Trinity," *Seattle Times*, June 9, 1995, available at http://seattletimes.nwsource.com/trinity/ (accessed April 18, 2007).

37. U.S. Department of Energy, Pacific Northwest National Laboratory, *Hanford Site: Environmental Report for Calendar Year 2003* (Washington, DC: Department of Energy, 2004), 4-25–4-26.

38. Michele Stenehjem Gerber, *On the Home Front: The Cold War Legacy of the Hanford Nuclear Site* (Lincoln: University of Nebraska Press, 1992), 115.

39. E. C. Tsiveglow and M. W. Lammering, "Evaluation of Pollutional Effects of Effluents from Hanford Works" (Cincinnati: Robert A. Taft Sanitary Engineering Center, U.S. Public Health Services, March 1961), 24, cited in Gerber, *On the Home Front*, 115.

40. Ibid., 78.

41. Susan Zwinger, *The Hanford Reach* (Tucson: University of Arizona Press, 2004), 48–49.

42. Associated Press, "Declassified Report on 1949 Nuclear Test Give Radiation Data," *Wall Street Journal*, Eastern Edition, May 5, 1989: 1.

43. Arjun Makhijani, "The United States," in *Nuclear Wastelands*, ed. Arjun Makhijani, Howard Hu, and Katherine Yih (Cambridge, MA: MIT Press, 1995), ch. 6, 249.

44. Odelia Funke, "National Security and the Environment," in Norman J. Vig and Michael E. Kraft, *Environmental Policy in the 1990's* (Washington, DC: Congressional Quarterly Press, 1994), ch. 15, 328–29.

45. James W. Hulse, *The Silver State: Nevada's Heritage Reinterpreted*, 3rd ed. (Reno: University of Nevada Press, 2004), 235.

46. R. McGregor Cawley, *Federal Land: Western Anger: The Sagebrush Rebellion and Environmental Politics* (Lawrence: University Press of Kansas, 1993), 109.

47. Howell Raines, "States Rights Move in West Influencing Reagan's Drive," *New York Times*, July 6, 1980: 7.

48. Associated Press, "Western Delegates Seek State Control of Lands," *New York Times*, September 8, 1979: 10.

49. James Dean Caudill, "The Sagebrush Rebellion: An Historical Perspective," M.A. thesis, Washington State University, Pullman, 1983.

50. Caudill, "The Sagebrush Rebellion," 84–107.

51. Cawley, *Federal Land*, 88.

52. Richard Burt, "On MX in NV and Utah: Pentagon Team Trying to Sell Plan Meets Resistance to Building Missile Sites in Desert," *New York Times*, January 17, 1980: A17.

53. Don W. Driggs and Leonard Goodell, *Nevada Politics and Government: Conservatism in an Open Society* (Lincoln: University of Nebraska Press, 1996), 2.

54. Michael H. Bowers, *Sagebrush State: Nevada's History, Government and Politics*, 2nd ed. (Reno: University of Nevada Press, 2002), 130.

55. Ibid., 129.

56. Michael Barone, with Richard Cohen, *The Almanac of American Politics 2004* (Washington, DC: National Journal Group, 2003), 988.

57. Ibid.

58. "Yucca Foes Cite Risk to Tourism, Water," *Las Vegas Review-Journal*, November 9, 1999, available at www.yuccamountain.org/archive/yucca1999.htm.

59. Keith Rogers and Sean Whaley, "Yucca Water Permit Denied," *Las Vegas Review-Journal*, February 3, 2000: 1A.

60. Matthew L. Wald, "Funds to Study Proposed Waste Site May Be Cut," *New York Times*, June 22, 1988: A19.

61. Tony Batt, Donrey Washington Bureau, "Energy Secretary Wants Audit to Examine Antinuclear Agency," *Las Vegas Review-Journal*, October 16, 1997: 7B.

62. Ed Vogel, Donrey Capitol Bureau, "Nuclear Agency May Need State Funds, Official Says," *Las Vegas Review-Journal*, January 15, 1998: 3B.

63. Ed Vogel, Donrey Capitol Bureau, "Legislative Panel Cuts Funding for Nuclear Projects Agency," *Las Vegas Review-Journal*, September 24, 1998: 4B.

64. Tony Batt, Donrey Washington Bureau, "Reid Wants Nuclear Official Fired," *Las Vegas Review-Journal*, March 2, 2000: 1A.

65. Jon J. Fialko, "Nevada Hones Effort to Block Nuclear Waste Dump," *Wall Street Journal*, Eastern Edition, July 5, 2001: A14.

66. Tim Anderson, "Nuclear Watchdogs Bring Cask to Nevada," *Reno Gazette-Journal*, August 2, 2000, available at www.rgj.com/news2/stories/news/965271912.php (accessed April 19, 2007).

67. Benjamin Grove, "No Time to Waste: Anti-nuclear Activists Are Ready to Spread Message Nationwide," *Las Vegas Sun*, July 6, 2001, available at www.lasvegassun.com/sunbin/stories/sun/2001/jul/06/512050024.html?"no%20time%20to%20waste" (accessed April 19, 2007).

68. A. Costandina Titus, "Bullfrog County: A Nevada Response to Federal Nuclear Waste Disposal Policy," *Publius: The Journal of Federalism* 20, no. 1 (1990): 123–35.

69. Ibid.

70. Ibid., 128.

71. Dayton Duncan, *Miles from Nowhere: Tales from America's Contemporary Frontier* (New York: Viking, 1993), 251.

72. Titus, "Bullfrog County," 125.

73. Associated Press, "Nevada County Is Held Illegal," *New York Times*, February 13, 1988: sec. 1, 7.

74. Titus, "Bullfrog County," 134.

8

The Energy Act of 1992 and
Yucca Mountain Radiation Standards

INTRODUCTION OF NUCLEAR WASTE PROVISIONS INTO THE ENERGY ACT OF 1992

During 1992 Congress was considering a comprehensive energy bill. Two provisions affecting the Yucca Mountain repository project were included in the House version of this bill (H.R. 776). One of these dealt with the problem of the delays in issuing permits by the State of Nevada. A second addressed the process involved in setting radiation standards for Yucca Mountain. These provisions were not included in the Senate version of the bill (S.B. 2166).

An amendment relating to delays in Nevada granting environmental permits, introduced by Representative John Dingell (D-MI), provided that no state permits would be required for characterization studies at the Yucca Mountain site. This was opposed vigorously by the Nevada delegation, which viewed it as an infringement of states' rights. In addition, Nevada Representative Bilbray (D-NV) claimed that the State of Nevada was not responsible for the delays at Yucca Mountain and cited a General Accounting Office report that blamed the Department of Energy (DOE) rather than the State of Nevada for the delays. The Nevada delegation apparently was not convincing, and the Dingell amendment passed on a voice vote.

The House version also included a provision that would reinstate the 1985 Environmental Protection Agency (EPA) radiation standards for disposal of nuclear waste, except for the parts that had been struck down by a federal court in 1987.[1] The conference committee, set up to resolve the differences between the House and Senate versions of what would become the 1992 Energy Act, was chaired by Senator J. Bennett Johnston (D-LA), whose byzantine maneuvers in 1987 resulted in Nevada's Yucca

Mountain being selected for a high-level nuclear waste repository. The Dingell amendment regarding Nevada's authority to require environmental permits was dropped from the conference committee bill. Johnston successfully introduced a provision in the conference bill that superseded the House bill provisions for radiation standards. This provision required the EPA to develop health and safety radiation standards specifically tailored to the Yucca Mountain site. They were to be based on and consistent with findings and recommendations of the National Academy of Sciences (NAS). Nevada Representative Vucanovich (D-NV) attempted to have this provision withdrawn by conferees but lost the vote to do so. Nevada Senators Reid (D-NV) and Bryan then renewed their threat to filibuster the entire energy bill when the conference committee bill was introduced into the Senate.[2] This filibuster effort was decisively halted when the bill was taken up by the Senate.[3] Johnston had attempted to insert specific radiation standards into the conference committee bill, but House negotiators opposed this effort. House conferees also "refused to accept a Senate proposal to preclude the Environmental Protection Agency from fully considering collective dose or human intrusion in setting a standard."[4]

In the Senate debate on the conference committee bill, Nevada Senator Harry Reid criticized both the procedure used to include the provision and the substance of the radiation standards provision. As to the procedure, Reid took issue with inserting the measure into the closed hearings of a conference committee without the benefit of hearings before relevant House and Senate committees or floor debate in both of these houses. Addressing the substance of the measure, Reid claimed that Johnston was representing the interests of the nuclear industry. The nuclear industry felt that the EPA standards adopted in the House bill would cost too much. Reid claimed that weakening the standards would result in increased risk to the residents of Nevada. Reid also objected to the provision that the new radiation standards would apply only to Yucca Mountain and wondered why Yucca Mountain should be subject to less stringent regulations than other nuclear facilities.

In response, Senator Johnston claimed that the 1985 EPA standard that the House version of the bill reinstated was established when it was assumed that the repository was going to be located below the level of saturated rock. Johnston said that the level set by the EPA in 1985 was not applicable to the Yucca Mountain situation. He also asserted that the EPA set standards that it felt were achievable and that the standards set by the EPA were much too stringent and were not health based. Johnston claimed that using the 1985 EPA standards at Yucca Mountain would require the use of canisters costing $3.2 billion. The conference bill eventually passed both houses and became law under the title "Energy Policy Act of 1992" (P.L. 102-486).

THE NATIONAL ACADEMY OF SCIENCES REPORT

In August 1995 the NAS published its report *Technical Bases for Yucca Mountain Standards,* mandated by the Energy Act of 1992.[5] It contained three principal recommendations. First, a standard should be set that limits the risk to individuals of adverse health effects. This is in contrast to the EPA's previous generic standard for geologic repositories (40 CFR 191) that is based on limits for dose to individuals and on radionuclide release to the environment. Second, the compliance time for the standard should be the time of peak risk, rather than at 10,000 years. The report noted that performance assessments suggested "that peak risks might occur tens to hundreds of thousands of years or even farther into the future." Third, it is not possible to assess the frequency of human intrusion into the repository far into the future. Therefore a risk-based calculation requiring an assessment of the frequency of human intrusion is not warranted, although a calculation of the consequences of an intrusion should be "calculated to assess the resilience of the repository to intrusion."[6] The NAS report went on to note that if the EPA followed its recommendation to issue standards based on individual risk, then the Nuclear Regulatory Commission would be required to revise its licensing regulations (10 CFR part 60) to be consistent with EPA standards. This is because the regulations in place at the time were directed in part to subsystem technical requirements, whereas a health standard based on risk to individuals depends only on the total system performance.

PUBLIC HEALTH AND ENVIRONMENTAL RADIATION PROTECTION STANDARDS FOR YUCCA MOUNTAIN, NEVADA

The 2001 Environmental Protection Agency Standards

On June 6, 2001, the EPA announced what it hoped would be its final rules for groundwater standards and radiation exposure to the public that must be met by the Yucca Mountain repository.[7] The Energy Policy Act of 1992 directed the EPA to develop these standards. The Nuclear Regulatory Commission then had to incorporate these final standards into its licensing regulations. The DOE must demonstrate compliance with these standards as part of its license application to store or dispose of radioactive material in Yucca Mountain. The standards limit radiation exposure from groundwater to four millirems per year, which is consistent with the Safe Drinking Water Act. The EPA notes that an aquifer beneath the planned repository will likely serve nearby Las Vegas in the 10,000-plus years that the repository's spent fuel remains dangerous. For all the potential pathways of exposure the limit corresponds to 15 millirems per year. (The Nuclear Regulatory Commission had suggested that its 25 millirem standard is adequate.[8] The average person receives about 300 millirems per year from natural radiation sources.) These standards are designed to protect residents closest to the repository at levels within the agency's acceptable risk range for environmental pollutants.[9] In a comment after the release of these rules, DOE Secretary Spencer Abraham is said to have remarked that "these are tough standards but we can meet them."[10] More specifically, the final rules consisted of three parts—(1) an Individual-Protection Standard, (2) a Human-Intrusion Standard, and (3) Groundwater Protection Standards:

1. The Individual-Protection Standard of 15 millirems per year (mrem/ yr) applies to a "reasonably maximally exposed individual" who lives in a publicly accessible area and has a diet and living style representative of present residents of the town of Amargosa Valley. This individual is assumed to drink two liters of water per day from wells in the area.

2. The Human-Intrusion Standard is concerned with exposure that might occur as a result of drilling without recognition of the intrusion. If such an intrusion is projected to occur before 10,000 years after disposal, it requires the same 15-millirem dose limit to a reasonably maximally exposed individual as does the Individual-Protection Standard.

3. The Groundwater Protection Standards set separate concentration limits (15 picocuries per liter) on alpha emitters and dose limits (four millirems) from combined beta and photon emitters. These limits are severable from the Individual-Protection Standard.

This might be an appropriate point to consider further the policy aspects of setting a dose or risk limit for effects from release from a repository. This topic is discussed on the basis of general considerations in the appendix on the principles governing radioactive waste management. It might be argued that the risk limit corresponding to a dose rate of 15 mrem/yr (the limit for the first 10,000 years) is unreasonably low compared with what society accepts for other activities and even compared with other radiation sources. As discussed above, there are much larger than 15 mrem/yr differences in background doses from state to state. For example, the government does nothing to discourage, much less prevent, citizens from moving to Denver from Washington, D.C., two cities whose average background radiation differs by considerably more than 15 mrem/yr. Another example comes from increased radiation exposure associated with airplane trips. One cross-country trip contributes 2.5 millirems, so that flight attendants and pilots making 50 cross-country roundtrips per year receive an additional 250 mrem/yr, more than a factor of ten higher than would be allowed for a nearby resident of Yucca Mountain. From these examples one might argue that the 15 mrem/yr limit in the EPA standard is unnecessarily stringent compared with other risks the government and society accepts.

These standards were only to apply to the period up to 10,000 years following disposal. The rules did require the DOE to calculate the peak dose of the reasonably maximally exposed individual that would occur after 10,000 years following disposal but within the period of geologic stability. These results had to be included in the Environmental Impact Statement for Yucca Mountain as an indicator of long-term disposal system performance.

Court of Appeals Rejects 10,000-Year Limit on Compliance Time

As discussed in our later chapter on court appeals, Nevada and the Natural Resources Defense Council filed suit against the EPA, saying that in restricting compliance to 10,000 years the advice of the NAS to extend compliance to the time of peak dose had not been followed. This suit was successful, with the D.C. Court of Appeals ruling in summer 2004 that the EPA had to revise its standard with regard to compliance time to be consistent with the NAS recommendation, as required by the Energy Act of 1992. Alternatively the court said the government could seek congressional action to override this act. This latter option has not been pursued.

The Environmental Protection Agency's Proposed Revisions

In summer 2005 the EPA issued proposed revisions to the compliance time part of its standards.[11] It proposed a two-tiered standard, with the original 15 mrem/yr limit for the first 10,000 years and a much less stringent limit of 350 mrem/yr for the period up to one million years.

The proposed revision of the standard is accompanied by a lengthy explanatory statement. The rationale for a two-tiered approach, with a much less stringent standard for later times, is based on the larger uncertainty in the projected performance of the repository over long periods of time. The EPA says that "given the increased uncertainty that is unavoidable in the capabilities of science and technology to project and affect outcomes over the next one million years, the concept of reasonable expectation underlying our standards implies that a dose limit for that very long period that is higher than the 15 mrem/yr limit that applies in the relatively 'certain' pre-10,000-year compliance period could still provide a comparable judgement of overall safety."[12] This relaxation of the dose limit in response to increased uncertainties seems to us rather peculiar. If one were designing a bridge whose steel and concrete performance became more uncertain with time, would one loosen or tighten the structural design standards if one realized that the bridge was going to have to provide safe transport for a longer period of time?

The rationale given for the choice of the numerical value of the standard is based on how much radiation exposure is tolerated for other unregulated activities. In particular the EPA's goal is to ensure that releases from Yucca Mountain will not lead to a total exposure of the reasonably maximally exposed individuals that exceeds the background level that other populations live with routinely. The EPA estimates that Amargosa Valley residents experience an average annual background dose of 350 mrem/yr. For comparison the EPA chose the State of Colorado, a western state claimed to be reasonably comparable to Nevada. The average annual background radiation for Colorado residents is 700 mrem/yr (dominated by the indoor radon contribution). This exceeds the Amargosa Valley background by 350 millirems, and the excess is the basis for the new standard for long times.

There is, however, an inconsistency in the rationale for the 350 mrem/yr limit. This arises from the fact that the distributions of both indoor radon levels and the results of different performance assessment runs exhibit a mean value appreciably larger than the median value. The value the EPA used for Colorado is based on the mean contribution of indoor radon, whereas the new standard for Yucca Mountain only requires that the median of the distribution for the assessment "runs" be less than 350 mrem/yr. If a consistent comparison with Colorado had been made, the median value of the indoor radon contribution would have been used, leading to a standard of about 200 mrem/yr rather than 350 mrem/yr.

Although the principle that designers of a repository should not be held to a higher standard than other sectors of society seems reasonable, it is not clear why this principle should be operative at times longer than 10,000 years and not at times less than 10,000 years. According to standard rule-making procedures now in effect, the EPA will have to consider any comments made on the proposed standards and then issue final standards. These final standards are subject to review by the Court of Appeals.

It is not clear that all of the proposed revisions would meet court approval, particularly the proposed change to use the median rather than the mean of the distribution of projections of repository performance, as well as the rather permissive 350 mrem/yr dose limit for the time period between 10,000 and one million years. The 350 mrem/yr dose limit is 23 times the 15 mrem/yr dose permitted before 10,000 years. Because in the proposed standards the former is based on the median of the projected dose distribution and the latter is based on the mean, the dose limit for longer times is effectively 40 to 50 times more permissive than the limit for the first 10,000 years.

NOTES

1. Holly Idelson, "High Noon at Yucca Mountain," *Congressional Quarterly Weekly Report*, October 10, 1992: 3142.

2. Holly Idelson, "Conferees at Last Find Harmony on National Energy Strategy," *Congressional Quarterly Weekly Report*, October 3, 1992: 3033.

3. Adam L. Clymer, "Bills Sent to Bush as 102nd Congress Wraps Up Its Work," *New York Times*, October 9, 1992: A1.

4. *Congressional Record*, October 5, 1992: H11399–401.

5. U.S. National Research Council, Committee on Technical Bases for Yucca Mountain Standards, *Technical Bases for Yucca Mountain Standards* (Washington, DC: National Academy Press, 1995).

6. Ibid., 2.

7. U.S. Environmental Protection Agency, "Public Health and Environmental Radiation Protection Standards for Yucca Mountain, Nevada," 40 CFR part 197, *Federal Register* 66, no. 114 (June 13, 2001): 32074.

8. Keith Rogers, "EPA Chief Says Yucca Mountain Standards in Works," *Las Vegas Review-Journal*, November 3, 2000: 6B.

9. Eric Pianin, "U.S. Sets Safety Rules for Yucca Nuclear Waste Site," *Washington Post*, June 6, 2001: A2.

10. Jeff Johnson, "EPA Retains Tough Standards for Radiation Exposure at Yucca Mountain," *Chemical and Engineering News* 79, no. 24 (June 11, 2001): 6.

11. U.S. Environmental Protection Agency, "Public Health and Environmental Radiation Protection Standards for Yucca Mountain, NV, Proposed Rule, 40 CFR Part 197," *Federal Register* 70, no. 161 (August 22, 2005): 49014–65.

12. Ibid., 49029.

9

The 2002 Approval of the Yucca Mountain Repository

Like the 1987 Nuclear Waste Policy Amendments Act, passed after the Chernobyl accident, congressional action in 2002 giving final approval of Yucca Mountain took place in a crisis environment. The terrorist attacks on the World Trade Center in New York City and the Pentagon in Washington, D.C., on September 11, 2001, increased the urgency of disposing of high-level nuclear waste in an underground repository. The attacks brought home the vulnerability of nuclear reactors, storage casks, and especially spent fuel storage pools to attacks by terrorists. Also, the Bush administration had announced an energy plan that included a policy of building more nuclear power plants. It was recognized that the development of satisfactory arrangements for spent fuel disposal was essential before more reactors were built.

Energy Secretary Abraham notified the governor of Nevada that he intended to recommend the Yucca Mountain site for a permanent repository on January 10, 2002. It is interesting to note that the secretary's transmittal letter not only asserted his belief that the site is technically suitable but also emphasized the importance of a repository to our national security. He stated that "we should consolidate the nuclear wastes to enhance protection against terrorist attacks by moving them to one underground location that is far from population centers."[1] In keeping with the Amendments Act of 1987, he did not need to comment on why the Yucca Mountain site is more suitable than other possible repository sites.

The Nuclear Waste Policy Act (NWPA) of 1982 required that the governor of the repository host state be given 30 days notice before recommendation of a site to the president. Abraham recommended the site to President George W. Bush on February 14, 2002. Only one day after receiving this recommendation, February 15, 2002, President Bush notified

Congress that he accepted the recommendation. This notification to Congress started the clock ticking. Governor Guinn had 60 days to veto the selection. Guinn took nearly the maximum time allowed and issued his Notice of Disapproval on April 8, 2002. Congress then had a maximum of 90 days to override the Nevada veto.

The vehicle for overturning the Nevada veto of the repository was a resolution, H.J.R. 87, that required a majority vote of each house of Congress. The procedure for overriding a repository host state veto, as well as the option for a state to veto hosting a repository, was mandated by the Nuclear Waste Policy Act of 1982. During the debates preceding the passage of this act a good deal of time had been spent on strength of the veto. The strongest veto considered was a veto that could not be overridden by the federal government. This was rejected as it raised the possibility that a site for a repository would not be found, given the resistance of states to hosting a repository. Another option was that a veto had to be upheld by at least one house of Congress. This was rejected, as there was concern that it might be unconstitutional.[2] A similar option, a veto that would require the passage of an override resolution by a majority of each house of Congress was finally adopted. The 1982 act also addressed a concern that a state veto would stand if either the speaker of the House or the Senate majority leader failed to take up the resolution. The act provided that all members could introduce the override resolution in their respective bodies. This resolution could not be amended and would not require conference committee action. The provisions of the act required congressional action in 60 days or less of continuous session after the Nevada veto.

Unlike the Nuclear Waste Policy Act of 1982 and the Nuclear Waste Policy Amendments Act of 1987 that were passed under time constraints just prior to adjournment, neither the hearings nor the debates were rushed. Opponents of the veto override, including the Nevada congressional delegation, the Nevada governor, and other Nevada officials, were offered ample opportunity to present their case at hearings in both houses of Congress. The House procedure differed from that of the Senate in that hearings before the subcommittees of the House Transportation and Infrastructure Committee provided a formal opportunity to discuss problems associated with transporting spent fuel from nuclear reactor sites to the Yucca Mountain repository. There was no corresponding formal opportunity to air transportation issues in the Senate. In the Senate, the norm that allows the Senate majority leader to control when legislation will be brought to the floor was violated.

Proponents of the veto override stressed fears of terrorist attacks on spent fuel storage pools and casks, the excellent safety record for transporting spent fuel, the need for additional power, the suitability of the Yucca Mountain repository site, and the legal obligation of the federal government to take custody of spent fuel from commercial reactors. Opponents of the veto override resolution cited the difficulties of protecting tens of thousands of spent fuel shipments from terrorist attacks, numerous unresolved scientific questions about the suitability of the repository, evidence that water transport time through the repository was much more rapid than originally thought, and the risks of seismic activity and of volcanic activity near the repository. Some opposed nuclear power and thought they could stop the building of additional nuclear power plants by blocking the development of nuclear waste disposal facilities.

The veto by the State of Nevada was overridden overwhelmingly in the House of Representatives and by a smaller margin in the Senate. In both the House and Senate, nearly all Republicans supported the veto override. Democrats split evenly 102 to 103 in the House, and the majority of Democrats opposed the resolution in the Senate.

HOUSE ACTION

The committee with jurisdiction for the veto override resolution was the Committee on Energy and Commerce, which on energy issues is the House counterpart of the Senate Energy and Natural Resources Committee. This committee was chaired by Representative Billy Tauzin (R-LA), a strong supporter of nuclear power. Testimony was presented at hearings of a subcommittee of this committee, the Subcommittee on Energy and Air Quality, chaired by Representative Joe Barton (R-TX), a supporter of the Yucca Mountain repository.[3]

The leadoff witness at the hearings was Energy Secretary Spencer Abraham.[4] Secretary Abraham first addressed the major controversies related to the Yucca Mountain repository. These included radiation standards, rainwater seepage into the repository, and possible seismic and volcanic activity in the vicinity of the repository site. Abraham claimed that the radiation standards for the repository were stringent and that the annual radiation exposure for people residing near the repository would be less than that received in two cross-country plane trips. On the rainwater seepage issue, Abraham said that if rainwater did seep down, it would be into a contained aquifer. Abraham also said that the Department of Energy (DOE) was satisfied that the risks of seismic or volcanic activity were very low. Abraham claimed that the energy needs of the United States were increasing and unless a way were found to dispose of spent fuel, new nuclear reactors would not be brought online. The 9/11 terrorist attacks raised the question of the vulnerability of spent fuel to terrorist attacks. Spent fuel was being stored in pools or dry casks at 131 sites. Abraham felt that for homeland security reasons it was desirable to consolidate as much of the dangerously radioactive spent fuel as possible in a deep underground repository.

Laura Chapelle of the National Association of Regulatory Utility Commissioners pointed out that some reactors would have to be shut down if a repository for the waste were not opened soon.[5] Commissioner Greta Dicus of the Nuclear Regulatory Commission (NRC) testified that she was satisfied that the DOE was ready to proceed with the Yucca Mountain repository licensing procedure.[6] Joe F. Colvin, president and CEO of the Nuclear Energy Institute, reminded subcommittee members of the legal obligation of the federal government to accept spent fuel in a repository by 1998. This obligation was incurred with the passage of the Nuclear Waste Policy Act of 1982. As a result of the government's inability to do so, ratepayers were paying for storage costs. Colvin estimated this additional expense to be $5 to $7 billion if the repository is opened in 2010 and more if it is opened later. Colvin pointed out that the DOE was facing lawsuits to recover storage costs.[7]

Jeffrey R. Holmstead, assistant administrator for air and radiation of the Environmental Protection Agency (EPA), first described the process for setting radiation standards for Yucca Mountain. Holmstead testified that the radiation standards for Yucca Mountain were developed in consultation with the DOE, the NRC, and the Office of Science and Technology Policy. The radiation standards, Holmstead claimed, were also generally consistent with the recommendations of the National Academy of Sciences. In the Energy Act of 1992, Congress had directed the EPA to contract with the National Academy of Sciences to make recommendations relating to radiation standards for Yucca Mountain. The EPA was directed, in this act, to take into account these recommendations in setting radiation standards. The EPA radiation standards, issued June 13, 2001, were among the most stringent in the world and could be implemented, Holmstead claimed.[8]

Ms. Gary Jones of the General Accounting Office claimed that 293 technical issues related to the repository had not yet been resolved and opposed the veto override. She suggested that it might be early 2006 before the DOE would be ready to apply for a license.[9] Jared L. Cohon, chairman of the Nuclear Waste Technical Review Board (NWTRB), stated that the NWTRB's view was that the technical basis for the performance of the Yucca Mountain repository was "weak to moderate." Cohon and the other members of the NWTRB were particularly concerned about the lack of data related to corrosion of the waste packages in the proposed repository.[10]

Joan Claybrook, president of Public Citizen, a group founded by Ralph Nader, cited the mishandling of military nuclear waste by the DOE. Claybrook also claimed that the DOE could not demonstrate that the Yucca Mountain repository could effectively isolate high-level nuclear waste for the 250,000 years that it remains dangerously radioactive.[11] On April 23, 2002, the Energy and Air Quality Subcommittee of the House Energy and Commerce Committee voted to override the veto by a 24 to 2 vote. This was followed by a 41 to 6 vote of the full House Energy and Commerce Committee to override the veto.

Although the House Transportation and Infrastructure Committee did not have jurisdiction over the veto override resolution, House Speaker Dennis Hastert (R-IL) granted permission for this committee to hold hearings on transportation issues. The chairman of the House Transportation and Infrastructure Committee, Don Young (R-AK), though initially in support of the veto override resolution, had become concerned over the safety of transporting spent fuel across the country.[12] By means of these hearings opponents of the veto override hoped to bring nuclear waste transportation problems to the attention of the exceptionally large (75-member) Transportation and Infrastructure Committee. Also, it was hoped that media coverage of the hearings would bring spent fuel transportation problems to the attention of the general public.[13] The Nevada congressional delegation had emphasized the health and safety risks of transporting spent fuel, and this increased the interest of the transportation committee in expanding its jurisdiction over the issue.

Representative Shelley Berkley (D-NV) claimed that there would be 108,000 truck shipments of spent fuel, with one shipment leaving a nuclear reactor site every four hours after the Yucca Mountain repository opened. Berkley also testified that the DOE's own Environmental Impact Statement estimated that there would be between 50 and 300 accidents transporting the spent fuel. Representative William Pascrell Jr. (D-NJ) expressed concern that many of the nuclear waste transportation routes would pass through heavily populated areas. Representative Elijah Cummings (D-MD) reminded committee members of the fact that the Baltimore tunnel fire burned for four days and Baltimore commerce came to a halt for seven days. Cummings claimed that the Baltimore tunnel was on a potential DOE route for transporting nuclear waste.

Representative Vern Ehlers (R-MI) expressed the opinion that there was a greater risk of terrorist attacks against stationary dry storage casks at the reactor sites than against casks used to transport nuclear wastes. Governor Kenny Guinn (R-NV) testified that the DOE had not done an analysis of the terrorism risks associated with transporting spent fuel from reactor sites to the Yucca Mountain repository.

Expert witnesses provided testimony before a combined hearing of the Highways and Transit Subcommittee and the Railroad Subcommittee of the House Transportation and Infrastructure Committee. These witnesses included Lake Barrett, deputy director of the DOE's Office of Civilian Waste Management, who claimed that the record of transporting high-level nuclear waste in the United States was excellent.[14] Another expert witness, Edward R. Hamberger, president and CEO of the Association of American Railroads, the railroad industry's main trade group, claimed that the safety record of railroads for transporting hazardous materials was very good. Hamberger also mentioned that the railroad industry preferred not to transport spent fuel but that the Interstate Commerce Commission had ruled that its status as a common carrier required it to do so. Hamberger testified that the DOE disagreed with the preference of his association for using dedicated trains (trains in which all cars making up the train would be carrying spent fuel) for transporting spent fuel.[15] Allen Rutter, administrator of the Federal Railroad Administration, testified that approximately 1,100 shipments of spent fuel and other high-level nuclear waste had been transported safely by rail over a period of 45 years. Rutter also revealed that dedicated trains had been used.[16]

On May 8, 2002, the full House debated the override resolution. Representative Jim Gibbons (R-NV) raised a point of order against the override resolution, claiming it was an unfunded mandate. Unfunded Mandate Reform legislation, passed in 1995, prohibited the federal government from passing a bill that would impose more than $58 million in costs on state and local governments. Gibbons estimated the cost to state and local governments to be in the billions. Billy Tauzin, chairman of the House Energy and Commerce Committee, ruled that Gibbons's claim was without foundation as the Congressional Budget Office reported that it "did not identify any mandates in this resolution that would fall under the Unfunded Mandates Reform Act."[17]

In the debates some proponents of the override stated that the U.S. economy needed nuclear power and that approval of the Yucca Mountain repository was necessary if nuclear power were to continue to be used. Terrorism was also an important issue in the debates. Some stressed the risk of terrorist attacks on spent fuel stored in pools or casks at nuclear reactor sites. Others feared attacks on trucks or trains transporting spent fuel to the Yucca Mountain repository. Neither the DOE nor expert witnesses had compared the risks of on-site attacks with the risk of transportation-related attacks. Congress was without expert guidance on this issue. As a result representatives of states with spent fuel tended to support the override, whereas many of those on likely transit routes tended to oppose it. Some opponents of the veto felt it was premature to vote on the resolution, citing the 293 scientific and technical issues identified by the General Accounting Office that remained to be resolved. Some proponents of the override cited the past safety record in transporting spent fuel and the time and money already spent on Yucca Mountain. Several mentioned that 161 million people lived within 75 miles of existing on-site temporary storage sites and felt it was safer to move the waste to Yucca Mountain. Some of the latter stated that the spent fuel would then all be stored at one place (which was incorrect because spent fuel is too radioactive to be transported immediately and must be stored at the reactor site for five years).

Representative James McDermott (D-WA) made one of the strongest statements of the opponents in the debate. McDermott said: "This is being rushed through for one reason: The President has got the September 11 flag and he is waving it around and wrapping himself in it and saying we have got to have nuclear power, and if we do not get rid of the nuclear waste we cannot have nuclear power. So he sees his chance. He wants to ram this through in spite of the fact that the General Accounting Office says there are 293 problems."[18] The House voted 306 to 117 on the resolution, H.J.R. 87, to override the Nevada veto. The party breakdown of the vote—Republicans, 203 to 13, and Democrats, 102 to 103—shows over-whelming support by the Republicans and an even split by the Democrats. The strong support by Republicans of administration positions was common during the first term of President George W. Bush.[19]

SENATE ACTION

The Nevada veto override resolution then moved to the Senate. The Senate, just barely controlled by Democrats with a 50 to 49 margin, was expected to be more resistant to the override than the House. Many major bills have passed the House since the early 1990s only to be defeated in the Senate. Sinclair has described the Senate as "the major choke point in the legislative process."[20] In the previous year, 2001, Senator Harry Reid (D-NV) played an active role in the switch from Republican to Democratic control. Both Reid's persuasiveness and his willingness to relinquish the chairmanship of the Environment and Public Works Committee to James Jeffords (R-VT) are thought to have influenced Jeffords's decision to leave the Republican Party. Jeffords for some time had "deep disagreements" with the administration over energy and environmental policies.[21] Although Jeffords, upon leaving the Republican Party, officially became an Independent, he joined the Democratic caucus of the Senate, thereby giving the Democrats control of the Senate. Senator Tom Daschle, who then became Senate majority leader, announced soon after assuming this position that as long as the Democrats were in control, the Yucca Mountain repository would not be approved. Later, he would have to eat his words.

Hearings on the veto override resolution were held by the Senate Energy and Natural Resources Committee, the committee of jurisdiction in the Senate. Unlike the case in the House, there were no hearings before a Senate transportation subcommittee. Transportation issues, however, were presented and discussed at the hearings of the Senate Energy and Natural Resources Committee. At one of the hearings a nuclear reactor fuel assembly that had not been irradiated was introduced into the hearing room to illustrate that it would not explode.[22]

At the first hearing, Senator Bingaman, chairman of the Senate Energy and Natural Resources Committee, reviewed the history of the Yucca Mountain project. Bingaman said that 15 years ago Congress took the repository site selection out of the hands of the secretary of energy when it designated Yucca Mountain as the sole site. Bingaman pointed out that the secretary of energy must still determine if the Yucca Mountain site se-lected by Congress is suitable for the storage of high-level nuclear waste. He said that when the Nuclear Waste Policy Act of 1982 was passed 20 years ago Congress debated the state veto provision longer than any other provision of the act. The expedited procedure adopted for consideration of the act, Bingaman said, was designed to ensure that both houses of Congress would have an opportunity to vote on the question. Bingaman claimed that the burden of proof was on the administration and that Sec-retary Abraham would have to make the case for going forward. The task of the committee was to decide whether to allow the secretary of energy to file a license application with the Nuclear Regulatory Commission. The committee would have to decide whether the State of Nevada had identi-fied weaknesses in the case sufficient to terminate the program.[23]

The prepared statement of Secretary Abraham before the Senate com-mittee was similar to that presented at House hearings, and a summary will not be repeated here.[24] Nevada Governor Kenny Guinn did not ap-pear in person before the committee but submitted a statement and docu-ments, including a Statement of Reasons for his veto of the Yucca Moun-tain repository. This was the first time a governor had vetoed a presidential action. Guinn cited a number of scientific concerns, including possible corrosion of embedded casks. Among the documents submitted was an af-fidavit signed by John W. Bartlett, former director of the DOE's Office of Civilian Waste Management. This affidavit, signed just shortly before the hearings (February 4, 2002), included Bartlett's assertion that the DOE's site characterization data show that the rate of water infiltration into Yucca Mountain is of the order of 100 times greater than expected. Also included in the affidavit was the claim that because the Yucca Mountain site cannot be shown to be capable of long-term geologic isolation of high-level nu-clear waste, the DOE adopted new rules that permit the agency to rely en-tirely on man-made waste packages.[25]

Witnesses testifying at the Senate hearings who had not previously tes-tified before the House committees or House subcommittees on the Ne-vada veto override included Victor Gilinsky, Jim Hall, Richard Meserve, and Charles Groat. Victor Gilinsky, a former member of the NRC, tes-tified: "The most egregious of the pro-Yucca arguments has to do with spent fuel security—egregious because it exploits public fears in the wake of September 11th. People have been given the idea that spent fuel will be quickly moved from around the country to Yucca Mountain where it will be placed deep underground. The Mantra is 'better one site than 131.' It will be decades before the spent fuel could be shipped to Nevada."[26]

Jim Hall, former chairman of the National Transportation Safety Board, currently representing the Transportation Safety Coalition, opposed the veto override. The main reason for this opposition was that the DOE had no plan for transporting spent fuel to the Yucca Mountain repository. Hall's position was that Congress should demand a detailed transportation plan before considering the override vote. Hall also pointed out that the transportation risks cited by the DOE would not be evenly spread along the transportation routes. Although spent fuel shipments would originate from scattered locations, they would converge as they approached the repository site. Risk, therefore, would be greater closer to the repository. Another shortcoming mentioned by Hall was that no government agency had demonstrated the safety of the casks that would be used to ship spent fuel.[27]

Richard Meserve, chairman of the NRC, testified that deep geologic disposal is appropriate for spent fuel and that spent fuel could be safely transported to a repository. Meserve said that the DOE's Final Environmental Impact Statement on the site is "sufficient to allow a site recommendation." The NRC did not take a position on whether the repository should be located at Yucca Mountain.[28]

Charles Groat, director of the U.S. Geological Service, did not appear at the hearings. In a statement submitted to the committee, Groat supported the decision to recommend the Yucca Mountain repository. The statement included an assessment of the probability of a volcanic eruption at the site of 16 in one billion years. The statement also included a recommendation that surface structures at the repository site be earthquake resistant. This indicates that the U.S. Geological Service estimated that significant seismic activity was probable during the period the repository was being filled.[29] The testimony of Ms. Gary Jones of the General Accounting Office, Jared Cohon of the Nuclear Waste Technical Review Board, Jeffrey Holmstead of the EPA, and the Nevada congressional delegation is similar to that presented before House committees and will not be described again here.

In the question period Senator Hagel (R-NE) asked about the possibility of reprocessing spent fuel.[30] Abraham responded that highly radioactive by-products remain after reprocessing that would have to be disposed of.[31] Senator Thomas (R-WY) asked if, as some alleged, siting guidelines were changed to make it possible for Yucca Mountain to meet the guidelines.[32] Abraham replied that changes were made in response to congressional directives to the EPA and also as a result of regulations issued by the NRC.[33] Senator Craig (R-ID) asked about new technologies such as transmutation.[34] Abraham said he did not foresee a transition to new technologies in the near future and that transmutation would also generate a waste stream.[35] Senator Ensign (R-NV) was critical of the steep increase in cost estimates for the repository, rising from $35 billion in 1995 to $50 billion in 2001.[36] Secretary Abraham claimed that rule changes were a major contributor to the increased costs.[37]

Chairman Bingaman asked whether the DOE would be able to file an application for licensing with the NRC within 90 days after the site recommendation became effective. He pointed out that legislation required that the license application be completed within that time frame.[38] Abraham replied that the 90 days specified in the 1982 act was designed to make certain that the process moved forward and did not prohibit a later application.[39] Chairman Bingaman also asked: "To what extent will the repository rely on the geology of the mountain, to what extent will it rely on the waste packages, or drip shield or other manmade barriers to ensure that the waste remains sealed in the repository?"[40] Secretary Abraham replied: "The legislation that governs this issue has never, in any sense suggested that either a 100 per cent geological approach or 100 per cent manmade approach is called for. I think it has always contemplated a combination and that is what we are proposing.... Its natural barriers alone are going to protect the public health and safety by isolating 99.999999 per cent of radioactive material which is emplaced in it over 10,000 years."[41]

Senator Bingaman mentioned that the Nuclear Waste Technical Review Board classified the science of Yucca Mountain as "weak to moderate" and asked whether the secretary shared that assessment.[42] Secretary Abraham replied, "We take the NWTRB seriously. They offer perspectives on how to perfect it to an even higher standard." He indicated that the board had raised the question of whether the repository environment should be hot or cold and that the DOE was doing research on this question.[43]

Senator Nighthorse-Campbell (R-CO) expressed concern that nuclear waste trucks would go through downtown Denver and also through a section of I-70 that annually experienced a dozen or more large semitruck accidents.[44] Abraham responded that the DOE would consult with states and Indian tribes about routes.[45] Nighthorse-Campbell responded that alternate routes in Colorado were two-lane country roads and furthermore governors could not veto routes.[46] Senator Carper (D-DE) asked Meserve to assess the greatest risks associated with the transportation of spent fuel.[47] Meserve responded that ordinary traffic accidents posed the greatest risks and that he was also concerned over terrorist attacks.[48]

The Senate Energy and Natural Resources Committee, voting largely along party lines, voted 13 to 10 to override the Nevada veto of the Yucca Mountain site on June 5, 2002. This was a much closer vote than the House Energy and Commerce Committee vote or the full House vote. Nighthorse-Campbell, who had expressed concern about nuclear waste being trucked through Denver and the mountain passes of Colorado, was the only Republican committee member voting to sustain the Nevada veto. Three Democrats voted to override the veto. All three were from southern states whose representatives generally are moderate or conservative Democrats. Mary Landrieu was from Louisiana, which had once been under consideration for a repository site and might again become a candidate should Yucca Mountain be rejected. Jeff Bingaman represented New Mexico, which had an operating low-level and transuranic waste repository, the Waste Isolation Pilot Project (WIPP). Some in New Mexico feared that rejection of Yucca Mountain would result in WIPP becoming the default high-level waste repository. New Mexico was the site of the first atomic bomb explosion and also the home of Los Alamos, where the first atomic bombs were developed and assembled, and New Mexican residents perhaps were more comfortable with nuclear programs. Bingaman himself explained his vote by saying that he was willing to let the NRC make the decision. Bob Graham (D-FL), the third defector from the Democratic position, was from a state with several nuclear reactors with waste for disposal.

By June 26, 2002, Senate Majority Leader Tom Daschle had not called up the veto override resolution, and there was concern that he was going to let it die. Senator Frank Murkowski (R-AK) in a Senate floor speech indicated that the Nevada veto override resolution would be called up on July 9, 2002. At that point it had not yet been decided who would challenge the prerogative of the Senate majority leader to set the agenda for the Senate. Murkowski admitted that the procedure to be used was unusual but that it had been spelled out in the NWPA of 1982. He then proceeded to describe the history of the procedure for expediting consideration of the resolution incorporated in the 1982 act. The procedure allowed any member of the Senate to introduce the resolution, thus offering the opportunity to bypass the Senate majority leader. Details of the expediting procedure are described by Beth.[49] The procedure was first included in a 1980 act that did not pass. Later it was included in the Nuclear Waste Policy Act of 1982, which was enacted. Murkowski pointed out that this provision was not adopted in the wee hours of a meeting of a conference committee but was included with the introduction of the 1982 NWPA, over half a year before the act was passed. There were no objections to the expedited procedure being included in the act, Murkowski claimed. Senator George Mitchell (D-ME) felt it was necessary to include the expediting provision to prevent delay and obstructionism. Senator Murkowski pointed out that the Senate had the right to choose its rules and that the rule did not violate laws or the Constitution. Senator John Ensign (R-NV) said that expediting procedures attached to previous legislation, including the War Powers Act, were not acted upon and that although with these pieces of legislation senators could bypass the Senate majority leader, no one had chosen to do so.[50]

Although the expediting procedure allowed any senator to call up the resolution, there was an understandable reluctance of all senators to do so. Virtually all bills do not have an expediting procedure and depend on the goodwill of the majority leader to schedule legislation for debate and, more importantly, a vote. Historically, senators who violate norms have difficulty in getting their bills passed and getting recognition to participate in debates, as well as other sanctions. Senator Murkowski, who had decided to leave the Senate and run for governor of Alaska and would not experience long-term repercussions, introduced the resolution to proceed on July 9, 2002. The vote on the motion to proceed was the key vote, as Senate leaders on both sides of the issue had agreed not to have a roll-call vote on the override resolution. Senator Larry Craig (R-ID) estimated that the proponents of the Yucca Mountain repository picked up three to five votes by making the procedural vote the only roll-call vote on the repository.[51]

Although the motion to proceed is not debatable, both sides agreed to four and a half hours of debate as part of the agreement. Senator Harry Reid (D-NV), assisted by Senator John Ensign (R-NV), managed the debate for the opposition to the veto override, and Murkowski served as his counterpart for supporters.

In the Senate debate, parochial concerns played a major role. The senators were more succinct and focused than is usually the case. Few speakers, other than Senators Murkowski and Reid, the bill managers, responded to the remarks of the previous speaker. Senator Murkowski provided statistics about the number of metric tons of spent fuel stored in the states of senators who opposed approval of the Yucca Mountain repository. This had the effect of putting into the official record that the senator was in effect opposing the removal of this hazardous material from his or her state. These statistics could be used against these senators in subsequent campaigns. A few senators who favored the override had the mistaken impression that opening the Yucca Mountain repository would make it possible to consolidate the spent fuel at one site, despite the fact that it had been pointed out at hearings that spent fuel was too radioactive to be transported immediately after removal from a reactor. It had to be retained on-site for five or more years before it could be transported, and spent fuel would always be present at operating reactors. Over 30 senators participated in the debate on the override issue, a much larger number than was the case for the 1987 Nuclear Waste Policy Amendments Act that selected Yucca Mountain. Selective summaries and excerpts from the "debate" are presented in chronological order. Some remarks made by Senators Reid, Ensign, and Murkowski are omitted. The full text is available in the *Congressional Record*.[52]

Senator Ensign (R-NV) immediately took up procedural matters. With the help of the Congressional Research Office and former Senate Parliamentarian Robert Dove, whom the State of Nevada had hired to advise Reid and Ensign on procedural matters, Ensign claimed that never in the history of the Senate had anyone other than the majority leader or his designee successfully offered a motion to proceed with legislation. Ensign predicted that "if the motion to proceed prevails without the majority leader's consent, then his office has been impaired. His ability to control the agenda of the Senate which is the basis of his power and that of the majority party...would be dealt a devastating blow."

Senator Wellstone (DFL-MN), representing a state with three nuclear reactors, nevertheless opposed moving ahead with the program until transportation and security issues were dealt with. Wellstone mentioned that the DOE had estimated that as many as 1,000 truck and rail shipments of high-level nuclear waste would move through the Minnesota cities Minneapolis–St. Paul, Rochester, and Mankato. At this point Senator Murkowski waved a document entitled "The Spent Nuclear Fuel Transportation System," which he claimed was a comprehensive analysis. Senator Reid said the document Murkowski waved "was not worth the paper it was written on." He said that it talked about 4,300 shipments by train when they had no trains at Yucca Mountain. The document, unlike most DOE documents dealing with Yucca Mountain, was very brief and bore no date. It had very little detail and was obviously a product of the public relations office designed for mass consumption. Murkowski stated that "835 metric tons of spent nuclear fuel are stored in Minnesota."[53]

Senator Dayton (DFL-MN) observed:

> The design, the construction, the loading, the unloading and the safe transportation…of extremely poisonous nuclear waste must all be done perfectly—at least almost perfectly.… The standards for approval must be very high.… This project is nowhere near that standard today, not even close.… The law states that within 90 days after Congress's final approval…the Department of Energy shall submit its application to the Nuclear Regulatory Commission. According to the Secretary of Energy the Department is at least two years away from being able to submit that application. According to the private project contractor, Bechtel Corporation, DOE is four years or more away from being able to submit an acceptable application.… Clearly the lawmakers intended, and I believe wisely so, that Congress's final review of this project would be within 90 days or very shortly before the Department of Energy made its application to the Nuclear Regulatory Commission. In other words, after all the testing and design and evaluation had been completed.[54]

Senator Bingaman (D-NM) explained that the resolution to override the Nevada veto did not authorize construction of a repository or the transportation of nuclear waste. Bingaman claimed that the DOE still needed to persuade the Nuclear Regulatory Commission that the repository would be safe before construction could begin.

Bingaman, at the same time, stated that he did not feel it was an imminent threat to leave nuclear waste where it was in the short run but felt that it was an unacceptable long-term solution because it would require constant monitoring and replacement of storage containers for thousands of years. Bingaman stated that "the Nuclear Waste Technical Review Board testified that 'no individual technical or scientific factor has been identified that would automatically eliminate Yucca Mountain from consideration.'" He also stated that the Environmental Protection Agency testified that the radiation protection standards are "among the most stringent in the world." If the repository complies with them it will be fully protective of public health and the environment. The U.S. Geological Survey stated "The scientific work performed to date supports a decision to recommend Yucca Mountain for development of the nuclear waste repository" and that "no feature or characteristic of the site…would preclude recommending the site." The National Academy of Sciences has said "Geological disposal remains the only scientifically and technically credible long-term solution available to meet the need for safety without reliance on active management."[55]

Senator Boxer (D-CA) said she opposed Yucca Mountain before 9/11 and continued to oppose it as it was only 17 miles from the California border and Death Valley. "Scientific studies have shown," Boxer said, "that the regional aquifer surrounding Yucca Mountain discharges into Death Valley and that there is a risk of contaminating the water of Death Valley and the surrounding towns." She also expressed concern that a terrorist attack on a truckload of nuclear waste on a heavily populated stretch of I-15 between Los Angeles and Las Vegas would put many people at risk of being contaminated. In addition to repeating the arguments of other opponents of Yucca Mountain regarding the suitability of the site and the risks of transporting high-level nuclear waste, Boxer inserted into the record a list of organizations that opposed Yucca Mountain. (See Appendix F for the entire list.) The more prominent organizations included the American Public Health Association, the League of Conservation Voters, the National Parent Teacher Association, the National Wildlife Federation, Physicians for Social Responsibility, the Sierra Club, and the U.S. Public Interest Research Group (Nader's PIRG). Senator Murkowski responded that "the amount of spent fuel in California at the end of the year 2000 was 1,954 metric tons, not including 98 tons from the San Onofre nuclear reactor. There are 403 metric tons at shutdown nuclear reactors, 11 metric tons in dry storage."[56]

Senator Thomas (R-WY) said that "the repository site was selected because it was remote, 90 miles from population centers and had a climate conducive to storage. This is the one that we decided upon to be the best and this is where we are."[57] Senator Reid (D-NV) proceeded to describe some details about the first shipment to the Waste Isolation Pilot Project in New Mexico, a facility that stored military transuranic nuclear waste:

"WIPP is the most highly planned nuclear shipment we have ever had. Yet the first shipment went 28 miles the wrong way and was turned around by the local police department. The DOE satellite tracking system didn't work."[58]

Senator Stabenow (D-MI), who had defeated Energy Secretary Abraham in the last election, said that although she was eager to have nuclear waste moved out of Michigan, moving nuclear waste created new problems for the citizens of Michigan. She was particularly concerned about a plan to ship nuclear waste on barges on the Great Lakes. Senator Murkowski responded: "Currently, in the State of Michigan, there are 1,627 metric tons of which 58 tons are in shutdown reactors and 177 tons in dry storage."[59]

Senator Carnahan (D-MO) expressed concern that most of the nuclear waste shipments would pass through her state on Interstate 70, a highway designed for a 20-year lifetime but the age of which in 2002 ranged from 37 to 46 years. Carnahan mentioned that the DOE had recently used a route for shipment of high-level nuclear waste that went through St. Louis and Kansas City, with the shipments through St. Louis showing up at rush hours. Carnahan claimed that both the number and the severity of accidents on I-70 were increasing yearly and that the highway was in poor condition. Senator Murkowski responded: "388 metric tons of spent fuel is in the State of Missouri."[60]

Senator Crapo (R-ID) supported the veto override. Among the statements of senators who wanted to get rid of nuclear waste stored in their states, none was more compelling than that of this senator. Senator Crapo claimed that Idaho had 56.5 percent by volume and 11 percent by weight of all the high-level nuclear waste in the DOE inventory. This included spent fuel from the nuclear ships of the Navy, spent fuel and rubble from Three Mile Island, spent fuel from foreign nuclear reactors coming to the United States for nonproliferation purposes, spent fuel from Argonne West, and spent fuel from Idaho reactors.[61]

Senator Carper (D-DE) listed some of the advantages of nuclear power. The advantages Carper specified were that nuclear power does not create sulfur dioxide, mercury, nitrogen oxide, or carbon dioxide. Carper informed the senators that he would vote for the motion to proceed and would vote to override the Nevada veto if his vote was needed. Carper had voted to sustain the Nevada veto in committee. He stated that there were legitimate concerns about the transportation of nuclear waste as well as nuclear power.[62]

Senator Kyl (R-AZ) pointed out that "saying Yucca Mountain should not be built because nuclear waste would continue to be generated is like saying Phoenix should not have a garbage dump because people in Phoenix will continue to produce garbage."[63] Senator Dodd (D-CT) stated that he had supported the 1982 and 1987 Nuclear Waste Policy acts and would also support the veto override.[64] Connecticut had spent fuel to be disposed of.

Senator Voinovitch (R-OH) was under the impression that the establishment of a repository at Yucca Mountain would allow all of the nuclear waste to be stored at one location: "The site is on federal property with restricted access to the land and air space, and as a further safeguard, the Nellis Air Force Range is nearby. From a national security perspective one site is easier to defend than many facilities scattered throughout the nation."[65] Senator Allard (R-CO) was concerned that without Yucca Mountain the nuclear waste from the decommissioned Fort St. Vrain reactor, located in Colorado, would remain there indefinitely.[66]

Senator Domenici (R-NM) claimed that the record for transporting waste to the Waste Isolation Pilot Project in New Mexico was spectacular. Domenici expressed concern that spent fuel, which still contains immense amounts of residual energy, was being treated as waste and supported the plan to make it fully retrievable for 50 years.[67] Senator Hatch (R-UT) frankly stated that one of the top considerations in his decision to support Yucca Mountain was the possibility that if Yucca Mountain were not approved a temporary storage facility would be built on the Skull Valley Goshute Indian Reservation in Utah.[68]

Senator Nighthorse-Campbell (R-CO) explained that his opposition to Yucca Mountain was "deeply rooted in my strongly held belief in states rights. The State of Nevada strongly opposes storing waste at Yucca Mountain.... I cannot in good conscience vote to override a Governor's veto, when the long-term effect has the potential to destroy that state's economy."[69] Senator Kerry (D-MA) objected to abandonment of the process for site selection established by the Nuclear Waste Policy Act, the selection of Yucca Mountain in 1987 "for purely political reasons," lowering standards for Yucca Mountain by the EPA when it found that existing ones could not be met, underestimation of the water transit time, the nearly 300 scientific and technical questions identified by the General Accounting Office that must still be answered, and the lack of a transportation plan.[70]

Senator Lieberman (D-CT) opposed the motion to proceed on both procedural and substantive grounds. On procedural grounds, Lieberman did not want to violate the Senate norm of the right of the majority leader to schedule legislation. On substantive grounds, Lieberman did not think that the Yucca Mountain site was ready to be approved by Congress. Lieberman cited the Nuclear Waste Policy Act, which "instructs the Energy Department to submit an application to the Nuclear Regulatory Commission 90 days after Congress acts."[71]

Senator Jeffords (Ind.-VT), who had previously supported Yucca Mountain, indicated he had changed his position because he felt that the Yucca Mountain repository would not provide a comprehensive solution that would deal with nuclear waste generated in the future. Jeffords favored the development of regional repositories that would increase overall storage capacity and would also minimize the transportation of nuclear waste. Jeffords also was concerned that important water flow processes around Yucca Mountain were poorly understood.[72]

Senator Feinstein (D-CA) expressed concern that the casks containing spent fuel and stored in the Yucca Mountain repository would corrode over time and release radioactive material into the groundwater of a California county, Inyo County, and Death Valley National Park. Feinstein also cited the "weak to moderate" rating of the DOE scientific studies by the Nuclear Waste Technical Review Board.[73] Senator Akaka (D-HI) cited concerns the General Accounting Office raised about seismology and "long term chemical effects of heat, water and chemical processes in and around the containers."[74]

Senator Durbin (D-IL) explained why he was supporting the veto override although he had voted against an interim storage facility at Yucca Mountain previously. Durbin opposed temporary storage because it would require an additional move of spent fuel. Illinois had seven operating nuclear reactors that generated nearly half of the electricity used in the state. The spent fuel from these reactors was currently being stored in facilities at the reactor sites. None of these storage facilities was designed to store spent fuel permanently. Durbin felt that this arrangement was both an environmental hazard and a security risk.[75]

Senator Snowe (R-ME) said she had supported the 1982 and 1987 Nuclear Waste Policy acts and would continue to support the repository program by voting for the Nevada veto override. Senator Snowe mentioned that nuclear waste was still sitting at the site of the Maine Yankee reactor that had been decommissioned in 1996.[76] Senator Grassley (R-IA) felt that the risk of contaminating soil, surface water, and groundwater was greater if the spent fuel was stored at reactor sites than if it was stored at one repository.[77]

Senator Kohl (D-WI) supported Yucca Mountain for three reasons. First, nuclear waste would be removed from the decommissioned Dairyland Power Cooperative reactor. The second reason given by Kohl was: "The site has been proven safe after 20 years of study by the Department of Energy and the National Academy of Sciences." Third, electric ratepayers of Wisconsin had paid over $250 million for the site. (Note, part of the second reason was incorrect. The National Academy of Sciences had not proven that the Yucca Mountain repository was safe.) Kohl ended his statement with a qualifying observation: "Burying our waste problems for future generations to deal with is not something we should be proud of. I hope the Congress and the administration will continue to fund nuclear research that will investigate ways to neutralize this waste. The repository at Yucca Mountain doesn't have to be the last word on nuclear waste. I hope we can do better in the future."[78]

Senator Feingold (D-WI), though of the same party and state as Kohl, opposed the override. Feingold was concerned that Yucca Mountain would not hold all of Wisconsin's waste and mentioned the concerns of some constituents that Wisconsin might become the site for a second repository.[79]

Senator Levin (D-MI) wanted to move waste presently stored in Michigan on the shores of the Great Lakes to Yucca Mountain. Levin felt that terrorism and transportation issues could be addressed in the licensing process. Levin had the misconception that opening the Yucca Mountain repository would eliminate the need for storage at 131 sites. Levin stated: "It makes more sense to store the nation's high level nuclear waste in a single place than it does to leave it at 131 sites, spread all around the country, many close to significant population centers and all located on bodies of water including the Great Lakes and major river systems."[80]

Senator Leahy (D-VT) said that claims made in the 1970s that nuclear power would be cheap, reliable, and clean were not completely true and that nuclear power was neither cheap nor clean. He supported the override, stating that "while I know that some waste will always be located on site at operating plants, we must locate the bulk of the waste at a single secure site." Leahy also mentioned that 29 years' worth of spent fuel was being stored on the banks of the Connecticut River and that Governor

Dean and the Vermont Public Service Commission had urged him to support the veto override.[81]

Senator Craig (R-ID) contradicted Senator Ensign's claim that the expedited procedure under consideration had never been used. He said that on July 8, 1957, Senator Knowland of California, the Republican minority leader, made a successful motion to proceed to consideration of a bill that had been blocked by the Senate majority leader, Lyndon Johnson. Craig claimed that Johnson survived the assault on his leadership. The bill became the Civil Rights Act of 1957, which Craig claimed was one of the most critical pieces of legislation of a generation, if not in the history of this country. Craig, representing a state with a great deal of both defense and commercial high-level nuclear waste to be disposed of, claimed that the record of shipping 2,700 shipments of high-level waste was excellent and accused those who raised the transportation issue of using alarmist tactics. He said that the 70,000 metric ton cap for Yucca Mountain was a statutory cap, not a physical cap, and could be changed. Craig admitted in his statement that Yucca Mountain may not have been the best choice:

> It was determined…Yucca Mountain was, by far, the site that appeared to be the most desirable, other than, if you will, the large granite deposits in Vermont. Granite has unique shielding capability, and it is possible to assume that you could put repositories deep into the granite of Vermont and it would be an ideal situation. But our country did not go there. Our country decided not to have multiple repositories, but a single one, largely because of the politics of it.

Craig also expressed the concern that if the Nevada veto were not overridden, they would walk away from an industry that provides power without contributing to climate change.[82]

Senator Ensign (R-NV) pointed out that of the three finalist states for the permanent repository, Washington, Texas, and Nevada, Washington had the majority leader of the House and Texas had the speaker of the House. Politics decided that Nevada would get the repository, Ensign claimed.[83]

Senator Murkowski (R-AK) cited the editorial support of the *New York Times*, the *Washington Post*, and *The Oregonian* for the Yucca Mountain repository. He also described the history of the selection of the sites for the first repository. Murkowski mentioned that if Yucca Mountain were not approved, the sites selected earlier might be revisited as well as granite formations in Michigan and Vermont and salt formations in Louisiana.[84] Senator Inhofe (R-OK) pointed out that many nuclear reactor sites were running out of storage space and that nuclear waste would have to be transported to storage sites even if the Yucca Mountain repository were not built.[85]

Senate Majority Leader Daschle (D-SD) said he opposed Yucca Mountain because there were still too many unresolved questions about the wisdom and safety of creating a national nuclear waste dump at Yucca Mountain. Daschle also mentioned that transportation problems were of "huge concern" to many of the undecided senators. Daschle cited the "weak to moderate rating" of the technical basis by the Nuclear Waste Technical Review Board and the more than 200 unresolved issues cited by the General Accounting Office, which the DOE's own contractor, the Bechtel Corporation, did not feel would be resolved in time to meet the 2010 deadline. Daschle also mentioned the mild earthquake that had shaken Yucca Mountain two weeks before the debate. He expressed concern over danger of exposure to nuclear waste, saying: "This is extremely dangerous material…a person standing 3 feet from an unshielded nuclear waste cask will receive a lethal dose of radiation in 2 minutes." Terrorism was another concern of Daschle, who stated that "by shipping nuclear waste by trucks, rail and barge we may very well be creating hundreds, even thousands of dirty bombs." Daschle also said that there was no need to make a decision today, citing assurances of the NRC that nuclear waste can stay where it is for 100 years in dry cask storage.[86]

Senator Lott (R-MS), Senate minority leader, said that if France, Sweden, and Japan had solved the problems of transporting nuclear waste, the United States should be able to do so. Lott also mentioned that the federal government could "face billions of dollars in liability" by not accepting the waste by the mandated dates. Lott raised the possibility that private companies might start making arrangements for other types of repositories that might not be as safe. Lott also felt that nuclear power was the only realistic way of meeting global climate concerns.[87] Finally, Senator Maria Cantwell (D-WA) based her opposition to the veto override on the fact that Yucca Mountain would take very little of the 54 million gallons of high-level waste presently stored in underground tanks at Hanford, Wash.[88]

The roll-call vote to proceed in the Senate, which was the crucial vote, was 60 to 39 to override the Nevada veto (S.J.R. 34). To a large extent it was a party-line vote, with most Republicans supporting the Nevada veto override and most Democrats opposing the override. Republican senators were very supportive of the president in 2002, averaging 97 percent support for issues that President George W. Bush had taken a position on.[89] The Republican defectors, Ensign of Nevada, Nighthorse-Campbell of Colorado, and Chafee of Rhode Island, all represented states that did not have operating reactors but were positioned to have large numbers of nuclear waste trucks passing through them. Nighthorse-Campbell had decided not to run for reelection. Chafee, a northeastern Republican, often voted with Democrats.

Democratic defectors from the position of the Senate majority leader included Senators Bingaman (NM), Cleland (GA), Dodd (CT), Durbin (IL), Edwards (NC), Graham (FL), Hollings (SC), Kohl (WI), Landrieu (LA), Leahy (VT), Levin (MI), Lincoln (AR), Murray (WA), Nelson (FL), and Nelson (NE). All except Senator Bingaman represented states with civilian nuclear reactors and had spent fuel awaiting disposal.

Although Senator Ensign contacted nearly every Republican senator, he did not change a single Republican vote, despite the fact that he gave every Republican senator he contacted a list of which highways in their state would carry nuclear waste.[90] Senator Reid and Senator Ensign were assisted by lobbyists from both parties: John Podesta from the Clinton administration and Ken Duberstein from the Reagan administration.[91] Vigorous lobbying both for and against the override continued right up to the vote. The two Republican senators in addition to Ensign who voted against the repository, Chafee and Nighthorse-Campbell, opposed the repository before being contacted by Ensign. The vote margin was much larger than expected and may have been influenced by announcements of support for the repository on July 8, 2002, just one day before the vote, by three senators who had been sitting on the fence. Republican Senators Hatch and Bennett of Utah were under cross pressure but ended up voting for the repository. They were concerned that if the repository were not constructed in Nevada, a temporary storage facility would be built on the reservation of the Skull Valley band of the Goshute Tribe Indian in Utah. Senator Bennett said: "Given the choice that is before us, I would rather have the waste go through Utah than to Utah." The third senator to announce support on this date, Richard Durbin (D-IL), represented a state with the largest amount of spent fuel.[92] Durbin had previously been opposed to the Yucca Mountain repository, citing the risks associated with moving thousands of tons of high-level nuclear waste through Chicago's dense hub of railways and highways. He expressed even greater concern over nuclear waste being transported on barges on the Great Lakes or the Mississippi River.[93] Durbin claimed that although he had opposed Yucca Mountain previously, radiation standards were much tougher in 2002 than in previous bills.[94]

In summary, two themes emerge from the floor debate and the vote. The first is party affiliation, with the Republicans, for the most part, supporting the repository recommendation and the Democrats opposing it. Modifying this partisan split were the parochial interests of the states involved, with legislators from states with spent fuel to be disposed of tending to favor the repository recommendation and legislators anticipating impacts from the transportation of spent fuel through their states tending to oppose it. According to the *Congressional Quarterly Almanac*, "Several senators who voted for the resolution said their support had little to do with backing the desert repository. They were motivated more by the parochial desire to prevent waste from remaining in their own states."[95]

POLITICAL AFTERMATH OF THE 2002 ACT

Nuclear Regulatory Commission Appointments

Reid's use of holds on presidential nominees became more prominent after 2002, when it was no longer possible to obstruct legislation relating to the Yucca Mountain project. The practice of putting holds on nominations is similar to the practice of putting holds on bills, described previously. It allows a single member of the Senate to stop floor consideration of presidential nominations. It is an informal procedure, not a matter of the Senate rules.[96] Holds can be placed either permanently or temporarily. The procedure involves making a request of party leaders to refrain from taking up a nomination on the floor of the Senate and is a roadblock to confirmation. Party leaders are not required to honor the request. As a matter of custom they usually do so. There is a risk that if they do not do so, the senator who requested the hold may conduct a filibuster or object to unanimous consent requests, thereby tying up the work of the Senate. The identity of the senator requesting the hold is usually confidential.[97]

Although holds are most frequently used to assure that a senator is notified when a bill or appointment comes up for consideration, it is sometimes used for parochial purposes. A recent example is the hold placed by

Senator Larry R. Craig (R-ID) on the promotions of 212 Air Force officers in order to persuade the Pentagon to locate four C-130 transport planes at a National Guard base in Idaho.[98] Since the 1970s holds have been used with increasing frequency and started to become troublesome in the 1980s.[99] One of the holds by Senator Reid was associated with his effort to persuade President George W. Bush to nominate a member of Reid's staff for a position on the Nuclear Regulatory Commission. This staff member, Gregory Jaczko, a physicist, was Reid's science adviser and later his budget director. Jaczko was heavily involved in the effort to oppose the Yucca Mountain repository. The NRC has responsibility for licensing the Yucca Mountain repository before it can accept spent fuel from nuclear reactors. After President Bush sent the nomination of Vice Admiral John Grossenbacher to the NRC to the Senate in July 2003, Senator Reid is reported to have put a hold on the Grossenbacher nomination in response to the refusal of President Bush to nominate Jaczko for a position on the NRC.[100] After months of delay because of the refusal of Reid to withdraw his hold and of the president to nominate Jaczko, Grossenbacher was offered an interim appointment. Interim appointments do not require Senate confirmation. Grossenbacher did not accept this interim appointment and withdrew his name from consideration. Reid expanded his holds to other presidential nominees, including the former governor of Utah, Michael Leavitt, who had been nominated to head the EPA. On February 12, 2004, President Bush nominated Jaczko for a five-year term on the NRC. Reid then withdrew his hold on the Leavitt nomination, and the Senate voted to confirm Leavitt.[101]

The battle, however, was not over, as Pete Domenici (R-NM), chairman of the Senate Energy and Natural Resources Committee, which had primary responsibility for the Yucca Mountain project, opposed the Jaczko nomination, as did several other senators. By mid-May the Senate Environment and Public Works Committee had not held hearings on the Jaczko nomination, and in an effort to move the confirmation proceedings forward, Reid put holds on nominees for all environmental agencies. This had no effect, and so Reid expanded his holds to a blanket hold on all presidential nominees except for judicial and military positions.[102] By November 2004, 175 presidential nominations had been blocked by Senator Reid. Reid finally released his holds on these nominees when President Bush appointed Jaczko for an interim two-year term on the NRC. This would become effective in January 2005 and, because it was an interim appointment, would not require Senate confirmation.[103] Reid got much less than he sought in this deal, as President Bush promised opponents to the appointment that he would not reappoint Jaczko to the commission after his interim term expired and Jaczko was to recuse himself on Yucca Mountain issues for the first year of his interim term.

Once Reid got his man on the NRC, Senator Domenici, chairman of the Senate Energy and Natural Resources Committee and a strong supporter of the Yucca Mountain site, decided he could best get his side represented by getting one of his staff members nominated to the Nuclear Regulatory Commission. This he was able to do with far less effort and time than Reid. On January 20, 2005, President Bush nominated Peter Lyons, a nuclear physicist and aide to Senator Domenici, to the NRC. Lyons's appointment also was an interim appointment and did not require Senate confirmation.[104]

The Yucca Mountain Issue in the 2004 Presidential Campaign

Polls showed that the major party candidates were deadlocked in the 2004 presidential race. This situation led them to spend a great deal of time and effort in Nevada and other competitive states with few electoral votes. The Republican candidate, George W. Bush, promised Nevadans in his 2000 campaign for the presidency that he would not approve of the Yucca Mountain repository.[105] In the 2004 campaign the Democratic candidate, John Kerry, claimed that President Bush had broken his promise when he approved of Yucca Mountain. But Kerry also had problems with the Yucca Mountain issue. Kerry not only had voted in 1987 to designate Yucca Mountain for the repository but had supported the program with five other votes.[106] Senator Reid explained that Kerry had voted against Yucca Mountain when his vote was needed, but this statement may only have reinforced the suspicion of many that Kerry was a "flip-flopper." To make matters worse for the Democrats, Kerry was about to announce that John Edwards, who had voted to override the Nevada veto of Yucca Mountain in 2002, was his choice for the vice presidential nominee. Pressure was successfully applied to Edwards, who took the pledge to oppose Yucca Mountain.[107] Despite the efforts to make Yucca Mountain an issue in the presidential campaign in Nevada, the Republican candidate won by 414,939 to 393,372 votes for Kerry.

*2005 Budget Cuts and Senator Dominici's Proposal to Increase the
Nuclear Utility Rate Surcharge*

Substantial tax cuts enacted in 2001 and sharply increased expenditures associated with the Iraq War led to a huge increase in the deficit of the U.S.
government. This led to calls for reductions in domestic spending. The
budget for the Yucca Mountain repository did not escape this pressure.

For the 2004 fiscal year budget Representative Hobson (R-OH),
chairman of the Energy and Water Subcommittee of the House Appropriations Committee, and Senator Domenici (R-NM) were at loggerheads
over funding for Yucca Mountain. They finally reached agreement on $580
million for Yucca Mountain, which was 24 percent below the amount the
House recommended and 36 percent more than the Senate wanted.[108]

The DOE requested $880 million for FY2005.[109] This was a sharp
increase from the $577 million received for the project in FY2004. The
increase, according to the DOE, was necessary for preparing for the repository license application. The license application was scheduled to be
submitted to the NRC by the end of 2004. The House Appropriations
Committee voted to reduce the repository project funding to $131 million
for FY2005. This was the amount available from the Bush administration
that did not require new legislation to be passed. The Bush administration
expected Congress to pass legislation that would allow the DOE to have
direct control over the $14.5 billion in the Nuclear Waste Trust Fund. Be-
cause the secretary of energy serves at the pleasure of the president, this, in
effect, would transfer control of the fund from Congress to the executive
branch of government and ultimately to the president. Congress is generally unwilling to give up power, and this was no exception.

Faced with the possibility of significant disruption of the civilian spent
fuel disposal program, Senator Domenici proposed a one-year 60 percent increase in the surcharge on nuclear utility bills. (The apparent need
for additional revenue from utility bills was an artifact of the president's
budget, where an attempt had been made to wrest control of the Nuclear
Waste Fund from Congress. In effect, most of the year's waste fund revenue had been committed to bring down the overall budget deficit.) The
increase was expected to provide $446 million for the repository project,
bringing the total to $577 million. This is equal to the amount of funding
for FY2004 but much less than the $880 million requested by the DOE for
FY2005. Senator Reid threatened to filibuster the Domenici proposal.[110]

This proposal was also strongly opposed by the Nuclear Energy Institute, an organization that represents the nuclear power industry.[111] One can sympathize with the nuclear industry on this issue. It had already put $14.5 billion into the Nuclear Waste Trust Fund, and not an ounce of spent fuel had been placed in a repository thus far. Like Social Security funds, much of the Nuclear Waste Trust Funds had been used to bring down the deficit.

Representative Joe Barton (R-TX), chairman of the House Energy and Commerce Committee, introduced an amendment to the Energy and Water Appropriations bill that would allow Congress to get $750 million each year for the repository from a pool of money funded by an additional surcharge on nuclear power.[112] This amendment was not approved by House Rules Committee members, who decided to maintain the prohibition against legislating on appropriation bills.[113]

Another solution was suggested by Representative David Hobson (R-OH), chairman of the House Appropriations Subcommittee on Energy and Water Development. In a letter to Energy Secretary Spencer Abraham, Hobson asked if the administration could provide the money through executive action. The Office of Management and Budget (OMB) expressed an unwillingness to do so but suggested that it might be possible if both House and Senate committees agreed to the proposal. This would antagonize the full House and Senate, to put it mildly. The funding problem led to a sharp exchange between Hobson and Rick Merton, chief of the OMB's energy branch. Hobson claimed that the hole in the budget was caused by an OMB "gimmick" that required a legislative fix. Merton called Hobson's contention that he did not have money to fund Yucca Mountain "disingenuous."[114]

Funding of Yucca Mountain remained a controversial issue for over six months, well into the 2005 fiscal year. The impasse on this and other issues was finally resolved late on November 19, 2004, when Senate–House negotiators decided to appropriate $577 million for Yucca Mountain, the same amount as in FY2004.[115] In order to come up with the money and not go above the budget ceiling, funding came from commercial and defense waste disposal funds.[116]

The presidential recommendation and subsequent congressional override of Nevada's veto led to several lawsuits by Nevada. These are discussed in chapter 10 and were unsuccessful in changing the approval of the president's recommendation.

NOTES

1. U.S. Department of Energy, letter of notification to Governor Guinn and the Nevada Legislature from Spencer Abraham, Secretary of Energy, January 10, 2002, press release, available at www.fas.org/news/usa/2002/011002yucca.htm.

2. Luther J. Carter, *Nuclear Imperatives and Public Trust: Dealing with Radioactive Waste* (Washington, DC: Resources for the Future, Inc., 1987), 222.

3. House Committee on Energy and Commerce, Subcommittee on Energy and Air Quality, *A Review of the President's Recommendation to Develop a Nuclear Waste Repository at Yucca Mountain, Nevada, Hearing on H.J.R. 87*, 107th Cong., 2nd Sess., April 18, 2002 (Washington, DC: U.S. Government Printing Office, 2002).

4. Ibid., Testimony and Prepared Statement of the Secretary of Energy Spencer Abraham, 32–38.

5. Ibid., Testimony and Prepared Statement of Laura Chapelle, Chairperson, Michigan Public Service Commission, 206–16.

6. Ibid., Testimony and Prepared Statement of Greta Joy Dicus, Commissioner, U.S. Nuclear Regulatory Commission, 181–85.

7. Ibid., Testimony and Prepared Statement of Joe F. Colvin, President and CEO of the Nuclear Energy Institute, 210–15.

8. Ibid., Testimony and Prepared Statement of Jeffrey R. Holmstead, Assistant Administrator for Air and Radiation, Environmental Protection Agency, 186–89.

9. Ibid., Testimony and Prepared Statement of Ms. Gary Jones, Director, Natural Resources and Environment Team, U.S. General Accounting Office, 194–203.

10. Ibid., Testimony and Prepared Statement of Jared L. Cohon, Chairman, Nuclear Waste Technical Review Board, 189–94.

11. Joan Claybrook, President of Public Citizen, available at www.yuccamountain.org/pdf/claybrook041802.pdf (accessed April 17, 2007).

12. Ken Ritter, Associated Press, "Rep. Young Rethinking Yucca Vote," *Reno Gazette-Journal*, January 22, 2002, available at www.rgj.com/news/printstory.php?id=6436 (accessed April 18, 2007).

13. House Committee on Transportation and Infrastructure, Subcommittees on Highways and Transit and Railroads, *Transportation of Spent Fuel Rods to Yucca Mountain*, 107th Cong., 2nd Sess. (April 25, 2002), available at www.yuccamountain.org/leg/hearings.htm (accessed April 17, 2007).

14. Ibid., Statement of Lake Barrett, Deputy Director, Office of Civilian Radioactive Waste Management, April 25, 2002, available at www.yuccamountain.org/pdf/barrett042502.pdf (accessed April 17, 2007).

15. Ibid., Statement of Edward Hamberger, President and CEO of the American Railroad Association, April 25, 2002, available at www.yuccamountain.org/pdf/hamberger042502.pdf (accessed April 17, 2007).

16. Ibid., Statement of Allen Rutter, Administrator, Federal Railroad Administration, April 25, 2002, available at www.yuccamountain.org/pdf/rutter042502.pdf (accessed April 17, 2007).

17. Yucca Mountain Repository Site Approval Act, H.J.R. 87, 107th Cong., 2nd Sess., *Congressional Record* 148 (May 8, 2002): H2181.

18. Ibid., H2190.

19. Ibid., H2180–205.

20. Barbara Sinclair, "The '60 Vote Senate': Strategies, Process, and Outcomes," in *U.S. Senate Exceptionalism*, ed. Bruce I. Oppenheimer (Columbus: Ohio State University Press, 2000), 259.

21. Norman J. Vig, "Presidential Leadership and the Environment," in *Environmental Policy: New Directions for the 21st Century*, ed. Norman J. Vig and Michael Kraft (Washington, DC: Congressional Quarterly Press, 2003), 103.

22. Yucca Mountain Repository Development, Senate Committee on Energy and Natural Resources, *Hearings on S.J. Res. 34, Senate Hearing: 107-483*, 107th Cong., 2nd Sess. (May 16, 22, and 23, 2002), available at www.yuccamountain.org/leg/hearings.htm.

23. Ibid., Senator Bingaman, Opening Statement, May 16, 2002, 1–4.

24. Ibid., Energy Secretary Abraham, Testimony and Prepared Statement, May 16, 2002, 10–17; and Recommendation to the President, app. 2, 179–215.

25. Ibid., Governor Guinn of Nevada, Prepared Statement, May 22, 2002, 46–50; and Statement of Disapproval, app. 2, 216–20.

26. Ibid., Victor Gilinsky, former Commissioner, Nuclear Regulatory Commission, Testimony and Prepared Statement, May 22, 2002, 73–77.

27. Ibid., Jim Hall, former Chairman, National Transportation Safety Board, on behalf of the Transportation Safety Coalition, Testimony and Prepared Statement, May 22, 2002, 108–12.

28. Ibid., Richard Meserve, Chairman of the Nuclear Regulatory Commission, Testimony and Prepared Statement, May 23, 2002, 125–30.

29. Ibid., Charles Groat, Director of the U.S. Geological Service, letter to Robert Card, app. 2, 173–79.

30. Ibid., Senator Hagel, May 16, 2002, 29.

31. Ibid., Secretary Abraham, May 16, 2002, 26.

32. Ibid., Senator Thomas, May 16, 2002, 31.

33. Ibid., Secretary Abraham, May 16, 2002, 32.

34. Ibid., Senator Craig, May 16, 2002, 33.

35. Ibid., Secretary Abraham, May 16, 2002, 33–34.

36. Ibid., Senator Ensign, May 16, 2002, 38.

37. Ibid., Secretary Abraham, May 16, 2002, 38.

38. Ibid., Senator Bingaman, May 16, 2002, 17.

39. Ibid., Secretary Abraham, May 16, 2002, 17–18.

40. Ibid., Senator Bingaman, May 16, 2002, 18.

41. Ibid., Secretary Abraham, May 16, 2002, 18.

42. Ibid., Senator Bingaman, May 16, 2002, 18.

43. Ibid., Secretary Abraham, May 16, 2002, 18–19.

44. Ibid., Senator Nighthorse-Campbell, May 16, 2002, 20.

45. Ibid., Secretary Abraham, May 16, 2002, 20–22.

46. Ibid., Senator Nighthorse-Campbell, May 16, 2002, 22.

47. Ibid., Senator Carper, May 23, 2002, 136.

48. Ibid., Chairman Meserve, May 23, 2002, 136–37.

49. Richard S. Beth, "Nuclear Waste Repository Siting: Expedited Procedures for Congressional Approval," in *Nuclear Waste Disposal*, ed. Warren S. Melfort (New York: Nova Science Publishers, 2003), 1–24.

50. Senator John Ensign (R-NV), "Yucca Mountain," *Congressional Record* 148 (June 26, 2002): S6055.

51. Elaine Hiruo and Lira Behrens, "Senate Advances Yucca Mountain to Project Licensing Phase," *Nucleonics Week* 43, no. 28 (July 21, 2002): 1.

52. Yucca Mountain Repository Site Approval Act, S.J. Res. 34, 107th Cong., 2nd Sess., *Congressional Record* 148 (July 9, 2002): S6451–90.

53. Senator Wellstone (DFL-MN), *Congressional Record*, July 9, 2002: S6451–54.

54. Senator Dayton (DFL-MN), *Congressional Record*, July 9, 2002: S6453–54.

55. Senator Bingaman (D-NM), *Congressional Record*, July 9, 2002: S6454–55.

56. Senator Boxer (D-CA), *Congressional Record*, July 9, 2002: S6455–56.

57. Senator Thomas (R-WY), *Congressional Record*, July 9, 2002: S6457.

58. Senator Reid (D-NV), *Congressional Record*, July 9, 2002: S6458.

59. Senator Stabenow (D-MI), *Congressional Record*, July 9, 2002: S6458–59.

60. Senator Carnahan (D-MO), *Congressional Record*, July 9, 2002: S6459–60.

61. Senator Crapo (R-ID), *Congressional Record*, July 9, 2002: S6460–61.

62. Senator Carper (D-DE), *Congressional Record*, July 9, 2002: S6462.

63. Senator Kyl (R-AZ), *Congressional Record*, July 9, 2002: S6462.

64. Senator Dodd (D-CT), *Congressional Record*, July 9, 2002: S6463.

65. Senator Voinovitch (R-OH), *Congressional Record*, July 9, 2002: S6464.

66. Senator Allard (R-CO), *Congressional Record*, July 9, 2002: S6465.

67. Senator Domenici (R-NM), *Congressional Record*, July 9, 2002: S6466.

68. Senator Hatch (R-UT), *Congressional Record*, July 9, 2002: S6466.

69. Senator Nighthorse-Campbell (R-CO), *Congressional Record*, July 9, 2002: S6467.

70. Senator Kerry (D-MA), *Congressional Record*, July 9, 2002: S6467–88.

71. Senator Lieberman (D-CT), *Congressional Record*, July 9, 2002: S6468.

72. Senator Jeffords (Ind.-VT), *Congressional Record*, July 9, 2002: S6469–70.

73. Senator Feinstein (D-CA), *Congressional Record*, July 9, 2002: S6471–72.

74. Senator Akaka (D-HI), *Congressional Record*, July 9, 2002: S6472.

75. Senator Durbin (D-IL), *Congressional Record*, July 9, 2002: S6472.

76. Senator Snowe (R-ME), *Congressional Record*, July 9, 2002: S6473.

77. Senator Grassley (R-IA), *Congressional Record*, July 9, 2002: S6473.

78. Senator Kohl (D-WI), *Congressional Record*, July 9, 2002: S6475.

79. Senator Feingold (D-WI), *Congressional Record*, July 9, 2002: S6475.

80. Senator Levin (D-MI), *Congressional Record*, July 9, 2002: S6476.

81. Senator Leahy (D-VT), *Congressional Record*, July 9, 2002: S6475.

82. Senator Craig (R-ID), *Congressional Record*, July 9, 2002: S6477–78.

83. Senator Ensign (R-NV), *Congressional Record*, July 9, 2002: S6479–82.

84. Senator Murkowski (R-AK), *Congressional Record*, July 9, 2002: S8482–83.

85. Senator Inhofe (R-OK), *Congressional Record*, July 9, 2002: S6483–84.

86. Senator Daschle (D-SD), *Congressional Record*, July 9, 2002: S6486–87.

87. Senator Lott (R-MS), *Congressional Record*, July 9, 2002: S6487–88.

88. Senator Cantwell (D-WA), *Congressional Record*, July 9, 2002: S6488–89.

89. "Bush, Hill Back Nuclear Waste Site," *Congressional Quarterly Almanac Plus 2002*, 58 (Washington, DC: Congressional Quarterly, Inc.), 8.

90. Ibid., 8–10.

91. Stephen F. Hayes, "Nevada Goes Nuclear: But What Better Place to Store Radioactive Waste than the Middle of Nowhere," *Weekly Standard*, April 1, 2002: 25–29.

92. Eric Pianin and Helen Dewar, "Senate Approves of Storage of Nuclear Waste in Nevada," *Washington Post*, July 10, 2001: A1.

93. Eric Pianin and Helen Dewar, "In Nuclear Waste Site Debate, Visions of Transport Disaster, Yucca Mountain Foes Cite Fears of Terrorism and Spills," *Washington Post*, July 8, 2002: A3.

94. Michael Barone, *Almanac of American Politics 2004* (Washington, DC: National Journal Group, 2003), 533.

95. "Bush, Hill Back Nuclear Waste Site," 8–10.

96. Sinclair, "The '60-Vote Senate,'" 254.

97. Walter J. Oleszek, *Congressional Procedures and the Policy Process*, 5th ed. (Washington, DC: CQ Press, 2001), 192–94.

98. Lawrence C. Dodd and Bruce I. Oppenheimer, eds., *Congress Reconsidered*, 8th ed. (Washington, DC: CQ Press, 2005), 243.

99. Steven S. Smith, "Parties and Leadership in the Senate," in *The Legislative Branch*, ed. Paul J. Quirk and Sarah A. Binder (Oxford: Oxford University Press, 2005), ch. 9.

100. Steve Sibelius, "Democracy in Peril," *Las Vegas Mercury*, September 11, 2003, available at www.lasvegasmercury.com/2003/MERC-Sep-11-Thu-2003/22116997.html (accessed April 17, 2007).

101. Steve Tetrault (Stephens Washington Bureau), "Bush Nominates Reid Aide to the NRC," *Las Vegas Review-Journal*, February 13, 2004: 3B.

102. Steve Tetrault (Stephens Washington Bureau), "Reid Expands Hold on Nominees," *Las Vegas Review-Journal*, June 15, 2004: 4B.

103. Steve Tetrault (Stephens Washington Bureau), "Yucca Mountain Advisor to Reid to Get NRC Post," *Las Vegas Review-Journal*, November 21, 2004, available at www.reviewjournal.com/lvrj_home/2004/Nov-21-Sun-2004/news/25317027.html (accessed April 17, 2007).

104. Sun Washington Bureau, "Domenici Aide Appointed to NRC," *Las Vegas Sun*, January 20, 2005.

105. David S. Broder, "Tailoring Policy to Electoral Votes," *Washington Post*, March 10, 2002: B09.

106. Martin Kasindorf, "Kerry: Bush Broke Vow on Nev. Nuke Site," *USA Today*, August 11, 2004: 9.

107. Christina Almeida, Associated Press, "Kerry Tries to Energize Foes of Nevada Dump Site," *Los Angeles Times*, October 31, 2004: A14.

108. "Deal Reached on Nuclear Energy Bill," *Congressional Quarterly Almanac Plus, 2003*, 59 (Washington, DC: Congressional Quarterly, Inc., 2004), 251.

109. H. Josef Hebert, Associated Press, "Nevada Nuclear Waste Project Faces Problems," *Las Vegas Sun*, June 9, 2004, available at www.lasvegassun.com/sunbin/stories/text/2004/Jun/09/060910082.html (accessed April 17, 2007).

110. David Rogers, "Domenici Seeks Nuclear Power Fees: Surcharge Would Finance Yucca Mountain Storage but Might Hamper Bush," *Wall Street Journal*, June 21, 2004: B2.

111. Chris Baltimore, Reuters, "Yucca Nuclear Dump Funding Plan Draws Industry Ire," *Environmental News Service*, June 22, 2004, available at www.nucnews.net/nucnews/2004nn/0406nn/040622nn.htm#170 (accessed April 17, 2007).

112. Suzanne Struglinski, "Nuke Power Users Asked to Pay More to Fund Yucca," *Las Vegas Sun*, June 21, 2004, available at www.lasvegassun.com/sunbin/stories/text/2004/jun/21/517052989.html (accessed April 17, 2007).

113. Elaine Hiruo, "House Approves Energy Funding without Waste Fee Provisions," *Nucleonics Week* 45, no. 27 (July 1, 2004): 4.

114. Daniel Whitten, "OMB Could Move on Yucca Mountain Funds, but It's Unlikely to Do So," *Inside Energy*, May 2004: 3.

115. Suzanne Struglinski, "Spending Bill Includes $577 Million for Yucca," *Las Vegas Sun*, November 19, 2004, available at www.lasvegassun.com/sunbin/stories/text/2004/nov/19/517853131.htm (accessed April 17, 2007).

116. "Dispute Centers on Nuclear Waste," *Congressional Quarterly Almanac Plus, 2004*, vol. 61 (Washington, DC: Congressional Quarterly, Inc., 2005), 2–19.

10

Court Appeals

The Nuclear Waste Policy Act (NWPA) of 1982 mandated that the only course of appeal with regard to a repository at Yucca Mountain was to the U.S. Court of Appeals for the District of Columbia Circuit. This court is the highest court below the U.S. Supreme Court, and by identifying this court the act shortened the time that appeals could take before being resolved. The first suit that Nevada filed was in December 1989, when it asked the court to order the Department of Energy (DOE) to halt all work at Yucca Mountain, citing an earlier "veto" by Governor Miller. The DOE responded in court, claiming that the state's veto was "premature and without merit." In September 1990 the Court of Appeals rejected Nevada's suit, and this decision was upheld by the Supreme Court.[1] As the site characterization proceeded and the time for the secretary's possible recommendation approached, Nevada filed several suits. One was a challenge to DOE's revised siting guideline rules.[2] Another was against the Environmental Protection Agency's (EPA's) radiation health-protection standard for Yucca Mountain.[3] Among the grounds cited in the latter suit was a claim that the site boundary to be used for evaluating compliance was gerrymandered and that the 10,000-year time frame covered by the standard was too short. Spent fuel to be buried at Yucca Mountain contains long-lived radioactivities such as Np-237 and I-129 with half-lives exceeding a million years. The Natural Resources Defense Council also challenged the EPA's standard.[4] A third set of petitions was filed by the Nuclear Energy Institute (NEI) versus the EPA.[5] These suits were all filed in 2001.

Various Nevada officials and congressional officeholders had indicated for some time that Nevada would continue to fight the Yucca Mountain selection in court as well as in Congress if the president approved the secretary's recommendation. Indeed, the State of Nevada, joined by Clark County and the City of Las Vegas, filed suit against the Department of

Energy, Secretary of Energy Spencer Abraham, and President of the United States George W. Bush.[6] A second Nevada suit was filed against the Nuclear Regulatory Commission (NRC), claiming that its licensing rule is in violation of the NWPA as amended.[7] The court directed that these two 2002 cases, as well as the earlier Nevada suits regarding the DOE's siting guidelines and the EPA Yucca Mountain radiation protection standards, be heard in tandem before the same panel starting on January 14, 2004.

THE NEVADA SUIT AGAINST THE DEPARTMENT OF ENERGY, SECRETARY ABRAHAM, AND PRESIDENT BUSH

Statement of the Case and Nevada's Opening Brief

The major issue underlying this suit is whether DOE's final rules (*Code of Federal Regulations* 10 CFR parts 960 and 963) conflict with the NWPA statement that deep geologic isolation form the primary means of containment for the nation's nuclear waste. A second related issue is that the guidelines specify detailed geologic considerations for primary selection criteria and factors that would disqualify a site. As we shall see, these issues lead to controversy as to the role that engineered barriers, as distinct from geologic barriers, are allowed to play in the containment of nuclear waste.

Although the Nuclear Waste Technical Review Board had been pushing for more robust casks since 1990, the need for an enhanced role of engineered barriers, particularly drip shields, was increased by the finding in the mid-1990s that some fraction of surface rainwater traveled by unsuspected fast flow paths to the repository depth in less than 50 years.[8] This finding was based on analysis of the isotopic composition of chlorine in samples taken at various locations along the tunnel of the Exploratory Studies Facility. The methodology used and the results obtained have been presented earlier in the chapter on Yucca Mountain. Fast flow paths from the surface to the repository depth have two important implications. One is that in a likely wetter future climate the canisters will be subjected to increased moisture and corrosion. The second is that the existence of fast flow paths from the surface to the repository depth suggests that it is likely that such fast flow paths continue from the repository depth down to the water table. The depth of the water table below the burial tunnel is comparable to the depth of the burial tunnel from the surface. This then creates a path for nuclear waste leaking from compromised storage casks to reach the water table and eventually wells in the Amargosa Valley. To minimize this problem drip shields and more corrosion-resistant cask shells are being proposed. This greater emphasis on engineered barriers is part of Nevada's suit. The Cl-36 findings were cited by those members of the House of Representatives Committee on Energy and Commerce who voted against the approval of Yucca Mountain in May 2002.[9]

It should be mentioned that the Cl-36 findings are somewhat controversial. The Yucca Mountain Science and Engineering Report mentions that the aforementioned Cl-36 findings have not been reproduced by some preliminary analyses by another laboratory.[10] The U.S. Geological Survey validation studies failed to find elevated Cl-36 in the samples they examined.[11] In a March 5, 2003, letter to Margaret Chu, director of the Office of Civilian Radioactive Waste Management, Michael Corradini, chairman of the Nuclear Waste Technical Review Board, reaffirmed their earlier recommendation that the DOE resolve the contradictory Cl-36 analyses. The board, while recognizing that current modeling of the repository behavior takes a conservative approach by assuming the presence of fast flow paths, "continues to believe that the DOE should persist in its efforts to reach scientific consensus on the results of the chlorine-36 analyses and the implications of those results for fluid flow in Yucca Mountain."[12] As discussed in the Yucca Mountain chapter, this issue is still unresolved.

Nevada et al. argue in their Opening Brief that the DOE should have disqualified Yucca Mountain as not being geologically suitable for a repository.[13] The Opening Brief, in reviewing the "Original Repository Rule-making Activity," points out that the NWPA (Section 112[a]) required the DOE to specify qualifying and disqualifying conditions as part of its rule making. The Opening Brief quoted from the 1984 DOE rule: "A site shall be disqualified if the pre-waste emplacement groundwater travel time from the disturbed zone [the underground waste area] to the accessible environment is expected to be less than 1000 years along any pathway of likely and significant radionuclide travel."[14]

In 1987 Congress, in one of the amendments of the NWPA, provided that Yucca Mountain would be the only site characterized. Nevada asserts that Congress did nothing to change the physical siting requirements it had enacted in the NWPA in Section 112(a). It asserts that the DOE acknowledged in December 1988 that the Nuclear Waste Policy Amendments Act did not alter the need to "apply site suitability guidelines developed pursuant to the requirements of Section 112(a)."[15] (Remember, however, that the particular criterion for being disqualified quoted above was a DOE

rule, created in response to congressional action, not part of the act itself.) Nevada points out that as late as 1995 DOE confirmed the 10 CFR
part 960 guidelines "as the primary criteria required by section 113(b) of
the NWPA to be used to determine the suitability" of Yucca Mountain.[16]
(The 10 CFR part 960 siting guidelines govern how technical factors such
as geohydrology and geochemistry should be taken into account in evaluating a site for a geological repository. The guidelines referred to here were
finalized in late 1983 and early 1984. They were revised in 2001 when part
963, specific to Yucca Mountain, was issued.) In 1996, however, the DOE
was faced with a number of problems. Congress cut the Yucca Mountain
budget by 40 percent, the D.C. Circuit Court ruled that the DOE had an
"unconditional obligation" to dispose of utilities' spent fuel by the NW-
PA's 1998 statutory deadline, and the Cl-36 evidence for fast flow paths had
been found.[17] (In its Opening Brief, Nevada characterizes this situation as
the "Perfect Storm"!) Nevada charges that at this point the DOE dropped
site characterization work and "placed all its efforts into developing a repository 'system' design that could ostensibly meet NRC license requirements for a construction permit by relying almost totally on engineered
barriers."[18] In 1996 (and again in 1999) unsuccessful attempts were made
to persuade Congress to drop the part 960 guideline rules or the Section
112(a) act guidelines.[19]

In 1998 Nevada's governor urged the DOE to disqualify the Yucca
site pursuant to the groundwater travel time requirements of the DOE's
part 960 guidelines for evaluating the suitability of the site.[20] In reply, the
secretary of energy conceded that up to 20 percent of all water moving
through the repository would reach the water table in less than 1,000 years
but stated that "additional study is warranted" and that a disqualification
decision would be "premature."[21] It is interesting to note that in Governor
Miller's 1998 letter he refers to a 1989 letter he sent to then-Secretary James
Watkins. In that earlier letter he said there were three factors that Nevada
believed provided sufficient cause for removal of the Yucca Mountain site
from further consideration. These factors were "1) the potential for future
human intrusion; 2) the potential for tectonics, including faulting and volcanism, to disrupt the site; and 3) rapid groundwater travel time from the
repository to the accessible environment."[22] Note that this last factor was
mentioned prior to the discovery of fast travel-time paths based on Cl-36
measurements.

In late 1999 the DOE published proposed amendments to part 960 and announced a new proposed part 963 applicable only to Yucca Mountain. Part 963 completed the shift from site suitability criteria to a Total System Performance Assessment that would demonstrate compliance with the EPA's dose limit for the 10,000-year regulatory compliance period. The amendments to part 960 and the new part 963 were issued in final form on November 14, 2001, only two months before the secretary issued to the president his site recommendation for Yucca Mountain.[23]

In its Summary of Argument, Nevada says these new guidelines essentially abandon "NWPA's mandate that the site's geology form the primary isolation barrier. But because Congress has spoken to the precise question at issue, there is no occasion for this Court to accord deference to DOE's strained construction of the NWPA." The Summary of Argument goes on to say,

> Sections 112 and 113 obligated DOE to issue guidelines governing the suitability determination and the recommendation of sites for repositories that both establish "detailed geologic considerations" to serve as "primary criteria" in site selection and specify the physical factors that would qualify or disqualify a site from development. Pertinent legislative history, from the initial efforts of Congress through the enactment of the NWPA and later amendments, show a clear Congressional commitment to a repository deep underground, relying on multiple, independent barriers, including primarily the geology of the site.[24]

But in the following paragraph Nevada concedes that the NWPA, as distinct from the initial guideline rule making, may be ambiguous on the primary reliance on the geology of the site. This paragraph of the Summary of Argument reads: "Even if the NWPA left this point ambiguous, however, DOE's earlier consistent position, and its sharp break with that position in its new Guidelines, strongly argues against according DOE's new position any deference. Not only does the NWPA not delegate fundamental policymaking to DOE, it was intended to wrest such policymaking away from the Executive Branch."[25]

It is not clear to us that the NWPA's reference to establishing guidelines for the selection of sites that "shall specify detailed geologic considerations that shall be primary criteria" implies primacy over engineered barriers or to other criteria such as cost or geographical location. It does appear that at the time the secretary made his recommendation and the president endorsed the recommendation, the part 960 rule regarding disqualification if water transport took less than 1,000 years was still in place.

It is interesting to note that the issue of the role of engineered barriers relative to geologic barriers came up in the Senate Committee on Energy and Natural Resources hearing on affirming the president's approval of Yucca Mountain over Nevada's veto. This hearing and the context of Energy Secretary Abraham's testimony are discussed in chapter 9. Referring to the Yucca Mountain repository, the committee chairman asked to what extent the repository relies on the geology of the mountain and to what extent it will rely on waste packages, or drip shields, or other man-made barriers. Secretary Abraham replied, "Natural barriers alone are going to protect public health and safety by isolating 99.999999 per cent of the radioactive material which is emplaced in it over 10,000 years." He went on to say, "Just by its geological factors alone it brings the potential exposure below that which we have legally permitted to be the case for nuclear workers. It is still, at that point, higher than the Environmental Protection Agency's standards, which are extraordinarily strict, which is why, based on those standards, we have added additional engineered barriers to accomplish the final small ingredient of protection that I referenced earlier."[26] The first of these statements is somewhat disingenuous. One could also say that the amount of radioactivity expected to escape to the environment in the absence of the additional engineered barriers would be many times higher than that projected with the engineered barriers in place. With respect to the comparison with nuclear workers, the occupational exposure limit is 330 times larger than that for the public in the vicinity of Yucca Mountain.

The occupational exposure limit for nuclear workers is 5,000 millirems per year (mrem/yr), whereas the EPA has set a limit of 15 mrem/yr for the "reasonably maximally exposed individual" outside the repository boundaries.[27] To put the latter limit in perspective, on the average an individual in the United States receives about 300 mrem/yr from natural background radiation. If one moves from New York or Chicago to Denver, one receives an annual increase larger than that allowed for the "reasonably maximally exposed individual" close to Yucca Mountain. This comparison supports Secretary Abraham's characterization of the EPA standards as "extraordinarily strict." On the other hand, the 15 mrem/yr EPA limit only applies to the first 10,000 years. DOE performance assessments indicate that the exposure of the "reasonably maximally exposed individual" continues to rise after 10,000 years, only reaching a maximum (which exceeds 15 mrem/yr) after several hundred thousand years.[28]

The Nevada suit was not the first attempt to disqualify Yucca Mountain on the basis of the groundwater transport time revealed by the Cl-36 findings. In late 1998 the Nuclear Information and Resource Service organization filed a petition with then–Secretary of Energy Bill Richardson asking that Yucca Mountain be disqualified as a nuclear waste repository. This petition was supported by representatives of over 200 environmental and consumer organizations.[29]

The Government Responds to the State of Nevada et al., and Nevada Replies

In February 2003 attorneys for the DOE and the Department of Justice issued their Brief for the Respondents.[30] One might describe their response as defense in depth. Their simplest defense is to argue that congressional passage of the joint resolution (H.J.R. 87), also called the Yucca Mountain Repository Development Act, overriding Nevada's disapproval makes moot all of the petitioners' challenges to the Guidelines and Recommendations of the NWPA.[31] Nevada, in its Petitioners' Reply Brief, asserts that the joint resolution simply vetoed Nevada's disapproval of the president's site designation, restoring its effectiveness.[32] It is perhaps worth noting that the phrasing of the joint resolution goes back to Sec. 115 of the 1982 NWPA. Presumably as backup in case the court rejected the argument that the joint resolution has made moot the petitioners' challenges, the government argues that the court would lack jurisdiction to entertain the challenges to the Guidelines and Recommendations.[33] The government further argues that enactment of the joint resolution ratified the secretary of energy's determination to base his recommendation on an assessment of the total system performance (as distinct from meeting subsystem requirements).[34]

Of more relevance to our previous discussion, the government goes on to argue that the "DOE's site suitability criteria for Yucca Mountain are consistent with the requirements of the NWPA."[35] It claims that the statutory provisions contain no mandate to place primary reliance on geologic barriers. On the contrary, the provisions are interpreted to indicate "that the suitability determination of the Secretary was to be based on the likelihood that Yucca Mountain would meet NRC's licensing criteria, which in turn require the repository to utilize multiple barriers, both geologic and engineered, to qualify for a license."[36] In keeping with the National Academy of Science (NAS) recommendations, the NRC approach for multiple barriers does not specify numerical goals for the performance of individual barriers.[37] (The 1992 Energy Policy Act required the NRC to modify its technical requirements to be consistent with an NAS study mandated by the 1992 act.)[38] Nevada replies that just because the NAS recommended a systems approach for NRC licensing, this does not mean the DOE could no longer use guidelines that included requirements for individual barriers.[39]

With respect to groundwater travel time, an issue the petitioners had focused on and we have discussed earlier in this chapter, the government argues that the NRC's elimination of its quantitative subsystem requirements made many of the DOE's corresponding guidelines inappropriate, including the groundwater travel time disqualification. Again, however, the government presents a backup argument. It asserts that the DOE never made a determination that the groundwater travel time from the disturbed zone to the accessible environment would be less than 1,000 years. Although the DOE conceded that its models indicated that "small amounts of water potentially moving in 'fast paths'" could reach the environment in less than 1,000 years, it concluded most water would take substantially longer.[40] Nevada in its Petitioners' Reply Brief claims that the DOE confessed in 1998 "that up to 20-percent of all water moving through the repository would reach the underlying water table in less than 1000 years." The Petitioners' Reply Brief goes on to say, "Nevadans may be forgiven for their lack of relief that only 20-percent of any contaminated ooze seeping through the repository will actually make its way to their drinking water sometime in this millennium."[41] This suit was eventually heard along with several others. The issues raised in this particular suit were declared moot in 2004, as discussed later in this chapter.

NEVADA CHALLENGES THE CONSTITUTIONALITY OF THE JOINT RESOLUTION

Statement of the Case and Nevada's Opening Brief

In this suit, Nevada et al. argue that Congress in passing the joint resolution overriding Nevada's veto violated principles of federalism and state sovereignty.[42] The limitation of the powers of the federal government is stated explicitly in the Tenth Amendment of the U.S. Constitution, so this is known as a "Tenth Amendment" case. The Tenth Amendment reads in its entirety: "The powers not delegated to the United States by the Constitution, nor prohibited by it to the States, are reserved to the States respectively, or to the people." Federalism is a system of government in which power is divided between a central and regional governments. In the United States, the regional governments (states) delegate certain powers to the central government while retaining others. In the United States these powers are set out in the Constitution, primarily in Article I. Amar has paraphrased the Tenth Amendment as, "We the People, acting collectively, have delegated some powers to the federal government, have allowed others to be exercised by state governments, and have withheld some things from all governments."[43]

Nevada had previously cited the Tenth Amendment in a lawsuit (*Nevada v. Watkins*) following the passage of the 1987 Amendments Act. The U.S. Court of Appeals for the Ninth Circuit rejected the complaint in 1990, concluding, "The tenth amendment does not limit Congress' authority to enact the 1987 NWPA amendments."[44] A petition to the U.S. Supreme Court for a rehearing was denied.[45] Typically Tenth Amendment lawsuits have been unsuccessful.

In the present suit Nevada argues that the joint resolution, also known as the Yucca Mountain Repository Development Act, invades the sovereign prerogative of the State of Nevada.[46] In the suit, filed May 1, 2003, with the U.S. Court of Appeals, District of Columbia, Nevada not only draws on the Tenth Amendment but also claims that a proper federalism analysis draws on the entire Constitution. It claims that "the Constitution mandates fair and equal regard for the sovereignty of the States and forbids the national government from singling out a state for an arbitrary invasion of its sovereignty."[47] Nevada argues that the legislation singles it out to bear a unique burden, not because it is best situated to bear that burden in accord with general, neutral criteria applicable to all states "but only because the rest of the States, acting through the national government, have cynically concluded 'better him than me' and have arbitrarily imposed the burden on that single State as an unapologetic act of naked political will."[48]

The Government's Response

The initial line of defense by the government was to argue that the 1990 judgment in the previously mentioned *Nevada v. Watkins* case precludes relitigation of the same issues occasioned by the passage of the 2002 joint resolution.[49] In the event this argument was not to be accepted, the government goes on to argue that "Congress was empowered, pursuant to its plenary authority to control the use of federal land, to approve Yucca Mountain as the site of a repository, and it decision violates neither the Tenth Amendment nor principles of federalism."[50] Furthermore it is argued that the joint resolution "is also a constitutional exercise of Congress' powers to regulate interstate commerce and provide for the national defense."[51]

An interesting sidelight to this case revolves around the fact that Clark County and the City of Las Vegas joined Nevada as petitioners in the suit. The government points out that the county and the city are subordinate units of state government and do not have standing to pursue the claim presented in the petitioners' brief. Nevada says that the government is mistaken, citing recent cases where units other than states have standing.[52]

NEVADA AND THE NATURAL RESOURCES DEFENSE COUNCIL V. THE ENVIRONMENTAL PROTECTION AGENCY

To understand the basis for these suits we have to review some legislative history. (See chapter 3.) In 1992 Congress passed the Energy Policy Act, which charged the Environmental Protection Agency with establishing health-based standards specific to Yucca Mountain. The legislation further directed the EPA to contract with the NAS to conduct a study and provide recommendations on what standards would protect public health and safety and to use these recommendations in establishing its new standards. In 1995 the NAS released its report.[53] On June 6, 2001, the EPA announced its final health standards for Yucca Mountain, some of which were at variance with recommendations of the NAS report.[54] Six months later the NRC promulgated its licensing criteria (10 CFR part 63) for Yucca Mountain based on the EPA's specific Yucca Mountain standard.

Subsequent to EPA's issuance of its Yucca Mountain standards, several suits were filed challenging various aspects of these rules. We will focus here on one of the issues raised in a Joint Brief of the State of Nevada and the Natural Resources Defense Council (NRDC), joined by six other organizations, "Environmental Petitioners."[55] This issue is the length of time for which compliance with the radiation dose limits must be met. The EPA, in 40 CFR 197.20, states that the DOE must demonstrate that there is a reasonable expectation that for 10,000 years following disposal, the reasonably maximally exposed individual will receive no more than 15 mrem/yr from releases from the repository. This time limit is very controversial, because the performance assessment for the Yucca Mountain site recommendation shows that the expected dose continues to rise rapidly after 10,000 years and does not reach its maximum until times of the order of 300,000 years. (See chapter 7.)

The choice of a 10,000-year compliance time goes back to 1985 when the EPA issued generic rules for a geologic repository, *Code of Federal Regulations* 40 CFR part 191. (Previously in 1983 the NRC had issued licensing criteria based on release rates evaluated at 1,000 years after repository closure [10 CFR part 60], but 10 CFR part 60 was later revised to be consistent with the EPA's 10,000-year compliance time in 40 CFR part 191.)[56] The Waste Isolation Pilot Plant was licensed on the basis of this 10,000-year compliance time.

The NAS report, mandated by Congress in 1992 and released in 1995, considered the compliance time in some detail. The NAS report states, "We believe that there is no scientific basis for limiting the time period of the individual risk standard to 10,000 years or any other value. We recommend…that compliance assessment be conducted for the time when the greatest risk occurs, within the limit imposed by long-term predictability of both the geologic environment and the distribution of local and global populations. Indeed, the 10,000-year limitation might be inconsistent with protection of public health."[57] It identified the recommendation that the compliance time should extend to the time that the peak risk is expected as perhaps the most significant difference between its recommendations and the EPA's generic repository standards of 40 CFR 191. In making this recommendation, the NAS addressed the common argument that beyond 10,000 years the uncertainties in repository performance assessment become too large to allow performance regulation. The NAS concluded that assessment of many aspects of repository performance is possible for much longer times, with an ultimate restriction determined by the long-term stability of the geologic environment, perhaps one million years at Yucca Mountain. The NAS found no scientific basis for limiting the risk standard to 10,000 years.[58]

The EPA, despite the congressional mandate of the Energy Policy Act to "set generally applicable standards…based upon and consistent with the findings and recommendations of the National Academy of Sciences," rejected the peak risk compliance time recommendation and retained the 10,000-year compliance time of its previous rules for generic repositories.[59]

In the preamble to its new standards for Yucca Mountain (40 CFR part 197) the EPA devotes considerable attention to its choice of compliance time.[60] It cites both "policy" issues and the technical reliability in performance projections for longer times. With respect to the policy issues, it emphasizes not only consistency with its earlier establishment of 10,000 years for geologic disposal in generic repositories but also its use of 10,000 years in the regulation of nonradioactive hazardous waste. It calls attention to the use of a 10,000-year period in international geologic disposal programs.

It is curious to note that in the aforementioned preamble to the Yucca Mountain standards the EPA appears to make two misinterpretations of the NAS recommendations. In the first of these, the EPA says, "Though NAS based its recommendation on scientific considerations, it recognized that such a decision also has policy aspects, and that we might select an alternative more consistent with previous Agency policy."[61] In fact NAS does not say anything about selecting an alternative more consistent with *previous* agency policy. The NAS does suggest that the EPA might choose to establish *consistent* policies for managing risks from the disposal of both long-lived hazardous nonradioactive materials and radioactive materials.[62] This cannot be taken as an endorsement of previous policy, as the NAS was fairly explicit in rejecting EPA's previous justification for a 10,000-year compliance time for radioactive waste.

With regard to a second misinterpretation, Nevada and the NRDC call attention in a Final Joint Brief submitted to the Court of Appeals to an "incorrect" statement in the EPA preamble to its final rule. The Final Joint Brief claims that the EPA says that the NAS report found "'no scientific basis' for identifying performance scenarios based on possible future climate regimes."[63] It goes on to say, "The report never made that claim. Instead, the reference to 'no scientific method' in the cited text…actually refers to speculation about the future of human society."[64]

Nevada and the NRDC in their briefs emphasize the congressional mandate in the Energy Policy Act to set standards to "protect health and safety" and dismiss EPA's policy justification. They claim that the 10,000-year time limit has never been scientifically justified. Nevada recalls that in 1985 the EPA, in explaining part 191's generic geologic repository rules' 10,000-year time frame, said, "Natural barriers are expected to provide the primary protection for longer time frames such as 100,000 years." It should be noted that the Total System Performance Assessments for the volcanic tuff geologic medium of Yucca Mountain do not support this expectation. A DOE performance assessment quoted by Nevada and the NRDC forecast the total peak dose rate to an average individual 20 kilometers from the repository to be as follows:

- 0.04 mrem/yr at 10,000 years
- 5 mrem/yr at 100,000 years
- 300 mrem/yr at 1,000,000 years[65]

The EPA standard in place at this time called for a limit of 15 mrem/yr for the first 10,000 years.

The government in one of its reply briefs tries to justify the 10,000-year compliance time by referring somewhat imprecisely to the Energy Policy Act's charge to NAS to address the question of whether it is possible to predict whether the repository's barriers would be breached as a result of human intrusion over a period of 10,000 years.[66] Nevada points out this has nothing to do with the repository performance in the absence of human intrusion, claiming no serious disagreement with the scientific unpredictability of human activity.[67]

In addition to the lawsuits filed by Nevada and co-petitioners, a rather different lawsuit against the EPA was filed by the Nuclear Energy Institute, a trade association for the nuclear power industry. This lawsuit challenges EPA's separate groundwater standard, which is in addition to the all-pathways individual protection standard. NEI claims that the Energy Policy Act does not authorize such a separate standard and asks the court to invalidate the groundwater standard and sever it from the remainder of the rule. The NEI's motivation in this challenge becomes more apparent after the EPA challenged NEI's standing to bring such a suit. In response to this challenge to its standing, NEI claims it has standing because its "members faced unnecessary DOE and NRC design, licensing, construction and operation activities." NEI also claims that the "groundwater standard increases the complexity of the repository's design and licensing, delaying its completion."[68] Delay in the repository will increase storage cost to NEI members.

NEVADA V. THE NUCLEAR REGULATORY COMMISSION

As mentioned previously, six months after the EPA issued its standards unique to Yucca Mountain, the Nuclear Regulatory Commission issued its rules specific to Yucca Mountain, 10 CFR part 63. Nevada filed two suits related to these rules.

Nevada's first suit challenges the NRC's 10 CFR part 63 Yucca Mountain licensing regulation, claiming that it violates the NWPA in several regards, particularly by failure to require that the repository's geologic setting form the primary barrier for the isolation of wastes.[69] This is the same issue that dominates Nevada's suit against the Department of Energy, Secretary Abraham, and President Bush, discussed above. Nevada argues in the present suit that 10 CFR part 63 authorizes the licensing of Yucca Mountain "even if DOE cannot demonstrate that Yucca's physical characteristics will provide the primary waste isolation capability, or that the repository has incorporated multiple, independent barriers to prevent release of wastes. Instead, Part 63 allows Yucca to be licensed on the basis of an assessment of how effectively the 'total' repository 'system' will work."[70] It should be noted, however, that the NAS recommended that the health standard be based on risk to individuals from releases from the repository, and hence on total system performance, not on the performance of specific subsystems such as engineered barriers or geological barriers. Thus one might conclude that the issue that the court would have to resolve here is whether the 1992 Energy Policy Act's mandate to follow NAS's recommendations supersedes requirements in the Nuclear Waste Policy Act.

Nevada also challenges the Yucca Mountain licensing regulation for precluding consideration of the period (hundreds of thousands of years rather than the 10,000-year period required for compliance) when the radiation dose to individuals in the accessible environment will be highest according to Total System Performance Assessments. It claims that this "wholly arbitrary feature of Part 63 is unlawful under provisions of NWPA, the AEA [Atomic Energy Act], and NEPA [National Environmental Policy Act] protecting public health and safety."[71] This compliance time issue is of course the same issue that forms much of the basis for the suit against the EPA discussed in the previous section. It is not clear whether the NRC had any option other than to follow the EPA's compliance time standard, as the Energy Policy Act requires it to modify, by rule, "its technical requirements and criteria...to be consistent with the [EPA's] Administrator's standards."[72]

A second, more technical, suit challenges the NRC's denial of a 2002 petition by Nevada asking the NRC to revise part 63.[73] The Court of Appeals has consolidated this second suit with the earlier suit against the NRC.

The NRC's Brief for the Federal Respondents first asks the court to dismiss the first suit on the grounds that Nevada failed to file it by an appropriate deadline.[74] (At issue here is whether the Hobbs Administrative Review Act 60-day limit after issuance of the rule deadline or an NWPA timeline is applicable.)[75] In the event the court were to fail to dismiss the case on timeline grounds, the NRC Brief for the Federal Respondents also challenges Nevada's interpretation of the NWPA's Section 112(a). It quotes from this section: "The Secretary [of Energy]…shall issue general guidelines for the recommendation of sites for repositories. Such guidelines shall specify detailed geologic considerations that shall be primary criteria for the selection of sites in various geologic media." The NRC says that this shows that this statutory obligation is imposed only on the DOE.[76] Furthermore, the NRC argues that "as a matter of logic, that geology should be primary in choosing sites for characterization does not mean that it should be *the* primary barrier against the release of radiation."[77]

THE COURT HEARS ORAL ARGUMENT

Petitions to courts of appeal are assigned to three-judge panels drawn from a larger panel of judges in a particular jurisdiction. The NWPA had specified that any appeal would have to be directed to the Court of Appeals for the District of Columbia. The court decided to combine all of the Yucca Mountain cases and hear them at the same time. The panel for the Yucca Mountain cases comprised Judge Harry T. Edwards, appointed by President Carter; Karen LeCraft Henderson, appointed by President G. H. W. Bush; and David Tatel, appointed by President Clinton. The panel heard oral argument on January 14, 2004. The nominally three-hour period stretched to three and one-half hours.

The questions by the judges indicated their leaning on some of the issues. Both Edwards and Tatel repeatedly asked the government why the EPA rejected the NAS recommendation for a much longer compliance time than 10,000 years. Judge Edwards asserted that the NAS was "absolutely clear…that 10,000 years is incorrect."[78] Although at least two of the judges appeared sympathetic with Nevada and the NRDC's arguments on the EPA standards, they seemed unsympathetic to Nevada's constitutional argument that Congress acted unfairly and infringed on state sovereignty in passing the joint resolution overriding Nevada's veto. Nevada had also challenged a DOE suitability guideline that did not require the primacy of geologic isolation. Judge Edwards indicated that this challenge had become moot with the passage of the 2002 joint resolution.[79] Newspaper coverage of this case, like most court cases, gave more coverage to the filing of the case and the verdict than legal arguments presented during the trial.[80]

THE COURT DECIDES

On July 9, 2004, the Federal D.C. Court of Appeals issued its much-anticipated decision on all the Yucca Mountain petitions in a 100-page unanimous opinion.[81] Most of the cases under consideration were initiated by the State of Nevada, with participation in some cases by Clark County, the City of Las Vegas, the NRDC and other environmental organizations, and the NEI. Although the government respondents (DOE, NRC, EPA, president) prevailed in almost all of the cases, the one they lost will have serious consequences for the Yucca Mountain repository. It will surely delay the licensing and opening, and may even call into question the viability, of a repository at Yucca Mountain.

Briefly, the court rejected Nevada's challenges concerning the primacy of the geologic barrier, the use of Total System Performance Assessments that did not break out geologic and engineered barrier contributions separately, the constitutionality of congressional action designating Nevada alone to take waste ("Tenth Amendment" issue), and the EPA's establishment of a separate groundwater standard (NEI case). It ruled that Nevada's complaints about the site-selection-related actions of executive branch officials, federal agencies, the secretary of energy, and the president were moot as a consequence of the subsequent 2002 congressional resolution approving Yucca Mountain.

The court, however, rejected the EPA's 10,000-year compliance period as clearly not consistent with the NAS recommendations. The 1992 Energy Policy Act requires that the EPA standards were to be "based upon and consistent with" NAS recommendations. As discussed above, the NAS had concluded that there was no scientific basis for a 10,000-year compliance period and recommended that compliance assessment be conducted for the time when the greatest risk occurs. DOE models indicate that the largest exposures will not occur until after 100,000 years. The court "vacated" the EPA and NRC regulations insofar as they include a 10,000-year compliance period. The court said the EPA would either have to come up with (and get court approval of) a new standard or secure congressional action negating the requirement of consistency with NAS recommendations.

We first review, in slightly more detail, the issues on which Nevada et al. lost. In an earlier section we have outlined a number of site suitability issues that Nevada claims the DOE, the secretary of energy, and the president did not properly take into account in their actions with regard to Yucca Mountain. In particular, the role of engineered barriers versus geologic barriers and the implications of fast water paths were at issue. The "primacy" of geologic barriers came up again in an NRC suit discussed above. The court asserted that

> Nevada's challenges to DOE's site-suitability criteria, the Secretary's recommendation, the FEIS [Final Environmental Impact Statement], and the President's recommendation are all directed to the fundamental question of whether the Yucca site was properly selected for development as a repository. Congress's enactment of the 2002 veto override Resolution, however, has rendered the question moot. The Resolution affirmatively and finally approved the Yucca site for a repository, thus bringing the site-selection process to a conclusion. No determination as to the soundness of the administrative and executive actions leading up to the Resolution's enactment would undo the Resolution's binding effects.[82]

Thus the wording of the resolution did more than simply override Nevada's veto. It led to a finality of the site selection process that allowed the court to avoid such technical issues as the fast-path water transport implied by the Cl-36 studies and the role of engineered barriers. The court's rather strong statement quoted above perhaps goes beyond what some members of Congress thought they were voting on. Senator Bingaman said during the floor debate that "a vote for the motion to proceed on the resolution is not a final vote to put nuclear waste in Yucca Mountain. It is a vote to let the technical experts at the Nuclear Regulatory Commission decide whether Yucca Mountain is, in fact, safe."[83]

With respect to the constitutional challenge discussed above, the court rejected the government's first line of defense based on the earlier 1991 *Nevada v. Watkins* case. Rather, the court ruled on the merits of the challenge. Central to the court's conclusion is that the repository is to be located on federal land. It calls attention to the Property Clause of the U.S. Constitution providing that "Congress shall have Power to dispose of and make all needful Rules and Regulations respecting the Territory or other Property belonging to the United States."[84] With respect to Nevada's claim that the Constitution generally mandates fair and equal regard when it decides to use federal property in a manner that imposes "a unique burden on a particular State," the court found no constitutional basis for this claimed mandate.[85]

We return now to the issue where the court ruled in favor of Nevada et al., the EPA's 10,000-year compliance time standard. This issue has been discussed extensively earlier in this chapter. We do not find the court's decision on this issue surprising, as the NAS report seemed quite clear and explicit in rejecting a 10,000-year compliance time. Indeed, the court stated that the EPA "unabashedly rejected NAS's findings, and then went on to promulgate a dramatically different standard, one that the Academy had expressly rejected."[86]

As an alternative to the EPA coming up with a new standard, the court offered the somewhat surprising suggestion that the EPA could seek congressional approval for overturning the requirement of consistency with NAS recommendations.[87] Such congressional action seems problematical, although the Senate did recently, on a very close vote, approve reclassification of high-level waste at Savannah River, allowing simpler and cheaper but perhaps not as safe disposal techniques. (This reclassification is dependent on successful reconciliation with a somewhat different House bill.)

There are also difficulties with regard to creating a new standard with a longer compliance period. The DOE stated in its Final Environmental Impact Statement as well as in the Yucca Mountain Science and Engineering Report that releases in the 100,000- to one million–year time frame would significantly exceed the EPA's 15 mrem/yr allowable individual dose. It might be difficult for the DOE to engineer barriers that would bring the projected dose down to the 15-mrem level at the time of peak dose. Alternatively the EPA could consider a larger maximum individual dose. The NAS was considerably less specific in suggesting what the dose (or risk) limit should be as compared with its compliance time recommendation. (The NAS prefers to use risk rather than dose when considering health protection. Using current dose-risk relations, a dose of 20 mrem/yr corresponds to a health effect risk of one chance in 100,000 per year of developing a fatal cancer.) The NAS did not directly recommend a level of acceptable risk, commenting that what is acceptable is a public policy rather than a scientific issue. It does refer to risk levels used previously by nuclear regulators both within and outside of the United States. It goes on to suggest that a risk level in the one part in a million to ten parts in a million per year range might be a reasonable starting point in drawing up a standard. The 15 mrem/yr limit in the present EPA standard corresponds to about 7.5 parts in a million, near the high end of this risk range.

The reaction to the court's decision was mixed, not surprisingly considering the divergence of interests regarding this issue. The immediate response of Bob Loux, head of Nevada's Agency for Nuclear Projects, was, "I believe this effectively kills the process. I think everyone will recognize that its futile to proceed because they can't write a standard Yucca Mountain can meet." Nevada's Attorney General Brian Sandoval said the decision means "Yucca Mountain is dead."[88] On the other hand, Spencer Abraham, secretary of energy, said he was confident the government could move ahead now that the court has "dismissed all challenges to the site selection. Our scientific basis for the Yucca Mountain project is sound." He indicated that the DOE would work with the EPA and Congress to "determine appropriate steps to address" the call for a new radiation standard.[89]

Editorial reaction to the court decision was also mixed. The *Washington Post* expressed skepticism that Congress would address the issue.[90] The *New York Times* asserted that "Congress needs to change the law and allow the EPA to set the compliance period at 10,000 years, roughly twice as long as recorded human history."[91] Western U.S. newspapers were less strongly supportive of changing the law. The *Denver Post* and the *San Francisco Chronicle* expressed the need for further scientific consideration in their editorials.

Court of Appeals decisions can be appealed within 45 days of the issuance of a decision. A rehearing by the full panel of court judges can be requested. It was generally thought that both sides might appeal the parts of the decisions that went against their positions. But after the deadline passed, only one entity had filed an appeal. The Nuclear Energy Institute, an advocacy organization for the nuclear energy industry, filed a petition asking for a rehearing on the EPA's compliance standard. In particular, the NEI challenged the court's rejection of a 10,000-year compliance time. It also challenged the court's decision to let the separate groundwater standard remain in place. One consequence of the NEI's appeal was that the EPA standard would remain in place until the appeal was resolved. This might have given the NRC the necessary authority to accept a license application from the DOE, a step that had been in some doubt since the court's decision.

NEI's appeal, however, was dealt with very promptly. On September 1, 2004, the court rejected the appeal, simply stating, "The petition for rehearing is denied." This meant that their July 9 ruling would take effect on September 8, 2004. The only remaining legal option was to take the case to the U.S. Supreme Court. The deadline for such an appeal was November 29, 2004, and no appeals were filed. Although the NEI had indicated earlier that it might appeal to the Supreme Court, its spokesman, Mitch Singer, said that its attorneys had concluded that the chance of the case being heard was not great. Singer also said that it was not yet decided whether NEI will lobby Congress to revise the radiation standard.[92]

When questioned about the government decision not to appeal the court's decision, the DOE's spokesman, Joe Davis, said, "Our general belief is that the framework the court decision required is a workable deal. Our best way to proceed is not to engage in litigation but to allow the Environmental Protection Agency to develop a regulatory response. Whatever standard they come up with, our commitment is to ensure the repository will meet the standard."[93]

The State of Nevada continued its challenge to Yucca Mountain–related activities. On September 8, 2004, Nevada filed a new suit with the D.C. Court of Appeals claiming that the DOE did not follow federal environmental policy when it proposed building a railroad from near Caliente to Yucca Mountain.[94] This particular suit is somewhat surprising, as the choice of this route (Caliente Corridor) and mode (rail) would seem to have the least impact on the populous area around Las Vegas. It is consistent with the general posture of the state, which has used any means possible to slow down or stop Yucca Mountain, including cutting off the water supply for site characterization activities. This posture may have compromised its effectiveness in challenging major controversial decisions.

NOTES

1. Terrence R. Fehner and Jack M. Holl, "Department of Energy 1977–1994: A Summary History," Department of Energy (Washington, DC: Office of Scientific and Technical Information, 1994), 60.

2. U.S. Court of Appeals, District of Columbia Circuit, Case no. 01-1516, 2001.

3. Ibid., Case no. 01-1425, 2001.

4. Ibid., Case no. 01-1426, 2001.

5. Ibid., Case nos. 01-1258, -1268, and -1295, 2001.

6. Ibid., Case no. 02-1077, 2002.

7. Ibid., Case no. 02-1116, 2002.

8. On the Nuclear Waste Technical Review Board, see David Bodansky, *Nuclear Energy: Principles, Practices and Prospects*, 2nd ed. (New York: Springer-Verlag, 2004), 305; on rainwater travel, see S. S. Levy, J. T. Fabryka-Martin, P. R. Dixon, B. Liu, H. J. Turin, and A. V. Wolfsberg, "Chlorine-36 Investigations of Groundwater Infiltration in the Exploratory Studies Facility at Yucca Mountain, Nevada," in *Scientific Basis for Nuclear Waste Management XX—Symposium*, ed. W. J. Gray and I. R. Triay (Pittsburgh: Materials Research Society, 1997), 901–8.

9. House Committee on Energy and Commerce, "Report 107-425," accompanying H.J. Res. 87, 107th Cong., 2nd Sess. (May 1, 2002).

10. U.S. Department of Energy, *Yucca Mountain Science and Engineering Report Rev. 1: Technical Information Supporting Site Recommendation Consideration* (DOE/ RW-0539-1; Washington, DC: U.S. Department of Energy, Office of Civilian Radioactive Waste Management, February 2002), available at www.ocrwm.doe.gov/documents/ ser_b/index.htm.

11. J. B. Paces, Z. E. Peterman, L. A. Neymark, G. J. Nimz, M. Gascoyne, and B. D. Marshall, "Summary of Chlorine-36 Validation Studies at Yucca Mountain, Nevada," in *Proceedings of the 10th International High-Level Radioactive Waste Management Conference (IHLRWM)*, March 30–April 2, 2003, Las Vegas (La Grange Park, IL: American Nuclear Society, 2003), 348.

12. Michael Corradini, Chairman of the Nuclear Waste Technical Review Board, letter to Margaret Chu, Director of the Office of Civilian Radioactive Waste Management, March 5, 2003, available at www.nwtrb.gov/corr/mlc006.pdf.

13. State of Nevada et al., "Petitioners' Opening Brief: Petition for Review from Final Decisions, Actions, and Failures to Act of United States Department of Energy and Final Decisions and Actions of the President of the United States," *State of Nevada, et al., Petitioners, v. United States Department of Energy, et al., Respondents*, December 2, 2002, available at www.state.nv.us/nucwaste/news2002/nv021203.pdf.

14. Ibid., 20.

15. Ibid., 22.

16. On Nevada's action, see ibid., 26; for the DOE's confirmation, see U.S. Department of Energy, "Use of the 10 CFR Part 960 Siting Guidelines in Evaluating the Suitability of the Yucca Mountain Site," *Federal Register* 60, no. 18 (September 14, 1995): 47738.

17. State of Nevada et al., "Petitioners' Opening Brief," December 2, 2002, 27–28.

18. Ibid., 30.

19. Ibid., 31.

20. Bob Miller, Governor, State of Nevada, letter to Bill Richardson, Secretary of Energy, December 4, 1998, available at www.state.nv.us/nucwaste/yucca/nuctome1.htm.

21. State of Nevada et al., "Petitioners' Opening Brief," December 2, 2002, 34.

22. Miller, letter to Bill Richardson.

23. U.S. Department of Energy, "General Guidelines for the Preliminary Screening of Potential Sites for Nuclear Waste Repositories," 10 CFR part 960, *Federal Register* 66, no. 220 (November 14, 2001): 57304; U.S. Department of Energy, "Yucca Mountain Site Suitability Guidelines," 10 CFR part 963, *Federal Register* 66, no. 220 (November 14, 2001): 57298.

24. State of Nevada et al., "Petitioners' Opening Brief," December 2, 2002, 41–42.

25. Ibid., 42.

26. Yucca Mountain Repository Development, Senate Committee on Energy and Natural Resources, *Hearings on S.J. Res. 34,* 107th Cong., 2nd Sess. (May 16, 2002), 18.

27. On the occupational exposure limit, see U.S. Nuclear Regulatory Commission, "Standard for Protection against Radiation: Occupational Dose Limits," 10 CFR 20.1201, *Federal Register* 56 (May 21, 1991): 23396; on the limit outside repository boundaries, see U.S. Environmental Protection Agency, "Public Health and Environmental Radiation Protection Standards for Yucca Mountain, NV, 40 CFR Part 197, Final Rule," *Federal Register* 66, no. 114 (June 13, 2001): pt. 197.20, 32134.

28. U.S. Department of Energy, *Yucca Mountain Science and Engineering Report Rev. 1,* fig. 4-187.

29. Nuclear Information and Resource Service, press release, November 17, 1998, available at www.nirs.org/press/11-17-1998/1.

30. U.S. Department of Justice, "Brief for the Respondents: On Petitions for Review from Decisions of United States Department of Energy and Decision of the President of the United States," *State of Nevada, et al., Petitioners, v. United States Department of Energy, et al., Respondents,* February 2003, available at www.state.nv.us/nucwaste/legal/nl030224cons.pdf.

31. Ibid., 11.

32. State of Nevada et al., "Petitioners' Reply Brief: Petition for Review from Final Decisions, Actions, and Failures to Act of United States Department of Energy and Final Decisions and Actions of the President of the United States," *State of Nevada, et al., Petitioners, v. United States Department of Energy, et al., Respondents,* May 13, 2003, 1, available at www.state.nv.us/nucwaste/news2003/pdf/nvag030514_replybrief.pdf.

33. U.S. Department of Justice, "Brief for the Respondents," 12.

34. Ibid., 14.

35. Ibid., 12.

36. Ibid., 12.

37. Ibid., 59.

38. The Energy Policy Act of 1992, P.L. 102-486, 102nd Cong., 1st Sess. (October 24, 1992), Title VIII—High-Level Radioactive Waste, Sec. 801 USC 10141.

39. State of Nevada et al., "Petitioners' Reply Brief," May 13, 2003, 31.

40. U.S. Department of Justice, "Brief for the Respondents," 63.

41. State of Nevada et al., "Petitioners' Reply Brief," May 13, 2003, 38–39.

42. U.S. Court of Appeals, District of Columbia Circuit, Case no. 03-1009, 2003.

43. Akhil Reed Amar, *The Bill of Rights* (New Haven: Yale University Press, 1998), 119.

44. *Nevada v. Watkins*, 914 F. 2d 1545 (9th Cir., 1990).

45. *Nevada v. Watkins*, 501 U.S. 1225 (1991).

46. Yucca Mountain Repository Site Approval Act, Public Law No. 107-200, 116 Stat. 735 (2002).

47. State of Nevada et al., "Petitioners' Opening Brief: Petition for Review of Joint Resolution Designating Yucca Mountain, Nevada as Nuclear Waste Repository Site," *State of Nevada, et al., Petitioners, v. United States of America, et al., Respondents*, May 1, 2003, 33, available at www.state.nv.us/nucwaste/news2003/pdf/nvag03-1009.pdf.

48. Ibid., 54.

49. U.S. Department of Justice, "Initial Brief for the Respondents: On Petition for Review of the Yucca Mountain Development Act, Pub. L. 107-200," *State of Nevada, et al., v. United States of America, et al., Respondents*, June 2003, 22, available at www.state.nv.us/nucwaste/news2003/pdf/nvag030610.pdf.

50. Ibid., 28.

51. Ibid., 58.

52. State of Nevada et al., "Petitioners' Reply Brief: Petition for Review of Joint Resolution Designating Yucca Mountain, Nevada as Nuclear Waste Repository Site," *State of Nevada, et al., Petitioners, v. United States of America, et al., Respondents*, June 26, 2003, 30, available at www.state.nv.us/nucwaste/news2003/pdf/nvag030626.pdf.

53. U.S. National Research Council, Committee on Technical Bases for Yucca Mountain Standards, *Technical Bases for Yucca Mountain Standards* (Washington, DC: National Academy Press, 1995).

54. U.S. Environmental Protection Agency, "Public Health and Environmental Radiation Protection Standards for Yucca Mountain, NV, 40 CFR Part 197, Final Rule," *Federal Register* 66, no. 114 (June 13, 2001): 32074–135.

55. State of Nevada and Natural Resources Defense Council, "Joint Brief of Petitioners State of Nevada and Natural Resources Defense Council, et al.," *State of Nevada, et al., Petitioners, v. United States, et al., Respondents; Natural Resources Defense Council, et al., Petitioners, v. Christine Todd Whitman, et al., Respondents; Nuclear Energy Institute, Inc., Petitioner, v. United States, et al., Respondents*, May 3, 2002, available at www.state.nv.us/nucwaste/legal/epa/File%201%20-%2005_03_02.pdf.

56. U.S. Nuclear Regulatory Commission, "Disposal of High-Level Radioactive Wastes in Geological Repositories Technical Criteria, Final Rule," *Federal Register* 48 (June 21, 1983): 28194.

57. U.S. National Research Council, Committee on Technical Bases for Yucca Mountain Standards, *Technical Bases for Yucca Mountain Standards*, 55.

58. Ibid.

59. Energy Policy Act of 1992, Sec. 801.

60. U.S. Environmental Protection Agency, "Public Health and Environmental Radiation Protection Standards for Yucca Mountain, NV," 32096–99.

61. Ibid., 32099.

62. U.S. National Research Council, Committee on Technical Bases for Yucca Mountain Standards, *Technical Bases for Yucca Mountain Standards*, 56.

63. State of Nevada and Natural Resources Defense Council, "Final Joint Brief of Petitioners State of Nevada and NRDC et al.," *State of Nevada, et al., Petitioners, v. United States, et al., Respondents; Natural Resources Defense Council, et al., Petitioners, v. Christine Todd Whitman, et al., Respondents; Nuclear Energy Institute, Inc., Petitioner, v. United States, et al., Respondents*, October 1, 2002, 45, available at www.state.nv.us/nucwaste/legal/epa/File%206%20-%2010_01_02.pdf; U.S. Environmental Protection Agency, "Public Health and Environmental Radiation Protection Standards for Yucca Mountain, NV," 32124.

64. State of Nevada and Natural Resources Defense Council, "Final Joint Brief of Petitioners State of Nevada and NRDC et al.," 45.

65. Ibid., 40.

66. U.S. Department of Justice and U.S. Environmental Protection Agency, "Brief of Respondent, United States Environmental Protection Agency: On Petition for Review of Final Rule of the United States Environmental Protection Agency," October 1, 2002, 41, available at www.state.nv.us/nucwaste/legal/epa/File%207%20-10_01_02.pdf.

67. State of Nevada and Natural Resources Defense Council, "Final Reply Brief of Petitioners State of Nevada and NRDC et al.," *State of Nevada, et al., Petitioners, v. United States, et al., Respondents; Natural Resources Defense Council, et al., Petitioners, v. Christine Todd Whitman, et al., Respondents; Nuclear Energy Institute, Inc., Petitioner, v.*

United States, et al., Respondents, October 1, 2002, 21–22, available at www.state.nv.us/nucwaste/legal/epa/File%205%20-%2010_01_02.pdf.

68. Nuclear Energy Institute, Inc., "Reply Brief of Petitioner—Nuclear Energy Institute, Inc.: On Petition for Review of Final Regulation Issued by the U.S. Environmental Protection Agency," *Nuclear Energy Institute, Inc., Natural Resources Defense Council, and State of Nevada, Petitioners, v. United States Environmental Protection Agency, Respondents*, October 1, 2002, 1, 5, available at www.state.nv.us/nucwaste/legal/epa/File%204%20-%2010_01_02.pdf.

69. U.S. Court of Appeals, District of Columbia Circuit, Case no. 02-1116.

70. State of Nevada et al., "Petitioners' Opening Brief: Petition for Review from Final Decisions and Actions of United States Nuclear Regulatory Commission," *State of Nevada, et al., Petitioners, v. United States Nuclear Regulatory Commission, Respondent*, January 27, 2003, 4, available at www.state.nv.us/nucwaste/news2003/pdf/nvago30128final.pdf.

71. Ibid., 38.

72. Energy Policy Act of 1992, 801(b)(1).

73. U.S. Court of Appeals, District of Columbia Circuit, Case no. 03-1058.

74. U.S Nuclear Regulatory Commission, "Brief for the Federal Respondents: On Petition to Review Two Orders of the U.S. Nuclear Regulatory Commission," *State of Nevada, et al., Petitioners, v. U.S. Nuclear Regulatory Commission and the United States of America, Respondents*, April 9, 2003, available at www.state.nv.us/nucwaste/legal/nrc/nrc030409.pdf.

75. See United States Code 28 USC 2342.

76. U.S. Nuclear Regulatory Commission, "Brief for the Federal Respondents," 45.

77. Ibid., 46.

78. Suzanne Struglinski, "Judges Question EPA's Yucca Standard," *Las Vegas Sun*, January 14, 2004, available at www.lasvegassun.com/sunbin/stories/text/2004/jan/14/516175028.html.

79. Suzanne Struglinski, "No Knockout on Yucca," *Las Vegas Sun*, January 15, 2004, available at www.lasvegassun.com/sunbin/stories/sun/2004/jan/15/516182392.html.

80. Lynn Mather, "Courts and American Popular Culture," in Kermit L. Hall and Kevin T. Mc Currie, *The Judicial Branch* (New York: Oxford University Press, 2005), ch. 9, 243.

81. Court of Appeals for the District of Columbia, Opinion of the Court, July 9, 2004, available at http://pacer.cadc.uscourts.gov/docs/common/opinions/200407/01-1258a.pdf.

82. Ibid., 90.

83. Senator Bingaman, *Congressional Record–Senate*, July 9, 2002: S6454.

84. Court of Appeals for the District of Columbia, Opinion of the Court, 81–82.

85. State of Nevada et al., "Petitioners' Opening Brief," May 1, 2003, 54; Court of Appeals for the District of Columbia, Opinion of the Court, 79.

86. Court of Appeals for the District of Columbia, Opinion of the Court, 26.

87. Ibid., 31.

88. Suzanne Struglinski, "Yucca in for Long Delay: Radiation Standards Too Low," *Las Vegas Sun*, July 9, 2004, available at www.lasvegassun.com/sunbin/stories/text/2004/jul/09/517149080.html.

89. Juliet Eilperin, "New Plan Ordered for Yucca Mountain," *Washington Post*, July 10, 2004: A4.

90. Editorial, "Yucca Mountain," *Washington Post*, July 11, 2004: B6.

91. "Roadblock at Yucca Mountain," *New York Times*, August 23, 2004: A22.

92. Suzanne Struglinski, "Yucca Standard Won't Be Appealed," *Las Vegas Sun*, November 29, 2004, available at www.lasvegassun.com/sunbin/stories/text/2004/nov/29/517899896.html.

93. Steve Tetreault, "U.S. Government to Sit Out Challenge of Radiation Ruling," *Las Vegas Review-Journal*, August 24, 2004: 1B.

94. Suzanne Struglinski, "Yucca Standard Won't Be Appealed," *Las Vegas Sun*, September 8, 2004.

11

Transportation of Spent Fuel
to Yucca Mountain

The 63,000 metric tons of civilian spent fuel and 7,000 metric tons of defense waste slated for Yucca Mountain are presently located in 39 states. It is envisioned that this material will be transported over a period of 24 years. All of the waste to be transported is in solid form. The fuel from civilian power reactors will be pellets in fuel rod assemblies, and the defense waste will be mostly vitrified waste from reprocessing. These waste forms will be transported in special steel casks, as discussed in more detail later in this chapter. The casks are designed both to provide radiation shielding to protect drivers and the public and to provide structural integrity in case of an accident. As will also be discussed later, the Department of Energy (DOE) envisions that the principal mode of transport will be by rail, although some truck shipments will also be required from sites without rail access. The costs of transportation are to be paid from the Nuclear Waste Fund authorized by the Nuclear Waste Policy Act of 1982. This fund is based on a tax on utilities producing nuclear power.

The transportation of spent fuel has been a subject of a great deal of concern. There are numerous reasons for this. One is that there is a considerably larger number of people who can come into relatively close contact with radioactive material during transportation than who live close to a reactor or to a possible repository site. Second, there are constant reminders of the possibility of truck or rail accidents by the frequent occurrence of nonnuclear transport accidents. Another reason is that transport takes place in a venue with unlimited public access, in contrast to reactors or disposal sites. This access has made transportation a popular target for antinuclear protestors, particularly in Europe, where considerable amounts of radioactive material have been transported to and from reprocessing plants. Since the World Trade Center attacks of September 11, 2001, the possibility of terrorist attacks during transport have introduced a heightened element of concern in the United States. There is also the possibility of a serious enough accident to cause contamination that would be expensive to remediate. Estimates of the cleanup cost range up to $2 billion for a severe accident in an urban area.[1]

The Nevada congressional delegation has tried to increase the awareness of the risks of terrorists attacking nuclear waste shipments. They have exaggerated the number of shipments, speaking of "more than 108,000 shipments."[2] (This estimate assumes transport of the entire projected national inventory of 119,000 metric tons of heavy metal rather than the authorized limit of 70,000 metric tons.)[3] A transportation accident in Nevada could have an impact on its tourist industry. More than half of the revenue of the State of Nevada comes from tourism. In late 2001 the state hired a public relations agency to run a national public information campaign to alert citizens of other states to the risk from transporting waste to Yucca Mountain.[4] The Environmental Working Group, a Washington, D.C.–based organization challenging the DOE's Yucca Mountain plans, built a website that allowed users to learn how close nuclear waste might pass by their neighborhoods if shipped to Nevada. The website project was supported in part by a $200,000 grant from *Las Vegas Sun* editor Brian Greenspan.[5] It was based in part on possible truck and rail routes in the Yucca Mountain Environmental Impact Statement. Although Clark County (the seat of Las Vegas) and Nevada's governor and congressional delegation oppose a repository at Yucca Mountain, some of the rural counties are less opposed. Nye County, the host county for the repository, is neutral about the repository. Lincoln County, to the east of Nye County, has in the past supported hosting a site for the transfer of rail shipments to heavy-haul trucks.[6]

There was considerable effort by states in the mid-1990s to select preferred highway and rail routes and to identify the infrastructure necessary to accommodate and monitor shipments. It was thought at this time that Yucca Mountain might begin to accept waste in 1998. With the announcement some years ago that the earliest time that waste might be accepted would be 2010 there has been less activity in this area. The U.S. Department of Transportation (DOT) has regulations governing highway routing, which require carriers to use "preferred" routes that include the Interstate Highway System. State routing agencies, however, have the option of designating alternative routes that do not necessarily involve Interstate

System routes. Iowa and Nebraska designated alternate routes before 1997. Colorado may not have a viable alternative route. The Nuclear Regulatory Commission (NRC) requires the shipper of spent fuel to provide written notification to the governor (or the governor's designee) seven days in advance of any shipment through the state. Schedule and routes are not announced publicly and are disseminated only on a "need to know" basis. Armed escorts through heavily populated areas and visual surveillance of shipments during stops are required.[7] The DOE is required to provide technical assistance and funds to states for training public safety officials of the appropriate local government units. It does not provide for equipment or staff costs. Much of the states' planning was done under the auspices of regional sections of the Council of State Governments. Fairly detailed reports have been issued for the Midwest and northeastern regions.[8]

In late 2001 or early 2002 the DOE issued a brochure entitled "Spent Nuclear Fuel Transportation."[9] This is the document that Senator Frank Murkowski brandished on the floor of the Senate during the debate on overriding the Nevada veto of Yucca Mountain. The report recounts the past history of safe transport of nuclear materials to the Waste Isolation Pilot Plant and elsewhere. It also illustrates the puncture, free-drop, thermal, and immersion criteria transportation casks must satisfy (see below). In contrast to Nevada's reference to 108,000 truck shipments, this report projects 4,300 shipments over 24 years. This much smaller number implies an average of 16 tons of spent fuel per shipment and hence implies predominantly shipment by multicar trains.

The NRC and the DOT share regulatory responsibility for the shipment of radioactive materials. The DOT regulates carriers and transport operations while a radioactive material package is in transit. The NRC is responsible for overseeing the design, manufacture, use, and maintenance of shipping containers (casks) for spent nuclear fuel and for certain other types of radioactive material shipments. Regulations limit radiation levels to a dose rate of 10 millirems per hour at a distance of about 6.5 feet from the edge of the truck bed or railcar to which a cask is attached.[10] To put this number in perspective, one would have to stand at this distance for more than ten hours to receive the same amount of radiation as the extra yearly radiation a resident of a city at an elevation of 5,000 feet gets from cosmic rays, radioactivity in the surroundings, and radionuclides deposited internally, compared with a resident of a city at sea level.[11] Spent fuel casks are designed to be leak-tight and to be able to withstand specific insults in accident scenarios. For a cask to be certified,

> package designers must demonstrate to the NRC that the cask can survive a sequence of four hypothetical accident tests:
>
> > 1) Impact: a 30-foot drop onto an unyielding surface in a direction to cause maximum damage (equal to 30 mph speed);
> >
> > 2) Puncture: a 3-foot drop onto a 6-inch diameter steel shaft to cause maximum damage;
> >
> > 3) Fire: exposure to an all-engulfing fuel fire (1475°F) for 30 minutes; and
> >
> > 4) Submersion: a tested cask is held underwater at 3-feet depth for 8 hours (relates to criticality control as water is a neutron moderator and enhances the potential for a nuclear chain reaction).
>
> After the tests, the external dose rate may not increase to more than 1 rem/hr at 3.3 feet from the cask surface.[12]

Again to put the latter dose rate into perspective, one would have to remain within 3.3 feet of the damaged cask for at least 500 hours to receive a lethal dose.

Regulations do not require that this demonstration must be performed physically. Up until now only simulations have been performed on designs of casks expected to be used in spent fuel transport to Yucca Mountain. This has been a matter of concern, and the chairman of the NRC, testifying before a Senate committee on May 23, 2002, said that the commission plans "full-scale testing of a cask to confirm computer models of cask response to severe accident conditions."[13] Other concerns are whether the 30 miles per hour speed specification on an unyielding surface (equivalent to a head-on collision of two vehicles each going 30 miles per hour) is too low and whether the fire exposure temperature specification is too low (a recent tunnel fire in Baltimore had sustained temperatures higher than 1,475°F). The chairman mentioned the latter incident when reporting that the commission was analyzing appropriate national transportation accidents.[14] The submersion test mentioned above (three-foot depth) does not address the consequences of an accident where a cask falls into much deeper water during barge transport. A separate regulation requires that casks be able to withstand pressures equivalent to a water depth of greater than 600 feet.[15]

In March 2000 the NRC released a new risk assessment study, "Re-examination of Spent Fuel Shipment Risk Estimates."[16] In 1977 the NRC· had issued "Final Environmental Statement on the Transport of Radioactive Materials by Air and Other Modes."[17] The 2000 study obtained estimates for the risk of both railway and highway shipments that are lower than those estimated in 1977.[18] When one takes into account the fact that many fewer rail than truck shipments are required to move all the spent fuel, the rail risk is much less than the truck risk. The authors of the study report concluded that "spent fuel transportation regulations adequately protect public health and safety."[19]

As part of the process for possible presidential approval and congressional review, the DOE prepared a Final Environmental Impact Statement (FEIS) for Yucca Mountain.[20] It was released in February 2002. This assessment dealt with the transportation of spent fuel to the repository as well as impacts from the presence of the fuel in the repository. The DOE did not attempt at this time to determine exact modes and routes but, rather, to establish a range of impacts for sample scenarios. (The State of Nevada, Clark County, and the City of Las Vegas have challenged in court DOE's failure to formally select preferred modes and routes in the FEIS.)[21] Two kinds of scenarios were considered in the FEIS, a mostly legal-weight truck scenario and a mostly rail scenario. For the mostly legal-weight truck scenario there would be 53,000 shipments (2,200 annually assuming a 24-year transportation campaign), whereas the mostly rail scenario would involve approximately 10,700 shipments (450 annually).[22] As there is no rail access to Yucca Mountain or to some reactor sites at the present time, for the mostly rail scenario either a branch line would have to be built or the material would have to be transferred to heavy-haul trucks somewhere along an existing rail line. Both of these possibilities were included in the range of possible impacts presented. The topography of Nevada and the layout of the Interstate Highway System led to several scenarios involving transport through or on the outskirts of Las Vegas.

The impacts evaluated in the FEIS include both those from incident-free transport and those from accidents. Incident-free impacts arise from exposure to workers and the public from the small fraction of radiation penetrating through the transport cask walls. Impacts of accidents include fatalities not necessarily associated with the release of radioactivity as well as from radiation exposure involving a loss of shielding and the release of

TABLE 11.1. Estimated National Transportation Impacts

IMPACT	TRUCK	RAIL
Incident-free latent cancer fatalities		
Involved worker	12	3
Public[a]	3	1
Latent cancer fatalities from accidents		
Public	0.00023	0.00045
Traffic fatalities[b]	5	3
Latent cancer fatalities from maximum		
foreseeable accident	0.55	5
Frequency of occurrence of most serious		
Accidents per year	2.2×10^{-7}	2.8×10^{-7}

Note: The values shown are for 24 years of operation, and for both a mostly legal-weight truck scenario and a mostly rail scenario.

Source: U.S. Department of Energy, Final Environmental Impact Statement for a Geologic Repository for the Disposal of Spent Nuclear Fuel and High-Level Radioactive Waste at Yucca Mountain, Nye, County, Nevada (DOE/EIS-0250; Washington, DC: U.S. Department of Energy, Office of Civilian Radioactive Waste Management, 2002), vol. 1, sec. 6, tab. 6-1, available at www.ocrwm.doe.gov/documents/feis_2/vol_1/ch_06 index1_6.htm.

[a]These latent cancer fatalities would result from very low doses to a very large population.

[b]This does not include 10 to 17 fatalities that could occur from repository workers commuting and transporting construction materials to the repository.

some of the contents of the cask. The estimates presented in the FEIS are reproduced in Table 11-1.

Perhaps surprisingly, the incident-free radiological impacts far exceed (by factors of 1,000 or more) those from radiological causes associated with accidents. The estimated latent cancer fatalities for workers and the public of 15 for the mostly legal-weight truck scenario and four for the mostly rail scenario can be compared with the expected nonradiological accident fatalities associated with these shipments of five and three, respectively.

As a worst-case scenario, the FEIS also presented (last two lines of Table 11-1) the impact of the most serious reasonably foreseeable accident. Although such an accident is thought to only have a probability of two to three chances in ten million of occurring per year, it could result in up to five fatalities. Again, the number of fatalities would be similar to the normal traffic hazards of 53,000 truck shipments or 10,700 rail shipments of nonradioactive material. The environmental damage and cleanup costs could be considerable, however.

An example of the kind of scenario considered to define a maximum reasonably foreseeable accident is a collision with impact velocities of 60 to 90 miles per hour. Another example is a situation in which a collision would not occur but where the temperature of a rail cask would rise to between 1,400°F and 1,800°F. This temperature range encompasses the reported temperature of 1,500°F in the Baltimore, Md., tunnel fire. A comparison of the numbers in the body of the table with the numbers in footnote b provides some perspective on the impact of the transport of spent nuclear fuel relative to that of daily commuting and delivery associated with an industrial activity of this magnitude not involving radioactive materials.

Of heightened interest since the September 11, 2001, attack is the possibility of a terrorist attack during transportation. Although the FEIS was published some months after the September 11 attack, most of the analysis in it was performed prior to the attack. The report does include the possible consequences of a saboteur "using a device" on a truck or rail cask. It concludes that such an event could cause 48 latent cancer fatalities in an assumed population of a large urban area.[23] Not considered is the impact of possible panic induced by public fears of nuclear radiation. As a consequence of the September 11 attack, the DOE and other agencies are re-examining safety and security issues for transportation shipments. Nevada has estimated that the impacts of a terrorist attack could be much larger than the estimates in the FEIS.[24]

Final decisions on modes and routes for transport have been slow in coming. The DOE had indicated for some time that it would prefer to use railroads. In making this choice the DOE considered human health and environmental impacts.[25] In testimony before the combined House Highway and Transit Subcommittee and the Railroad Subcommittee of the House Transportation and Infrastructure Committee, Lake Barrett, deputy director of the DOE Office of Civilian Radioactive Waste Management, said there might be 175 shipments per year over a 24-year waste emplacement schedule. There is no railway line to the Yucca Mountain site. Several possible routes for branch rail lines were described in the FEIS for Yucca Mountain. There was some disarray at the DOE regarding transportation following presidential and congressional approval of Yucca Mountain. In fall 2002 plans seemed to envision outsourcing much of the transportation activities. In September the DOE issued a Draft Statement of Work for a transportation integration contractor. It asked for comments and indicated that it planned to release a request for proposal on a performance-based transportation integration contract in 2003.[26] But a month or so after the close of the comment period the DOE posted a message on its Industry Interactive Procurement System website that it was revising its acquisition approach and that it no longer anticipated issuing a request for proposal during fiscal year 2003.[27] During a March 2003 budget hearing before the House Energy and Water Subcommittee, Margaret Chu acknowledged, "The transportation program has been in a coma for years."[28]

In December 2003 Margaret Chu reaffirmed the rail preference in a presentation to the Nevada legislature's Commission on High-Level Radioactive Waste.[29] A week later the DOE applied to the Bureau of Land Management to obtain a mile-wide corridor more than 300 miles long from near Caliente to Yucca Mountain.[30] This corridor, known as the Caliente Corridor, is one of five rail line alternatives listed in the FEIS. It is nearly the longest and was estimated to be the most costly of the five, with a life-cycle cost of $880 million in 2001 dollars.[31] A decision by the secretary of the interior on the DOE request would follow environmental studies that might take 18 months to two years.[32]

On April 8, 2004, the DOE published in the *Federal Register* a "Record of Decision" selecting the "mostly rail" scenario as the transportation mode and the Caliente Corridor as the route for the required rail line within Nevada.[33] It also announced its intent to prepare an Environmental Impact Statement for the alignment, construction, and operation of the rail line from near Caliente to the Yucca Mountain repository site.

The reaction of state officials was surprisingly negative, inasmuch as the DOE had chosen one of the most expensive options to avoid transportation through or near the Las Vegas metropolitan area. Transporting waste through or near Las Vegas had been a concern of many opponents. Bob Loux, director of the state's Nuclear Projects Office, said the state would try to challenge the rail plan. He said he believes that there are too many logistical problems with the rail route and that the DOE will eventually decide to ship nuclear waste to Yucca Mountain almost exclusively by truck, adding that shipping by truck would not be as safe.[34] Senator Harry Reid said, "There is absolutely no way that they can safely transport nuclear waste regardless of how they want to do it." Senator Ensign said the DOE was moving ahead prematurely.[35] The reactions of local officials of the counties through which the rail corridor would pass were less negative to the proposal. The mayor of Caliente, Kevin Phillips, said his town would welcome having the railhead built nearby.[36] Officials of the three counties affected, Esmeralda, Lincoln, and Nye, have held meetings concerning the impacts of the proposed rail line and what mitigation resources they might request from the DOE. They have agreed to ask for $330,000 to study the economic impact of the route and to survey landowners and users near the proposed corridor.[37]

In 2006 the DOE announced that it was also considering another rail route known as the Mina Corridor. It is a north–south route in western Nevada. It has the advantage of being less topologically challenging but requires permission from the Walker River Paiute Indians.[38] This tribe recently announced that it will not allow nuclear waste to be transported on rail through the reservation.[39]

Nevada has acted on its threat to challenge the rail plan. On September 8, 2004, the state filed suit against the DOE for its transportation decision.[40] The U.S. Court of Appeals for the District of Columbia Circuit on August 8, 2006, denied Nevada's petition for review, concluding that "some of Nevada's claims are unripe for review and the remaining claims are without merit."[41]

One issue regarding rail transport that was discussed during congressional hearings on the Nevada veto override bill was the use of dedicated trains (only carrying nuclear waste) versus general freight service (trains with both nuclear waste cars and general freight cars). On July 18, 2005, the DOE issued a Policy Statement that it will use dedicated train service for its rail transport of spent nuclear fuel and high-level radioactive waste to Yucca Mountain.[42] It cited safety, security, and operational benefits from using dedicated trains while maintaining that general freight rail transport was also safe and secure.

The National Academy of Sciences initiated an independent assessment of the risk of nuclear waste shipments in 2003. This was in the context of the U.S. DOE's program to develop a permanent repository at Yucca Mountain and a private program to develop an interim storage facility in Utah for spent fuel from commercial power reactors. During the course of the study its scope was expanded pursuant to a congressional request to include an examination of the procedures used by the DOE for selecting routes for transporting research reactor spent fuel between its facilities within the United States. The study was performed by an appointed Committee on Transportation of Radioactive Waste, operating under the National Research Council's Nuclear and Radiation Studies Board and

Transportation Research Board.[43] The study was paid for by the DOE, the NRC, the DOT, the National Cooperative Highway Research Program (a state-administered fund), and the Electric Power Research Institute, a utility-funded organization.

The committee's report, *Going the Distance? The Safe Transport of Spent Nuclear Fuel and High-Level Radioactive Waste in the United States,* was published in 2006. In its summary the committee stated that it "could identify no fundamental technical barriers to the safe transport of spent fuel and high-level radioactive waste." (In this context "safe" refers to the avoidance of radiation release because of incidents such as accidents, equipment failure, and human error as well as the radiation exposure of workers and the public during transportation. It does not include consequences of sabotage and terrorist attacks during transport, as the committee was unable to access classified and otherwise restricted information relevant to these issues. The committee recommended an independent examination of these security issues prior to the commencement of large-quantity shipments.) The committee concluded that the radiological health and safety risks associated with both normal transport conditions and accidents are "well understood and generally low, with the possible exception of risks from releases in extreme accidents involving very long duration fully engulfing fires."[44] This last qualification arose from consideration of the environment created by the Baltimore, Md., tunnel fire mentioned earlier. The committee endorsed the use of full-scale testing of transportation packages to understand how they will perform under both current regulatory conditions and more extreme conditions. It strongly endorsed DOE's decisions to ship waste mostly by rail and to use dedicated trains. The committee called attention to the challenge of public acceptance of waste transportation, urging transportation implementers to take early proactive steps.

The possibility of terrorist attacks on shipments of high-level waste has become of considerably more concern in recent years. Two considerations in this regard are the vulnerability of waste shipments relative to waste storage at reactor sites and the relative vulnerability of rail versus truck shipments. Ballard has addressed the first issue and argues that waste shipments provide the more attractive target, for it is impossible to provide the same level of security as at fixed sites. To this statement might be added that an attack on a shipment near a heavily populated area could affect more people than an attack on a storage site where there are fewer people in the immediate vicinity. Ballard concludes that the "massive number of shipments, predictable schedules, identifiable cargoes, and the overall length of the transportation routes" are factors that contribute to the risks of the shipment of wastes to a repository at Yucca Mountain.[45]

It is very difficult to predict the relative likelihood of a terrorist attack on a rail shipment as compared with a truck shipment. The U.S. Department of Energy in its Final Environmental Impact Statement for Yucca Mountain presents estimates from a 1999 Sandia National Laboratories study of the consequences of sabotage attacks on transportation casks.[46] For a legal-weight truck shipment an attack in an urban environment was projected to result in 48 fatal cancers, and for a rail shipment, to result in nine fatal cancers. These estimates are based on cask designs under consideration at the time of the study. In view of the fact that cask specifications are in a state of flux because of the DOE's recent proposal to utilize newly designed Transportation, Aging, and Disposal canisters, and the fact that terrorists have access to increasingly sophisticated weapons, these estimates must be considered very uncertain.

As mentioned above, the 2006 *Going the Distance?* National Research Council report stated that the committee felt it could not evaluate the likelihood and consequences of terrorist attacks without access to secret information. It did say that such a study should be performed. It is unlikely that specific and authoritative information on the possible impact of terrorist attacks will be available to the public.

NOTES

1. U.S. Department of Energy, *Final Environmental Impact Statement for a Geologic Repository for the Disposal of Spent Nuclear Fuel and High-Level Radioactive Waste at Yucca Mountain, Nye, County, Nevada* (DOE/EIS-0250; Washington, DC: U.S. Department of Energy, Office of Civilian Radioactive Waste Management, 2002), app. J, J-72.

2. Representative Shelley Berkley (Nevada), Prepared Witness Testimony, House Committee on Commerce and Energy, Subcommittee on Energy and Air Quality Hearings, *A Review of the President's Recommendation to Develop a Nuclear Waste Repository at Yucca Mountain, Nevada*, 107th Cong., 2nd Sess. (April 18, 2002), available at http://energycommerce.house.gov/reparchives/107/hearings/04182002Hearing505/Berkley927.htm.

3. R. J. Halstead and F. Dilger, "How Many Did You Say? Historical and Projected Spent Nuclear Fuel Shipments," paper presented at the Waste Management 2003 Symposium, February 2003, Tucson, available at www.state.nv.us/nucwaste/news2003/pdf/nv030225b.pdf.

4. Michael Janofsky, "A Transit Crossroads Eyes Yucca Mountain," *New York Times*, April 20, 2002: A12.

5. Steve Tetreault, "Yucca Mountain: Internet Site Tracks Paths to Repository," *Las Vegas Review-Journal*, June 11, 2002: 2B.

6. C. Ryan and E. Koch, "Rural Counties Work on Yucca Pact," *Las Vegas Sun*, October 15, 2003, available at www.lasvegassun.com/sunbin/stories/text/2003/oct/15/515741759.html.

7. U.S. Nuclear Regulatory Commission, "Physical Protection of Plants and Materials," *Code of Federal Regulations* 10 CFR 73.37 (January 1, 2006), available at www.gpoaccess.gov/cfr/retrieve.html.

8. Council of State Governments, Midwestern Office, "Radioactive Waste Transportation: A Guide for Midwestern Legislators" (DOE/RW/00286-10), 1996; Council of State Governments/Eastern Regional Conference, Northeast High-Level Radioactive Waste Transportation Task Force, "Transportation Routes: High-Level Radioactive Waste Transportation Routes in the Northeastern States," January 1998, available at www.csgeast.org/pdfs/nhlrwt/transroutes.pdf.

9. U.S. Department of Energy, "Spent Nuclear Fuel Transportation" (Washington, DC: U.S. Department of Energy, Office of Public Affairs, n.d.).

10. David Bodansky, *Nuclear Energy: Principles, Practices, and Prospects*, 2nd ed. (New York: Springer-Verlag, 2004), 263.

11. G. Friedlander, J. W. Kennedy, F. S. Mathias, and J. M. Miller, *Nuclear and Radiochemistry*, 3rd ed. (New York: Wiley, 1981), 239.

12. Bodansky, *Nuclear Energy*, 264.

13. Richard Meserve, Chairman, Nuclear Regulatory Commission, Testimony before the Senate Energy and Natural Resources Committee, *Yucca Mountain Repository Site Approval Act: Hearings on S.J. Res. 34*, 107th Cong., 2nd Sess. (May 23, 2002).

14. Ibid.

15. U.S. Nuclear Regulatory Commission, "Packaging and Transportation of Radioactive Material," *Code of Federal Regulations* 10 CFR 71.61 (January 1, 2006), available at www.gpoaccess.gov/cfr/retrieve.html.

16. J. L. Sprung, D. J. Ammerman, N. L. Breivik, R. J. Dukart, F L. Kanipe, J. A. Koski, G. S. Mills, K. S. Neuhauser, H. D. Radloff, R. F. Weiner, and H. R. Yoshimura, "Reexamination of Spent Fuel Shipment Risk Estimates," Spent Fuel Project Office, Office of Nuclear Material Safety and Safeguards, U.S. Nuclear Regulatory Commission

(NUREG/CR-6672; Washington, DC: Superintendent of Documents, U.S. Government Printing Office [dist.], 2000).

17. U.S. Nuclear Regulatory Commission, "Final Environmental Statement on the Transportation of Radioactive Material by Air and Other Modes" (NUREG-0170; Washington, DC: U.S. Nuclear Regulatory Commission, December 1977).

18. Sprung et al., "Reexamination of Spent Fuel Shipment Risk Estimates," ES-9, 10.

19. Ibid., 9-4.

20. U.S. Department of Energy, *Final Environmental Impact Statement for a Geologic Repository for the Disposal of Spent Nuclear Fuel and High-Level Radioactive Waste at Yucca Mountain, Nye County, Nevada.*

21. State of Nevada et al., "Petitioners' Opening Brief: Petition for Review from Final Decisions, Actions, and Failures to Act of United States Department of Energy and Final Decisions and Actions of the President of the United States," *State of Nevada, et al., Petitioners, v. United States Department of Energy, et al., Respondents*, December 2, 2002, available at www.state.nv.us/nucwaste/news2002/nv021203.pdf.

22. U.S. Department of Energy, *Final Environmental Impact Statement for a Geologic Repository for the Disposal of Spent Nuclear Fuel and High-Level Radioactive Waste at Yucca Mountain, Nye County, Nevada*, S-69.

23. Ibid., S-70; errata sheet, 13.

24. R. J. Halstead, presentation to the Committee on Nuclear Transportation, Transportation Research Board of Board of Radioactive Waste Management, National Academy of Sciences, July 25, 2003.

25. U.S. Department of Energy, "Record of Decision on Mode of Transportation and Nevada Rail Corridor for the Disposal of Spent Nuclear Fuel and High-Level Radioactive Waste at Yucca Mountain, Nye County, NV," *Federal Register* 69, no. 68 (April 8, 2004): 18559.

26. "Draft Work Scope Outlines Tasks for Transportation Integration Contractor (Yucca Mountain)," *HazMat Transport News* 23, no. 10 (October 2002).

27. U.S. Department of Energy Industry Interactive Procurement System, available at http://doe-iips.pr.doe.gov/iips/busopor.nsf/.

28. Steve Tetreault, "Lawmaker: Yucca at Risk over Routes," *Las Vegas Review-Journal*, March 21, 2003: 3B.

29. Mark Waite, "State Leadership Looks at Benefits," *Pahrump Valley Times*, December 12, 2003.

30. Steve Tetreault, "Yucca Mountain: DOE Seeks Land for Rail Corridor," *Las Vegas Review-Journal*, December 30, 2003, available at www.reviewjournal.com/lvrj_home/2003/Dec-30-Tue-2003/news/22896192.html.

31. U.S. Department of Energy, *Final Environmental Impact Statement for a Geologic Repository for the Disposal of Spent Nuclear Fuel and High-Level Radioactive Waste at Yucca Mountain, Nye County, Nevada.*

32. Tetreault, "Yucca Mountain: DOE Seeks Land for Rail Corridor."

33. U.S. Department of Energy, "Record of Decision on Mode of Transportation and Nevada Rail Corridor for the Disposal of Spent Nuclear Fuel and High-Level Radioactive Waste at Yucca Mountain, Nye County, NV," *Federal Register* 69, no. 68 (April 8, 2004): 18557.

34. Ken Ritter, "DOE Picks Rail Option; Caliente Corridor to Nevada Nuke Dump," *Las Vegas Sun*, April 5, 2004, available at www.lasvegassun.com/sunbin/stories/text/2004/apr/05/040510849.html.

35. Steve Tetreault, "Yucca Mountain: DOE Formalizes Nuclear Waste Plan," *Las Vegas Review-Journal*, April 6, 2004: 1B.

36. Ed Vogel, "Mayor Says Yucca Shipments Would Benefit Caliente," *Las Vegas Review-Journal*, April 20, 2004: 1B.

37. Associated Press, "Rural Panel Wants Funds to Study Yucca Mountain Plan," *Las Vegas Sun*, May 1, 2004, available at www.state.nv.us/nucwaste/arch2004.htm.

38. Steve Tetreault, Stephens Washington Bureau, "DOE to Publish Rail Plan for Yucca," *Las Vegas Review-Journal*, October 12, 2006: 1B.

39. Steve Tetreault and Keith Rogers, "Yucca Passage Dealt Setback," *Las Vegas Review-Journal*, April 18, 2007: 1A.

40. Suzanne Struglinski, "State Sues over Yucca Rail Line," *Las Vegas Sun*, September 8, 2004.

41. U.S. Court of Appeals for the District of Columbia Circuit, Case no. 04-1309, "On Petition for Review of an Order of the Department of Energy," *State of Nevada, Petitioner, v. Department of Energy, Respondent,* August 8, 2006, 3, available at www.state.nv.us/nucwaste/news2006/pdf/appeals20060808nepa.pdf.

42. U.S. Department of Energy, "Department of Energy Policy Statement for Use of Dedicated Trains for Waste Shipments to Yucca Mountain," 2005, available at www.state.nv.us/nucwaste/news2005/pdf/doe050718rail.pdf.

43. The Board on Radioactive Waste Management was reorganized in February 2005 as the Nuclear and Radiation Studies Board.

44. U.S. National Research Council, Committee on Transportation of Radioactive Waste, *Going the Distance? The Safe Transport of Spent Nuclear Fuel and High-Level Radioactive Waste in the United States* (Washington, DC: National Academies Press, 2006), 2, 4. A summary of this report is accessible at http://newton.nap.edu/.

45. James David Ballard, Prepared Statement before the Committee on Energy and Natural Resources, *Yucca Mountain Repository Site Approval Act: Hearings on S.J. Res. 34*, 107th Cong., 2nd Sess. (May 22, 2002), 11, available at www.state.nv.us/nucwaste/news2002/nn11704.pdf.

46. U.S. Department of Energy, *Final Environmental Impact Statement for a Geologic Repository for the Disposal of Spent Nuclear Fuel and High-Level Radioactive Waste at Yucca Mountain, Nye County, Nevada*, 6–152.

: 12

High-Level Nuclear Waste Disposal
in Other Countries

It is constructive to compare the progress in other countries with that in the United States in their planning and implementation of high-level nuclear waste disposal. Many of the issues are similar, although the governmental involvement may take on a somewhat different character from country to country. Also the mix of types of nuclear waste may vary some from country to country depending on the extent to which reprocessing of nuclear fuel elements takes place.

At the present time the only nations close to a final decision about what to do with nuclear waste are Finland, Sweden, and the United States. John Paffenbarger, of the energy company Constellation Generation Group in Baltimore, conducted an analysis of nuclear power in Organisation for Economic Co-operation and Development countries for the International Energy Agency.[1] Jeff Johnson reports in an article in *Chemical and Engineering News* that Paffenbarger found that although there is growing demand in this group of 30 countries to reach a waste solution, there is also growing concern by the populations about practical aspects of actually implementing a plan.[2] Paffenbarger went on to say, stressing that he was expressing his own views, "What that has meant is that timetables are always set beyond the reach of current politicians."[3]

In this chapter we will discuss the status of waste disposal plans in most of the countries with the largest nuclear power programs. But it must be remembered that it may be some of the smaller countries with modest nuclear power programs that will have the most difficulty in permanently disposing of their waste. Although some have contracted with Britain and France for reprocessing, such contracts call for the return of both the plutonium and the fission product waste to the originating country. The cost of permanent waste disposal does not scale with the amount of waste to be disposed of, and many small countries may have difficulty in funding disposal costs. As discussed at the end of this chapter, there have been attempts to organize an international repository. Such attempts have so far been unsuccessful, and the political difficulty in persuading a potential host country to accept waste from other countries seems to be increasing. The only country that at present seems somewhat receptive is Russia. Russia's past failures in radioactive material custodianship raise questions about this route as a solution.

CANADA

As of January 2007 Canada had 18 operational nuclear reactors, most of which were located in the province of Ontario.[4] They are all of the heavy-water-moderated CANDU (Canadian deuterated uranium) design. The future of nuclear power in Canada is unclear. Canada has ratified the Kyoto Protocol and is committed to reduce its emissions of greenhouse gases by 6 percent below its 1990 level by 2012. Bratt has argued that this can only be achieved by including a nuclear power component.[5] He points out that although some officials such as natural resources ministers have acknowledged this, nuclear power has not been mentioned in government strategy documents such as a 2002 "Climate Change Plan for Canada."[6] Nor is it mentioned in a more recent 2005 update.[7]

In 1978, the government of Canada directed Atomic Energy of Canada Limited to develop a plan for deep geological disposal. The plan would involve sealed containers for either fuel elements or solidified high-level wastes. These containers would be designed to last at least 500 years and be emplaced 500 to 1,000 meters underground in plutonic rock of the Canadian Shield. Plutonic rock is a class of igneous rock that has solidified far below the earth's surface. All access tunnels and shafts would be ultimately sealed so that the disposal facility would be passively safe, not dependent on institutional controls.[8] In the late 1980s plans were laid for an environmental assessment of this disposal concept. This assessment by an independent panel was pursuant to the Environmental and Review Process Guidelines Order issued by the Canadian Environmental Agency. Establishing the terms of reference (the charge to the review panel) for this assessment was contentious, as has been discussed by Murphy and Kuhn.[9] The final terms of reference released in 1989 were somewhat broader than originally proposed. It charged the Environmental Assessment Panel not only with reviewing the safety and science of deep geological disposal but also with a broader range of nuclear fuel waste management issues. However, the issues to be addressed were basically technical and did not include most political and societal issues. The report of this panel was not released until 1998. The panel concluded that although the safety of the Atomic Energy of Canada Limited concept had been adequately demonstrated from a technical perspective, from a social perspective it had not. It further concluded that the current proposal for deep geologic disposal does not have the required level of public acceptance to be adopted as Canada's approach for managing nuclear fuel wastes.[10] Murphy and Kuhn emphasize that by coming to this latter conclusion the panel "broke out of the constraints imposed on them by the Terms of Reference and redefined the nature and scope of what constitutes an environmental assessment."[11] The panel also recommended the creation of a nuclear fuel waste management agency to assume responsibility for managing and coordinating the full range of activities required to deal with nuclear fuel wastes in the long term. It recommended that a search for a specific site not proceed at the present time.

In December 1998 the federal government cabinet announced that it would not set up a government agency to manage nuclear waste. There was considerable concern that the federal government not take direct responsibility for nuclear waste. An internal memo warned that the federal government should leave industry to deal with the radioactive waste problem, under government regulation.[12]

In an effort to understand the lack of public acceptance for deep geologic disposal, Murphy performed in-depth interviews of various stakeholder organizations grouped into First Nations (Native Americans in U.S. parlance), nongovernmental organizations (NGOs), federal and local governments, industry, academics, and consultants. All groups felt that there had been an increasing role of public participation in spent fuel management. Murphy reported, however, that First Nations and NGOs wanted more influence, whereas "industry and some government respondents expressed dismay about the unwillingness of people to accept traditional authority positions."[13] On the specific issue of deep geological disposal, several respondents commented that over the years since 1978 societal views were shifting from permanent geologic disposal toward monitored storage and retrievability.

The Canadian Parliament enacted a national Nuclear Fuel Waste Act in summer 2002. It requires the nuclear energy corporations, including

Atomic Energy of Canada Limited, to create a waste management organization whose purpose is to "(a) propose to the Government of Canada approaches for the management of nuclear fuel waste; and (b) implement the approach that is selected" by the government. "Management"
means "long-term management by means of storage or disposal, including handling, treatment, conditioning or transport for the purpose of storage or disposal." It also requires that a trust fund be set up to finance this
management, setting initial contributions from nuclear energy corporations and Atomic Energy of Canada Limited as well as annual payments.
Within three years after the date that this act came into force (November
15, 2002) the waste management organization was required to submit to
the minister a study of proposed approaches for the management of nuclear fuel waste as well as its recommendation as to which proposed approach should be adopted. The proposed approaches were required to include (a) deep geological disposal in the Canadian Shield (igneous rock),
(b) storage at nuclear reactor sites, and (c) centralized storage, either above
or below ground. Each proposed approach must include a comparison of
the benefits, risks, and costs of that approach as well as ethical, social, and
economic considerations associated with that approach. The general public, and in particular aboriginal peoples, must be consulted on each approach.[14] It appears that this act distances the government from operational responsibility while retaining ultimate control on the approach to
be implemented. The government is not required to follow the recommendations of the Nuclear Waste Management Organization.

In preparation for its final report and recommendations published in
November 2005, the Nuclear Waste Management Organization issued several interim reports. The first of these, a discussion document entitled *Asking the Right Questions* issued in November 2003, focused on engagement
with the public and how to assess alternative technical methods. A second discussion document, *Understanding the Choices*, was issued in August
2004. It drew heavily on an Assessment Team report issued in June 2004.

With respect to public engagement, *Understanding the Choices* reported that Canadians generally approved the identification of issues put
forth in "Asking the Right Questions." The public did express a need for
a better understanding of the health and environmental hazards posed by
spent nuclear fuel, in particular the risk posed by transportation. They also
wanted more information on opportunities to reuse or recycle used nuclear
fuel. Although they agreed that the three options (storage at reactor site,

centralized surface or near-surface storage, and deep geological disposal) of the Nuclear Waste Fuel Act should receive the primary focus, they flagged partitioning (requiring reprocessing) and transmutation as being of particular interest.

The "Executive Summary" of the *Understanding the Choices* report provides a good summary of the strengths and weaknesses of the three principal options. We have discussed these and other options in more detail in chapter 2. Briefly, at-reactor storage has the advantage of not requiring transportation. Nuclear expertise and infrastructure are available in the short term. A principal disadvantage is the fact that the spent fuel will remain hazardous long after institutional control can be expected to be maintained. This raises very serious security, environmental, and safety issues. Centralized storage could allow for site selection based on waste management considerations. Short-term institutional controls would be more practical, but the long-term problem shared with at-reactor storage persists. In addition there would be transportation risks. Deep geological disposal is expected to result in permanent disposition without the need for long-term institutional controls. The site can be chosen on the basis of waste management considerations. Both short- and long-term security concerns are minimized. As with centralized storage, there will be transportation risks. Another limitation of geologic disposal is that it is difficult to prove from scientific and engineering considerations that isolation of the waste from the environment can be guaranteed over the very long period of time that the waste will be hazardous. (The "Executive Summary" is not adequately forthcoming about the length of time the waste remains hazardous. It is for hundreds of thousands of years, rather than the "thousands of years" appearing repeatedly in the report.)

The nine-member Assessment Team has given a preliminary assessment of these three options with respect to several objectives of waste management. The deep geological repository and centralized storage options received the highest scores for fairness. For other objectives the team distinguished between near-term (less than 175 years) and longer-term scores. With respect to public health and safety, deep geological disposal received the highest scores for both the short and long term. On-site storage received the lowest score for the long term. The scores for community well-being and economic viability were similar for all categories except for long-term deep geologic disposal, which received a higher score. Deep geologic disposal received the highest scores for both security and environmental integrity objectives.

In summary, the average scores of the Assessment Team indicate that deep geologic disposal meets the objectives better than the other two options. This conclusion has to be tempered by the fact that the range of scores among the different team members for a particular objective and option often was quite broad. The report attributes this to differing views among members "concerning future environmental and social conditions in Canada as well as questions regarding how well the approach might actually perform."[15]

The next step by the Nuclear Waste Management Organization was the release in May 2005 of a draft report and in November 2005 of a final report, *Choosing a Way Forward*.[16] This document focuses on the three options discussed above. The storage at reactors and centralized storage options were deemed to be expected to perform well over the near term (at least for 175 years), during which time strong institutions and active management could be relied on. It was not felt that institutional support could be counted on for times of the order of tens of thousands of years. Deep geological disposal employing a combination of natural and engineered barriers was deemed to perform well in the very long term.

The specific recommendations for long-term management include the following characteristics:

- Centralized containment and isolation of the used fuel in a deep geologic repository in suitable rock formations, such as the crystalline rock of the Canadian Shield or Ordovician sedimentary rock;
- Flexibility in the pace and manner of implementation through a phased decision-making process, supported by a program of continuous learning, research and development;
- Provision for an interim step in the implementation process in the form of shallow underground storage of used fuel at the central site, prior to final placement in a deep repository.[17]

Furthermore, the Nuclear Waste Management Organization said it would implement the above approach by seeking a willing community to host the central facilities. Interestingly, it also said it would focus site selection on those provinces that have nuclear reactors. This contrasts with the situation in the United States, where states with operating reactors have been quite successful in keeping themselves from being considered for a repository.

Another interesting aspect of the recommendation is the suggestion that Ordovician sedimentary rock (shale) as well as Canadian Shield crystalline rock (granite) would be suitable geological hosts. Sedimentary rock underlies much of southern Ontario, the province with the large majority of nuclear power plants. Canada commissioned a study of this rock formation by Martin Mazurek of the Institute of Geological Sciences, University of Bern, Switzerland. The formation under consideration is approximately 400 million years old. Mazurek reports that "hydrochemical evidence indicates very long underground times of formation waters" and "flow does not occur or is very limited. Solute transport is probably dominated by diffusion." He concludes, "Ordovician shales and limestones occurring beneath southern Ontario provide a highly suitable environment to host a deep geological repository for spent fuel."[18]

Reprocessing was screened out as not a viable option for Canada at this time. Difficulties mentioned included cost, the production of wastes even more difficult to manage, and the potential for separating out weapons-usable plutonium.[19]

The draft report contained an illustrative timeline. This timeline is so leisurely that one wonders whether decisions made in the near term will outlive likely changes in the government. According to this timeline the siting process would not be initiated for approximately ten years. A decision as to whether to construct a centralized storage facility would not occur for approximately 20 years. Both the draft and the final report suggest that emplacement in a deep geologic repository would only begin in about 60 years.

FRANCE

France has long relied on nuclear energy as its primary source of electricity. It has approximately 59 reactors in operation.[20] These account for about 75 percent of the electricity production in France, the highest percentage for any country in the world. In April 2004 the French government announced that as these reactors reach the end of their useful life they would be replaced with new reactors.[21]

Nuclear activities in France have traditionally raised much less public resistance than in other countries, particularly compared with neighboring Germany. Some years ago Kitschelt analyzed antinuclear movements in France, West Germany, Sweden, and the United States in terms of political opportunity structures.[22] France was judged relatively low with respect to the openness of political regimes to new demands. On the operational side, the greater centralization and governmental control of the nuclear establishment made opposition difficult. A less independent judiciary also thwarted opposition. Only recently has the governmental "decide, announce, defend" approach been weakened.

France has chosen to reprocess its spent nuclear fuel ever since the introduction of nuclear power plants. Some of the plutonium is used to make mixed-oxide fuel, but more plutonium is being produced than is presently being recycled as reactor fuel. The fission product waste is being vitrified for eventual disposal. France also reprocesses spent fuel for other countries, but the waste from this is not permitted to be disposed of in France and is returned to the country of origin. In 1999 Prime Minister Lionel Jospin formed a high-level governmental panel to conduct a study concerning the economic aspects of the nuclear industry. In particular, he asked that the later stages of the nuclear fuel cycle, including reprocessing, be addressed. Broader issues concerning electricity production and CO_2 emission were to be studied. The study report was issued in July 2000.[23] With respect to the reprocessing issue, the study concluded that a very small saving, approximately 1 percent in the total electricity costs to 2050, could be achieved if reprocessing were to be terminated in 2010. It noted that much of the capital investment in the nuclear reprocessing infrastructure has already been made.

It had long been assumed that the high-level fission product waste from reprocessing would be disposed of in a geological repository. A first attempt to characterize four different geological sites was suspended in 1990 because of public opposition. Christian Bataille, a member of Parliament, was asked by the Parliamentary Office for Scientific and Technological Decisions to reexamine the subject of radioactive waste disposal. After much consultation, he issued a report that emphasized responsibility, transparency (openness and accountability), and democracy. This report was followed by the introduction of a bill before the Parliament that was passed into law in December 1991. The law set a 15-year framework for conducting radioactive waste management research. The law established three research directions to be pursued. The partition and transmutation of the long-lived elements are to be investigation by the Commissariat a l'Energie

Atomique (CEA). Disposal in deep geological formations is being studied by the French agency for radioactive waste management, Agence nationale pur la gestion des déchets radioactifs (ANDRA). Immobilization and conditioning processes, as well as long-term near surface storage, are also being investigated by the CEA.

With respect to deep geological disposal, three sites were identified that had favorable geological as well as political and social conditions that might make a repository acceptable to the communities concerned. All three sites, Meuse/Haute-Marne, Gard, and Vienne, are in clay formations. Preliminary surveys begun in 1994 confirmed that they were suitable candidates for further study. ANDRA filed applications in mid-1996 for the construction and operation of underground laboratories at each of the sites. In 1998 the government approved one site at the border of Meuse and Haute-Marne in northeastern France.[24] In December 1998 the government also dropped Gard and Vienne as possible sites because of geological reasons.[25] A search for a granite site in Brittany and in central France encountered strong local opposition and has been abandoned.[26] French law requires local communities to agree to siting of underground research laboratories in their neighborhood.[27] The 1991 act also provides financial incentives to communities willing to accept underground laboratories. Bataille was able to offer communities the prospect of getting up to FF 60 million per year once a facility has been developed.[28] Thus far this does not seem to have been sufficient incentive for some communities. The Haute-Marne (Bure) underground laboratory is the only one that has been constructed. In preparation for the 2006 waste management decision, ANDRA in June 2005 produced a report including a feasibility assessment for clay formations, based largely on work conducted at this laboratory. The formation at this site is 155 million years old and is homogeneous with no faults. A performance assessment shows that only three nuclides, I-129, Cl-36, and Se-79, escape from the host medium. The peak dose to a critical group occurs after about 500,000 years and is several orders of magnitude lower than the 25 millirems per year (mrem/yr; 0.25 millisieverts per year [mSv/yr]) regulatory limit.[29] The ANDRA report also includes a part on the suitability of granite rocks based on the literature on French granites and on investigations carried out by ANDRA under research partnerships with foreign laboratories. Draft legislation announced in 2006 requires that waste be disposed of in a geological repository but does not specify a specific site. It proposes licensing a repository by 2015, with operations targeted for 2025.[30]

GERMANY

Germany presently has 17 reactors in operation, which account for 30 percent of electricity production.[31] Reactors in the old east German Democratic Republic were closed after reunification. These were pressurized water reactors of Russian origin. Until the recent election in September 2005, the coalition government in power included the Green Party, which has long called for an end to nuclear power. The environment minister during this period, Jürgen Trittin, was a member of the Green Party. As part of the coalition agreement, the government agreed to phase out nuclear power in Germany. The first reactor shutdown under this agreement occurred on November 14, 2003. Trittin said on this occasion that "nuclear energy has no future in Germany."[32] The phaseout agreement is not without contention, however. The economics minister prior to the 2002 election, Werner Mueller, pointed out the difficulty in meeting greenhouse gas emissions goals by 2020 at the same time as phasing out nuclear power.[33] During the 2005 election campaign, now-Chancellor Angela Merkel promised to change the law requiring the nuclear shutdown. As of late 2006 she had been unable to fulfill this promise.[34]

The federal government has affirmed its commitment to establish permanent disposal facilities irrespective of the planned nuclear phaseout (by 2025) in Germany. Utilities are permitted to transport spent fuel to centralized interim storage sites at Gorleben, Lubmin, and Ahaus until temporary storage facilities at or close to reactor sites can be constructed. International transport of reprocessing products from spent fuel processed under contract in France or England continued until July 1, 2005. After July 1, 2005, spent fuel could not be transported to either a reprocessing plant or an interim storage site except in special circumstances where licensed interim storage was not yet available on-site.

The safety standards for licensing a repository were issued in 1983. No time frame for compliance demonstration was specified.[35]

Planning for a permanent repository had focused on a salt mine near Gorleben in Lower Saxony, about 100 kilometers northeast of Braunschweig. The Gorleben project had its beginnings in 1974 with the announcement of an "Integrated Waste Management Concept." Spent fuel management, a reprocessing plant, and disposal facilities were to be centered at a single site. The choice of Gorleben was formally announced on February 22, 1977. In 1979 plans for a reprocessing plant were dropped. Deep test drilling began that year, following issuance of a state license.[36] The former German Democratic Republic identified a similar site in a salt dome at Morsleben.[37]

Considerable exploratory work has been performed at Gorleben. A preliminary report from an international team of experts commissioned in December 1999 to advise on the suitability of the site declared that there was no reason the Gorleben mine could not meet all necessary criteria for long-term storage of spent fuel. This response was in contrast to the position of the environment minister, Trittin, who on February 22, 2000, called for a moratorium on exploration activities at Gorleben and established a commission to define permanent disposal criteria. On June 14, 2000, the federal government and the utilities agreed to suspend underground investigations for three to ten years.[38] Other geologic sites in addition to salt will be considered. The Gorleben site has been criticized because of a lack of comparison with other geological formations. There has also been public pressure to provide a retrievability option. The moratorium has not been without criticism. The Internationale Länderkommission Kerntechnik (International Committee on Nuclear Technology), a panel of experts established by the states of Baden-Wurttemburg, Bavaria, and Hesse in 1999, argued that because the results obtained so far provide no technical grounds for ruling out the site, a Total Systems Performance Assessment should be carried out.[39] Wolf-Dieter Krebs, chairman of the German Nuclear Society, strongly criticized the suspension. Referring to hard-liners among the opponents of nuclear energy, he said, "The suspension of investigations of the Gorleben salt dome shortly before the expected confirmation of its suitability as a site for a final radioactive waste repository is nothing more than an ill-conceived attempt to pacify precisely these people."[40]

In Germany the states (länder) are more powerful than in the United States.[41] This may make repository siting more difficult.

UNITED KINGDOM

Britain has 19 operating reactors, producing about 20 percent of its electricity.[42] However, the long-range future of nuclear power in Britain is in doubt. In February 2003 the government published an Energy White Paper, *Our Energy Future—Creating a Low Carbon Economy.*[43] It emphasized renewables and energy efficiency. While recognizing that nuclear power is currently an important source of carbon-free electricity, it did not propose building new nuclear power plants. It cited economic considerations and the nuclear waste problem for this recommendation. In late 2005 Prime Minister Tony Blair announced that Britain may reverse its present reluctance to build new nuclear power plants.[44] In May 2006 he endorsed a new generation of reactors.[45]

Britain reprocesses much of its spent fuel, although the justification for doing so is often challenged.[46] Reprocessing takes place at Sellafield, where two reprocessing plants are located. The high-level waste from reprocessing is stored in cooled stainless steel tanks. Work has begun on incorporating this waste into glass blocks (vitrification). The blocks are sealed in stainless steel canisters for dry storage. According to current government policy the waste will be stored above ground for at least 50 years before disposal. Nuclear power, the nuclear fuel cycle, and nuclear waste disposal in the United Kingdom have had a long and troubled history. There have been serious environmental problems, including a fire at a nuclear power plant in Windscale. There have been significant releases of both air- and waterborne radioactivity from fuel reprocessing facilities at Sellafield (née Windscale) on the northwest coast of England across from Ireland. It has been claimed that, prior to Chernobyl, Sellafield was the source of most cesium-137 contamination of North European waters, resulting in the largest population exposure from waste disposal in the nuclear industry.[47] More recently, a "serious incident" on April 18, 2005, at the main reprocessing plant (THORP) at Sellafield resulted in it being shut down for months. This led some officials of its owner, the Nuclear Decommissioning Authority, to recommend that the plant be permanently shut down.[48] The division of responsibility for nuclear activities between the governmental and private sectors has also proven troublesome and unstable.

Britain has not had the will or political skill to effectively deal with the final disposal of nuclear waste. Little attention was paid to disposal of high-level waste until the 1976 publication of the "Sixth Report of the Royal Commission on Environmental Pollution," known as the Flowers Report. It called attention to the increasing quantities of nuclear wastes being generated and the U.K. Atomic Energy Authority's expectation that considerably more reactors would be needed by the end of the century.[49] The report concluded that "there should be no commitment to a large programme of nuclear fission until it has been demonstrated beyond reasonable doubt that a method exists to ensure the safe containment of long-lived highly radioactive wastes for the indefinite future."[50] The Royal Commission recommended that two new administrative bodies should be created; an independent advisory body to monitor waste management activities and report to the government and an executive independent statutory body to oversee the whole process of waste disposal. In partial response to these recommendations, a Radioactive Waste Management Advisory Committee was established in 1978, and in 1982 the Nuclear Industry Radioactive Waste Management Executive (Nirex) was established with responsibility for disposing of long-lived waste.[51] In 1995 Nirex sought permission to construct an underground research laboratory at Sellafield. The application was first denied by the local planning authority, and the denial was later upheld by the secretary of state for the environment, who is responsible for developing policies for managing and disposing of long-lived nuclear waste.

This setback led to a reexamination of radioactive waste management policy in the United Kingdom. The first effort in this direction was undertaken by a House of Lords Select Committee on Science and Technology. The House of Lords in the United Kingdom has little real political power. Perhaps because of its lack of power, it has been able to issue a number of rather perceptive reports largely free of political bias. The current tendency toward the creation of more life peers rather than additional hereditary peerages also leads to greater participation by and competence of member lords.[52] The aforementioned committee issued a report in March 1999 that concluded that one or more underground repositories were necessary within the next 50 years.[53] The report's proposal to offer compensation for a hosting community drew opposition from the environmental community as being too much of a goal-driven process with the use of compensation to "buy" acceptance.[54]

As an aside, it is interesting to note a separate activity that occurred soon after the issuance of the House of Lords committee report. This was a Consensus Conference, held in May 1999. It was made up of a randomly selected Citizen's Panel that was charged with forming an opinion on nuclear waste policy. The panel studied the issues and held a two-day hearing. It rejected the idea of deep disposal, favoring retrievability.[55] The conference conclusions were nonbinding and appear to have had little influence on later developments. It does illustrate the variety of public views and the likely difficulty in achieving political acceptability of any solution.

The 1999 House of Lords report proposed the preparation of a wide-ranging consultation document. Soon after, devolution of some political power to the divisions of the United Kingdom brought some other players into this process. Scotland, Wales, and Northern Ireland assumed some responsibilities in the area of nuclear waste management. They participated in preparation of the report "Managing Radioactive Waste Safely: Proposals for Developing a Policy for Managing Solid Radioactive Waste in the UK." This report does not recommend specific disposal methods or sites. Rather, it calls for a fresh start: "We want to inspire public confidence in the decisions and the way in which they are implemented. To do that, we have to demonstrate that all options are considered; that choices between them are made in a clear and logical way; that people's values and concerns are fully reflected in this process; and that information we provide is clear, accurate, unbiased, and complete." It goes on to

> propose to set up a strong, independent and authoritative body to advise us on what information there is, what further information is needed, and when enough information has been gathered for decisions to be made on how the UK's radioactive waste should be managed. For example, should it be put in an underground repository? or stored, until we know more about its risks and better ways of dealing with it? or some other option or combination? After that, we can start a debate on where in the UK we should keep this waste in the long term.[56]

It set out a time schedule that would lead to selection of a disposal option in 2006 and passage of any needed legislation in 2007.

The government's response started to take shape with the announcement on July 29, 2002, by the Department of Environment, Food and Rural Affairs of a new "Committee on Radioactive Waste Management" (CoRWM). This committee has been asked "to oversee a review of options for managing solid radioactive waste in the United Kingdom and to recommend to Ministers the option, or combination of options, that can provide a long-term solution, providing protection for people and the environment."[57]

On December 10, 2004, the Science and Technology Committee of the House of Lords issued a report "Radioactive Waste Management."[58] The report focuses on the charge to, composition of, and progress by the

Committee on Radioactive Waste Management. It is rather critical of all three of these items. With respect to the charge to the CoRWM, the report expresses astonishment that it was told, in effect, to start "with a blank sheet of paper."[59] The House of Lords report suggests that in view of extensive previous studies and discussion in the United Kingdom and abroad, the committee should have been instructed to concentrate on various alternatives for underground repositories, reflecting international opinion that deep geological disposal is the preferred method for permanent disposal of high-level waste. In fact, one of the first accomplishments of the committee was to draw up a list of options for long-term management of "higher active" wastes.[60] The list includes statements on the extent of current knowledge and experience, and potential benefits and problems, with each option. The inclusion on this list of some unrealistic options, such as incineration (only suitable for low-level waste) and disposal in space (generally rejected on the basis of safety and cost considerations), supports the House of Lords report's concern that the charge to the committee was too unfocused.

With respect to the composition of CoRWM, the report notes that its mandate ("Terms of Reference") mentions that its members should include those with expertise in "scientific and technical issues such as earth science, materials and their properties, and civil engineering; radiation protection principles and their implementation; radionuclides and how they affect the environment."[61] The House of Lords committee did not feel that these skills were represented in the present composition of the committee.

With respect to the progress made by the Committee on Radioactive Waste Management up to 2004, the report expresses concern regarding the "undue emphasis given to investigating methodologies of decision-making and public stakeholder engagement at the expense of identifying the right scientific and technical solution."[62] David Ball, a member of CoRWM, resigned in spring 2005, citing similar concerns about the committee.[63] (We feel the same criticism could be made of the similar ongoing process in Canada.) Although recognizing that the committee is charged with both proposing a technical solution and inspiring public confidence in that solution, the House of Lords report goes on to express doubt as to the extent of public interest and engagement until possible sites are identified. More recently, after the committee released its short list of options for long-term management of nuclear wastes, the World Nuclear Association said, "These state the obvious, focus on deep geological disposal, and continue the elaborate procrastination of recent years."[64]

In July 2006 CoRWM released a major report, *Managing Our Radioactive Waste Safely: CoRWM's Recommendations to Government.*[65] It reaffirms geological disposal, defined as burial underground (200–1,000 meters) with no intention to retrieve the waste once the facility is closed.[66] It recognizes that interim storage must play an integral part in the long-term management strategy.

With regard to siting long-term radioactive waste facilities, the committee recommends that community involvement "should be based on the principle of volunteerism, that is, an expressed willingness to participate."[67] The report does not indicate at what level of government such community decisions should be taken. The experience at Yucca Mountain in the United States shows that this can be an important matter. The county in which Yucca Mountain is located, Nye, is much more accepting of the proposed repository than is the State of Nevada.

The committee professes to not having adopted an approach of incentives for communities to volunteer but goes on to suggest the enhancement of the well-being of such communities through mechanisms such as "Community Packages that provide the resources to support both the short and long term well-being of the community."[68] The distinction between the latter mechanism and an incentives program seems small.

The next step is for the government of Britain to act on these recommendations. The committee urges progress without delay.

The government has also asked United Kingdom Nirex Limited (Nirex) to look at some aspects of long-term management of high-level waste and spent fuel. Historically Nirex, an independent body responsible for supporting government policy on radioactive materials, has focused on low- and intermediate-level waste. As part of its new charge it has developed a generic repository concept based on the Swedish plan discussed later in this chapter.[69]

The radiation protection guidance in Britain sets a risk target (cancer fatalities and serious genetic effects) of 10^{-6} per year. The guidance does not prescribe an overall timescale for which meeting this target must be demonstrated.[70]

In addition to the establishment of the Committee on Radioactive Waste Management policy committee, the government established a new Nuclear Decommissioning Authority. This authority is responsible for treating and packaging waste from civil nuclear fuel reprocessing and for cleaning up the sites and the surrounding land. The authority will relieve British Nuclear Fuels Ltd. of responsibility for the power reactors and for the Sellafield reprocessing plant, although British Nuclear Fuels Ltd., through its new subsidiary, the British Nuclear Group, will continue to operate many of the sites under license.

SWEDEN

Sweden is of particular interest both because of the early political opposition to nuclear power and because Sweden has made steady sustainable progress in defining the technical aspects of a permanent geological repository and in determining siting possibilities. It has ten operating reactors that produce about 45 percent of Sweden's electrical power.[71] Hydroelectric provides the majority of the remaining power. Sweden has the highest percentage of nuclear power reliance of any country other than France and Belgium.

Up until the 1970s, nuclear waste received virtually no attention from either the nuclear industry or the government. It was assumed that spent fuel would be reprocessed, and it was hoped that foreign facilities could be used. It was even hoped, partly on the basis of foreign reprocessing and waste disposal services available at the time of writing of a government report published in 1971, that the waste from foreign reprocessing would not have to be returned to Sweden.[72] This hope was somewhat short-lived, and later a recommendation to start preliminary planning for a domestic reprocessing plant was made by another committee. However, reprocessing has not been seriously pursued as an option for Sweden.

An influential figure in bringing the nuclear waste problem to public attention in the early 1970s was Hannes Alfvén (winner of the Nobel Prize in Physics in 1970 for his work in plasma physics). In 1973 the leader of Sweden's Center Party, Thorbjörn Fälldin, invited Alfvén to be the principal speaker at the party's annual national congress. Here Alfvén "talked about the dangers of radiation, about waste problems and the thousands of years it has to be isolated from the biosphere."[73] Nuclear issues figured prominently in the election of 1976, at which time the Social Democratic Party was defeated after 43 years of governance. Marianne Löwgren has commented that "to a large extent this historic overturning of the Social Democratic Party rule in the 1976 election was due to the appeal of the

Center Party's strongly antinuclear platform."[74] In 1975 the government had announced, and the Parliament (Riksdag) approved, a plan for a dozen nuclear reactors, in spite of public opposition.[75] A few weeks prior to the election, Törbjorn Fälldin, leader of the Center opposition party, promised that if he became prime minister a study of nuclear hazards would be commissioned and that a popular referendum on the future of nuclear power might follow.[76] But the new coalition government was split over nuclear energy, with the Center Party opposed and the other two in favor.[77] A temporizing measure established an Energy Commission, which was supposed to develop a comprehensive energy program.

A much more substantive action was the passage of the Stipulation Act in April 1977. This act transferred the responsibility of nuclear waste management from the state to the nuclear industry. The act required reactor operators to present an acceptable scheme for waste management in order to obtain a license. This could be satisfied by presenting either a contract for reprocessing together with a plan for deposition of the radioactive waste from reprocessing or a plan for final storage of unprocessed fuel.[78] In either case final storage must be achieved with "absolute safety."[79] This act was tested the following year when the government denied an application to operate the Ringhals 3 reactor, concluding that further geological investigation was required to prove that "an area, or areas, exist in Sweden which are of such nature that final storage in compliance with the requirements put down in the Act is possible.... On the grounds of what has been said above, the application cannot be granted for the present."[80] After further investigations (and a change in government), and in spite of an unfavorable report from a panel of geologists, a majority of the Swedish Nuclear Power Inspectorate recommended approving the application. This the government did in June 1979.[81] It is interesting to note that one of the issues that concerned the panel of geologists was the discovery of more crack zones in bore cores than had been marked on Swedish Geological Survey maps. To compensate for this, the Nuclear Fuel Safety organization (KBS) reduced the assumed water permeability in unfractured rock by a factor of 1,000 so as to keep the transport time for the groundwater from the repository to the surface greater than 400 years.[82] This issue of transport time has also come up at Yucca Mountain, as discussed in our chapter "Court Appeals." Another interesting sidelight was provided by two reviewers from the Jet Propulsion Laboratory of the California Institute of Technology, who made the radical suggestion: "In order to properly understand the nature of the geology and the path of groundwater flow, it is necessary to make so many boreholes that the site is no longer suitable for its original purpose, that is, for a high level waste repository."[83] The Three Mile Island accident, which occurred the day after the Swedish Nuclear Power Inspectorate recommendation, diverted attention from the nuclear waste issue to the nuclear reactor safety issue. In response to public concern, a referendum on the future use of nuclear power was announced for March 1980.[84] This decision to hold a referendum effectively removed the nuclear issue from the regularly scheduled September 1979 election, at which time Center Party leader Fälldin was narrowly returned to power as the head of a new coalition government.[85]

The culmination of almost a decade of intense debate was the advisory referendum of March 1980. As it turned out, the results of the referendum were not as definitive as might have been expected. The various political parties supported one of three alternatives. They have been summarized by Zinberg as follows:

> *Alternative I.* Supported by the Moderate Party and business organizations (pronuclear). This proposed that all twelve reactors—those already operating as well as those under construction and those in the planning stage—be used until ready to be decommissioned in approximately twenty-five years. This alternative stressed Sweden's dependence on foreign oil (70%) and the need for industrial expansion to ensure full employment.
>
> (18.9% in favor.)
>
> *Alternative II.* The Social Democrats and the Liberals also proposed twelve reactors and advocated phasing them out by the year 2010. In addition, on the back of the ballot, they stressed the need to move away from electricity intensive industries and housing, to in increasing the use of renewable resources and to turn the nuclear industry from private to public ownership. Conservation would be vigorously promoted.
>
> (39.1% in favor.)
>
> *Alternative III.* The Center and Communist Parties requested a phasing out of the six reactors currently in operation within ten years. No other would be completed or built. Conservation would be stressed and there would be a substantially increased investment in renewable sources of energy.
>
> (38.7% in favor.)

As further noted by Zinberg, various segments of the national and international press gave different emphases in reporting the results of the referendum. As an example, she reports the following headlines:

"AN OVERWHELMING MAJORITY OF SWEDES VOTED AGAINST ANY FURTHER EXTENSION OF NUCLEAR POWER IN A SPECIAL ADVISORY REFERENDUM" (*Nature*, 3/27/80)

"SWEDEN APPEARS TO ENDORSE NUCLEAR ENERGY" (*International Herald Tribune*, 3/24/80)[86]

Later in 1980, the Parliament decided to phase out the existing reactor program by the end of the life of the newest reactors, calculated as the year 2010.[87] This date has never been officially changed, although there is general recognition that complete phaseout is unlikely to be achieved by that date. Fueling of the last two reactors was approved in 1984, with their satisfaction of the Stipulation Act being based on the favorable reviews of the 1983 KBS-3 plan for a geological repository.[88] Parliament also changed the wording of the Stipulation Act by replacing a requirement to show "how and where the absolutely safe disposal of HLW [high-level waste] can be done" with one to "show that a method exists for the management and final deposition…that can be approved regarding safety and radiation protection."[89] By 1985 the nuclear reactor program was complete, with 12 reactors in operation.

In 1997, an energy bill was passed that advanced the phaseout of nuclear power. It also provided considerable subsidies for renewable energy sources and energy conservation programs. The bill created the Swedish Energy Agency to oversee the subsidies and to ensure safe closure of Sweden's 12 reactors.[90] It stipulated that one reactor, Barsebaeck 1, be closed by July 1998, and called for closure of Barsebaeck 2 by July 2001 providing loss in capacity could be made up through energy efficiency and new energy capacity from renewable sources. These reactors had been built quite close to a major population center, Malmö, and are among the older Swedish reactors. Legal battles between the utility that owned the plants and the government were finally settled by the Swedish Supreme Court, which ruled Barsebäck 1 should be shut down by November 30, 1999. This shutdown occurred as ordered. In December 2000, the Parliament set a deadline of the end of 2003 for shutting down the other reactor at this site, Barsebäck 2.[91] This deadline slid, but in 2004, after several years of negotiations with the utilities, the government withdrew from the negotia-tions and announced that Barsebäck 2 would shut down in 2005.[92] Pres-sure to close the second reactor came not only from the Swedish Center Party but also from the mayor of Copenhagen. Copenhagen, Denmark, is only about 25 miles across a sound from the Barsebaeck site. An energy bill passed by the Parliament on June 11, 2002, set no dates for closing the re-maining ten reactors. Studies cited by Lofstedt indicate that a majority of the Swedish public opposes an early phaseout and considers global warm-ing to be more dangerous for Sweden than continued use of nuclear pow-er.[93] It should be noted that Sweden's citizens presently have a somewhat different view of nuclear issues as compared with the citizens of other Eu-ropean Union countries. A survey regarding radioactive waste was taken at the request of the European Commission Directorate-General for Energy and Transport in each of the 15 member countries in 2001. Swedes were the least worried about radioactive waste handling and the most trusting of their national waste management agencies.

The Swedish Nuclear Fuel and Waste Management Co. (Svensk Kärn-bränslehantering AB [SKB]), founded in 1980 by the four Swedish nuclear industries, is responsible for all aspects of the handling and final disposal of nuclear waste in Sweden. This includes the operation of the Central In-terim Storage Facility for Spent Nuclear Fuel, the transport of spent fuel, and the construction of a permanent repository.[94] SKB operates under the supervision of three government authorities: the Swedish National Board for Spent Nuclear Fuel, the Swedish Nuclear Power Inspectorate, and the Swedish Institute for Radiation Protection. Each of these governmental au-thorities has politically appointed boards. Löwgren has observed that such political appointments to independent governmental agencies are one of "the prime means by which the inclusive and consensual style of policy-making is transferred to the administrative sphere, while the interference of sponsoring ministries is strongly resisted."[95]

Sweden's present practice regarding spent nuclear fuel is to let it cool one year at the reactor site and then transport it to the Central Interim Storage Facility for Spent Nuclear Fuel at Oskarshamn, on the Baltic coast 150 miles south of Stockholm. (It has never been envisioned in the United States that on-site cooling would ever be for as short a time as one year.) The interim storage facility consists of subsurface excavated caverns that are filled with water. It was opened in 1985 with a capacity of 3,000 tons but is presently being expanded. There was little public opposition to the creation of this monitored retrievable storage facility, perhaps because it was expected that nuclear power would be phased out as a result of the 1980 referendum and because of the fact that spent fuel could be shipped by sea rather than by rail or truck. Sweden's reactors are located on the coast, and transport of spent fuel between reactor sites and the interim storage facility is performed by a specially built ship with double hulls and double rudders, the *M/S Sigyn*. The concern of opponents in the United States that interim monitored retrievable storage facilities might become de facto permanent does not seem to have been voiced strongly in Sweden. The spent fuel is to be stored underwater at the interim storage facility for 30 years and then eventually to be moved to a permanent repository.

The basic design of the permanent repository was decided about 1983 and is described in a document known as KBS-3. It differs from the Yucca Mountain plan in many respects. The canisters will be placed below the water table in granite bedrock about 1,650 feet below the surface, whereas at Yucca Mountain the canisters will be placed above the water table. An inner iron canister (for mechanical strength) will be surrounded by an outer welded copper canister. Copper is a suitable cladding in the chemically reducing environment below the water table. The space around the canisters will be filled with the clay bentonite, which has the property of swelling when wet and will seal the space between the rock and canisters.[96] In another departure from Yucca Mountain plans (although not the thinking of the U.S. Nuclear Waste Technical Review Board), the cooling prior to emplacement and the separation between canisters will assure that the temperature does not exceed 80 degrees C. The repository is expected to accommodate 9,300 metric tons of spent fuel. In preparation for a permanent repository, the Swedish Nuclear Fuel and Waste Management Co. has constructed a Hard Rock Laboratory at Äspö, an island near the Oskarshamn nuclear power plant. Among the tests being performed there is a canister retrieval test, where a canister of natural size was placed in a deposition hole and surrounded with bentonite. The bentonite is presently being saturated with water, which may take between three and five years. The canister is fitted with a heater to simulate the expected fuel heating. After water saturation SKB plans to demonstrate how a canister can be freed and removed. In another test a copper test vessel is surrounded by bentonite doped with radioactive tracers to study diffusion.[97]

Swedish regulations specify that the annual risk of harmful effects from a repository must not exceed 10^{-6} for a representative member of the most exposed group. The conversion from risk to dose is prescribed as 0.073 per sievert (Sv), leading to a dose limit of about 0.014 mSv/yr (1.4 mrem/yr).[98]

Siting proceeded in several steps. The first was the selection of municipalities for feasibility studies. Under Swedish law municipalities have the final determination on land use issues. The governments of a number of the municipalities first approached declined to accept feasibility studies in their jurisdiction.[99] Six municipalities for which feasibility studies were completed were Tierp, Älvkarleby, and Östhammer (all near the Forsmark nuclear power plant); Nyköping (near the Studsvik nuclear research center); and Oskarshamn and Hultsfred (near the Oskarshamn power plant).[100] Two other municipalities where feasibility studies were performed, Storuman and Mala, rejected further participation early on. This was a consequence of referenda held in 1995 and 1997.[101] As the next step, SKB nominated three sites for further characterization, including drilling of boreholes. Swedish law requires that the municipalities involved also give approval for site characterization. By 2002 two municipalities had agreed (Östhammar and Oskarshamn), and the third, Tierp, had voted against site investigation. Tierp is about 30 miles northeast of Östhammar. It is interesting to note that Östhammar and Oskarshamn already host nuclear power plants, whereas Tierp does not. Oskarshamn also hosts the interim storage facility. This suggests that familiarity with nuclear facilities allays some fears. Perhaps some residents hoped that establishment of a permanent repository might reduce the likelihood that the reactors in the municipality would be shut down, weakening the local economy. On the other hand, one political representative of Oskarshamn, where the interim storage site is located, expressed the fatalism of some: "In our municipality people are saying that everybody knows where the final storage will be located. We need help to change this attitude. When we try to discuss the questions in an open way, people just say that everything is already determined: It is going to be here!"[102] The site characterization investigations are expected to take around five years, and the Swedish Nuclear Fuel and Waste Management Co. estimates that a license application will be submitted in 2007 at the earliest.[103] Swedish law does not spell out clearly the criteria to be used in making the final site selection, nor is it specific as to what body will make the selection.[104]

A distinguishing feature of the Swedish waste disposal program is that the fund established for the disposal of nuclear waste is fully segregated from the utilities and from the government. This is in contrast to the United States, where unspent fees collected from producers each year go into the general fund, with the promise that as part of the "Nuclear Waste Fund" they will be available in future years for waste disposal purposes.[105]

FINLAND

Although Finland only has four operating reactors, it is of special interest because of the progress it has made on nuclear waste management. In 2001 the Finnish Parliament gave final approval to the siting of a deep geological repository at Olkiluoto. Finland is also the only European country to commit itself in recent years to building a new reactor, with the Parliament voting in 2002 107 to 92 to approve a new reactor.[106]

The important steps in developing a nuclear waste management plan can be summarized as follows.[107] In 1983 the government made a policy decision that excluded storage as a long-term method and required that a site for a final repository be selected by the year 2010. In 1987 the Nuclear Energy Act defining the responsibilities of various actors in the nuclear waste arena was passed. This act holds the producers of nuclear waste responsible for its disposal and makes the governmental Radiation and Nuclear Safety Authority the independent safety regulator. The local municipality in which a proposed site lies was given an absolute veto.[108]

In response to the requirement that the producers of nuclear waste have the responsibility for its disposal, the two nuclear power plant operators in Finland formed the organization Posiva Oy. This organization has the responsibility for siting, construction, and operation of the repository.

An amendment in 1994 to the Nuclear Energy Act prohibited the import or export of radioactive waste, requiring the final disposal of any spent fuel produced in Finland to take place in Finland. Environmental Impact Assessments of potential sites, including public involvement, took place in 1997–98. At this time four sites were under consideration for hosting the repository. Posiva Oy chose the Olkiluoto site near two existing nuclear reactors. The Council of Eurajoki, the municipality within which Olkiluoto lies, approved by a 20 to 7 vote hosting the repository in 2000. The Finnish Parliament ratified the governmental recommendation of Olkiluoto in May 2001. Future steps include underground rock characterization studies preparatory to application for a construction license.

The repository at Olkiluoto will be in igneous bedrock at a depth of about 500 meters. The repository concept has drawn on the Swedish plan, with waste containers to be encapsulated in copper and buried in a chemically reducing atmosphere by virtue of being below the water table. The first waste might be emplaced in 2020.

The radiation protection regulations are structured to treat different time regimes separately. For an "initial assessment period that is adequately predictable with respect to assessment of human exposure but that shall be extended to at least several thousand years," the annual dose to the most exposed members of the public shall remain below 0.1 mSv (10 mrem).[109] For longer time periods, specifically including extreme climate changes associated with the glacial cycle, radiation protection criteria are cast in the form of limits on the amounts of specific radionuclides that are allowed to reach the accessible environment.

The relatively smooth and steady progress in addressing the nuclear waste problem in Finland invites an examination of the factors that made this possible. This question was addressed by Isaacs in the concluding talk of the workshop "Stepwise Decision Making in Finland for the Disposal of Spent Nuclear Fuel."[110] Other contributions to the workshop had emphasized the importance of public involvement in an open and transparent process. Isaacs emphasized the importance of public belief in the competence and good intentions of the implementers and regulators. The implementers and regulators must build this confidence over an extended period of time and must show willingness to change program elements in response to legitimate public concerns. The early governmental decision to give a potential host municipality an absolute veto was important in assuring public participation in the environmental assessment process.

Other factors that played a role in Finland's success may be more unique to that country. The isle of Olkiluoto had benefited economically from the successful building and operation of two nuclear power plants. Also the issue of nuclear waste management did not become politicized in Finland. The final approval of Olkiluoto was supported by both major political parties in a 154 to 3 vote.

JAPAN

Japan has 55 nuclear power plants in operation, which produce about 29 percent of its electricity.[111] Nuclear power in Japan has not been without incident. There had been increasing public concern regarding the nuclear fuel cycle since a fatal accident at the Tokai uranium-processing plant in September 1999.[112] In early 2003 Tokyo Electric Power had to temporarily close down 13 of its 17 nuclear reactors for inspection as a consequence of discovering cracks at some reactors. The discovery that safety records had been falsified at several of its nuclear plants for more than 15 years led to the resignation of top executives of Tokyo Electric Power.[113]

Japan ranks third in nuclear generation behind the United States and France. Its policy is to reprocess nuclear waste. Initially spent fuel was reprocessed under contract in England and France. These contracts require that the high-level waste resulting from reprocessing be returned to Japan. Such shipments have resulted in protests, particularly when it was reported that waste from British Nuclear Fuels Limited had been mislabeled and that waste from the French reprocessing agency COGEMA included waste from the reprocessing of European reactor fuel. A major reprocessing plant, costing about $20 billion, is nearing completion in Rokkasho (Rokkashomura), Aomori Prefecture. In November 2004 prefecture officials signed an agreement to allow testing of the facility.[114] Currently the plant is in the stage of final commissioning tests, and operation is expected to start in late 2007.[115]

The policy to reprocess and use the recovered Pu as mixed oxide (MOX) in power plants is being questioned more now on economic grounds. There are few reactors that can presently use MOX fuel, and reactor operators do not find it economically competitive. There is considerable but not universal local political opposition to using MOX. In May 2001, the residents of Kariwa in Niigata voted to reject the introduction of MOX fuel at the nearby Kashiwazaki-Kariwa nuclear power plant. Although the referendum is not legally binding, government officials recognize they need to get the backing of local people before proceeding.[116] The prefectural governments of Fukushima and Niigata have moved to defer the use of MOX fuel within these prefectures.[117] A plan to use MOX at a Genkai reactor was, however, approved in early 2006 by the local assembly and by the governor of the Saga Prefecture in which the Genkai municipality resides.[118] The use of MOX fuel at Genkai would not begin until 2011.[119]

In 2004 it was revealed that the Ministry of Economy, Trade and Industry had covered up a 1994 report that said that reprocessing spent fuel would cost four times as much as simply burying it. As *The Economist* puts it, "The ministry, which is keen on the reprocessing plan, buried the report instead."[120]

Japan has initiated generic research on geological disposal. The Mizunami Underground Research Laboratory will be built in granite in Gifu Prefecture.[121] An agreement was reached in November 2000 to build a second laboratory in sedimentary rock at Horonobe.[122] It is not intended that these underground laboratories become permanent repositories.

In June 2000 new legislation relating to the final disposition of radioactive waste was enacted. The "Specified Radioactive Waste Final Disposal Act" required consultation with prefecture governors and heads of local municipalities when preliminary studies of the proposed sites are made. It also called for the establishment of a new organization to manage high-level waste. This organization, the Nuclear Waste Management Organization of Japan (NUMO) was constituted in October 2000. It is under the jurisdiction of the Ministry of Economy, Trade and Industry, which will have to approve any final disposal plan.[123] Although Burnie and Smith have called the 2000 legislation vague and unrealistic, NUMO appears to have understood its mandate to be substantive.[124] Accepting deep geological disposal as internationally recognized as the safest and most reliable method of isolating high-level waste, NUMO acknowledges it is responsible for identification of the disposal site, construction, operation and maintenance of the repository, closure of the facility, and postclosure institutional control.[125] An intent to start repository operations before 2040 has been mentioned.[126] The repository costs will be covered by a 0.2 yen/kWh surtax on nuclear-generated electricity.[127]

The procedure for site selection was announced in 2002.[128] It will occur in three stages, the first of which will result in selection of "Preliminary Investigation Areas." This stage will start with an "open solicitation" approach for finding candidate sites. The Nuclear Waste Management Organization believes that "the support of local communities is essential to the success of this highly public, long-term project."[129] In December 2002 application information was sent to 3,239 municipalities. As of March 27, 2003, 193 inquiries but no applications had been received. There is no deadline for application—it was hoped a first group would be defined after two years.[130] But by spring 2006 no municipalities had volunteered.[131] The 2002 procedure specified that a literature survey for volunteered sites and comments from authorities of municipalities and governors of prefectures would inform the selection of Preliminary Investigation Areas. This selection was expected to take place about 2007. The act requires that if the literature survey uncovers clearly identified active earthquake faults, proximity (~15 kilometers) to recently active volcanoes, uplift of more than 300 meters during the last 100,000 years, Quaternary unconsolidated deposits, or economically valuable mineral resources, the site will be disqualified. The second stage will involve surface investigations including drilling. This will lead to selection of "Detailed Investigation Areas" (2008–12). The third stage will involve investigations in underground facilities. After further consultation with municipalities and prefectures a final repository selection is anticipated between 2023 and 2027.

RUSSIA

The present Russian Federation has 31 nuclear power plants, with three more under construction.[132] The Ministry of Atomic Energy (Minatom) is responsible for nuclear reactors, reprocessing, and waste disposal. There are an additional somewhat smaller number of plants in countries that were part of the former Soviet Union, principally in Ukraine. A 2001 survey reports over 25,000 tons of spent fuel currently in storage.[133] The Russian reactors are primarily of two types, a pressurized water reactor (VVER) and a graphite-moderated, boiling water–cooled reactor (RBMK). (The Chernobyl reactor was of the latter type.) The VVER reactors have generated the larger fraction of the total spent fuel. It has been the policy to reprocess VVER reactor spent fuel but not RBMK fuel.

As a major nuclear weapons producer, Russia like the United States has a long history of reprocessing spent fuel for military purposes. Russia, however, has been responsible for most of the release of radioactivity to the environment. Bradley has estimated that Russia has discharged about 1.7 billion curies to the environment, exceeding by more than a factor of 100 U.S. releases or Chernobyl reactor accident releases.[134]

The Environmental Protection Act of 1991 prohibited the importation of radioactive material that results in long-term storage or burial on Russian soil. A presidential decree of April 21, 1993, however, allows for the importation of spent fuel from former Soviet republics. By 1995, Bulgaria, Hungary, and Ukraine had sent spent fuel for reprocessing.[135] Also, proposals to establish an international repository in Russia appear from time to time. Legislation to allow the importation of high-level waste for permanent storage was passed by the Russian Parliament and signed by President

Putin on July 10, 2001. There is considerable opposition to this plan. An attempt to force the government to hold a referendum on the importation of nuclear fuel was made at the time this issue was being considered by the Parliament—2.5 million signatures were obtained, but the Central Electoral Commission disallowed 600,000 of the signatures and prevented the referendum from being held.[136]

A special commission to approve and oversee any spent fuel importation has been set up by President Putin. There will be five members each from the Duma (lower house), the Federation Council (upper house), the government, and presidential nominees. It will be chaired by Dr. Zhores Alferov, vice president of the Russian Academy of Sciences and a Nobel laureate.[137]

A potentially lucrative possibility is for Russia to take charge of the 33,000 metric tons of U.S.-origin spent fuel accumulated at non-U.S. sites that the United States originally pledged to take back. Alex Burkart, deputy director of the State Department's Office of Nuclear Energy Affairs, is quoted by Webster as saying, "We cannot expect to see the United States giving consideration to taking irradiated U.S.-origin fuel supplied for electricity generation back for storage and disposition, in Yucca Mountain or elsewhere."[138] Although it would be politically difficult to bring this waste back to the United States, it is still governed by a 1954 nonproliferation law that prevents any agreement involving reprocessing by nations that originally received fuel from the United States (Brazil, the Czech Republic, India, Japan, Mexico, Slovenia, South Korea, Switzerland, Taiwan, and the European Union).[139] Although Russia had originally planned to reprocess imported spent fuel, proposals are now being floated by Minatom to store U.S.-origin spent fuel at Krasnoyarsk until a permanent geologic repository can be built. The Lawrence Livermore Laboratory has participated in joint studies with Russian entities on plans for geological repositories in the Krasnoyarsk and Mayak vicinity.[140] Burkhart has said, "We would not necessarily expect the permanent repository to be available immediately, and we can see a period of long-term storage as part of any scheme. But any scheme should involve specific plans for, and specific commitment of sufficient resource to, the development of a geologic repository."[141] Jardine et al. have proposed that spent fuel from Taiwan, including some U.S.-origin fuel, be stored and eventually disposed of in a geological repository in Russia.[142] Taiwan has a near-term need for spent fuel storage and eventual disposal. It also has considerable financial resources accumulated in its nuclear waste fund that could be used to help develop a geological repository in Russia. The United States could have a number of interests in such a development, including disposition of U.S.-origin fuel, facilitating Russian spent fuel storage and geological disposal capabilities, and supporting future energy security for Taiwan.[143]

The United States has become increasingly concerned about Russia building a nuclear power plant at Dushehr in Iran. In an attempt to discourage the Russians from continuing their assistance to Iran, the United States has expressed willingness to ship U.S.-controlled spent nuclear fuel to Russia for storage. In February 2003, U.S. State Department spokesman Richard Boucher said, "If the Russians end their sensitive cooperation with Iran, we have indicated we would be prepared to favourably consider such transfer, an arrangement potentially worth several billion US dollars in revenue to Moscow."[144] Russia did not respond favorably to this suggestion and on April 24, 2003, announced willingness to buy back spent nuclear fuel burned in the Iranian reactor.[145] But Russia also acknowledged that Iran is buying the fuel and it therefore becomes Iranian property.

Although some high-level waste has already been disposed of in a less-than-satisfactory manner (injection of "high-level liquid waste" into deep wells and sinking of submarines with reactor fuel still on board), the long-term plan is for geological disposal.[146] Several organizations have been studying various aspects of geological disposal. There has been some countrywide screening of favorable areas. More emphasis, however, has been placed on site-specific investigations at locations where waste has been accumulating, particularly Mayak (near Chelyabinsk) and also Krasnoyarsk. There is also considerable spent fuel and other waste at a site near Andreeva Bay in northwest Russia.[147]

In addition to the Mayak area (in the Ural Mountains), sites close to the Krasnoyarsk Mining–Chemical Combine in Siberia are also being considered. The Khlopin Radium Institute has examined the granitoid Nizhnekanskiy Massif in the latter area. Based on rock near the surface, the water permeability, heat conductivity, and radionuclide sorption properties seem to be adequate for a repository. The institute proposed that the next step would be to drill deep boreholes of two–three kilometers depth for further geological and hydrological characterization.

As in many other countries, there is increasing public involvement in nuclear matters in Russia. Opposition by environmental groups to the aforementioned deep injection of high-level waste, and also to the construction of new nuclear reactors, has developed. More recently opposition to the import of spent nuclear fuel has been intense.

INDIA

India has 16 operating reactors producing about 3 percent of the country's electricity.[148] India does not have many fossil fuel resources and therefore plans a large expansion of its nuclear reactor fleet. Seven more reactors are presently under construction.[149]

India's uranium resources are also somewhat limited, but it has considerable thorium resources. India has an active research program for developing a thorium fuel cycle.[150] As part of this cycle, U-233 will be bred from thorium in a fast reactor. India presently has a small research fast reactor and is building a larger fast reactor. This reactor will be fueled with mixed uranium-plutonium oxide with a blanket of thorium and uranium to breed U-233 and plutonium.[151]

Spent fuel from the existing pressurized heavy-water reactors is already being processed at facilities at Trombay (near Mumbai, née Bombay), Tarapur (on the west coast north of Mumbai), and Kalpakkam (on the southeast coast of India). The plutonium will be used to fuel the fast breeder reactors. Vitrification (in a borosilicate matrix) has already commenced at Tarapur and Trombay.[152] A storage and surveillance facility for vitrified waste has been commissioned at Tarapur and Trombay. Interim storage for at least 30 years is anticipated.[153] It is planned to eventually dispose of this waste in a geological repository. Crystalline rock is the favored medium, with a site near Kalpakkam one of the sites under consideration.[154]

CHINA

The People's Republic of China presently has ten operating reactors.[155] These provide about 2 percent of the electricity produced in the country. Five more reactors are under construction, and more are planned.

Already in the 1980s China committed itself to a fuel cycle involving reprocessing. A pilot reprocessing plant is under construction at Lanzhou, and a centralized spent fuel storage facility has already been constructed at this site.[156] Geologic disposal has been investigated since 1985. A requirement that high-level radioactive waste be disposed of in a deep geological repository was codified by a 2003 law.[157] Preliminary investigations have focused on sites in Gansu Province near the Gobi desert in northwestern China.[158] A site is expected to be selected by 2020, after which an underground research laboratory will be constructed at this site. Actual disposal might commence about 2050. There is no information available as to the role of the public in the siting process.

INTERNATIONAL REPOSITORY PROPOSALS

The concept of international disposal of nuclear waste is attractive for a number of reasons. Some countries have rather small nuclear power programs, and the expense of characterizing a deep geological repository site as suitable and of constructing a facility may be prohibitive. It is estimated that a deep geological facility would cost over $1 billion no matter how small the volume of wastes to be disposed of.[159] Some countries may not have suitable geological features. A single international repository might provide better security with respect to theft or terrorism than might be the case with more dispersed disposal in several countries. There are, however, people who hold the view that all countries that produce nuclear waste should dispose of it in their own country.

On the other hand, there are potential problems and difficulties associated with creating international repositories. McCombie has discussed some of the questions that arise from such concerns.[160] He concludes there are no ethical or legal grounds for dismissing international disposal, although he respects the legal right for individual countries to legislate against waste import. The most difficult problem is political acceptance. This cannot be achieved unless a convincing case can be made for the safety of a proposed repository. Political acceptance, however, will also probably have to be coupled to assurances of economic gain for the host country. McCombie also mentions some possible liabilities associated with proposals for international repositories. Countries with active national repository projects may worry that there might be future pressures on them to open up their repositories and hence become the site of an international repository. Another concern is that the prospect of an international repository, no matter how uncertain, might lead some countries to be less committed to preparing a national disposal plan.

In 1998 it was revealed that Pangea Resources was developing a proposal for an International Repository to be located somewhere in the flat, arid Australian outback, probably in South Australia or in Western Australia.[161]

Pangea Resources pointed out that southwestern Australia has a number of physical attributes that make it ideal for a repository, including geologic stability and an arid climate, and it is not likely to be subject to glaciation. On the other hand, Australia does not have any nuclear power plants and thus does not feel obligated to provide for waste disposal on this ground. Australia does mine and export uranium, and some have argued that this places some burden on Australia to play a role in the nuclear fuel cycle. The Australian government took the position that there is no relationship between selling uranium and taking responsibility for waste produced by its use.[162] Pangea's proposal quickly drew strong political opposition. In 1999 Western Australia passed legislation prohibiting the storage or disposal of nuclear waste in the state. South Australia passed similar legislation the following year. The Australian national Senate passed a motion in 1999 opposing Pangea's proposal on the grounds "that such a repository poses significant threats to Australia's environment, public safety and sovereignty."[163]

Following governmental rejection Pangea Resources ceased operations in Australia. A new organization, Pangea International Association, was formed as an international forum for consensus building and issues resolution for an international repository.[164] Later in 2002 this association evolved into the Association for Regional and International Underground Storage with support from Belgium, Bulgaria, Hungary, Japan, and Switzerland.[165] Charles McCombie has been a principal in all three of these organizations. McCombie has laid out the general concept for an International Repository.[166] As mentioned above, Russia is interested in serving as a repository for other countries. Its approach does not envision sponsorship or control by an international body or group of outside countries. Czerwinski has also mentioned South Africa, Argentina, and western China as possible locations.[167] The National Research Council has summarized the status of some proposals for international repositories.[168] One difficulty organizations interested in such repositories face is funding. Not many countries are willing to contribute to international efforts without assurance that eventually there will be a repository open to them. Such assurance is difficult to give.

OVERVIEW

The picture that emerges from this review of nuclear waste policy in foreign countries is that most countries are considerably behind the United States in terms of facing up to high-level waste disposal. Finland and Sweden are the furthest along in terms of a commitment to a particular technology (geologic disposal of nonprocessed spent fuel) and political acceptance of site characterization. Many other countries reprocess their spent fuel or contract with France or Great Britain to reprocess their spent fuel. Those that contract with other countries are required to take back the plutonium and high-level waste. It is doubtful that reprocessing makes economic sense in the present environment of cheap uranium. The creation of larger-volume waste streams and the possibility of accidents and reprocessing plant contamination are also drawbacks. Britain has had particular problems in this regard. The only commercial reprocessing plant in the United States, West Valley in New York, left a legacy of contamination from the very modest amount of reprocessing that took place there before the United States abandoned reprocessing of commercial spent fuel. The French reprocessing facility at La Hague currently releases 99 percent of the I-129 fission product in spent fuel out to sea.[169]

But an even larger problem seems to be developing. An increasing backlog of plutonium from reprocessing is developing in many countries. This is a consequence both of a shortage of reactors that are capable of using plutonium or mixed-oxide fuel (uranium and plutonium) and of increasing political resistance from communities near reactors to have plutonium used as fuel in those reactors capable of using it. The so-called Fast Reactor program in France, which would have used plutonium, has been terminated. Plans to burn mixed-oxide fuel in existing reactors in Japan have met successful opposition.

Another development is increasing public concern with regard to nuclear issues, with respect both to having nuclear power and to the disposal of nuclear waste. Historically there has been a considerable contrast in public involvement among different countries, as, for example, in the neighboring countries of France and Germany. But such differences are decreasing, with the French public showing more interest in nuclear issues. In Russia more than two million people signed a petition calling for a referendum on the import of foreign spent fuel. Although the Central Election Commission rejected this petition on the grounds that too many of the signatures were invalid, environmentalists continue to protest this rejection.[170] Japan has had difficulty in getting local governments to volunteer their municipalities as preliminary investigation areas for a repository.

In Sweden, however, support for terminating nuclear energy is weakening, and Finland has started building a new reactor. In spring 2006 Tony Blair indicated that new nuclear power has to be part of the planning for Britain's energy future.

There has also been a tendency in recent years for governments to distance themselves somewhat from the waste disposal problem. Both Canada and Britain have shifted the responsibility for designing, building, and operating repositories more toward the nuclear industry, while keeping a safety oversight role.

It is interesting to note that in many European countries (e.g., Britain, Finland, the Netherlands, Sweden, and Switzerland) the risk or dose limit for a most-exposed member of the public is considerably more stringent than that suggested by the International Commission on Radiation Protection or proposed in the United States. The timescale for which regulations apply and the manner in which expected repository performance is to be demonstrated vary somewhat from country to country. Typically, however, the limit for the annual risk of serious harm is set at 10^{-6} per year. By this is meant that there should only be one chance in a million that an individual exposed for one year to this radiation source should develop cancer or a heritable genetic defect in their lifetime. This risk level is considerably more restrictive than that which society accepts for a number of other activities.

Using the 1990 International Commission on Radiation Protection factor of 0.073/Sv for converting risk to dose, one obtains a dose limit of 0.014 mSv/year, or 1.4 mrem/year for an annual risk of 10^{-6}.[171] (This conversion factor is dominated by the contribution of fatal cancers [0.050/Sv], with smaller contributions from nonfatal cancers [0.01/Sv] and serious hereditary effects [0.013/Sv].) This dose limit of 0.014 mSv/year is more stringent than the constraint suggested by the International Commission on Radiation Protection of 0.3 mSv/year by a factor of 20.[172] The equivalent dose limit (expressed in mrem rather than in mSv) of 1.4 mrem/year is a factor of ten more stringent than the dose limit of 15 mrem/year that the U.S. Environmental Protection Agency has proposed for Yucca Mountain for the first 10,000 years after closure. The U.S. Environmental Protection Agency's proposed standard for greater than 10,000 years is 250 times more permissive than a 1.4 mrem/yr limit.

NOTES

1. Nuclear Energy Agency, "Nuclear Power in the OECD" (Paris: Organisation for Economic Co-operation and Development, Nuclear Energy Agency, 2001), 248.

2. Jeff Johnson, "Yucca Mountain," *Chemical and Engineering News* 80, no. 27 (July 8, 2002): 20–27.

3. Ibid., 23.

4. World Nuclear Association, "World Nuclear Power Reactors 2005–07 and Uranium Requirements," January 2007, available at www.world-nuclear.org/info/reactors.html.

5. Duane Bratt, "Implementing Kyoto in Canada: The Role of Nuclear Power," *Energy Journal* 26 (January 2005): 107.

6. Government of Canada, "Climate Change Plan for Canada," 2002, available at www.gcsi.ca/downloads/ccpbrief.pdf.

7. Government of Canada, "Moving Forward on Climate Change: A Plan for Honoring our Kyoto Commitment" (Ottawa: Government of Canada, April 13, 2005).

8. Natural Resources Canada, Backgrounder, "Nuclear Fuel Waste in Canada," Natural Resources Canada 98/94 (a), available at www.nrcan-rncan.gc.ca/media/archives/newsreleases/1998/199894a_e.htm.

9. B. L. Murphy and Richard G. Kuhn, "Setting the Terms of Reference: Environmental Assessments Canadian Nuclear Fuel Waste Management," *Canadian Public Policy* 27 (2001): 249–66.

10. Canadian Environmental Assessment Agency, news release, March 13, 1998, available at www.acee-ceaa.gc.ca/010/0001/0001/0012/0003/nr980313_e.htm; see also www.ceaa-acee.gc.ca/010/0001/0001/0012/0001/report_e.htm.

11. Murphy and Kuhn, "Setting the Terms of Reference," 254.

12. Tom Spears, "Costly Cleanup Could Sink Industry," *Kingston Whig-Standard*, February 20, 1999, available at www.energyprobe.org/EnergyProbe/index.cfm?DSP=content&ContentID=136.

13. B. L. Murphy, "Stakeholder Involvement in NFW Management: The Relationship between Democracy and Uncertainty," in *Proceedings of the 9th International High-Level Radioactive Waste Management Conference (IHLRWM)*, April 29–May 3, 2001, Alexis Park Resort, Las Vegas (La Grange Park, IL: American Nuclear Society, 2001).

14. Nuclear Fuel Waste Act, 49-50-51 Elizabeth II Chapter 23, 2002, available at www2.parl.gc.ca/HousePublications/Redirector.aspx?File=31&RefererUrl=%2fHousePublications%2fPublication.aspx%3fDocId%3d2330923%26Language%3de%26Mode%3d1.

15. Nuclear Waste Management Organization (Canada), *Understanding the Choices*, August 2004, 75, available at www.nwmo.ca/adx/asp/adxGetMedia.asp?DocID=164,163, 159,18,1,Documents&MediaID=1515&Filename=NWMO_DD2_e.pdf.

16. Nuclear Waste Management Organization (Canada), *Choosing a Way Forward*, Draft Study Report, May 2005, available at www.nwmo.ca/adx/asp/adxGetMedia.asp ?DocID=1224,1026,20,1,Documents&MediaID=2341&Filename=NWMO_DSR_E. pdf; Nuclear Waste Management Organization (Canada), *Choosing a Way Forward*, Final Report, November 2005, available at http://www.nwmo.ca/adx/asp/adxGetMedia.asp ?DocID=1487,20,1,Documents&MediaID=2703&Filename=NWMO_Final_Study_ Nov_2005_E.pdf.

17. Nuclear Waste Management Organization (Canada), *Choosing a Way Forward*, Final Report, 44.

18. M. Mazurek, "Long-Term Used Nuclear Fuel Waste Management—Geoscientific Review of the Sedimentary Sequence in Southern Ontario," Technical Report TR 04-01, Institute of Geological Sciences, University of Bern, Switzerland, 2004, 6, available at www.nwmo.ca/default.aspx?&DN=713,237,199,20,1,Documents&Print=true.

19. Nuclear Waste Management Organization (Canada), *Choosing a Way Forward*, Final Report, 388.

20. World Nuclear Association, "World Nuclear Power Reactors 2005–07 and Uranium Requirements."

21. Declan Butler, "Energy: Nuclear Power's New Dawn," *Nature* 429, no. 7087 (2004): 238.

22. H. P. Kitschelt, "Political Opportunity Structures and Political Protest: Antinuclear Movements in Four Democracies," *British Journal of Political Science* 16 (1986): 57–85.

23. Jean-Michel Charpin, Benjamin Dessus, and René Pellat, "Economic Forecast Study of the Nuclear Power Option," 2000, available at www.plan.gouv.fr/organisation/.

24. U.S. National Research Council, Committee on Disposition of High-Level Radioactive Waste through Geological Isolation, Board of Radioactive Waste Management, Division on Earth and Life Studies, *Disposition of High-Level Waste and Spent Nuclear Fuel: The Continuing Societal and Technical Challenges* (Washington, DC: National Academy Press, 2001).

25. Robert Jan van den Berg and Herman Damveld, "Discussions on Nuclear Waste," Laka Foundation, Amsterdam, 2000, available at www.laka.org/.

26. U.S. National Research Council, Committee on Disposition of High-Level Radioactive Waste through Geological Isolation, Board of Radioactive Waste Management, Division on Earth and Life Studies, *Disposition of High-Level Waste and Spent Nuclear Fuel*, 56.

27. Tim McEwen, "Selection of Waste Disposal Sites," in *The Scientific and Regulatory Basis for the Geological Disposal of Radioactive Waste*, ed. D. Savage (New York: J. Wiley and Sons, 1995), 222.

28. P. J. Richardson, "A Review of Benefits Offered to Volunteer Communities for Siting Nuclear Waste Facilities," Geosciences for Development and the Environment, United Kingdom, March 1998, prepared for Sweden's nuclear waste program.

29. S. Mayer, B. Faucher, and J.-M. Hoorelbeke, "Dossier 2005: ANDRA's Feasibility Study of Geological Disposal," in *Proceedings of the 11th International High-Level Radioactive Waste Management Conference (IHLRWM)*, April 30–May 4, 2006, Las Vegas (La Grange Park, IL: American Nuclear Society, 2006), 1164–72.

30. "Headlines: International Briefs," *Radwaste Solutions* 13 (May–June 2006): 9.

31. World Nuclear Association, "World Nuclear Power Reactors 2005–07 and Uranium Requirements."

32. Stephen Graham, Associated Press, "Germany Snuffs Out Nuclear Plant," *Seattle Times*, November 15, 2003: A10.

33. Mark Hibbs, "Economy Chief Says Germany Can't Phase Out Nuclear and Cut Carbon," *Platts Nucleonics Week* 42, no. 48 (November 29, 2001): 1.

34. Nuclear Power, "Half Life," *The Economist* 381, no. 8503 (November 11, 2006): 71–72.

35. D. Gay and K.-J. Röhlig, "Handling of Timescales in Safety Assessments of Geological Disposal: An IRSN-GRS Standpoint in the Possible Role of Regulatory Guidance," in *The Handling of Timescales in Assessing Post-closure Safety of Deep Geological Repositories*, Workshop Proceedings, April 16–18, 2002, Paris (Paris: Nuclear Energy Agency/Organisation for Economic Co-operation and Development, 2002), 91–98.

36. A. Blowers, D. Lowry, and B. D. Solomon, *The International Politics of Nuclear Waste* (New York: St. Martin's Press, 1991), 263.

37. McEwen, "Selection of Waste Disposal Sites," 213.

38. U.S. National Research Council, Committee on Disposition of High-Level Radioactive Waste through Geological Isolation, Board of Radioactive Waste Management, Division on Earth and Life Studies, *Disposition of High-Level Waste and Spent Nuclear Fuel*.

39. News Update, "Gorleben: Why Stop Now?" *Nuclear Engineering International* 47, no. 576 (July 2002): 12.

40. European Nuclear Society, "Germany Agrees to Limit Working Lives to 32 Years," *Nucleus*, July–August 2000: 1, available at www.euronuclear.org/pdf/nucleus_04_2000.pdf.

41. A. L. Campbell and J. K. Morgan, "Federalism and the Politics of Old-Age Care in Germany and the United States," *Comparative Political Studies* 38, no. 8 (2005): 807–914.

42. World Nuclear Association, "World Nuclear Power Reactors 2005–07 and Uranium Requirements."

43. U.K. Secretary of State for Trade and Industry, *Our Energy Future—Creating a Low Carbon Economy*, February 24, 2003, available at www.dti.gov.uk/files/file10719.pdf.

44. Alan Cowell, "British Review of Energy to Include Atomic Power," *New York Times*, November 30, 2005.

45. P. Wintour and D. Adam, "Blair Presses the Nuclear Button," *The Guardian*, May 17, 2006, available at www.guardian.co.uk/science/story/0,,1776498,00.html.

46. Stan Openshaw, Steve Carver, and John Fernie, *Britain's Nuclear Waste: Siting and Safety* (London: Bellhaven Press, 1989), 26; Friends of the Earth, *British Nuclear Fools: The Case against Reprocessing* (London: Friends of the Earth, 1992).

47. Nick Cassidy and Patrick Green, *Sellafield: The Contaminated Legacy* (London: Friends of the Earth, 1993), 28.

48. Oliver Morgan, "Close Nuclear Leak Plant for Good, Says Sellafield," *The Guardian*, May 15, 2005, available at http://politics.guardian.co.uk/print/0,385;8,5193810-107983,00.html.

49. Royal Commission on Environmental Pollution, "Flowers Report," 1976, quoted in Openshaw, Carver, and Fernie, *Britain's Nuclear Waste*, 48.

50. Ibid.

51. Ibid., 36.

52. Frank Wilson, *European Politics Today* (Englewood Cliffs, NJ: Prentice Hall, 1990), 80.

53. U.K. House of Lords Science and Technology Committee, "Science and Technology—Third Report," March 10, 1999, available at www.publications.parliament.uk/pa/ld199899/ldselect/ldsctech/41/4101.htm.

54. van den Berg and Damveld, "Discussions on Nuclear Waste."

55. Ibid.

56. U.K. Department for Environment, Food and Rural Affairs, "Managing Radioactive Waste Safely: Proposals for Developing a Policy for Managing Solid Radioactive Waste in the UK," Department of the Environment, National Assembly for Wales, and Scottish Executive, September 2001, available at www.defra.gov.uk/environment/consult/radwaste/pdf/radwaste.pdf.

57. U.K. House of Lords Science and Technology Committee, "Radioactive Waste Management," December 10, 2004, 5, available at www.publications.parliament.uk/pa/ld200304/ldselect/ldsctech/200/200.pdf.

58. U.K. House of Lords Science and Technology Committee, "Radioactive Waste Management."

59. Ibid., 6.

60. U.K. Committee on Radioactive Waste Management, "The Options for Long-Term Management of Higher Active Solid Radioactive Wastes in the United Kingdom," November 2004, available at www.corwm.org.uk/pdf/Options.pdf.

61. U.K. Committee on Radioactive Waste Management, "Terms of Reference," 2004, 12, available at www.corwm.org.uk/content-261.

62. U.K. House of Lords Science and Technology Committee, "Radioactive Waste Management," 4.

63. Geoff Brumfiel, "Forward Planning," *Nature* 440, no. 7087 (2006): 989.

64. "UK Plods Ahead on Wastes," *Newsletter, World Nuclear Association* 3, no. 3 (May–June 2005), available at www.win-global.org/news/WIN_News_3_05.pdf.

65. U.K. Committee on Radioactive Waste Management, *Managing Our Radioactive Waste Safely: CoRWM's Recommendations to Government*, July 2006, available at www.corwm.org.uk/content-1092.

66. Ibid., 11.

67. Ibid., 12.

68. Ibid., 7.

69. A. McCall and S. King, "Generic Repository Concept Development and Assessment for UK High-Level Waste and Spent Nuclear Fuel," in *Proceedings of the 11th High-Level Radioactive Waste Management Conference (IHLRWM)*, April 30–May 4, 2006, Las Vegas (La Grange Park, IL: American Nuclear Society, 2006), 1173–79.

70. R. Wilmot, "Survey of the Role of Uncertainty and Risk in Current Regulations," in *Management of Uncertainty in Safety Cases and the Role of Risk*, Workshop Proceedings, February 2–4, 2004, Stockholm (Paris: Nuclear Energy Agency, Organisation for Economic Co-operation and Development, 2004), 71.

71. World Nuclear Association, "World Nuclear Power Reactors 2005–07 and Uranium Requirements."

72. Göran Sundqvist, *The Bedrock of Opinion: Science, Technology and Society in the Siting of High-Level Nuclear Waste* (Dordrecht: Kluwer Academic Publishers, 2002), 59–60.

73. Ibid., 70.

74. Marianne Löwgren, "Nuclear Waste Management in Sweden: Balancing Risk Perceptions and Developing Community Consensus," in *Problems and Prospects for Nuclear Waste Disposal Policy*, ed. E. Herzik and A. H. Mushkatel (Westport, CT: Greenwood Press, 1993), 107.

75. Blowers, Lowry, and Solomon, *The International Politics of Nuclear Waste*, 274.

76. Luther J. Carter, *Nuclear Imperatives and Public Trust: Dealing with Radioactive Waste* (Washington, DC: Resources for the Future, Inc., 1987), 292.

77. T. B. Johansson and P. Steen, *Radioactive Waste from Nuclear Power Plants* (Berkeley: University of California Press, 1981), 5.

78. Ibid., 7.

79. Carter, *Nuclear Imperatives and Public Trust*, 293.

80. Johansson and Steen, *Radioactive Waste from Nuclear Power Plants*, 8.

81. Ibid., 9; Blowers, Lowry, and Solomon, *The International Politics of Nuclear Waste*, 276.

82. Sundqvist, *The Bedrock of Opinion*, 91; KBS is the acronym for Nuclear Fuel Safety in Swedish, Kärn-Bränsle Säkerhet.

83. Ibid., 151.

84. Carter, *Nuclear Imperatives and Public Trust*, 298.

85. Ibid.

86. Dorothy S. Zinberg, "Public Participation: U.S. and European Perspectives," in *The Politics of Nuclear Waste*, ed. E. W. Colglazier Jr. (New York: Pergamon Press, 1982), 178–79.

87. Blowers, Lowry, and Solomon, *The International Politics of Nuclear Waste*, 277.

88. Carter, *Nuclear Imperatives and Public Trust*, 304.

89. Löwgren, "Nuclear Waste Management in Sweden," 114.

90. Ragnar E. Lofstedt, "Playing Politics with the Energy Policy: The Phase-Out of Nuclear Power in Sweden," *Environment* 43 (May 2001): 21.

91. Ibid.

92. Ariane Sains, "Sweden to Order Barsebaeck-2 Closed," *Nucleonics Week* 45, no. 41 (October 7, 2004): 1.

93. Lofstedt, "Playing Politics with the Energy Policy," 21.

94. U.S. Department of Energy, Office of Civilian Radioactive Waste Management, "Sweden's Radioactive Waste Management Program," June 2001, available at www.ocrwm.doe.gov/factsheets/doeymp0416.shtml.

95. Löwgren, "Nuclear Waste Management in Sweden," 115.

96. U.S. Department of Energy, Office of Civilian Radioactive Waste Management, "Sweden's Radioactive Waste Management Program."

97. Tommy Hedman, "The Swedish Program Enters the Site Selection Phase," *Radwaste Solutions* 10 (March–April 2003): 53.

98. A. Hedin, "Methodology for Risk Assessment of an SNF Repository in Sweden," in *Management of Uncertainty in Safety Cases and the Role of Risk, Workshop Proceedings*, February 2–4, 2004, Stockholm (Paris: Nuclear Energy Agency, Organisation for Economic Co-operation and Development, 2004), 211.

99. Lennart Sjöberg, Mattias Viklund, and Jana Truedsson, "Attitudes and Opposition in Sitting a High Level Nuclear Waste Repository, Facility Siting: Issues and Perspectives" *Academia Sinica*, Earthscape, available at www.earthscape.org/r1/sjl01.

100. Mikael Jensen, private communication, 2003.

101. O. Olsson, K. Ahlbom, and P. Wikberg, "Progress of the Investigations of Potential Repository Sites in Sweden," in *10th International High-Level Radioactive Waste Management Conference (IHLRWM)*, March 30–April 3, 2003, Las Vegas (La Grange Park, IL: American Nuclear Society, 2003), 83–89.

102. Sundqvist, *The Bedrock of Opinion*, 3.

103. European Nuclear Society, "Sweden with Two Possible Sites for High Level Radioactive Waste Disposal," *Nucleus*, June 2002, available at www.euronuclear.org/pdf/Nucleus_02_2002.pdf.

104. Sundqvist, *The Bedrock of Opinion*, 5.

105. Neil Chapman and Charles McCombie, *Principles and Standards for the Disposal of Long-Lived Radioactive Wastes* (Amsterdam: Pergamon, 2003), 54.

106. Lizette Alvarez, "Finland Is Nothing If Not Pragmatic and Law Abiding," *New York Times*, December 12, 2005: A10.

107. Nuclear Energy Agency, *Stepwise Decision Making in Finland for the Disposal of Spent Nuclear Fuel*, Workshop Proceedings, November 2001, Turku (Paris: Nuclear Energy Agency, Organisation for Economic Co-operation and Development, 2002).

108. J. Vira, "Step-Wise Decision-Making on Trial: The Case of Finland," in *Proceedings of the 9th International High-Level Radioactive Waste Management Conference (IHLRWM)*, April 29–May 3, 2001, Las Vegas (La Grange Park, IL: American Nuclear Society, 2001).

109. E. Ruokola, "Consideration of Unlikely Events and Uncertainties in the Finnish Safety Regulations for Spent Fuel Disposal," in *Management of Uncertainty in Safety Cases and the Role of Risk*, Workshop Proceedings, February 2–4, 2004, Stockholm (Paris: Nuclear Energy Agency, Organisation for Economic Co-operation and Development, 2004), 123.

110. T. Isaacs, "Thematic Report on Strategic Decision Making," in *Stepwise Decision Making in Finland for the Disposal of Spent Nuclear Fuel*, Workshop Proceedings, November 2001, Turku (Paris: Nuclear Energy Agency, Organisation for Economic Co-operation and Development, 2002), 125.

111. World Nuclear Association, "World Nuclear Power Reactors 2005–07 and Uranium Requirements."

112. M. Schreurs, *Environmental Politics in Japan, Germany, and the United States* (Cambridge: Cambridge University Press, 2002), 222.

113. Ken Belson, "Why Japan Steps Gingerly in the Mideast," *New York Times*, September 17, 2002: W1.

114. Ichiko Fuyuno, "Nuclear Agreement Paves Way for Fuel Recycling in Japan," *Nature* 422, no. 7017 (December 2, 2004): 539.

115. Japan Nuclear Fuel Limited, "Operational Progress (as of End of March 31, 2006)," available at www.jnfl.co.jp/english/progress.html.

116. David Cyanoski, "Referendum Stalls Japanese Nuclear Power Strategy," *Nature* 411, no. 6839 (June 14, 2001): 729.

117. Uranium Information Center, "Nuclear Power in Japan," Briefing Paper #79, Melbourne, Australia (April 2007), available at www.uic.com.au/nip79.htm.

118. "Town Approves MOX Reactor Plan; OK Expected from Saga Governor," *Japan Times*, February 18, 2006.

119. "Genkai, Saga Grant Request to Burn MOX," *Japan Times*, March 27, 2006.

120. "Bursting Point," *The Economist* 372 (August 14, 2004): 55.

121. G. F. D. McCrank, K. Sugihara, K. Ota, S. Mikake, T. Amano, K. Koide, and S. Takeda, "The MIU Research Laboratory, Japan Geoscience Activities during Construction and Operation," in *Proceedings of the 9th International High-Level Radioactive Waste Management Conference (IHLRWM)*, April 29–May 3, 2001, Las Vegas (La Grange Park, IL: American Nuclear Society, 2001).

122. S. Masuda, "Evolution of Geological Repository Program in Japan," in *Proceedings of the 9th International High-Level Radioactive Waste Management Conference (IHLRWM)*, April 29–May 3, 2001, Las Vegas (La Grange Park, IL: American Nuclear Society, 2001).

123. Ibid.

124. Shaun Burnie and Aileen Mioko Smith, "Japan's Nuclear Twilight Zone," *Bulletin of the Atomic Scientists* 57, no. 3 (May–June 2001): 58.

125. See www.numo.or.jp; U.K. Department for Environment, Food and Rural Affairs, "Managing Radioactive Waste Safely."

126. U.S. National Research Council, Committee on Disposition of High-Level Radioactive Waste through Geological Isolation, Board of Radioactive Waste Management, Division on Earth and Life Studies, *Disposition of High-Level Waste and Spent Nuclear Fuel*; Masuda, "Evolution of Geological Repository Program in Japan."

127. "Headlines: International Updates," *Radwaste Solutions* 11 (March–April 2004): 12.

128. Nuclear Waste Management Organization of Japan, "Open Solicitation for Candidate Sites for Safe Disposal of High-Level Radioactive Waste," Tokyo, December 2002, available at www.numo.or.jp.

129. Ibid., 2.

130. Sumio Masuda, remarks at Global Issues Salient to Geologic Disposal Progress—International Panel, *10th International High-Level Radioactive Waste Management Conference*, March 30–April 3, 2003, Las Vegas (La Grange Park, IL: American Nuclear Society, 2003).

131. Makoto Kajikawa, personal communication, April 2006.

132. World Nuclear Association, "World Nuclear Power Reactors 2005–07 and Uranium Requirements."

133. U.K. Department for Environment, Food and Rural Affairs, "Managing Radioactive Waste Safely."

134. Don J. Bradley and David R. Payson, eds., *Behind the Nuclear Curtain: Radioactive Waste Management in the Former Soviet Union* (Columbus, OH: Battelle Press, 1997), 18–19.

135. Ibid., 87.

136. Igor Kudrik, "Russia Open for Nuclear Waste Import," the Bellona Foundation, July 11, 2001, available at www.bellona.no/en/international/russia/nuke_industry/waste_imports/21326.html.

137. World Nuclear Association, "Nuclear Power in Russia," April 2007, available at www.world-nuclear.org/info/inf45.html.

138. Paul Webster, "Minatom: The Grab for Trash," *Bulletin of the Atomic Scientists* 58, no. 5 (2002): 36. •

139. Atomic Energy Act of 1954, Ch. 11, Sec. 123 a.(7), 1954.

140. Webster, "Minatom."

141. Ibid., 36.

142. L. J. Jardine, W. G. Halsey, and C. F. Smith, "Technical Framework to Facilitate Foreign Spent Fuel Storage and Geologic Disposal in Russia," submitted to "HLW, LLW, Mixed Wastes and Environmental Restoration—Working towards a Cleaner Environment Conference," February 27–March 2, 2000, Tucson.

143. Ibid.

144. Charles Digges, "US Publicly Offers SNF to Russia If Moscow Abandons Iran," the Bellona Foundation, February 5, 2003, available at www.bellona.no/en/international/russia/nuke_industry/waste_imports/28221.html.

145. Igor Kudrik, "Russia to Buy Back Spent Nuclear Fuel Burnt in Iranian Reactor," the Bellona Foundation, April 24, 2003, available at www.bellona.no/en/international/russia/nuke_industry/waste_imports/29396.html.

146. Bradley and Payson, *Behind the Nuclear Curtain*, 463, 489.

147. "Headlines: International Briefs," *Radwaste Solutions* 12 (March–April 2005): 8.

148. World Nuclear Association, "World Nuclear Power Reactors 2005–07 and Uranium Requirements."

149. Ibid.

150. Uranium Information Centre, "Nuclear Power in India and Pakistan," UIC Nuclear Issues Briefing Paper #45, May 2006, available at www.uic.com.au/nip45.htm.

151. Ibid.

152. Kanwar Raj, "Commissioning and Operation of High Level Radioactive Waste Vitrification and Storage Facilities: The Indian Experience," *International Journal of Nuclear Energy Science and Technology* 1, nos. 2–3 (2005): 148–63, available at http://inderscience.metapress.com/media/pe669ujopp4tumbobk91/contributions/n/9/t/v/n9tvnnka28k1r73a.pdf.

153. Ibid.

154. Eureka County (Nevada) Yucca Mountain Information Office, available at www.yuccamountain.org.

155. World Nuclear Association, "World Nuclear Power Reactors 2005–07 and Uranium Requirements."

156. Ibid.

157. Huazhu Zhang, "Present Situation and Perspective of China's Geological Disposal of High-Level Radioactive Waste," in *Geological Repositories: Political and Technical Progress*, Workshop Proceedings, December 7–10, 2003, Stockholm, Nuclear Energy Agency Report No. 5299 (Paris: Organisation for Economic Co-operation and Development, 2005), 37–40.

158. Ibid.

159. Charles McCombie, "International and Regional Repositories: The Key Questions," in *Proceedings of the 9th International High-Level Radioactive Waste Management Conference (IHLRWM)*, April 29–May 3, 2001, Las Vegas (La Grange Park, IL: American Nuclear Society, 2001).

160. Ibid.

161. I. Holland, "Waste Not Want Not? Australia and the Politics of High-Level Nuclear Waste," *Australian Journal of Political Science* 37, no. 2 (2002): 283–301.

162. Holland, "Waste Not Want Not?"

163. Ibid., 286.

164. "Pangea Resources Metamorphisizing into International Repository Forum," *Nuclear Waste News* 22, no. 5 (January 31, 2002): 41.

165. See www.arius-world.org; "Pangea Becomes Support Group for Multinational Repositories," *Nuclear Waste News* 22, no. 20 (May 16, 2002): 198.

166. McCombie, "International and Regional Repositories."

167. K. Czerwinski, lecture notes, Massachusetts Institute of Technology, Cambridge, MA, 2001.

168. U.S. National Research Council, Committee on Disposition of High-Level Radioactive Waste through Geological Isolation, Board of Radioactive Waste Management, Division on Earth and Life Studies, *Disposition of High-Level Waste and Spent Nuclear Fuel*.

169. Pierre Bacher, quoted in Ann MacLachlan, "French Hail Strides in P&T but Question Strategy, Cost," *Platts Nuclear Fuel* 30, no. 5 (February 28, 2005): 10.

170. Webster, "Minatom."

171. *Recommendations of the International Committee on Radiological Protection*, ICRP Publication 60, Annals of the ICRP 21, nos. 1–3 (Oxford: Pergamon Press, 1991).

172. *Radiation Protection Recommendations as Applied to the Disposal of Long-Lived Solid Radioactive Waste*, ICRP Publication 81, Annals of the ICRP 28, no. 4 (Oxford: Pergamon Press, 1998).

⠇ Appendix A

Organizations Concerned with Nuclear Waste Issues

U.S. AGENCIES, COMMISSIONS, AND DEPARTMENTS

The Nuclear Regulatory Commission

The Nuclear Regulatory Commission (NRC) was established with the breakup of the Atomic Energy Commission (AEC) in 1976 when it was somewhat belatedly realized that the AEC could not effectively serve as both the advocate for and the regulator of nuclear power. Birkeland has pointed out that prior to the breakup of the AEC and the establishment of the NRC, "nuclear policy was monopolized by the Atomic Energy Commission, the nuclear utilities, the builders of nuclear power plants, the civil and military establishment and the Joint Committee on Atomic Energy (JCAE)."[1] The JCAE was one of the more powerful joint committees of Congress. This monopoly began to break up in the 1970s as interest groups and the public became increasingly concerned about the cost and safety of nuclear power. The Three Mile Island nuclear reactor accident in Pennsylvania in 1979 and the multimillion-dollar default on nuclear power plant bonds in Washington State in 1982 greatly accelerated these concerns with both safety and cost.

The NRC is made up of five members who are nominated by the president and must be confirmed by the Senate. They serve five-year staggered terms with one member retiring every year. An executive director administers the agency, distancing the commissioners from routine administrative functions.[2] The commission is advised by an Advisory Committee on Nuclear Waste. The five members of the Advisory Committee on Nuclear Waste are appointed by the commission, and it operates independently of the NRC staff.[3]

The NRC regulates civilian nuclear reactors, repositories for non-military wastes, and other facilities, including licensing. It also regulates handling of nuclear wastes generated by nonmilitary facilities as well as uranium mining and milling. In 2001, the budget of the NRC was approximately $510 million, and it employed approximately 2,800 persons.[4] The NRC is responsible for licensing the Yucca Mountain repository and for supervision of the waste disposal process at the repository should it be approved.

Environmental groups have been critical of the NRC's supervision of nuclear reactors and nuclear waste repositories and generally feel that it sides too often with the nuclear power industry.[5] The NRC has also been criticized for responding sluggishly and with disproportionately small penalties to violations of safety rules. Rosenbaum notes that after the Three Mile Island reactor accident in Pennsylvania, the NRC responded more quickly and with stronger penalties to infractions.[6] Rosenbaum also mentions the General Accounting Office criticism of the NRC for not shutting down reactors with chronic problems.[7]

The Department of Energy

The Department of Energy is a Cabinet department headed by the secretary of energy, who is nominated by the president and confirmed by a majority vote of the Senate. Among the Cabinet secretaries, the position of energy secretary is less prestigious than most. Although the technical and scientific responsibilities of the DOE are significant, many energy secretaries have been political appointees. Most have been lacking in or have had weak technical credentials. Despite this, nearly all of the presidential nominees for the position of energy secretary have been confirmed by unanimous or nearly unanimous votes of the Senate. A brief summary of the background and accomplishments of each energy secretary is given in Appendix D.

Among the responsibilities of the department are insuring delivery of electricity, energy source development (which has primarily been concerned with fossil fuel and nuclear energy sources), disposal of "legacy" military nuclear wastes, and disposal of commercial nuclear reactor spent fuel. Until the Three Mile Island nuclear reactor accident in Pennsylvania in 1976, the department was primarily responsive to the energy industry and to energy industry associations. After the Three Mile Island accident environmental and public interest groups began to "weigh in" on Energy

Department policies and the nomination and confirmation of the energy secretary.

The Energy Department has been criticized by both official and non-official sources. In 2001, the General Accounting Office issued a report that was very critical of the DOE. Among the problems cited were major cost overruns, significant schedule delays, confusion about the roles and responsibilities of headquarters and field staff, poor oversight of contractors, unsatisfactory arrangements for regulating worker safety, and inadequate results in its efforts to clean up the military nuclear waste.[8] Political scientist Walter Rosenbaum has called attention to the "disastrous mismanagement of the military nuclear weapons facilities" by the DOE and predicts that the cleanup costs may reach over $250 billion and take a century. Rosenbaum attributes the DOE problems to both the system and the leadership. He claims that the DOE has conflicting responsibilities and has lacked strong leadership. Constant internal reorganization, Rosenbaum claims, has left the staff of the DOE demoralized and confused about its mission.[9]

The energy industry has been critical of the DOE for delays in opening the permanent repository for commercial spent fuel at Yucca Mountain, Nevada. The 1982 Nuclear Waste Policy Act mandated that this repository accept commercial spent fuel by 1998. The repository is still not open and probably will not accept waste until 2017, if ever. During the Clinton administration bills were introduced in the House three times by Republicans to abolish the DOE.

Environmental Protection Agency

The Environmental Protection Agency (EPA) was created by the U.S. Congress in 1970 in response to growing public concern about air, water, and land pollution. The agency develops and enforces regulations enacted by Congress. It is an executive branch agency headed by an administrator appointed by the president and confirmed by a majority vote of the Senate. Fluctuations in party control of Congress and of the presidency have been accompanied by variations in environmental protection laws and regulations as well as their enforcement.

The EPA's mandate to regulate the release of radioactive material from nuclear waste repositories was made explicit in the Nuclear Waste Policy Act of 1982. The EPA was directed to establish standards for protection of the offsite environment, and the Nuclear Regulatory Commission was directed to establish licensing regulations consistent with these standards.

The EPA responded to this direction in 1985 by the issuance of Title 40, part 191, of the *Code of Federal Regulations* (CFR). (EPA regulations are found in Title 40; NRC and DOE regulations, in Title 10. Specific sections are usually designated by abbreviations such as 40 CFR 191.) The standards set forth in this issuance included an individual protection dose limit of 25 millirems per year to any member of the public in the accessible environment for 1,000 years after disposal. It also had containment requirements that limited the projected release of radioactivity to the accessible environment for 10,000 years after disposal.

These standards were challenged in court by the Natural Resources Defense Council, joined by some states and other organizations. In 1987, a federal court ruled in favor of the appellants, and much of 40 CFR 191 was vacated and sent back to the EPA for revision. Late in 1987, Congress selected Yucca Mountain as the only site to be further characterized as a potential repository. The EPA had not come forward with its revisions by 1992, at which time Congress enacted the Energy Policy Act of 1992. This act directed the Environmental Protection Agency to develop radiation standards specific to Yucca Mountain but also required it to base these standards on advice from a study it commissioned from the National Academy of Sciences (NAS). The NAS issued its recommendations in 1995.[10] Finally, in 2001 the EPA issued new standards specific to Yucca Mountain.

As discussed in chapter 10, the Natural Resources Defense Council, joined by the State of Nevada, again challenged the new standards on a number of grounds. In 2004 the District of Columbia Court of Appeals rejected the part of the standards that only required compliance for 10,000 years, citing the National Academy of Sciences' advice that compliance should last to the time of projected peak dose. The court directed the EPA to revise this part of its standard and submit a revised standard to the court for review. In late summer 2005 the EPA issued a draft revision and, as required by law, sought comment from interested parties. This draft revision is discussed in chapter 7. As of March 2007 the EPA had not issued its final standard for court review.

We conclude that the EPA has had a mixed record for developing radiation standards that can withstand judicial scrutiny. In several instances courts have ruled that the standards issued were not sufficiently protective of the public or responsive to congressional direction.

National Academy of Sciences/National Research Council

The National Academy of Sciences as well as the National Academy of Engineering and the Institute of Medicine are congressionally chartered nonprofit institutions that provide science, technology, and health policy advice. The academies elect their own membership. There is considerable prestige associated with being elected to an academy. The National Research Council is the principal operating arm of the aforementioned institutions and is administered by them through the National Research Council Governing Board.[11] (We avoid the use of the acronym NRC for the National Research Council as the same acronym is used for the Nuclear Regulatory Commission.) The council often contracts with governmental entities to perform specific studies. The National Academies Press makes many of the National Research Council reports available on its website.[12]

The *Technical Bases for Yucca Mountain Standards* report, originating in a mandate of the Energy Act of 1992, has had a defining role in the effort to create a high-level waste repository.[13] The committee generating the report consisted of 15 members. They were drawn from academic (7), nongovernmental (5), and industrial (3) organizations.

National Council on Radiation Protection and Measurement

The National Council on Radiation Protection and Measurement evolved from an informal body to become a congressionally chartered body in 1964. Although its objectives are specified by public law, it is a private corporation rather than a governmental body. It does not receive congressional appropriations, but as an educational and scientific body it is tax exempt. Its 100 members serve staggered six-year terms and elect their successors on the basis of their scientific expertise. It researches and makes recommendations on a broad range of issues including units and measurements, medical practices, and occupational and public radiation-protection standards. It typically issues several reports each year. The council's recommendations are utilized by such governmental bodies as the Nuclear Regulatory Commission, the Public Health Service, and the Environmental Protection Agency.[14]

INTERNATIONAL ORGANIZATIONS

There are several international organizations that play a role in the development and statement of principles for radioactive waste management.

The International Atomic Energy Agency

The International Atomic Energy Agency (IAEA) was established by the United Nations to ensure world cooperation in the peaceful use of nuclear energy. It has established policies for the prevention of diversion of nuclear materials to weapons production and has developed safety guidelines in relation to the key components of the nuclear cycle. Though IAEA guidelines and regulations have no legal jurisdiction, in practice member countries often comply with their recommendations.

The International Commission on Radiological Protection

This commission is an independent body of medical and scientific experts. The Main Commission, comprising 12 members and a chair, elects its own members under rules subject to the approval of the International Society of Radiology. These rules require that three to five members must be changed every fourth year. During 2001–5 the chairman and members were drawn from ten countries. The commission publishes regularly updated recommendations on the effects of radiation exposure on health. Its work is highly respected, and its recommendations are often used in establishing national regulations on radiation protection.

The Nuclear Energy Agency of the Organisation for Economic Co-operation and Development

The Nuclear Energy Agency (NEA) of the Organisation for Economic Co-operation and Development was created to promote cooperation among member states in furthering the development of nuclear power. The Radioactive Waste Management Committee of the NEA considers radioactive waste disposal issues. In 1995 it issued a report, "The Environmental and Ethical Basis of Geological Disposal."[15] It concluded that from an ethical standpoint society's responsibility to future generations is best served by final disposal rather than long-term storage. It also reaffirmed that a geological disposal strategy can be designed that is responsive to environmental considerations.

Recently the European Union has started the process of establishing common standards for the management of nuclear waste. Its European Commission proposes legislation to the Council of Ministers, the body that approves legislation for the European Union. In spring 2003 the European Commission issued a proposal that "effectively requires member countries to plan for geological disposal of high-activity waste, unless it has a proven alternative technology, which does not include long-term sur-face storage."[16] Export of waste to another country having an acceptable disposal facility would be allowed. The proposal requires a choice of a dis-posal site by 2008 and an operational repository by 2018.

NOTES

1. Thomas A. Birkeland, *An Introduction to the Policy Process: Theories, Concepts and Models of Public Policy-Making* (Armonk, NY: M. Sharpe, 2001), 227–28.

2. Dan B. Wood and Richard W. Waterman, "The Dynamics of Political Control of the Bureaucracy," *American Political Science Review* 85, no. 3 (1991): 801–28.

3. See www.nrc.gov/about-nrc/regulatory/advisory/acnw.html.

4. Walter A. Rosenbaum, *Environmental Politics and Policy*, 5th ed. (Washington, DC: Congressional Quarterly Press, 2001), 87.

5. Ibid.

6. Ibid., 285.

7. Ibid.

8. General Accounting Office, "Department of Energy: Fundamental Reassessment Needed to Address Major Mission, Structure, and Accountability Problems," Report to the Subcommittee on Energy and Water Development, Committee on Appropriations, House of Representatives (GAO-02-51; December 2001).

9. Rosenbaum, *Environmental Politics and Policy*, 87–89.

10. U.S. National Research Council, Committee on Technical Bases for Yucca Mountain Standards, *Technical Bases for Yucca Mountain Standards* (Washington, DC: National Academy Press, 1995).

11. See www.nationalacademies.org/nrc/.

12. See www.nap.edu.

13. U.S. National Research Council, Committee on Technical Bases for Yucca Mountain Standards, *Technical Bases for Yucca Mountain Standards*.

14. See www.ncrponline.org.

15. Nuclear Energy Agency, Radioactive Waste Management Committee, "The Environmental and Ethical Basis of Geological Disposal" (Paris: Organisation for Economic Co-operation and Development/Nuclear Energy Agency, 1995).

16. International, "EU Directives Adopted; No Option but Geological Disposal," *Nuclear News* 46, no. 3 (March 2003): 74.

Principles Guiding Radioactive Waste Management

We start this discussion drawing on the statements issued by two broadly based international organizations mentioned in the introduction to chapter 2. Most of the nuclear waste–producing countries participate in these organizations. In 1995, the International Atomic Energy Agency (IAEA) identified nine principles of radioactive waste management.[1] The first two principles state that waste shall be managed in such a way as to secure an acceptable level of protection for human health and for the environment. More specific principles require waste to be managed in such a way that predicted impacts on the health of future generations will not be greater than the relevant levels of impact that are acceptable today and further require that the waste management not impose undue burdens on future generations. These two principles are often referred to as providing for intergenerational equity.

It is interesting to note that, in a slightly more recent statement, the Radioactive Waste Management Committee of the Organisation for Economic Co-operation and Development's Nuclear Energy Agency makes an aspect of these principles even more explicit by asserting that there seems to be "no ethical basis for discounting future health and environment damage risks."[2] This statement is taken from a "Collective Opinion" of experts from 15 countries and several international organizations. Their findings have been issued in a 1995 report, "The Environmental and Ethical Basis of Geological Disposal of Long-Lived Radioactive Wastes: A Collective Opinion of the Radioactive Waste Management Committee of the OECD Nuclear Energy Agency." This "Collective Opinion" rejects storage strategies that require long-term surveillance and care by future societies whose structural stability cannot be presumed. As will be elaborated on shortly, these considerations severely limit the ethically acceptable alternatives for disposal of radioactive waste. The "Collective Opinion" concludes that geological disposal satisfies intergenerational equity principles.

The "Collective Opinion" statement also emphasizes intragenerational equity, mentioning the "involvement of various sections of contemporary society in a fair and open decision-making process related to the waste management solutions to be implemented."[3] (We note that this statement would seem to make unethical the enactment of the U.S. 1987 Amendments Act provision, prior to final scientific evaluation of all sites under consideration, designating Yucca Mountain to be the only nuclear waste repository site to be further characterized.)

A number of developments in the years following the 1995 position papers of the Organisation for Economic Co-operation and Development and the International Atomic Energy Agency led to a reexamination of the indefinite storage and monitoring versus permanent disposal issue by the IAEA. These included difficulties in establishing permanent repositories, the expansion of surface storage facilities in some countries, and heightened concern about security and safety. The result of this reexamination was presented in "The Long Term Storage of Radioactive Waste: Safety and Sustainability; a Position Paper of International Experts."[4] It reaffirms that the isolation of long-lived waste is best achieved by geological disposal. It concludes that the societal infrastructure required to assure the safety of material in monitored storage is unlikely to last for the long time period needed. A few years earlier the National Research Council of the U.S. National Academy of Sciences came to a similar conclusion, saying, "Geological disposal remains the only scientifically and technically credible long-term solution available to meet the need for safety without reliance on active management. It also offers security benefits because it would place fissile materials out of reach of all but the most sophisticated weapons builders."[5]

NEGLIGIBLE INCREMENTAL DOSE AND COLLECTIVE DOSE

The two concepts of negligible incremental dose and collective dose have not received as much attention in ethical principle considerations as they deserve. An incremental dose is a dose from some particular activity above the dose that the same person or population receives from other sources, generally background sources. If the incremental dose is quite small compared with the background dose, it is sometimes declared to be negligible (or at a so-called *de minimus* level) and may be ignored as far as regulatory or protective action is concerned. Though such a declaration may be non-controversial if only a small number of people are exposed to a small incremental dose, such a declaration becomes more problematical when many people are exposed to a small dose.

It is useful when dealing with the impact of exposing a sizable number of people to an incremental dose to define the collective dose. The collective dose is simply the sum of the individual doses over all the members of a population. An example of the unreasonableness of setting a negligible incremental dose at the individual dose level is given by the release of a radioactive gas whose lifetime is long compared with the mixing time in the atmosphere, so that its effect may put every person in the world at risk. Using generally accepted linear dose-response values discussed later in this book, even an incremental dose of only one 1,000th of natural background would lead to about 1,000 cancer fatalities per year for a world population of seven billion people.

It would seem from this example that it does not make sense to set "negligible" incremental dose levels at the individual dose level when sizable populations are involved. This is not, however, the view of some policy makers. A National Academy of Sciences (NAS) panel, charged by Congress in its 1992 Energy Policy Act (see Chap. 3, Sec. D) to advise the Environmental Protection Agency on its establishment of radiation protection standards for Yucca Mountain, endorsed the adoption of a risk equivalent of a negligible individual incremental dose level.[6] The NAS panel did not endorse a collective dose (or equivalent risk) standard.[7] In dismissing a collective standard the panel mentioned uncertainties in the generally accepted dose-response model and difficulties in estimating the future size of large population groups.

The International Commission on Radiological Protection (ICRP) makes recommendations that inform radiological protection standards in many countries.[8] For example, the U.S. Environmental Protection Agency's proposed standards for Yucca Mountain incorporate dose weighting factors and methodology recommendations from the ICRP. The ICRP takes a somewhat different position on collective doses than the NAS panel. The commission has considered the suggestion that sources that give rise to very small individual doses to many people could be exempted from regulatory concern. It points out that "in the context of waste management, this approach tends to ignore large collective doses delivered at long ranges, often in other countries."[9] Although the commission recognizes that this method of exemption is in use, sometimes only implicitly, it states explicitly that it does not recommend its use. It acknowledges, however, the possible difficulty in reducing small but widespread doses with reasonable deployment of resources.

The U.S. National Council on Radiation Protection (NCRP) comes to a similar conclusion in a report on collective dose.[10] Its concluding recommendation includes the statement that collective dose should be considered as one of the means for assessing the acceptability of a facility. It is also recommended that all doses should be included in calculations of collective doses as there is no conceptual basis for excluding any individual doses, however small, from a collective dose calculation. This statement is in conflict with a slightly earlier NCRP report that recommended that an annual effective dose of 0.01 sieverts (1.0 millirems) or less be considered a negligible incremental dose per source or practice.[11] The more recent report concluded that because collective dose depends on demographic variables as well as radiation doses, regulatory limits should not be set in terms of collective dose.

Thus the response to a particular collective dose becomes a trade-off of the societal benefit associated with the activity responsible for the radiation source and the harm arising from that source. This value judgment can only be made if the collective dose associated with a proposed activity is calculated and made available.

APPLICATION OF GENERAL PRINCIPLES TO RADIATION STANDARDS

The general principles we have discussed have specific relevance to the setting of the radiation standards for protecting the public from the hazards of a repository. Among the issues that arise are the following: What (governmental) entity should set the standards? What risk level is appropriate? How does one extrapolate the dose–risk relationship to low doses where experimental data are unattainable? How does one apply intergenerational equity to the very long times (hundreds of thousands of years) that nuclear waste is hazardous? Should one compare the possible social harm of moving ahead too slowly with nuclear energy with that of the hazards of nuclear waste disposal? We discuss all but the last of these issues briefly. The last issue involves much broader issues than encompassed by this book.

Most countries have concluded that the governmental entity that sets the public health and safety standards should be independent of the organization that has the responsibility for the actual management and disposal of the hazardous waste. In the United States, the Environmental Protection Agency is responsible for promulgating rules regarding radioactive waste, and this responsibility for repositories was made explicit in 1982. The authority to set generally applicable standards for repositories was modified in 1992 when Congress directed the Environmental Protection Agency to take into account recommendations of the National Academy of Sciences and set standards specific to Yucca Mountain. In the United States a third governmental entity, the Nuclear Regulatory Commission, has the semi-judicial role through its licensing authority to see that the standards are met.

A more difficult issue is that of what risk level is appropriate. Although radiation standards are usually specified in terms of the radiation dose rate (often expressed in units of millirem per year, mrem/yr, or in more modern international nomenclature, units of sieverts per year, Sv/yr), these can be translated into risk factors assuming a relationship between dose and the probability of developing a fatal cancer. (Cancer is the chief hazard of radiation exposure.) This relationship can be determined empirically from observed consequences of known radiation exposures. Although a more quantitative discussion of this issue for Yucca Mountain will be presented later, we observe now for orientation purposes that dose rate limits for repositories typically correspond to between one in 100,000 and one in a million probability of developing a fatal cancer from a year's exposure to the maximum dose permitted. This can be compared with the corresponding probability of one in 6,000 for developing a fatal cancer for the general public from natural background sources. (We have used a "consensus" risk factor of 0.05 probability of developing a fatal cancer per sievert of dose as suggested by Bodansky).[12] Although the conversion of dose rate to risk is moderately well known for intermediate and high dose rates, as the dose rate gets lower there comes a point where the health effects become so rare as to be statistically unobservable for available study group sizes. This has led to considerable controversy as to how to extrapolate the risk factor–dose relationship to the lowest doses. This extrapolation is important as the number of people exposed to low doses becomes larger as the dose becomes smaller. Most national and international advisory bodies have favored assuming a linear extrapolation from medium and high doses down to zero risk at zero dose.[13] This is known as the linearity hypothesis. There are those that argue that there may be a dose threshold below which there is no appreciable health risk. The National Commission on Radiation Protection and Measurements has concluded that "the data…provide insufficient grounds for rejecting the linear-nonthreshold dose-response model as a basis for assessing the risks of low-level ionizing radiation in radiation protection."[14] An international body, the U.N. Scientific Committee on the Effects of Atomic Radiation, has also concluded that the linear dose-response model is the most scientifically defensible approximation.[15] It seems to us that for regulatory purposes the linearity hypothesis is the most responsible assumption at this time. But as indicated earlier, it will never be possible to determine the dose–risk relationship empirically for the lowest doses.

Once these low-dose and long-timescale issues are decided in some manner, one must still address the initial issue we raised as to what risk level is appropriate for those affected by a repository. It seems to us that the allowable risk factor should be comparable to that allowed for other hazardous activities. The regulation of hazardous materials becomes complicated, however, because some effects are additive, for example, those from smoking and those from auto emission pollution. The allowable risk factor should also take into account the uncertainty of the risk factor. It should not be significantly more stringent than that for activities that society chooses not to regulate. We have suggested in chapter 7 (on Yucca Mountain) that the dose rate standards for Yucca Mountain are somewhat more stringent than dose rates associated with some societal choices that are not regulated.

NOTES

1. International Atomic Energy Agency, *IAEA Safety Fundamentals: The Principles of Radioactive Waste Management* (Vienna: International Atomic Energy Agency 1995), extract from Safety Series no. 111-F, reproduced as Annexe I of the Nuclear Energy Agency's "Collective Opinion" document.

2. Nuclear Energy Agency, "The Environmental and Ethical Basis of Geological Disposal of Long-Lived Radioactive Wastes: A Collective Opinion of the Radioactive Waste Management Committee of the OECD Nuclear Energy Agency" (Paris: Organisation for Economic Co-operation and Development, 1995), 8, available at www.nea.fr/html/rwm/reports/1995/geodisp.html.

3. Ibid., 5.

4. International Atomic Energy Agency, "The Long Term Storage of Radioactive Waste: Safety and Sustainability; a Position Paper of the International Experts" (Vienna: International Atomic Energy Agency, 2003), available at www-pub.iaea.org/MTCD/ publications/PDF/LTS-RW_web.pdf.

5. U.S. National Research Council, Committee on Disposition of High-Level Radioactive Waste through Geological Isolation, Board of Radioactive Waste Management, Division on Earth and Life Studies, *Disposition of High-Level Waste and Spent Nuclear Fuel: The Continuing Societal and Technical Challenges* (Washington, DC: National Academy Press, 2001), available at http://books.nap.edu/books/0309073170/ html/index.html.

6. U.S. National Research Council, Committee on Technical Bases for Yucca Mountain Standards, *Technical Bases for Yucca Mountain Standards* (Washington, DC: National Academy Press, 1995), 60–61. This panel was actually a committee of the National Research Council, the operating arm of the National Academy of Sciences. The report of this panel is generally referred to in court briefs and Environmental Protection Agency and Nuclear Regulatory Commission rule-making documents as the "NAS Report." See Appendix A for more detail on the National Academy of Sciences and the National Research Council.

7. U.S. National Research Council, Committee on Technical Bases for Yucca Mountain Standards, *Technical Bases for Yucca Mountain Standards*, 61, 64.

8. The International Commission on Radiological Protection is a nonprofit organization that elects its own members. See the appendix on organizations for more details.

9. International Commission on Radiological Protection, "1990 Recommendations of the International Commission on Radiological Protection," in *Annals of the ICRP* 21, nos. 1–3, ICRP Publication 60 (Oxford: Pergamon Press, 1991), 65.

10. U.S. National Council on Radiation Protection and Measurements, "Principles and Application of Collective Dose in Radiation Protection," NCRP Report No. 121 (Bethesda, MD: National Council on Radiation Protection and Measurements, 1995). Although chartered by Congress, the National Council on Radiation Protection and Measurements is a nonprofit public service organization that does not receive congressional appropriations and elects its own members. (See Appendix A.)

11. U.S. National Council on Radiation Protection and Measurements, "Limitation of Exposure to Ionizing Radiation," NCRP Report No. 116 (Bethesda, MD: National Council on Radiation Protection and Measurements, 1993).

12. David Bodansky, *Nuclear Energy: Principles, Practices and Prospects*, 2nd ed. (New York: Springer-Verlag, 2004), 103.

13. Ibid., 97.

14. U.S. National Council on Radiation Protection and Measurements, "Evaluation of the Linear-Nonthreshold Dose-Response Model for Ionizing Radiation," NCRP Report No. 136 (Bethesda, MD: National Council on Radiation Protection and Measurements, 2001), 205.

15. U.N. Scientific Committee on the Effects of Atomic Radiation, *Sources and Effects of Ionizing Radiation: United Nations Scientific Committee on the Effects of Atomic Radiation: UNSCEAR 2000 Report to the General Assembly, with Scientific Annexes* (New York: United Nations, 2000), vol. 2, 160.

: Appendix C

A Visit to Yucca Mountain

After an early breakfast, we boarded one of several buses for a tour of the Yucca Mountain repository site. This tour was sponsored by the Tenth International High-Level Radioactive Waste Conference of the American Nuclear Society, meeting in Las Vegas, Nev., in spring 2003. Among the participants on the bus were officials with nuclear waste or nuclear radiation safety organizations of several European countries. The Yucca Mountain host on our bus was Abe Van Luik, senior policy adviser to the Yucca Mountain project. He would prove to be a valuable resource and provider of interesting commentary.

As we drove west from the Texas Station Casino and Hotel conference site, our driver informed us his name was Joe and that he expected to be addressed as "Joe," rather than as "driver" or some other less personal name. After a few miles we turned south rather than north, and I became curious about the route we were taking. Soon we pulled in to a strip mall and stopped at a Department of Energy Yucca Mountain Information Center. This is one of several such centers, one of which we had visited in Pahrump, Nev., southwest of Yucca Mountain. The Las Vegas center had a number of educational exhibits and considerable literature for distribution. But our principal purpose for being here was for security processing. We were given badges on strings to wear around our neck. We reboarded the bus and started northwest toward US 95. Once we left the urban Las Vegas area we were in a wide desert valley between two mountain ranges, with the highest range to the west being dominated by Mt. Charleston. It had rained in the last few weeks, and the desert was unusually green. Many yucca trees were blooming, and the creosote bushes had tiny yellow flowers if one looked closely. About an hour north of Las Vegas we left the highway and entered the Nevada Test Site reservation at the Mercury entrance. We were instructed to put away our cameras while in the vicinity

of the gate, although we were permitted to use them later on at the repository site. In earlier years the community of Mercury within the gate had
housed 10,000 people, but presently it was occupied by few people. We
continued on another ten miles or so over increasingly hilly terrain until
we reached a collection of temporary-looking low buildings at the North
Portal of the exploratory tunnel.

We were taken into a large assembly room where later employees provided us with box lunches. At the controlled back exit we received the
safety equipment for our trip into the tunnel—hard hat, safety glasses,
earplugs, and a heavy belt with flashlight and an oxygen-generating pack.
We were then loaded into (or perhaps one should say onto, as there was
no top) one of several railcars with benches that pulled up just outside of
the tunnel entrance. We were advised to insert our earplugs, as the train
would be fairly noisy in the constrained environment of the tunnel. The
tunnel entrance was fairly large, with a huge air ventilation duct at the top
of the tunnel. We had been advised to bring warm clothes, as the motion
of the train created a cool wind, although later when we dismounted we
would find the air temperature comfortable for walking. The rock walls,
composed of volcanic tuff, were a uniformly gray color. The integrity of
the rock varied along the length of the tunnel. In some places near the entrance mesh and supporting structures were apparent. Farther in the walls
were generally unsupported. Some fractures in the rock were noted at various places along the length of the tunnel. We did not see any signs of
dampness, contrary to some expectations. Several miles into the tunnel we
dismounted and went down a connecting side tunnel, stopping at several
places along this tunnel where various experiments were being performed.
The most ambitious experiment had been going on for several years. It was
an experiment to measure the effect of heat on the neighboring rock and
its entrapped water. An excavation similar in size to that to be occupied by
a waste container was heated to over the boiling point of water and held at
this temperature for two years. Boreholes were drilled in several directions
to measure the temperature gradient as a function of distance into the rock
and to measure the humidity. After two years the heating had been terminated, and the response of the rock to cooling was being measured. After
visiting several other side excavations we remounted the train and rode
back to our entry point at the North Portal.

At lunch we sat opposite an official of an East Coast nuclear power
plant. He mentioned there had been a booth at the conference where a

company was trying to sell casks that could be used to store waste indefinitely at reactor sites. His response was that he wanted to get rid of the
waste, which he considered bait for a possible terrorist attack, rather than
to store it. He also mentioned his dismay when some of his reactor's waste
that had been sent to the West Valley reprocessing plant was shipped back
when that project was aborted. He also mentioned that his company had
to pay for storage costs of the returned spent fuel.

After lunch we boarded the buses and were taken to the South Portal of the exploratory tunnel. This tunnel is approximately five miles long,
with two shorter entrance and exit legs at nearly right angles to the longer
section where most of the studies are being performed. It was drilled by a
variant of a commercial mine borer, affectionately known as the "Yucca
Mucker." It had started at the North Portal and emerged several years later
at the South Portal, where it now stood forlornly. It was for sale, but no
buyer had come forward who was willing to take it away. It is very large,
with the front cutter 25 feet in diameter, and it weighs more than 700 tons.
It was fabricated in Kent, Wash., and transported in pieces on 50 trucks.
Rails were laid as the boring proceeded. The borer pulled a car with places
for scientists and technicians to take samples and to make measurements
from as it moved along. The excavated material was removed by train back
out the North Portal.

Our final stop at the repository site was reached by a gravel road that
took us to the summit of Yucca Mountain. The summit is at an elevation
of 4,946 feet, about 2,000 feet higher than Amargosa Valley to the west.
To the north and east are successive ranges of low mountains. To the west
stretches the Amargosa Valley, home to about 3,000 people spread out over
several hundred square miles. There is some agricultural activity, including
a large dairy farm. The Amargosa Valley is downstream from the repository
and where any water from the repository will appear. The Amargosa River
is mostly invisible underground. Beyond Amargosa Valley is the drop off
to Death Valley, where any residual water in the Amargosa River ends up.
The most surprising and striking sight from the summit, however, was the
presence of a number of cinder cones, some perhaps as close as a dozen
miles. Most were said to be about a million years old, but one of the closest, the Lathrop Wells cinder cone, is only about 80,000 years old. These
cones attest to the volcanic history of the area. Tectonic activity, in the
form of both earthquakes and volcanic eruption, is one of the major concerns of critics of the Yucca Mountain repository.

: Appendix D

U.S. Secretaries of Energy

Congress created the Department of Energy (DOE) in 1977, absorbing the Energy Research and Development Administration (ERDA), the Federal Energy Administration, and the Federal Power Commission. ERDA and the Nuclear Regulatory Commission were the successors to the original Atomic Energy Commission. The Atomic Energy Commission had been both a developer and a regulator of nuclear activities, and the split was a response to the incompatibility of these two roles. The new Department of Energy had about 20,000 employees and a budget of over $10 billion.[1] The DOE has major responsibilities in both applied and basic science. Its responsibilities span such diverse activities as funding high-technology laboratories, managing the Strategic Petroleum Reserve, designing and constructing nuclear weapons, and overseeing nuclear waste disposal.

The secretaries of energy are appointed by the president and must be confirmed by the Senate. The 11 secretaries of energy with the dates they took office and the president who appointed them are listed below:

James R. Schlesinger	1977	Carter
Charles W. Duncan Jr.	1979	Carter
James B. Edwards	1981	Reagan
Donald Paul Hodel	1982	Reagan
John S. Herrington	1985	Reagan
James D. Watkins	1989	George H. W. Bush
Hazel R. O'Leary	1993	Clinton
Federico F. Peña	1997	Clinton
Bill Richardson	1998	Clinton
Spencer Abraham	2001	George W. Bush
Samuel W. Bodman	2005	George W. Bush

As will be seen from the brief biographies that follow, the secretaries have differed considerably in their field of training and in their previous experience in the energy field. Two common denominators emerge from a study of their backgrounds. Half were trained as lawyers, and most had little if any experience in the energy field or in the sciences. Schlesinger, Hodel, and O'Leary had the most previous experience in the energy field. The secretary of energy position has not always been held in high regard. At the 2005 Senate Energy and Natural Resources Committee hearings on the confirmation of Samuel Bodman as secretary of energy, Committee Chairman Pete Domenici supported Bodman and remarked, "There have been a few (nominees) that I believe had the qualifications to be a secretary of energy, which means that my view is that there were more that didn't."[2] In recent years Cabinet secretaries have often been symbols of diversity, presidential confidantes, or representatives of interest groups, although some were experienced administrators. The energy secretaries are no exception to this. There have been several attempts over the years, both by President Reagan and later by Congress, to abolish the Department of Energy.

JAMES SCHLESINGER

Schlesinger obtained B.A., A.M., and Ph.D. degrees in economics from Harvard. For the following eight years he taught economics at the University of Virginia. He then moved to the RAND Corporation, rising to director of Strategic Studies. He served as chairman of the Atomic Energy Commission, a predecessor to the DOE, between 1971 and 1973. He then became director of the Central Intelligence Agency and, soon thereafter, secretary of defense. In 1976 President-Elect Carter asked Schlesinger to draft a plan for the establishment of the Department of Energy, and in August 1997, he became the department's first secretary. He organized the new department along groupings based on their evolution from research and development through application and commercialization, rather than on fuel type. With regard to nuclear matters, during his first year the DOE proposed to take title to civilian spent fuel for a onetime storage fee. This proposal would have required both a temporary and a permanent storage site. During his last year an Interagency Review Group on Nuclear Waste Management released its findings, declaring that the primary objective should be to isolate nuclear waste from the biosphere. Following his term as secretary he has been active in both private industry and the Center for Strategic and International Studies. In a 1985 speech he argued for regulatory reform for nuclear power, including legislation to mandate the standardization of plant design.[3] In 1999 he testified before the Armed Services Committee of the U.S. Senate in opposition to the Comprehensive Test Ban Treaty. He has served on many commissions and has received many awards. He is also credited with originating the remark, "Everyone is entitled to their own opinion…but no one is entitled to their own facts."[4]

CHARLES DUNCAN

Charles Duncan obtained a B.S. in chemical engineering from Rice University. He held a number of industrial executive positions before going to Washington as a deputy secretary of defense in 1977. Two years later he was named secretary of energy. Early in his term he announced the reorganization of the DOE so as to manage programs by technologies or fuels. Subsequent to his service as secretary he served on the Board of Directors of a number of corporations and was the business member of the Texas State Board of Education.

JAMES B. EDWARDS

Edwards obtained a doctor of dental medicine from the University of Louisville. He was an oral surgeon in Charleston, S.C., where he became active in Republican politics. He served in the state Senate and was elected governor of South Carolina in 1975. He became secretary of energy in January 1981. During a debate in the presidential campaign the previous fall, Ronald Reagan advocated abolishing the DOE, saying it had not "produced a quart of oil or a lump of coal or anything else in the line of energy."[5] In October 1981 President Reagan, as part of his Program for Economic Recovery, more formally proposed abolishing the Department of Education as well as the Department of Energy. Although Secretary Edwards supported the abolition of the DOE, the effort languished. In a reversal from Schlesinger's organization, Edwards regrouped research and development programs by major fuel sources.[6] He also reaffirmed the nuclear power option. Toward the end of their first year, President Reagan announced a nuclear energy policy that anticipated the establishment of a facility for the storage of high-level radioactive waste. Reagan also lifted the ban on commercial reprocessing of nuclear fuel. In 1982 the DOE assumed control of the former nuclear fuel–reprocessing complex in West Valley, N.Y., so as to implement a nuclear waste solidification demonstration project. After Edwards's term as secretary he served as president of the Medical University of South Carolina for 16 years.

DONALD HODEL

Hodel received a B.A. from Harvard and a J.D. from the University of Oregon School of Law. Prior to going to Washington he was head of the powerful Bonneville Power Administration (BPA), which markets electricity for the Bureau of Reclamation, Army Corps of Engineers, and publicly owned utilities in the Pacific Northwest. Initially the BPA was concerned mostly with hydroelectric power from the many dams on the Columbia River. In the late 1960s and 1970s the BPA pushed for a large nuclear power program. In 1976 Hodel encouraged utilities to join the program by saying that the BPA would no longer be able to guarantee adequate power to the region after 1983.[7] Utilities responded by signing up for the Washington Public Power Supply System (WPPSS). During Hodel's tenure WPPSS started building five nuclear power plants, but by 1983 enormous cost overruns and slacking demand led to the abandonment of most of the partially completed reactors and default on bonds valued at $2.25 billion. This was the largest bond default in U.S. history. In 1982 Hodel was named secretary of energy. In 1983 the DOE established the Office of Civilian Radioactive Waste Management. In 1985 he left the DOE to become secretary of the interior. After leaving Washington he formed an energy and natural resources consulting firm. In 1995 he testified before a House subcommittee that the DOE should be abolished.[8] He was named president of the Christian Coalition in 1997.

JOHN HERRINGTON

Herrington was trained as a lawyer, receiving his LL.B. and J.D. in 1964 from the University of California Hastings College of Law. For several years he was a deputy district attorney in Ventura County, Calif. In 1967 he opened his own law office in Walnut Creek, Calif. During Reagan's 1980 presidential campaign Herrington was a full-time volunteer advance man. Following Reagan's election he was appointed as deputy assistant to the president for presidential personnel. In 1985 he was named secretary of energy. At his confirmation hearing he confessed he did not know much about energy beyond having put insulation on his water heater. Despite this the Senate confirmed him by a 93 to 1 vote, with Senator Proxmire the sole dissenting vote. This validates the observation that "the Senate gives Presidents wide latitude in selecting Cabinet members."[9]

During Herrington's term in office the DOE initiated an administrative "land withdrawal" procedure for the Waste Isolation Pilot Plant (WIPP) in New Mexico. The DOE also tried to establish a monitored retrieval storage site in Tennessee. While he was secretary the Nuclear Waste Policy Amendments Act of 1987 was passed. This act to a large extent governs nuclear waste disposal policies at the present time. After his time of service as secretary he remained active in Republican politics. In the mid-1990s he was the California party chairman and in January 1997 was a candidate for chair of the Republican National Committee.[10] In 1997 he, along with former Energy Secretary Don Hodel, supported a bill to abolish the Department of Energy.[11] Although this effort was again unsuccessful, it should be mentioned that a significant reallocation of resources took place during the Reagan years. In the department's 1980 budget defense activities accounted for 36 percent and energy research and development for 45 percent of the total budget. In the final Reagan budget for 1990, these figures were 60 percent (including 7 percent for defense waste management) and 16 percent, respectively.[12]

JAMES D. WATKINS

Watkins had a long and distinguished career in the U.S. Navy, rising to commander in chief, U.S. Pacific Fleet. He holds a B.S. from the U.S. Naval Academy and a master's degree in mechanical engineering from the Naval Postgraduate School. He served in Rickover's nuclear-powered submarine program and was commanding officer of the Navy's first nuclear-powered surface ship.[13] In 1982 he was appointed chief of naval operations by President Reagan. In 1988 President George H. W. Bush appointed him secretary of energy. At his confirmation hearing Senator Bennett Johnston charged that the department's program lacked aggressive leadership and was in "shambles."[14] As secretary he put forward plans to strengthen environmental protection and waste management activities at DOE facilities. He brought together responsibilities previously scattered in other offices in a new Office of Environmental Restoration and Waste Management.[15] However, he strongly opposed the dismantlement of the Shoreham (N.Y.) nuclear power plant. This plant, completed but never opened, was felt by the local communities and the state as being too close to major urban areas. With regard to Yucca Mountain, he tried to take a more conciliatory stance with the State of Nevada. "I think we were moving too aggressively and did not give them a chance," Watkins observed, "and they really felt they were being put upon. And, I think to a certain extent they were right."[16] Nevada, however, was not moved very much by these expressions. Toward the end of his appointment, the General Accounting Office praised Watkins's organizational and management changes establishing clearer lines of responsibility but commented that much more needed to be done to change the "culture" of the department.[17]

HAZEL O'LEARY

O'Leary obtained a law degree from Rutgers University in 1966. She worked for the U.S. Federal Energy Administration and the DOE under Ford and Carter. She was responsible for federal programs designed to conserve energy and protect the environment. Her husband, John, who died in 1987, had been involved in the WIPP controversy, first as New Mexico's natural resources secretary and later as a DOE official.[18] From 1989 to 1993 she was an executive of the Northern States Power Co. She was appointed secretary of energy in 1993 and was the first woman and the first African American to hold that post. (Dixie Lee Ray was the only woman to head the Atomic Energy Commission, a predecessor organization to the Department of Energy.) During the selection process of his first secretary of energy, President-Elect Clinton observed that although most of the department's budget currently was devoted to nuclear issues, the future demanded "a different direction and a different policy."[19] The administration's first budget reflected this view, with nuclear programs receiving cuts and energy efficiency, natural gas research and development, and technology transfer receiving increases. The environmental restoration and waste management program request totaled $6.5 billion and became the largest program in the department. (The latter program received criticism from Senator B. Johnston, who characterized the cleanup effort as a "grand and glorious mess.")[20] In November 1993 the DOE, the Environmental Protection Agency, and the State of Washington reached accord on a Hanford

Tri-Party Agreement.[21] This agreement has often been cited as a successful resolution of the interests of the various stakeholders, who had considerable input in its drafting. Secretary O'Leary worked at changing the culture of the DOE, an effort started by her predecessor. As secretary of energy she brought a new degree of openness and pressed for and achieved the declassification of many old records.

FEDERICO PEÑA

Peña obtained both a bachelor's degree in 1969 and a law degree in 1972 from the University of Texas at Austin. He went into private law practice in Denver, and in 1978 he was elected to the Colorado House of Representatives. He served as mayor of Denver from 1983 to 1991. In 1993 he was appointed Clinton's secretary of transportation, and from there he moved into the Department of Energy as secretary in 1997. He was the first Hispanic American to hold either of these offices.

BILL RICHARDSON

Richardson did his undergraduate work at Tufts University. He went on to obtain an M.A. degree in international diplomacy from the Fletcher School of Law and Diplomacy at Tufts in 1971. He worked on the staff of the U.S. Department of State and then the Senate Foreign Relations Committee before moving to New Mexico. He was elected to the U.S. House of Representatives in 1982, where he served until being named ambassador to the United Nations in 1997. In 1998 he was named secretary of energy. He thus became the head of a department he had severely criticized in the past. In 1992, during the debate on the land withdrawal legislation for WIPP, then-Congressman Richardson said: "As we open the first DOE facility in 30 years, do we trust DOE to manage this facility with all the safety, health and environmental oversight that is required? The answer is a resounding 'no.'"[22]

Richardson was the first secretary to ask Congress to provide compensation for current and former Energy Department workers who had become ill because of radiation exposure as a result of their work at nuclear facilities. In his memoir he identifies having obtained compensation for DOE contract workers for job-related illnesses as the accomplishment he is most proud of.[23] He negotiated agreements with Russia to improve nuclear nonproliferation safeguards. He was quoted toward the end of his term as saying, "What worries me most in this job is what to do with 50 years' worth of nuclear waste."[24]

As a congressman and as U.N. ambassador, Richardson acquired a reputation as a successful negotiator. During this period he won the release of hostages, American servicemen, and prisoners in North Korea, Iraq, and Cuba.[25] In January 2003, soon after being sworn in as the newly elected governor of New Mexico, he was asked by North Korean representatives to meet with them at a time when the administration was distancing itself from negotiations as a result of North Korea's decision to proceed with a nuclear program in violation of agreements with the Clinton administration. He has continued to be involved in negotiations with North Korea as recently as early 2007.

SPENCER ABRAHAM

Abraham became secretary of energy in 2001. He received a J.D. in 1979 from the private Thomas M. Cooley Law School in Lansing, Mich. He taught at this law school for two years after graduation and then became chairman of the Michigan Republican Party, an office he held until he became deputy chief of staff to Vice President Dan Quayle. For a short time he was cochairman of the National Republican Congressional Committee, and in 1995 he was elected by Michigan voters to the U.S. Senate. During his period as senator he supported an unsuccessful effort to abolish the Department of Energy. In 2000 he lost his bid to serve a second term as senator from Michigan and shortly thereafter was named by President-Elect George W. Bush to head the DOE. He continued Richardson's pursuit of nonproliferation agreements, signing agreements with Kazakhstan and Uzbekistan. He moved rapidly to deal with the high-level nuclear waste problem. In February 2002 Abraham recommended to President Bush that Yucca Mountain be approved as the permanent repository for spent fuel from nuclear reactors. He defended his recommendation at congressional hearings following Nevada's veto of President Bush's approval of Yucca Mountain.

On November 14, 2004, following President Bush's reelection, Abraham submitted a letter of resignation. In this letter he listed among his successes the development of the nation's first comprehensive energy plan in over a decade, plans for acceleration of the cleanup of former weapon sites, pressing ahead on the Yucca Mountain project, and the acceleration and expansion of nonproliferation programs.[26] The energy plan was orchestrated by Vice President Cheney, and the alleged dominant participation of industry representatives in its formulation has led to considerable controversy. Congress has had before it, but not passed, a bill incorporating most of its recommendations. Some of the plans for accelerating the cleanup of former weapons sites have also created considerable controversy. In particular, a DOE proposal to grout and leave in place solid residue in liquid waste tanks generated a lawsuit by the Natural Resources Defense Council and the State of Idaho. Although a District Court in Idaho ruled in the plaintiff's favor, this ruling was overturned by the Ninth Court of Appeals in November 2004. The Court of Appeals said that the issue was not yet "ripe." An amendment prohibiting the DOE from reclassifying the high-level waste to be left in tanks in South Carolina and Idaho failed narrowly in the Senate in summer 2004. The amendment was vigorously championed by Senator Maria Cantwell of Washington State. Reclassification is required to allow grouting and leaving in place the high-level waste resulting from the reprocessing of spent reactor fuel. Secretary Abraham's efforts to curb nuclear proliferation have received considerable praise.[27] Although only secretary of energy for four years, Abraham was the longest-serving energy secretary.

SAMUEL W. BODMAN

Bodman was nominated on December 10, 2004, by President Bush to replace Spencer Abraham as secretary of energy. Bodman is a chemical engineer by training, with degrees from Cornell University and the Massachusetts Institute of Technology (MIT). Following a six-year academic stint at MIT, he has spent most of his career as a businessman, primarily in the chemical and investments industries. At the time of his nomination he was deputy secretary of the U.S. Treasury Department. Prior to February 2004 he had been deputy secretary of commerce.[28] Senator Pete Domenici, chairman of the Senate Energy and Natural Resources Committee, which holds confirmation hearings, correctly predicted a "swift and smooth" confirmation for Bodman.[29] Some environmental groups such as the Sierra Club, however, were concerned that Bodman took a hands-off position on global warming when he oversaw the National Oceanic and Atmospheric Agency as deputy secretary of commerce.[30]

During his second year as secretary, the administration proposed a radical change in its nuclear waste disposal policy as part of a new initiative to offer nuclear fuel to other countries. This initiative, the Global Nuclear Energy Partnership, included an ambitious plan to replace the direct disposal of spent nuclear fuel with the reprocessing and burn up of plutonium and other actinides in fast nuclear reactors.

NOTES

1. Terrence R. Fehner and Jack M. Holl, "Department of Energy 1977–1994: A Summary History," Department of Energy (Washington, DC: Office of Scientific and Technical Information, 1994).

2. Tony Batt, Stephens Washington Bureau, "Panel Quickly Approves Bodman," *Las Vegas Review-Journal,* January 27, 2005: 5A.

3. Jeff Gealow, "Schlesinger Delivers Lecture," *The Tech* 105, no. 47 (November 5, 1985): 1, available at www-tech.mit.edu/V105/N47/nuke.47n.html.

4. John L. Ferri, letter to the editor, "A 'Christian Nation' My Ass," *Towanda Daily Review,* April 8, 1998, available at http://home.epix.net/~jlferri/nation.html.

5. Fehner and Holl, "Department of Energy 1977–1994," 31.

6. Ibid., 33.

7. John. A. Baden and Eric H. Espenhorst, "Whoops: An Expensive, Valuable History Lesson," *Seattle Times,* April 12, 1995: B5.

8. American Institute of Physics Public Information Division, 1985, available at www.infomag.ru/dbase/B006E/950529-002.txt.

9. Walter J. Oleszek, *Congressional Procedures and the Policy Process,* 5th ed. (Washington, DC: CQ Press, 2001), 286.

10. Gene Randall, CNN TIME All Politics News, "Crowded Field Vies for Republican Party Chair," November 22, 1996, available at www.cnn.com/ALLPOLITICS/1996/news/9611/22/1bennett.randall.ip/index.shtml.

11. Donald Devine, *Washington Times,* June 20, 1997.

12. Fehner and Holl, "Department of Energy 1977–1994," 52.

13. Chuck McCutcheon, *Nuclear Reactions: The Politics of Opening a Radioactive Waste Disposal Site* (Albuquerque: University of New Mexico Press, 2002), 106.

14. Fehner and Holl, "Department of Energy 1977–1994," 59.

15. James A. Thurber and Timothy C. Evanson, "Subsystem Politics and the Nuclear Weapons Complex: Congressional Oversight of DOE's Environmental Restoration Program," in *Problems and Prospects for Nuclear Waste Disposal Policy,* ed. E. B. Herzik and A. H. Mushkatel (Westport, CT: Greenwood Press, 1993), 121–38.

16. Fehner and Holl, "Department of Energy 1977–1994," 59.

17. Ibid., 74.

18. McCutcheon, *Nuclear Reactions*, 152.

19. Fehner and Holl, "Department of Energy 1977–1994," 78.

20. Ibid., 88.

21. Ibid.

22. "Waste Isolation Pilot Plant Land Withdrawal Act," *Congressional Record* 138 (July 21, 1992): H6298.

23. Bill Richardson with Michael Ruby, *Between Worlds: The Making of an American Life* (New York: G. P. Putnam's Sons, 2005), 259–65.

24. "EUROTECH Stakes EKOR's Future on Its Ability to Contain Nuclear Fuel Mass and Radioactive Debris at Chernobyl," *Business Wire*, December 13, 1999, available at www.thefreelibrary.com/Business+Wire/1999/December/14-p53.

25. White House, "President Clinton Names Ambassador Bill Richardson as Secretary of the U.S. Department of Energy," press release, June 18, 1998, available at www.bnl.gov/bnlweb/pubaf/pr/1998/whpr061898.html.

26. U.S Department of Energy, Office of Public Affairs, "Abraham Thanks President Bush for the Privilege to Serve the Nation," November 14, 2004, available at www.energy.gov/news/1543.htm.

27. Greg Schneider, "Abraham Leaving Energy Department," *Washington Post*, November 16, 2004: A6, available at www.washingtonpost.com/wp-dyn/articles/A52857-2004Nov15.html; Editorial, "Secretary Abraham's Tenure," *Washington Times*, December 22, 2004, available at http://washingtontimes.com/op-ed/20041221-084702-5645r.htm.

28. See www.energy.gov/news/4757.htm?photo=4767.

29. Bob Deans, "Bodman Tapped to Head Energy," *Atlanta Journal-Constitution*, December 11, 2004: A3.

30. Ibid.

⋮ Appendix E

U.S. Department of Energy Guidelines for Repository Site Recommendations

On November 14, 2001, the Department of Energy issued final rules establishing policies for recommendation of repository sites.[1] The "General Guidelines for the Preliminary Screening of Potential Sites for Nuclear Waste Repositories" (10 CFR part 960) was revised, and a new part 963, "Yucca Mountain Site Suitability Guidelines," was promulgated.

The most extensive revision was to the "Basis for Site Evaluations" section that deals primarily with the relative importance of natural and engineered barriers in comparative site evaluations.[2] The revised rule states that "engineered barriers shall be considered only to the extent necessary to obtain realistic source terms for comparative site evaluations based on the sensitivity of the natural barriers to such realistic engineered barriers." It goes on to state, "The comparisons shall assume equivalent engineered barrier performance for all sites compared and shall be structured so that engineered barriers are not relied upon to compensate for deficiencies in the geologic media. Furthermore, engineered barriers shall not be used to compensate for an inadequate site; mask the innate deficiencies of a site; disguise the strengths and weaknesses of a site and the overall system; and mask differences between sites when they are compared." This section does not apply to Yucca Mountain, as Congress in 1987 decided that only Yucca Mountain was to be considered for the first repository. It would apply if the secretary of energy, the president, or Congress should decide Yucca Mountain is unsuitable and a new search for a site was initiated or if a search for a second site was begun.

The purpose of the new part 963 is to establish Department of Energy methods and criteria for determining the suitability of the Yucca Mountain site for the location of a geologic repository. Parts of this rule reflect the increasing importance of engineered barriers and of probabilistic analyses of expected performance that have emerged as the Department of Energy site characterization and Environmental Protection Agency and Nuclear Regulatory Commission rule making has progressed. For example, *barrier* is defined as

> any material, structure or feature that prevents or substantially reduces the rate of movement of water or radionuclides from the Yucca Mountain repository to the accessible environment, or prevents the release or substantially reduces the release rate of radionuclides from the waste. For example, a barrier may be a geologic feature, an engineered structure, a canister, a waste form with physical and chemical characteristics that significantly decrease the mobility of radionuclides, or a material placed over and around the waste, provided that the material substantially delays movement of water or radionuclides.

> *Total System Performance Assessment*
>
> means a probabilistic analysis that is used to: 1) Identify the features, events and processes (except human intrusion) that might affect the Yucca Mountain disposal system and their probabilities of occurring during 10,000 years after disposal: 2) Examine the effects of those features, events, processes, and sequences of events and processes (except human intrusion) on the performance of the Yucca Mountain disposal system; and 3) Estimate the dose incurred by the reasonably maximally exposed individual, including associated uncertainties, as a result of releases caused by all significant features, events, processes, and sequences of events and processes, weighted by their probability of occurrence.

The new rule goes on to reassert that in conducting a Total System Performance Assessment the Department of Energy will consider only events that have at least one chance in 10,000 of occurring over 10,000 years.

These definitions, in keeping with the final Environmental Protection Agency and Nuclear Regulatory Commission rules, means that the relative contributions of natural and engineered barriers is not to be considered in the determination of the suitability of Yucca Mountain as a geologic repository. This aspect has aroused considerable concern in Nevada officials who oppose the repository. However, it is more of an expected consequence of the 1987 congressional action designating Yucca Mountain as the only site to be further characterized and less a result of subsequent rule making by the Environmental Protection Agency, Nuclear Regulatory Commission, or Department of Energy. The difference in emphasis on natural barriers between part 960 (applicable to future repository site selection) and part 963 (for establishing the suitability of Yucca Mountain) highlights the extent to which the role of the geological and hydrological properties of the site were ignored in Congress's selection of Yucca Mountain.

NOTES

1. U.S. Department of Energy, "General Guidelines for the Preliminary Screening of Potential Sites for Nuclear Waste Repositories," 10 CFR part 960, *Federal Register* 66, no. 220 (November 14, 2001): 57304; U.S. Department of Energy, "Yucca Mountain Site Suitability Guidelines," 10 CFR part 963, *Federal Register* 66, no. 220 (November 14, 2001): 57298.

2. U.S. Department of Energy, "General Guidelines for the Preliminary Screening of Potential Sites for Nuclear Waste Repositories," part 960.3-1-5.

: Appendix F

Organizations Opposed to the Yucca Mountain Repository

20/20 Vision, Washington, DC
Alliance for Nuclear Accountability, Seattle, WA
American Lands Alliance, Washington, DC
American Public Health Association, Washington, DC
American Rivers, Washington, DC
Americans for Democratic Action, Washington, DC
Center for Safe Energy, Earth Island Institute, Berkeley, CA
Clean Water Action, Washington, DC
Defenders of Wildlife, Washington, DC
Earth Action Foundation, Takoma Park, MD
Earthjustice, Oakland, CA
Environmental Defense, New York, NY
Environmental Working Group, Washington, DC
Fellowship of Reconciliation, Nyack, NY
Free the Planet! Washington, DC
Friends of the Earth, Washington, DC
Government Accountability Project, Seattle, WA
Grandmothers for Peace International, Elk Grove, CA
Greenpeace, Washington, DC
Honor the Earth, St. Paul, MN
Indigenous Environmental Network, Bemidji, MN
Institute for Energy and Environmental Research, Takoma Park, MD
International Association of Firefighters, Washington, DC
League of Conservation Voters, Washington, DC
League of United Latin American Citizens, Washington, DC
National Coalition of Native Americans, Prague, OK
National Education Association

National Environmental Trust, Washington
National Parent Teacher Association
Natural Resources Defense Council, Washington, DC
National Wildlife Federation, Washington, DC
Nuclear Information and Resource Service, Washington, DC
Pax Christi USA, Erie, PA
Peace Action, Washington, DC
Physicians for Social Responsibility, Washington, DC
Presbyterian Church (USA), National Ministries Division, Washington, DC
Psychologists for Social Responsibility, Washington, DC
Public Citizen, Washington, DC
Safe Energy Communication Council, Washington, DC
Scenic America, Washington, DC
Sierra Club, Washington, DC
Union of Hebrew Congregations/Religious Action Center of Reform Judaism, Washington, DC
United Church of Christ, Office for Church in Society, Washington, DC
United Methodist Church, General Board of Church and Society, Washington, DC
U.S. Public Interest Research Group, Washington, DC
Wilderness Society, Washington, DC
Women Legislators' Lobby, Washington, DC
Women's Action for New Directions, Washington, DC
Women's International League for Peace and Freedom, Philadelphia, PA

Source: Congressional Record, July 9, 2002: S6456. This material was inserted into the Congressional Record by Senator Barbara Boxer (D-CA).

⠿ Appendix G

Supporters of the Yucca Mountain Repository

ORGANIZATIONS

60 Plus Association
African American Environmental Association
American Public Power Association
Council for Citizens against Governmental Waste
Covering Your Assets Coalition
Edison Electric Institute
Frontiers of Freedom
Hispanic Business Roundtable
International Brotherhood of Electrical Workers
Latino Coalition
National Association of Manufacturers
National Association of Neighborhoods
National Black Chamber of Commerce
Nuclear Energy Institute
Seniors Coalition
United Seniors Association, Inc.
U.S. Hispanic Chamber of Commerce
Utility Workers Union of America

NEWSPAPER EDITORIALS

Albuquerque Journal
(Allentown) Morning Call
Chicago Sun Times
Chicago Tribune
Cleveland Plain Dealer
New York Times
Tennessean
Wall Street Journal
Washington Times
Wilmington Morning Star

Source: Joe F. Colvin, President and CEO, Nuclear Energy Institute, Prepared Statement, in A Review of the President's Recommendation to Develop a Nuclear Waste Repository at Yucca Mountain, Nevada, Hearing, House Committee on Energy and Commerce, Subcommittee on Energy and Air Quality, 107th Cong., 2nd Sess., April 18, 2002 (Washington, DC: U.S. Government Printing Office, 2002), 214–15.

Selected Bibliography

Baumgartner, Frank R., and Bryan D. Jones. *Agendas and Instability in American Politics*. Chicago: University of Chicago Press, 1993.

Blowers, Andrew, David Lowry, and Barry D. Solomon. *The International Politics of Nuclear Waste*. New York: St. Martins Press, 1991.

Bodansky, David. *Nuclear Energy: Principles, Practices and Prospects*. 2nd ed. New York: Springer-Verlag, 2004.

Bowers, Michael W. *The Sagebrush State: Nevada's History, Government and Politics*. 2nd ed. Reno: University of Nevada Press, 2002.

Bradley, Don J. *Behind the Nuclear Curtain: Radioactive Waste Management in the Former Soviet Union*. Columbus, OH: Battelle Press, 1997.

Carter, Luther J. *Nuclear Imperatives and Public Trust: Dealing with Radioactive Waste*. Washington, DC: Resources for the Future, 1987.

Chandler, Steven D. *Radioactive Waste Control and Controversy: The History of Radioactive Waste Regulation in the U.K.* Amsterdam: Gordon and Breach Science Publishers, 1997.

Chapman, Neil, and Charles McCombie. *Principles and Standards for the Disposal of Long-Lived Radioactive Wastes*. Boston: Pergamon, 2003.

Colglazier, E. W., Jr. "Policy Conflicts in the Process for Siting Nuclear Waste Repositories." In *Annual Review of Energy*, 13:315–57. Palo Alto: Annual Reviews, 1988.

Colglazier, E. W., Jr., ed. *The Politics of Nuclear Waste*. New York: Pergamon Press, 1982.

Dodd, Lawrence C., and Bruce I. Oppenheimer, eds. *Congress Reconsidered*. 8th ed. Washington, DC: CQ Press, 2005.

Domenici, Pete V. *A Brighter Tomorrow: Fulfilling the Promise of Nuclear Energy*. With Blythe J. Lyons and Julian J. Steyn. Lanham, MD: Rowman and Littlefield Publishers, 2004.

Driggs, Don W., and Leonard E. Goodall. *Nevada Politics and Government: Conservatism in an Open Society*. Lincoln: University of Nebraska Press, 1996.

Duffy, Robert J. *Nuclear Politics in America: A History and Theory of Government Regulation*. Lawrence: University Press of Kansas, 1997.

Dunlap, Riley E., Michael E. Kraft, and Eugene A. Rosa, eds. *Public Reactions to Nuclear Waste*. Durham: Duke University Press, 1993.

Easterling, Douglas, and Howard Kunreuther. *The Dilemma of Siting a High-Level Nuclear Waste Repository*. Boston: Kluwer Academic Publishers, 1995.

Garwin, Richard L., and Georges Charpak. *Megawatts and Megatons: A Turning Point in the Nuclear Age*. New York: Alfred A. Knopf, 2001.

Herzik, Eric B., and Alvin A. Mushkatel, eds. *Problems and Prospects for Nuclear Waste Disposal Policy*. Westport, CT: Greenwood Press, 1993.

Hulse, James W. *The Silver State: Nevada's Heritage Reinterpreted*. 3rd ed. Reno: University of Nevada Press, 2004.

Jacob, Gerald. *Site Unseen: The Politics of Siting a Nuclear Waste Repository*. Pittsburgh: University of Pittsburgh Press, 1990.

League of Women Voters Education Fund. *Nuclear Waste Primer: A Handbook for Citizens*. Rev. ed. New York: Lyons and Burford, 1993.

Longley, Lawrence D., and Walter J. Oleszek. *Bicameral Politics: Conference Committees in Congress*. New Haven: Yale University Press, 1989.

MacFarlane, Allison M., and Rodney C. Ewing, eds. *Uncertainty Underground: Yucca Mountain and the Nation's High-Level Nuclear Waste*. Cambridge, MA: MIT Press, 2006.

McCutcheon, Chuck. *Nuclear Reactions: The Politics of Opening a Radioactive Waste Disposal Site*. Albuquerque: University of New Mexico Press, 2002.

Melfort, Warren S., ed. *Nuclear Waste Disposal: Current Issues and Proposals*. New York: Nova Science Publishers, 2003.

Murray, Raymond L. *Understanding Radioactive Waste*. 4th ed. Columbus, OH: Battelle Press, 1994.

National Research Council. *Technical Bases for Yucca Mountain Standards*. Washington, DC: National Academy Press, 1995.

Nordhaus, William D. *The Swedish Nuclear Dilemma: Energy and the Environment*. Washington, DC: Resources for the Future, 1997.

Norton, Philip. *The British Polity*. 3rd ed. New York: Longman, 1994.

Oleszek, Walter J. *Congressional Procedures and the Policy Process*. 5th ed. Washington, DC: CQ Press, 2001.

Oppenheimer, Bruce I., ed. *U.S. Senate Exceptionalism*. Columbus: Ohio State University Press, 2002.

Rosenbaum, Walter A. *Environmental Politics and Policy.* 5th ed. Washington, DC: CQ Press, 2002.

Saling, James H., and Audeen W. Fentiman, eds. *Radioactive Waste Management.* 2nd ed. New York: Taylor and Francis, 2001.

Sinclair, Barbara. *Unorthodox Lawmaking: New Legislative Processes in U.S. Congress.* Washington, DC: CQ Press, 2000.

Sundqvist, Göran. *The Bedrock of Opinion: Science, Technology and Society in the Siting of High-Level Nuclear Waste.* Dordrecht: Kluwer Academic Publishers, 2002.

U.S. Department of Energy. *Yucca Mountain Science and Engineering Report Rev. 1: Technical Information Supporting Site Recommendation Consideration.* DOE/RW-0539-1. Washington, DC: U.S. Department of Energy, Office of Civilian Radioactive Waste Management, February 2002. Available at www.ocrwm.doe.gov/documents/ser_b/index.htm.

U.S. National Research Council. *Technical Bases for Yucca Mountain Standards.* Report of Committee on Technical Bases for Yucca Mountain Standards. Washington, DC: National Academy Press, 1995.

Vig, Norman, and Michael E. Kraft, eds. *Environmental Policy: New Directions for the 21st Century.* 4th ed. Washington, DC: CQ Press, 2000.

Walker, J. Samuel. *Three Mile Island: A Nuclear Crisis in Historical Perspective.* Berkeley: University of California Press, 2004.

Weart, Spencer R. *Nuclear Fear: A History of Images.* Cambridge, MA: Harvard University Press, 1988.

"What's News." A continuously updated online listing of nuclear-related articles and agency notices. Available at the State of Nevada website or directly at www.state.nv.us/nucwaste/whatsnew.htm.

Wolfson, Richard. *Nuclear Choices: A Citizen's Guide to Nuclear Technology.* Rev. ed. Cambridge, MA: MIT Press, 1997.

Index

Abraham, Spencer, vi, 3, 44, 65, 115, 134–55, 166–86, 278–88

acceptable risk, 134

Adams, Brock, 60, 85

airplane trip radiation exposure, 135

Akaka, Daniel, 157

Allard, Wayne, 156

alloy 22, 15, 109

Alfvén, Hannes, 230

Amar, Akhil Reed, 181

Amargosa Valley, 41, 116, 134, 136, 174, 277, 301

Amendments Act. *See* Nuclear Waste Policy Amendments Act of 1987

American Nuclear Energy Council, 57

appropriations bills, 25, 43, 64, 84, 85, 86, 92, 98, 165, 166

Aspin, Les, 57

Association of American Railroads, 144

Atomic Energy Commission: Japan, 28–29; U.S., 2, 35–37, 117, 260, 278

Atomic Industrial Forum, 57

Atomic Safety and Licensing Board, 9, 101, 301

background radiation dose, 135–36, 178, 268–69, 271

Ballard, James David, 208–9

Barrett, Lake, 144, 205

barriers: engineered, 74, 108, 110, 114–15, 149, 174–80, 185–90, 219, 289–90; geological, 74, 110, 114–15, 149, 174–80, 184–90, 219, 289–90

Bartlett, John W., 147

Barton, Joe, 141, 166

basalt, 11–12, 37, 40, 65, 74

Bechtel Corporation, 153, 160

Bennett, Robert, 102, 161

Berkley, Shelley, 116, 143–44, 209

Beth, Richard S., 151

Bilbray, James H., 131

Bingamon, Jeff, 98, 115, 146–153, 161, 189

Bodansky, David, ix, 13, 23, 46, 112, 113, 271

Bodman, Samuel W., 278–79, 286

borehole disposal, 14

Boxer, Barbara, 154, 293

Broyhill, James T., 58

Bryan, Richard, 91–92, 124–25, 132

Bullfrog County (Nevada), 124–25, 129–30

Bureau of Indian Affairs, 8, 100–101

Bureau of Land Management, 8, 101, 105, 118–20

Bush, George H. W., 49, 59–60, 91, 97, 187, 278, 282; appointment of Nuclear Waste Negotiator, 97; Watkins appointment, 278; and Reid state sovereignty letter, 91; New Hampshire primary, 59–60

Bush, George W., 19, 117, 163–64, 174, 186, 278, 285, 286; Abraham appointment 278; Bodman appointment, 278; Energy Task Force formation, 4; Jaczko appointment to NRC, 163; Nevada lawsuits, 174, 186; nuclear

Thomas, Craig, 148, 154

Three Mile Island, 51–52, 121, 155, 232, 260–62

titanium drip shield, 109

Total System Performance Assessment (TSPA), 110–15, 290–91

transmutation, 7, 15, 21–29, 149, 218, 221; with accelerators, 23–28; in breeding, 23; in conventional (thermal) reactors, 22; economics of, 26–29; in fast reactors, 22–23; of I-129, 22, 24–25; of Np-237, 22, 24; of Tc-99, 22, 24–25; technical challenges, 26–29

Transport, Aging and Disposal (TAD) canisters, 209

transportation, 199–209; cask certification tests, 202; estimates of number of rail or truck shipments required, 203; estimates of transportation accidents, 203, 204; fire risks, 202, 205, 208; health effects of, 209; mostly rail decision, 205; state designation of routes, 200–201; state training responsibility, 201; in Sweden by ship, 235; terrorist attacks during, 205, 208, 209. *See also* casks, transportation; Yucca Mountain, transportation

tuff, 12, 37, 40, 61, 75, 78, 105–10, 185, 276

U.S. Geological Survey (USGS), 12, 65, 107, 154, 175

U.S. Public Health Service, 118, 264

Ubehebe crater, 108

Udall, Morris, vi, 82–87, 169

United Kingdom, 224–230; Atomic Energy Authority, 225; cesium-137 contamination, 225; Flowers report, 225–26; geological disposal, 228–29; House of Lords Select Committee on Science and Technology, 226; NIREX, 226, 229; percent electri-

city nuclear, 224; Radioactive Waste Management Advisory Committee, 226; reprocessing, 225, 230; Sellafield accident, 16, 225; THORP reprocessing plant, 225; Tony Blair, 225; Windscale accident, 225

Vacherie dome (Louisiana), 40, 61–62, 69

VanLuik, A., ix, 275

Vermont, 57, 86, 159, 160

veto override: Senate Energy and Natural Resources Committee, 150; House Energy and Commerce Committee, 143

Virginia, 57, 73, 86, 279

Voinovitch, George, 156

Vucanovich, Barbara, 133

Wald, Matthew, ix

Washington state, 23, 37, 40, 59, 60–65, 73–74, 76, 81, 118, 159, 260, 281–86

Waste Deposit Impact Committee (Deaf Smith County), 81

Waste Isolation Pilot Plant (WIPP), 11, 150, 155, 183, 201, 282–84

Watkins, James D., 176, 181, 189, 278, 282–83

Weart, Spencer, 2

Weinberg, Alvin, 2

Wellstone, Paul, 152

West Valley (New York), 16, 29, 50, 247, 77, 281

WIPP, 11, 150, 155, 183, 201, 282–84

Wisconsin, 57, 59, 73, 86, 99, 158

Wright, Jim, 86

Yakama Indian Tribe, 74, 81, 99

Yeager, Brooks, 59

Young, Don, 143

Yucca Mountain, 105–25; aquifer, 105, 134, 142, 154; budget cuts, 165–66, 176; characterization cost, 482; congressional capacity limitation, 40, 56, 79, 106, 159, 200; court appeals,